W9-BHR-685

A Treasure Hunting Text

FOR FURTHER READING

Charles Garrett and other treasure hunters give you an in-depth analysis, interspersed with exciting hints, useful tips and bold insights about the rewarding adventures of treasure hunting in these fine books. Each book holds a treasure of fine color and photos as well as important treasure hunting references.

The World's Richest Wrecks
Complete details on the richest ships and cargoes lost during the Age of Sail. 456 pages. By Robert and Jenifer Marx.

Modern Metal Detectors — Revised
Broad overview of metal detecting, with technical descriptions of instrument circuitry. 432 pages. By Charles Garrett.

The New Successful Coin Hunting
The world's most authoritative guide on finding valuable coins. 259 pages. By Charles Garrett.

Treasure Caches Can be Found
Learn to research, locate and recover abandoned treasure caches. 194 pages. By Charles Garrett.

Ghost Town Treasures
The lore of ghost town hunting with illustrations explaining how to locate hidden treasures. 156 pages. By Charles Garrett.

Treasure Hunting for Fun and Profit
Author explains how easy it is to find coins, jewelry, money caches, etc. today. 204 pages. By Charles Garrett.

Gold of the Americas
A history of gold and how the precious metal helped shape the history of the Americas. 168 pages. By Jennifer Marx.

Gold in the Ancient World
Historians and gold prospectors alike will benefit from the many centuries of gold history. 290 pages. By Jennifer Marx.

You Can Find Gold with a Metal Detector
Complete information on using detectors to find gold. 140 pages. By Charles Garrett/Roy Lagal.

Gold Panning is Easy
Inventor of the patented Garrett Gravity Trap Gold Pans, author shows the beginner how to find and pan gold. 134 pages. By Roy Lagal.

European Metal Detecting Guide
Includes tips, techniques, treasures, information on European antiquities laws and hundreds of color photos. 320 pages. By Stephen L. Moore.

Last Stand of the Texas Cherokees
An account of the greatest battle between Texas Rangers and Native Americans, plus relic recovery on the site by a team using Garrett metal detectors. 224 pages. By Stephen L. Moore.

Published by RAM Books
A Division of Garrett Metal Detectors

Charles Garrett and other professional treasure hunters also bring the hobby of metal detecting to life in treasure hunting and prospecting videos. To order a RAM book or a treasure hunting video, call 1-800-527-4011 or visit www. garrett.com for more information.

B·U·R·I·E·D
TREASURES
you can find

RAM
BOOKS

Over 7500 locations in all 50 states
BY ROBERT F. MARX

ISBN 0-915920-82-4
Library of Congress Catalog Card No. 93-84321
Buried Treasures You Can Find
© Copyright 1993, 1999
Robert Marx

Printed in Korea for worldwide distribution.

Tenth Edition Printing, December 2009

For FREE listing of related treasure hunting books write

Ram Publishing Company

P.O. Box 38649   •   Dallas, TX 75238

DEDICATION

Once again...to Charles Garrett,
who has done so much
...for treasure hunters everywhere
...and, has continued to be
a tremendous help to me

By Robert Marx

The Underwater Dig
The Lure of Sunken Treasure
Port Royal Rediscovered
Sea Fever: Famous Underwater Explorers
Shipwrecks in Mexican Waters
Shipwrecks in Florida Waters
Shipwrecks of the Western Hemisphere:1492-1825
Always Another Adventure
Pirate Port: The story of the Sunken City of Port Royal
They Dared the Deep: A History of Diving
The Battle of Lepanto:1571
The Battle of the Spanish Armada: 1588
The Treasure Fleets of the Spanish Main
Following Columbus: The Voyage of the Niña II
The Voyage of the Nina II
The Capture of the Treasure Fleet
Buried Treasure of the U.S.
Spanish Treasure in Florida Waters
Quest for Treasure: the Maravilla
Sunken Treasure: How to Find It

Buried Treasures You Can Find...

Contents

About the Author...

Editor's Note

Bob Marx gained his treasure hunting knowledge the old fashioned way — he earned it! For this reason any book he writes on the subject is bound to be interesting, useful and provocative. This new book which combines Bob's famed personal list of thousands of treasure sites all over the U.S. with the latest information on treasure hunting detectors is another winner from a most unusual and dynamic man.

Placing a label on Bob — even one so grandiloquent as *a legend in his own time* — is no simple task. The man defies categorizing. He is a dedicated historian and marine archaeologist...yet a helluva diver and daredevil adventurer. He can be grimly serious about the profession of marine archaeology and recovering artifacts from beneath the sea...yet treat remarkable personal achievements almost flippantly. His sense of history is truly astonishing.

Bob is one of the most successful and well known specialists in the field of marine archaeology, and he has an equally strong reputation for his work in naval and maritime history. He studied at UCLA and the University of Maryland and served in the U.S. Marine Corps where he was a diver and worked on salvage operations. His feats are almost legendary...exploration of sunken ships he has discovered all over the world...the highly acclaimed underwater study of Port Royal in the Caribbean, ravaged by a 1692 earthquake...advising leaders of industry and government.

Bob's numerous books, articles and scientific papers are amazing in their descriptions of various projects in which he has participated. Respected by archaeologists and sport divers alike, he has written more than 30 books and has published hundreds of scientific articles and reports. As his career has led him into a deeper interest in underwater archaeology, Bob has focused more of his personal attention on educating governments concerning the importance of not only protecting archaeological areas, but also actively supporting qualified projects.

Perhaps Bob Marx was described, if unknowingly, by a famous professional athlete who defended himself decades ago against the charge of boasting with this explanation: "If you done it...it ain't bragging."

Bob Marx has certainly *done it*!

Association with Robert Marx is indeed a privilege for Ram Publishing Company. We are confident that this book will prove to be one of his most notable.

Hal Dawson
Editor, RAM

Dallas, Texas
Summer 1993

By Robert Marx

Author's Note

Each of my books is truly a labor of love for me. I'm too busy to waste time writing about things that aren't really important. What's so special to me about this book – and *Buried Treasure of the U. S.* which preceded it – is their potential impact on the novice treasure hunter...the newcomer to our field. Treasure hunting is such a joy. I wish that everyone could know and love it the way that I do.

So many darn books claim to be the *only* one a person needs or the *first* one a person should read before taking up a new hobby. I'm not going to make that claim for *Buried Treasures You Can Find*. I will point out, however, that this book tells you *where* to find treasure and *how* to find it. If you follow the principles outlined in it, you *will* find treasure. As that third party presidential candidate liked to say...it's that simple; I rest my case.

But, this new book is written not just for the beginning treasure hunter. I've been seeking buried treasure most of my life, yet I still hope that I can learn something new each day. It's my wish that this book enables each of you to learn a little more – which will help you to find more treasure.

Since I wrote *Buried Treasures of the U.S.*, truly revolutionary improvements have been made in metal detectors. Because this progress permits all of us to become better treasure hunters, I decided to write this new "how-and-where" book combining my list of treasure sites with an explanation of the latest developments in treasure hunting, especially metal detection equipment.

Incidentally, the above-mentioned *Buried Treasures of the U.S.* is still a great book, filled with success stories galore. I

3

know that any treasure hunter will enjoy reading it. Just let me remind you that the detector information in that book is seriously out of date. This new *Buried Treasures You Can Find* presents the latest data on modern detectors along with directions for using them.

Speaking of detectors...I am grateful to Charles Garrett, the world's leading metal detector manufacturer, and to his engineers for their aid in helping me explain all the exciting developments in detector design and use to you. Charles is quite an author himself. There's no one better when it comes to writing about metal detectors and what can be accomplished with them. I've learned much from his books. They're interesting and worthwhile because he and I agree on "telling it like it is."

In fact, Charles has graciously accepted my invitation to provide an introduction that tells about treasure hunting and presents his views of just what it's all about. I know that you will enjoy it. I did.

Bob Marx

The Oriental Hotel
Singapore
Summer, 1993

Introduction — By Charles Garrett...

What is Treasure Hunting?

Bob Marx honors me and everyone associated with Garrett Metal Detectors with his dedication of this book and the request that I write an introduction to it. Bob is one of the great treasure hunters of all time, and we are proud to list him among our Garrett customers. He and the many Sea Hunter detectors he has used have found a veritable fortune beneath the waters of the world. In addition, these discoveries have literally helped rewrite history in several instances.

Enough about Bob! Let's talk about *Buried Treasures You Can Find*. Isn't it exciting to contemplate a book that locates for you literally hundreds of buried treasures that you can find. Yes, *you*.

This book is a dandy! Let me state that first and foremost. It's one that every treasure hunter and metal detector hobbyist should possess and study. Not only does it provide complete information about using the latest and most modern metal detectors, but it includes Bob's magnificent list of treasure hunting sites — throughout all 50 states. This list just can't be beat!

But, just exactly what is treasure hunting? It's difficult to define because it means different things to different people. Basically, treasure hunting is the search for — and recovery of — anything that *you* feel has value. Coins, costume jewelry, money caches and relics are all treasure just the same as gold and jewels. Your treasure can be simply a single item or a large cache. Your treasure can be anything you're searching for and desire.

Some people want (or, expect) to strike it rich the very first time they turn on a detector, while others are content to find rarely more than a few coins in the local park. Some individuals hunt with a detector for the excitement of digging a valuable treasure out of the ground, while others are fascinated by the "historical" discoveries they make. Some find pleasure in returning lost class rings and similar items to their rightful owners. Others enjoy displaying in their homes the treasures (and, junk) they have discovered. There are some who write magazine articles and enjoy sharing their treasure hunting techniques with others. Yet, some simply rejoice in getting out into God's great outdoors...any treasure they find is icing on the cake.

No matter what kind of treasure hunter you are, you will enjoy this book. And, you'll probably learn something from it.

If you're good with a metal detector, you're most likely an inquisitive person by nature. You want to find out what's around the next bend or under the next layer of soil. If so, great success in any field of treasure hunting can be yours with a quality metal detector. All you need now is knowledge.

First comes study and training. Learn all there is to know about the metal detector that you use – its searchcoils, accessories, modes of operation and capabilities. Put your examination into action with practice, practice and more practice. Then, carefully review the instructions given in this and other books. Incorporate them into your daily practice. Be ready to meet any general treasure hunting situations that might arise.

Treasure hunting has become a family hobby...husband, wife and children have all become dedicated hunters. Now, sometimes only the man of the household enjoys the hobby, but I know of wives who will hunt alone when the husband can't or won't. Often, children become more proficient than their parents. Hunters, fishermen, campers, vacationers and backpackers are adding metal detectors to their sports gear.

Treasure Hunting Is Healthful! Who can deny that outdoor activities are beneficial? Treasure hunting certainly takes you out of doors into the fresh air and sunshine. Scanning a detector over the ground all day, stooping to dig hundreds of targets, hiking several miles over the desert, or climbing a mountain to reach a ghost town...certainly such activities can become tiring. But, this is where an extra side benefit is realized. A "built-in" body building program is a valuable *plus* of treasure hunting. Leg muscles firm up, flab around the middle begins to diminish as excess pounds drop off, breathing improves and nights of restful sleep result. The good physical exercise that is absolutely required in successful treasure hunting can lead to a longer, healthier life.

Treasure Hunting is a Hobby for All Ages! Everyone can enjoy searching with a metal detector...men and women, boys and girls...from surprisingly young children to the most mature senior citizens. In fact, retired men and women all over the world are joining the ranks of metal detector owners in rapidly growing numbers. They realize that this is a relatively inexpensive hobby (that can even *pay for itself*) and that, moreover, it is *healthy* (see above). It's a hobby they can pursue at any time or any place, and it can involve as little or as much time and energy as they desire. A retired friend of mine tells me that he wouldn't go for a walk without his Garrett GTA detector...not that he necessarily always scans for treasure, but he can do so *if he happens to feel like it!*

Treasure Hunting Can Be Profitable! It is also simple and easy. Consider the hobby of coin hunting? The majority of all treasure hunters begin their new hobby by searching for coins. Countless millions of coins have been lost and await recovery by metal detectors. More coins are being lost every day than are being found...and this has been going on for centuries!

Most important to many of us is the awareness and enjoyment of nature's treasures that God placed upon the earth. Whether the "big prize" is found is really irrelevant. It's simply gratifying to see nature all around and to be a vital part of it. This could well be the greatest treasure anyone ever finds.

Educational factors related to treasure hunting can be stimulating. Relics and artifacts of bygone eras create many questions. Who were the people that once lived and prospered where faint memories of an old city or town remain? Where did they come from? Why was the area left deserted? These and many more questions can usually be answered with proper research and examination of the artifacts found.

Many persons who begin by scanning only for coins quickly extend their hobby into other areas of treasure hunting. Searching ghost towns and old houses for hidden money caches, and hunting in abandoned trash dumps for relics and rare bottles can be very rewarding. One treasure hunter found $41,000 in currency in a metal box that was cached in an old dumping ground. Another man in Idaho found a $20 gold piece estimated to be worth hundreds of thousands of dollars. Countless small fruit jar and "post hole" money caches are found each year.

Many find it amazing that the successful treasure hunter appears to expend no energy at all, while the mediocre treasure hunter runs about constantly in a helter-skelter fashion, chasing some sort of will-o-the-wisp...never being really satisfied or successful.

A metal detector must be used correctly and in the right places before it will pay off. Most successful finds result from research. Of course, a lot of treasure is found by accident, and all of us dream of finding the "big one" simply by stumbling over it. But, that is hardly the way to go about professional treasure hunting. Whether you are a coin hunter, cache or relic hunter, beach or underwater hunter or an electronic prospector, research is vitally important. It is a basic tool you cannot neglect to use if you want to enjoy success.

Charles Garrett, shown here in West Texas, has searched for — and found — treasure on every continent except Antarctica.

Research is a key to successful treasure hunting. Without proper and adequate research, you are shooting in the dark. Your efficiency and likelihood of successful recovery increase proportionately as the amount of your research increases. Without research you may not be as successful as you should or could be since 95% of a successful recovery usually depends on research. Always remember that you must go where the treasure is located. Even the world's finest metal detector can only inform you about what is beneath its searchcoil.

Most of the time, in order to find where any treasure is located, you must carry out a certain amount of research. You won't find treasure where it is not! You will find treasure where it is! In order to find it, you must study, read, and follow up leads. In short, do your research.

It's a sad, but true, fact that most treasure hunters do not go to the trouble to acquire correct data on treasure sites. They do not educate themselves on the correct use of metal detectors. They just don't hunt where the treasure is located or use the proper techniques. Usually, however, these people are the first to give up, perhaps blaming their failure on the detector.

For professional treasure hunters, however, the greatest difficulty comes from having to decide which of the dozens or hundreds of leads to follow. They try to avoid bum steers. They use their brains and they *think*. Common sense is a big factor in successful treasure hunting. Professional treasure hunters don't search for just one treasure. They keep many leads on the back burner and are always looking for promising new ones. Often in researching one story, you'll run across information that applies to another. The professional will select

The late L. L. "Abe" Lincoln became a legendary treasure hunter not so much because of his finds, but because of the wonderful stories he could tell.

several treasure leads to follow and collect all possible information about each of them. Then each one will be followed as far as possible, and the treasure hunter will let it lie dormant for a while, allowing the subconscious to work on it while waiting for new leads to develop. Maybe the professional only hits once a year, but often that is more than enough to repay the effort.

Many books have been written on this fascinating subject. Many of them have been published by Ram Publishing Company. Some of these should be on your bookshelf and should be read often. Use the order blank at the back of this book.

The dedicated and successful treasure hunter lives and breathes the hobby. It is always on his (or, her) mind. Consequently, everything he or she reads and everyone they talk with are potential sources of the fresh treasure leads and data they must have to help them in their work. They're always looking for ideas and tips that can point them to new finds.

If you are a coin hunter, for instance, you can find current coins all day long at the park, playground and along grassy strips near parking meters. If you really want to start finding old and rare, valuable coins, however, you must do your research. You must learn where the old settlers' campgrounds, carnival and fairground sites are located. These are the really valuable hot spots; here you will find treasure that makes hunting worthwhile. This same principle applies to any other kind of treasure hunting. If you are looking for gold, you have to search where precious metal has already been found. Gold and silver have been mined in many locations throughout the world, and to have the greatest chances of success, you must find the best places to prospect. Relic and cache hunters must also do their research. Find the hot spots, then put your expert detector knowledge to work. It will pay off!

If you have been hunting treasure for almost any length of time, you have probably run across mention of the word "patience." It's a proven fact! Absolutely and positively...unless you possess a great amount of patience and regularly put it into practice, you won't be as successful as you could be.

Experienced cache hunters have learned that success comes as infrequently as one in ten tries. Consequently, a person without patience to spare will surely give up long before success rolls around. Patience is a true key to making finds. If you plan to be successful, you'd better gather and store up plenty of it for yourself so that you can put it to use when needed.

Treasure hunting can be hard work. In fact, even the serious and dedicated treasure hunter sometimes finds it to be one of the hardest jobs a person can undertake — especially after a long day when the finds have been disappointing. Yet, this is no excuse for not searching!

You could sit on a rock all day long with patience to spare, but all you would accomplish is to keep the rock warm, for that rock will never hatch. To find treasure you must get out into the field, swing your detector from dawn to dusk and dig every signal, regardless of how weak or how strong.

Now, this doesn't mean you have to go at it night and day to enjoy hunting with a metal detector. Remember, how you enjoy this hobby is strictly up to you! Nobody has to "break a hundred" or win "two-out-of-three" to be a successful metal detector hobbyist! Many people get pleasure and healthy exercise just going to a park and scanning a searchcoil back and forth over the ground for only a little while with discrimination set to its maximum. Occasionally they will dig a coin or two. And, there's nothing wrong with that...if it's what you want. Yet, believe me, there is a far greater reward in hard work, sweat and the sound of money jingling in the pocket.

Almost a decade ago I wrote a book called *Modern Metal Detectors*, which has been revised recently. In both the original and revised versions I gave this advice which still holds true:

If you're willing to study...

If you're not afraid of hard work...

And, if you're even willing to sweat a little...

Success in hunting for treasure with a metal detector will be yours!

1 – Every Day...All Over the World

Treasure Is Being Found

A t a recent cocktail party a friend asked if, after a lifetime, I get bored searching for treasure. The answer is a resounding *No*. Since I took my first steps, scarcely a day has gone by when I haven't found some form of treasure, and it's the finding that keeps the pursuit exciting. Growing up in Pittsburgh I spent all my spare time searching for coins in playgrounds, parking lots and other places. When I was able to purchase a used World War II mine detector, my treasure hunting activities intensified. I even quit my paper route to devote more time to finding coins and jewelry. Once I got into the underwater shipwreck business in my early teens my land searches were reduced in number but I couldn't take my eyes off the ground wherever I walked.

I still have this problem today.

When I'm not at sea probing the depths for sunken treasure, I can often be found on a beach with a metal detector or walking along the side of a road scanning for coins. My wife claims that I miss so much of what is happening around me because I'm always looking down. I am so superstitious about finding money that I won't board a plane unless I first find a coin.

Jenifer and I go to Europe several times a year. She makes plans of things for us to see and do but inevitably treasure fever strikes, and we end up spending most of the time searching for treasures which may be ceramic shards, coins or even modern jewelry.

15

Our favorite search areas are construction sites or road repairs near historical parts of cities, especially in port areas. Someone else does the digging and exposing the ruins of old buildings, and all we have to do is look hard and pick up what others have missed or ignored. In less than a hour we once picked 70 ancient Roman coins out of a trench dug for sewer repairs near the Coliseum in Rome. Another time in Cadiz, Spain, we spent a day working an area where a dredge boat was depositing land fill along the shore. We found over 250 old coins, including 37 gold ones. We also found hundreds of artifacts dating as far back as the Phoenician period. All of these, like the coins, came from shipwrecks in the harbor.

In the years since I wrote *Buried Treasure of the United State*, from which this book has been adapted, there have been a number of exciting developments in searching for buried treasure. No matter where I read a newspaper around the world, I find reports of treasures found both on land and in the sea. Several months ago in Singapore I picked up the morning paper to see the glaring headline: "Archaeologist Finds Two and a Half Million Coins in China."

This is the largest hoard of ancient coins ever discovered anywhere. It was found when a farmer digging a well in Yongcheng County in Henan Province in central China accidentally fell into a 2d- century B.C. tomb. The walls of the tomb, the inhabitant of which has not been identified, were covered with paintings, including one of a nude woman. In addition to the millions of bronze coins there two well preserved wooden chariots and hundreds of ceramic objects. Far from finding himself suddenly wealthy, the hapless farmer was thrown in jail for disturbing an archaeological site. He remains there while archaeologists swarm over the site like locusts.

A newspaper story the following week reported another major find in China. Another tomb was discovered by a farmer plowing a field in Jiangxi Province. This one was even older — dating around 300 B.C. It yielded over 100 pieces of exquisite jade jewelry, 480 bronze bowls, 300 ceramic pots, weapons and tools. No coins were discovered on this site. Although most numismatic books credit the ancient nation of Lydia as the birthplace of coinage in the late 7th or early 6th century B.C., many scholars now believe that the Chinese produced the first coinage several centuries earlier.

A Japanese Treasure Hunt

In nearby Japan engraved maps, cryptic notes on parchment and a golden statue have kept a Japanese samurai family digging for treasure for three generations. Now in its 106th year it may be the longest continuous treasure hunt ever. The prize could be among the world's richest treasures – the entire stash of gold ingots of the Tokugawa shogunate, the feudal overlords who ruled Japan for the 265 years prior to 1868. Since 1887 the Mizuno family, whose ancestors worked in the treasury, has been searching for the gold under the barren slopes of Mount Akagi 60 miles north of Tokyo.

Nobody really knows just exactly how much is buried but estimates have valued the Japanese hoard as high as $1 1/2 *trillion*. Tomoyuki Mizuno, current leader of the family search, feels the gold originally belonged to the Japanese people and vows that if he finds it he will give every Japanese a share which he now estimates would be about $9,000.

Like other famous treasure troves, this story starts with the downfall of a dynasty – the Tokugawa shoguns. In 1866 the gold was moved to Akagi in hundreds of carts under the direction of the last shogun's chief financial advisor. Thousands of convicts were used to dig a tunnel into the heart of the mountain. The gold was deposited, the entrance sealed off and all of the convicts beheaded to keep the location secret.

The secret was kept for two decades until grandfather Mizuno discovered documents and maps revealing the approximate location of the treasure. What followed bears the classic hallmarks of a treasure hunt – anagrams and other cryptic clues planted to befuddle searchers not frightened off by several mysterious deaths. To date the only finds have been a small gold statue of Buddha, several bronze plates and some ceramic objects.

A recent article I saw just this morning in a local paper was entitled: "400-year-old Spanish coins found on beach." I almost skipped it because finds of Spanish colonial coins are commonplace on the east coast of Florida where I live. However, this find was made on the west coast of the state near Bradenton and is significant because Spanish coins have never been found in that area. Jim Bowsher on vacation from Ohio was using a metal detector to search an area on Anna Maria Island where a beach renourishment project had just begun. He discovered two Spanish copper coins dated 1598 and 1601, a musket ball, a brooch and a religious medallion – all no doubt coming from an offshore shipwreck. State archaeologists are excited because this is the first time Spanish colonial materials have come to light in that area.

Just a week ago a vacationing treasure hunter trying his luck on the opposite side of the country made an even more tantalizing find. His first three days of beachcombing near San Diego, California, yielded about a hundred modern coins, three gold rings, various keys and a set of false teeth. Not bad. But on the fourth day he hit paydirt when he found a small 4th-century A.D Roman bronze coin of the Constantinian era. Did the Romans reach California? Most unlikely; it probably was lost in recent times by a coin collector.

Two major expeditions in quest of incredible treasure hoards are underway even as I write – one in South America and one in Germany. In the remote Llanganati mountain range of central Ecuador, a treacherous area of the Andes, men are questing after an estimated 750 tons of treasure in the form of gold statues and ingots, jewelry and other art objects. The hoard was stashed in a cave by followers of the Inca ruler Atahualpa after he was killed in Peru by Spanish conquistadors in the 1530s. Ecuadorian Oswaldo Garces who grew up hearing the legend of the lost gold, dropped out of law school and spent several years researching the story. Backed by 28 corporate sponsors he recently set off seeking to unlock the secrets of this Inca treasure with advanced technology such as ground-penetrating radar and infrared scanners.

18

A World War II Treasure

One of the most important treasures of World War II is believed to be hidden in the heart of Germany – near Weimar, the historical birthplace of Martin Bormann, Hitler's deputy. The treasure hoard was amassed by Erich Koch, gauleiter of East Prussia, who looted museums and private collections throughout Europe as the German Army advanced. Among the tens of thousands of objects taken was the Amber Chamber, a truly priceless and almost unbelievable baroque and rococo masterpiece.

King Frederick I of Prussia conceived the unique chamber in 1701 as an appropriate gift to the Russian royal family upon sealing an alliance. It was a full-size room made entirely of amber, including 22 wall panels, intricate bas reliefs, busts, figures, monograms, candelabra, mirror frames and inlaid decorations depicting Tuscan scenes and landscapes from mythology. The Amber Chamber was installed in a palace in St. Petersburg where it remained until the Germans took it in 1941.

Koch assembled all the captured plunder, including the Amber Chamber in the Baltic port of Koenigsberg, now known as Kalingrad. But before the port was overrun by the Russians at the end of the war, the treasures were removed to Weimar and buried. Research indicates the hoard is buried beneath Karl Marx Square. An American group is currently using remote-sensing equipment to pin-point its location. They estimate worth of the treasure conservatively in the hundreds of millions of dollars and are determined to persevere until they find it.

The Germans weren't the only ones whose stolen and hidden plunder from the Second World War is still being sought. The Japanese buried loot throughout Southeast Asia. During the past five years more than a dozen large hoards of gold and other valuables have been uncovered in Indonesia alone. The finds were made by treasure hunters using metal detectors. The most valuable was made by an 11-year-old boy in eastern Java using his father's metal detector. He must have been the most thrilled kid ever when he found over a ton of gold ingots. In Malaysia another large treasure was unearthed two years ago by a British tourist armed with a detector and searching for coins near an old Dutch fort. He failed to find any colonial treasures but was more than content to discover over $7 million worth of gold ingots stamped Bank of Singapore 1940, which the Japanese had apparently looted and buried, since several Japanese weapons were found along with the gold.

Yamashita's Treasure

The most intense searching for buried Japanese World War II hoards goes on in the Philippine Islands where they are collectively referred to as Yamashita's Treasure. General Yamashita was called the Lion of Asia because his armies conquered most of the Far East – including China – before taking over the Philippines where they stored all the plunder from their previous conquests. Before the Japanese were dislodged from their strongholds in the Philippines by General MacArthur and his forces, they buried hundreds of hoards of treasures throughout this country. Marcos, the late dictator of the Philippines, used army troops to search for these treasures. At least four hoards, valued at several billion dollars, were located and account for a great deal of the loot Marco's is known to have deposited in Swiss banks. Numerous other hoards have been located in recent years, including one large solid-gold statue of Buddha. Dozens of groups are now continuing to scour the Philippines as they look for the remaining treasures.

In the British Isles rarely a month goes by without a major treasure discovery. Three stunning finds stand out in the last couple of years. In a field near the village of Hoxne in the county of Suffolk Eric Lawes, retired gardener, was looking for a lost hammer with a metal detector when he stumbled across a 1,600-year-old cache of Roman treasure valued at over $15 million. The amazed 70-year-old forgot his lost hammer as he unearthed hundreds of gold and silver coins, gold chains, gold and silver spoons, many gold ornaments and gem studded jewelry and a gold pendant encrusted with rubies weighing more than a pound.

An even older treasure hunter found an even more ancient treasure. Cecil Hodder, an 80-year-old former RAF squadron leader, was aware from old newspaper articles that in 1950 a farmer plowing a field a field at Ken Hill in eastern England had uncovered several heavy gold bracelets of Celtic origin, dating from 70 B.C. Hodder decided to search the field with his metal detector. It had been freshly plowed which made his task easier. In fact, within minutes his detector as going wild and by nightfall he had located over 50 gold bracelets, 170 gold rings, three gold ingots and several gold coins. By the time he quit, thinking he had found everything in the field, his collection totaled almost 600 priceless gold Celtic objects valued at over $25 million. He reported the find to the British Museum which sent a team to investigate the site. They stripped away the topsoil covering a three-acre area and discovered five other hoards buried deeper than Hodder's detector could penetrate.

Roger Minty, another lucky Englishman, on his first-ever treasure hunt with a borrowed detector was searching a field near Surrey, England, when he got such a massive signal that he thought he might have found an unexploded bomb. Much to his joy, however, careful digging revealed a cache of 6,701 medieval European coins of which 135 were gold and the rest silver. They were of French, English and Scottish manufacture and bore dates ranging from 1272 to 1455. Word of his find leaked out almost immediately and treasure hunters flocked to the area. Scarcely more than 50 yards from the spot where Minty had struck it rich one of them found a hoard of 1351 medieval coins.

While it would be exciting for the readers of this book to run off to such exotic places as the Philippines, Ecuador or England, most American treasure hunters are content to search closer to home. No matter where you live you are only minutes away from places where coins and other treasures can be found. They may not be hoards of Celtic gold or

Yamashita's Treasure, but you never know when you may pick up a rare coin of great value.

For example in 1992 Richard Trainito of Everett, Massachusetts, was metal detecting in a field with two friends. Fittingly, next to an oak tree he discovered a 1652 New England Oak Tree shilling valued at $3,000. And barely a year into his new hobby of metal detecting, Thomas G. Brown was combing an abandoned farm field near the Merrimack River in southern New Hampshire when he found a very rare colonial period coin known as a Pine Tree threepence dated 1652 and worth $35,000. Ron Attanasio of Gardnerville, Nevada, was detecting along an old trail about three miles from the Carson City Mint when he discovered a rare late 19th-century United States coin. His 1874-CC Seated Liberty dime was valued at $9,000.

While tens of thousands of treasure hunters search for individual coins and artifacts, a small number of others spend literally millions and use sophisticated electronic equipment to go after much larger treasures such as lost mines throughout the western United States and legendary hoards like Victoria Peak in New Mexico.

One of the most remarkable finds was made last year in remote southern Oman on the Arabian Sea. The lost city of Ubar, called "The Atlantis of the Sands" by Lawrence of Arabia, was discovered by analyzing hundreds of photographs taken by the space shuttle Challenger. Radar and optical cameras on the shuttle detected the site even though it had been buried and was deeply covered over by desert sands. The city had been inhabited between 2800 B.C. and 100 A.D. and is believed to be the earliest known shipping center for frankincense – one of the gifts given to Christ by the Wise Men.

Not all treasure hunts end on a happy note. Last summer boaters in the Abacos reported to Bahamian authorities sighting the sun- dried corpse of a man on a deserted cay . Officer Rick Redgrave was sent to investigate and found the remains of 61-year-old treasure hunter Todd Hobart, clutching an old treasure map in his hand. He had been on the island for a month searching for the treasure that French pirate Pierre Le Vecque robbed from a Spanish ship in 1628. He had run out of food and water but couldn't let himself give up the hunt which had dominated most of his life. An autopsy revealed Hobart died of a heart attack. Ironically he dropped dead only a few steps away from the treasure. After a helicopter came to pick up Hobart's body officer Redgrave was just about to leave the area when he noticed an "X" carved into a nearby rock. Underneath the rock he found the treasure that had obsessed Hobart – gold doubloons and diamonds valued at over $4 million.

Another search for pirate treasure which ended in disaster for the treasure hunters took place near Fort Meyers on Florida's gulf coast. After the men had spent 12 years searching without luck for the alleged buried hoard of legendary pirate Jose Gaspar, they stepped up their efforts. Bulldozers, backhoes and dynamite were used, and the expedition ended as the men were arrested and charged with ravaging Native American ruins dating back to 400 A.D. They were lucky to get off with five years probation.

Unfortunately, unscrupulous treasure hunters like these make it difficult for the rest of us. Recently the State of Florida banned the use of metal detectors in all 110 state parks. Many other states prohibit metal detectors and removal of any artifacts including stones. Before long all state and most local public lands will be off limits for treasure hunting. So, before you start searching – for one of the treasures described in this book or for anything else – make sure you are familiar with the laws and rules regarding the area where you plan to work.

If you are interested in buried pirate hoards and want to read more about the lives of the famous buccaneers, get a copy of my wife Jenifer's latest book entitled *Pirates and Privateers of the Caribbean,* available from Krieger Publishing Co., Box 9542, Melbourne, FL 32902. In other news of the Marx family, the Port Royal Sunken Treasure Museum recently opened in St. Petersburg Beach, Florida. It is dedicated to Port Royal in Jamaica, the infamous pirate stronghold in the Caribbean which sank into the sea in 1692 during an earthquake and tidal wave. Of course, an important part of my life has been dedicated to this fascinating subject. The museum contains numerous displays of sunken treasures from shipwrecks around the world, as well as an interactive exhibit where visitors can test their skills using metal detectors. Garrett Electronics has provided the detectors and videos showing how they can be used.

Can you find treasure? Absolutely...and, your chances of finding it are much better if get yourself a modern metal detector and learn how to use it properly.

Where can you find your treasure? As I've tried to point out in this chapter, treasure is being found today all over the world. You can find treasure literally anywhere.

The final 200-plus pages of this book contain my list that locates treasure sites in all 50 states. I offer no guarantees, but I know that if you use a modern metal detector properly, you *will find treasure*. Whether it's a handful of current coins on a public beach or a treasure cache hidden in a Rocky Mountain mineshaft or buried on a deserted Caribbean island is up to you. But, I have little doubt that eventually you'll strike it rich.

Happy treasure hunting!

2 – The Principles that Govern It...

Detector Operation

First of all, metal detectors are easy to use. Believe me! I've been finding treasure with them all my adult life – which goes back several decades – so, I should know. And, the modern one-touch detectors are so simple to operate that its sometimes uncanny.

In fact, metal detectors generally are incredibly easier to hunt with today than they were when I first began trying to find treasure with a war surplus U.S. Army mine detector. Now, that was a chore!

Plus, modern computerized circuitry will find *more* treasure and will find it quicker and easier. Over the years I've observed – and rejoiced – at the continuing improvements as they have been made in detector circuitry and design. Since metal detectors have been and continue to be a primary working tool for me, every improvement that is made in them helps me do my job better.

Progressive detector manufacturers have steadily improved the circuitry and design of their instruments. But, the advancements made just in the past few years have been truly breathtaking. You see, the metal detector has entered the computer age, and treasure hunting has never been simpler than with a computerized one-touch detector.

How easy are modern metal detectors to use? Press one touchpad, and you're ready to find treasure. You read correctly. That's all you must do – press just one touchpad. And, you may never have to touch another control as long as you hunt, even as you find countless treasures with that detector.

The remainder of Chapter 2 will discuss how a metal detector works. Now, It's not necessary to understand the scientific principles of metal detection to use a detector for treasure hunting. You can find coins, rings, jewelry, gold nuggets, caches or whatever you are searching for without understanding how your detector is operating. If you aren't interested in learning, skip *right now* to the next chapter which discusses the various kinds of detectors that are available and offers some suggestions about the type instrument that you should use to maximize your treasure hunting efforts.

That chapter is then followed by one which discusses just how to use a modern one-touch detector most effectively ... and, most profitably.

I'm serious; skip on over to Page 35 if you're not interested in learning about basic detector operations. But, stay with me if you want you want to find more treasure. You'll have a better comprehension of what your detector is doing, so that you can recognize why it just made that *peculiar* sound...so that you can understand a little better why it reacts the way it does to metals and minerals...so that you *know* what it's trying to tell you. Remember: a good metal detector will never lie; it will simply report what's lying beneath its searchcoil. Thus, good treasure hunters find it helpful to know just how a metal detector goes about finding metal and telling them what it has found.

To understand what a metal detector is and how it operates we need to know just what it is *not*. A detector is not an instrument (Geiger counter) that detects energy emissions from radioactive materials. It is not an instrument (magnetometer) that measures the intensity of magnetic fields. It does not "point" to coins, jewelry or any other kind of metal; it does not measure the abundance of metal. A metal detector simply detects the presence of metal and reports this fact.

These hunters on the trail of Nez Perce Indian treasure in Idaho benefit from knowing exactly what they can expect from their metal detectors.

When a coin or other treasure is made of metal – and, most of them usually are – a metal detector can signal their location a reasonable distance beneath its searchcoil. How all this comes about is somewhat more complicated. Every type of metal detector detects metal essentially by the transmission and reception of radio wave signals. This is basic: when a detector is turned on, a radio signal is transmitted from the detector's searchcoil, generating an electromagnetic field that flows out into any surrounding medium, whether it be earth, rock, water, wood, air or what-have-you. Electromagnetic field lines penetrate metal whenever it comes within the detection path. The extent of this detection depends upon the power used to transmit the signal and the resistance of the medium into which the signal is transmitted.

The electromagnetic field generated by the searchcoil's transmission causes something called *eddy currents* to flow on the surface of metal detected by this field. Generating these currents on the metal results in loss of power in the electromagnetic field, and this loss of power is immediately sensed by the detector's circuitry.

And, simultaneously, a secondary electromagnetic field is generated by the eddy currents into the surrounding medium. The normal electromagnetic field of the detector is further disturbed by electromagnetic field lines passing through metal and generating eddy currents.

These currents and the resulting distortion of the electromagnetic field are all sensed by a metal detector. A receiver in the searchcoil detects the signals at the same time the loss of generating power is being noted by the instrument. Circuitry of the metal detector simultaneously interprets all

Serious treasure hunters continually study the literature that is available on modern metal detectors and how they can be used most effectively.

of the sensations so that it can generate appropriate signals to the operator. The detection device instantly reports that some sort of metallic object appears to be present.

As noted above, electromagnetic signals from the detector's searchcoil cause eddy currents to flow on the surface of any metal object (or mineral) having the ability to conduct electricity. Precious metals such as silver, copper and gold have higher conductivities and, appropriately, more flow of eddy currents than iron, foil, tin or other less desirable metals. Since metal detectors can "measure" the amount of power that is used to generate eddy currents, the detector can "tell" which metals are the better conductors.

Quite simply, the quality of signals generated, received and interpreted by the metal detector and the ability of the treasure hunter to act upon them determine the difference between "digging junk" and finding treasure.

Sound complicated? Well, it is – sort of. And, let me hasten to add here that while all metal detectors utilize the same operating principles, they will not operate in the same manner – especially under field conditions. Better quality detectors will hunt deeper and be more sensitive to what they find. More about this later because it is important!

Penetration of the electromagnetic field into the "search matrix" (that area over which a metal detector scans) is described as "coupling." Such coupling can be "perfect" into air, fresh water, wood, glass and certain non-mineralized earth.

We all know that "perfection" is difficult to achieve, and the science of metal detecting is no different than anything else. The search matrix which a metal detector "illuminates" (through transmission and reception of signals) contains many elements and minerals...some detectable and some not, some desirable and some not. A metal detector's electronic response at any given instant is caused by all conductive metals and minerals and ferrous non-conductive minerals "illuminated" in the search matrix by the electromagnetic field.

Detection of minerals is, in most cases, undesirable. Two of the most undesirable are also two of the most common:

natural iron (ferrous minerals) found in most of the earth's soil and wetted salt found in much of the earth's soil and water. Not only do these minerals produce detection signals, but they inhibit the ability of instruments to detect metal. When iron minerals are present within the search matrix, the electromagnetic field is upset and signals are distorted. Iron mineral detection, therefore, has always presented a major problem to manufacturers and users of metal detectors. In the early days of metal detector treasure hunting it was particularly bad.

As the science of metal detection progressed, however, a primary design criterion measuring the improved abilities of any detector, therefore, was its ability to filter or eliminate responses from undesirable elements, informing the treasure hunter only of those from desirable objects. This is accomplished in a variety of ways depending upon the type of metal detector.

Ground Balancing

It is in this area of mineral elimination — we call it "ground balancing" — that many of the significant advances have been — and continue to be — made in the design of metal detectors. Electronic engineers have long known that this task could be accomplished through various methods of circuitry which properly manage the normal electrical phase relationship among resistive, inductive and conductive voltage. Management of this phase shifting makes detectors strikingly different from each other. The manner in which they can eliminate iron mineralization or other undesirable targets, while still permitting the discovery of coins and jewelry involves highly proprietary knowledge and circuitry protected by U.S. patents. Charles Garrett and his engineers, incidentally, hold a number of these patents, including some that are primary in the manufacture of metal detectors.

When you begin studying mineralization, target identification, field applications and other subjects, you'll be glad you learned this background material. It will help you to understand what your detector is telling you...why you hear certain

31

signals. You will become better able to determine if the object you have detected is one that you want to dig. Proper and highly efficient operation of a modern metal detector is not difficult. It does, however, require a certain amount of study, thought and field application.

Depth of Detection

The electromagnetic field transmitted by any detector flows into the search matrix, generating eddy currents on the surface of conductive substances. Detectable targets that sufficiently disturb the field are detected. Of course, the exact materials present in the search matrix and their resistance to electromagnetic signals will affect how deeply the electromagnetic field will penetrate.

Of all the above factors that determine how deeply a target can be detected only the electromagnetic field and the circuitry to interpret its disturbances are a function of the detector itself. Two other important factors, size and surface area, are determined by the individual targets.

Simply stated, the larger a metal target...the better and more deeply it can be detected. Larger detection signals come from targets that produce more eddy currents. An object with double the surface area of another will produce detection signals twice as strong as those of the smaller object, but it will not necessarily be detected twice as far. It is true, however, that a large target will produce the same detection signal as a small target positioned closer to the searchcoil.

Surface Area

Generally speaking, modern metal detectors are surface area detectors. They are not metallic volume (mass) detectors. How a detector "sees" a target will be determined to a large extent by the surface area of a metal target that is "looking at" the bottom of the searchcoil. You can prove for yourself that the actual volume or mass of a target has very little to do with most forms of detection.

Lay your detector down and turn it on. Now move a large coin toward the searchcoil with the face of the coin "looking at" the bottom of the coil. Note how far away the coin is detected. Next, move the coin back and turn it so that the narrow edge "looks at" the searchcoil's bottom. You will notice that when it is turned this way, the coin must come closer to the searchcoil to be detected. The mass of metal itself did not change, only the surface area of the coin facing the searchcoil. Another proof is to measure the distance a single coin can be detected. Then, stack several coins on the back side of the test coin and check to see how far this stack of coins can be detected. You'll find that the stack can be detected at only a slightly greater distance when the face of only one coin faces the searchcoil, illustrating that the larger volume of metal had very little effect on detection distance.

Fringe-area detection is a characteristic whose understanding will enable you to detect metal targets to the maximum depth capability of any instrument. The normal detection pattern for a coin may extend, say, nine inches below the searchcoil; the detection pattern for a small jar of coins may extend perhaps 18 inches. Within these areas of detection an unmistakable detector signal is produced.

But detection is also taking place outside the detection pattern. Signals from this detection, however, are too weak to be heard by the operator except in the fringe area directly adjacent to the outer edges of the normal detection pattern.

The ability to hear fringe-area signals results in greatly improved metal detection efficiency and success. If you want to hear such signals, a good set of headphones is a must, along with training yourself in the art of discerning those faint whispers of sound that can signal the presence of a target in your fringe area. You can develop the ability to hear these signals with practice, training, concentration and faith in your detector and its ability. Those of you who develop fringe area detection capability will discover treasures that other hobbyists miss. Combine this capability by using a modern computerized instrument that can detect deeper and more precisely, and you're part of a treasure hunting team that can't be beat!

How Detectors 'Report'

When a treasure hunter is scanning a searchcoil over the ground or in the water, a detector reports information on the targets it discovers in essentially three ways:

• Increases or decreases in audible volume (universal on all detectors);

• Graphic information presented on LCD meters (sometimes reported in a numerical "code");

• Meter deflections (types of meters can vary greatly, along with the amount and accuracy of the information they present).

This business of "reporting" is one that has changed dramatically over the years. Early treasure hunters had to rely on sound alone. They were urged to listen closely to their detectors so that they could learn to interpret these sounds. Then, came meters of varying abilities. Finally, we have LCD indicators, and I can assure you that those on quality detectors are *precise*! One family of detectors accurately reports both size and depth of every object detected. This is what's called reporting in detail.

But, the object of these reports by any detector — sounds alone from beginner models to precise LCD size-and-depth indications on the professional instruments — is to help you, the treasure hunter, determine what your detector has discovered...before you start to dig it up.

So, I urge you again to practice, practice, practice. Experiment and learn what your detector is trying to tell you. Remember, a quality detector will never lie. It's just up to you to interpret what it's saying and/or showing.

3 – Choosing The Right One...

Your Detector

The selection of a metal detector is more involved than just finding one that costs the most (or the least) or buying the one that a magazine article said found thousands of coins. You must have *quality*, and you should demand *value*. Both can be found! And, if you are diligent, you will recognize these essentials when you find them. Metal detectors are actually about as easy to learn to evaluate as they are to use. The purpose of this book is to make both these tasks easier for you – as well as to help you find a treasure.

Of course, as you've already observed I recommend a computerized one-touch detector – especially for a person just starting out in the hobby. Remember that your selection of any brand or type of metal detector should be based upon three proven features of any detector as well as quality and value:

- Ability
- Versatility,
- Capability.

Now, *quality* and *value* are never accidents. As you learn about detectors, your ability to recognize them will improve. Study the advertising and sales literature of all manufacturers. Make a chart, and list the various brands and types of detectors, their capabilities and the various available searchcoils. On the chart note what you like, and don't like, about each of them...also, their cost.

If a manufacturer says a detector will do a particular job, study his literature to determine if he gives you in-depth information regarding that detector and proving its capabilities. Or, has he just made a flat competitive statement that his detector can be used for this or that with no proof whatsoever? Visit or contact several detector dealers. Talk to them about the various kinds of detectors.

A popular adjective for detectors today seems to be "simple." I know one detector manufacturer that describes his instrument as "the ultimate in simplicity." Believe me, it isn't. Don't believe advertising claims. Turn on the detector for yourself and see if it's ready to hunt or if you have to set several controls or – perish the thought – load a computer program. I don't know about you, but having to *load* a program into my detector or to remember numerical codes to understand its signals ranks right up there with programming a VCR in simplicity.

Read this book carefully. You can also study the various magazines and other books about computers. Notice which detectors other hobbyists are using.

Don't believe such statements as "Oh, that particular detector is junk," and "You don't want that brand of detector." When you hear those kinds of statements, ask the person making them why he said that. Listen to his answer. Ask him for specifics and not generalities such as "Mine is the only one; all other brands of detectors are no good!" Judge for yourself the accuracy of such statements.

Talk to detector owners and dealers about metal detectors and then try to average out what they say. Don't take the word of just one person on which detector is best or which is the worst; talk to a lot of people. Perhaps a detector owner has experienced a problem with a detector. It may be serious, or only minor...or, in fact, the owner may have never learned how to use the detector correctly in the first place. Still, that person may forever be against a particular brand of detector...an opinion he or she expresses far and wide! Such information is scarcely the most desirable upon which to base your decision.

Select an instrument built by a progressive company that has a continuing program of detector improvement. Does the manufacturer test his own instruments? Does he get out into the field and use them under all kinds of situations? Does he travel to various locations to test varying soil conditions to insure his detectors work regardless of conditions? Are company engineers active in the field?

Pay no attention to unsubstantiated advertising claims. Those are simply *sell* statements and do nothing to increase your knowledge of detectors. The manufacturer who says his detectors are the best, above all others, should be asked to prove it. After all, HE made the statement, its up to HIM to prove it! And, while he is trying to do the impossible, go buy the best detector for you. If he claims that any instrument is a simple, one-touch detector, check it out for yourself to make certain that you're ready to hunt after touching one control.

How do you find this detector? Get your hands on one or more, and *try them out.*

Testing the Instrument

Turn the detector on. Is it ready to hunt? If not, what do you have to do to make it ready? Perhaps you must set an audio or a discrimination level; if this can't be done quickly and easily, you're already in trouble with the instrument. Ask the dealer for assistance. See if he is able to regulate the detector smoothly.

As you will learn from Chapter 5, there are several different kinds of treasure hunting. And, various detectors are specifically designed especially for particular types of hunting as pointed out in Chapter 6.

Unless you really know what you're doing with a detector, however, I suggest that you set aside any concern about getting just the "right" detector for the type hunting you intend to do. Get the right detector for *you.* More about this in Chapter 6.

Charles Garrett tells me that he believes more than two thirds of the men, women and children who use detectors hunt essentially just for lost coins. Now, that doesn't mean they will pass up any jewelry they find (or a pirate's chest filled with pieces of eight, for that matter)! But, the goal of most individuals is to enjoy a hobby that can pay for itself — and, to make it pay by finding coins. In fact, Charles adds that he's pretty confident that more than half of the instruments his company sells are never used for anything but coin hunting. For this reason, he has stated that *every* Garrett detector is designed to find coins. Perhaps that statement is true of other manufacturers. But, the point I'm making is that you should get a *general purpose* detector unless — as I noted above — you're pretty sure of yourself and what you want to accomplish with a detector.

There is no one particular brand or type of detector that is "just perfect" and that will do every job perfectly with total capabilities. There are, however, many types of detectors in all price ranges that will perform admirably in many situations and under extreme environmental conditions, and a few detectors that will do most jobs quite satisfactorily.

If possible, rent or borrow a detector of the type you wish to buy. Spend as many hours as possible using that detector to learn its characteristics and capabilities. There is no better way to find out for yourself if a particular detector is suited for you than to use it.

Concerning dollars and cents, please don't make the very common mistake of thinking that if you look around and choose the highest priced detector, you will be getting the best instrument. You may find yourself with one that's so complicated that you'll spend more time loading programs than treasure hunting!

Remember, you're looking for value. That means the most detector for the dollar.

So, instead of buying the most expensive or the lowest price instrument, determine a price *range* that fits your pocketbook. Then, diligently analyze all detectors priced within that range before buying the one that suits you best and measures up to your standards of quality and value.

Let's say that you've decided to spend from $400 to $600 on a new detector. Analyze and use the various models in that range. Compare them and judge their versatility, capability, quality and the ability to do the specific jobs you require. Then, purchase the detector that you find best suited to your metal detection wants and needs.

How much should you spend for a detector? Remember that you generally get what you pay for. Because a quality metal detector is a scientific instrument, you shouldn't expect it to come cheap. In fact, starting out with a cheap detector is a sure-fire way to shorten your detecting career. You'll quit in a hurry because you won't find anything.

Search for Value

When seeking that *right* detector for your type of hunting, one of your major considerations must always be value. Of course, value is the relationship between what an item costs and how well it performs. High quality detectors may seem expensive, but you'll never "lose your money" by purchasing one of them because you'll always have a high quality detector. On the other hand, if you buy a cheap, off-brand model, you'll essentially lose *all* your money because your so-called detector won't do any of the things you expect. You're left with nothing!

You can see that I'm evading the question I posed about price. Now, the detectors I use have a base price in the $1,000 range, even before I make expensive modifications. But, I'm a professional, and I must have quality and dependability. With a quality manufacturer you can certainly get everything you need for far less money. Right now, the basic "plain-Jane" quality detectors have suggested prices in the $200 range or just below that amount. Depending on your dealer, you may beat this price, but I wouldn't buy a model that has a list price of much less than $200. And, you'll probably want to pay more to get some of the features I discuss.

For example, you probably won't be able to buy a quality deepseeking (meaning, computerized) one-touch detector for this low price. But, the ease of operation you'll enjoy with this type of instrument and the deeper treasure you'll find are well worth the extra dollars. And, prices on the computerized one-touch models may become even less than they are today as the new models are developed.

Now, these "hundreds" of dollars may sound like a lot of money — and, it is — but, remember, that a quality metal detector will literally last a lifetime. I use mine constantly, and I'm continually amazed at how well they endure the treatment they're forced to receive. And, I can guarantee that you won't be ever be forced to buy bait, lures and balls or to pay greens fees or country club dues like you would with some other, more expensive, hobbies.

Above all, when you select a detector, you must depend upon the reputation of the manufacturer...the record a company has achieved over the years. It has happened many times that a detector with a square foot of printed circuit board was out-performed by a detector with a board the size of a playing card. And, think of what it may cost you to have that one square foot of printed circuit board repaired! Don't fall for the gimmick that "this detector has transistors in it that are the equivalent of a microprocessor." There's no such thing! To paraphrase the old song...there's nothing like a microprocessor. You may also be told that a particular detector has x-many more transistors than any competitive instrument. Someone may be trying to dump an engineering nightmare on you that wears out batteries every 30 minutes.

Knowledgeable and conscientious engineers continually strive to design circuitry with minimum components. The more components there are, the less reliable the product. And, I repeat, *nothing* does the work of a microprocessor in a detector except a microprocessor.

Be sure to examine the detector. Does it look like quality? Does it have jagged edges or unfinished parts? Is it ruggedly built or does the control housing flop on its handle? Pick up the detector and handle it. Does it feel like quality? Grasp the control housing and rock it back and forth. Is it solid or loose? Switch on the detector and check it out by adjusting the controls.

Speaking of controls, just how many are there? Will "one touch" really make this detector ready to hunt? You go into the field to find treasure, not to prove your expertise by manipulating controls on an electronic instrument. Are all controls absolutely necessary? Are they smooth to operate? When you put the detector through its paces over various targets, does it respond smoothly or are there sudden changes and squawks and squeals in the audio?

Quality construction should be demanded! If you suspect less-than-the-best construction in any single one of a detector's components, it may pay you to double-check everything else associated with this particular instrument.

The searchcoil should be well made with its components mated together properly. If there is a visible bonding seam, it should be a uniform bead properly applied. The stem mounting brackets on the searchcoil should be correctly aligned, and there should be two upright brackets, not just one. The method used for mounting the stem to the searchcoil should be simple, yet strong and functional, with only a reasonable twist of the wing nut or locking nut to hold the searchcoil securely in position...despite the bumps it is sure to take against the ground, stumps and bushes.

And, pay attention to the ease with which searchcoils can be changed. After you become proficient, you'll be doing this more and more.

When you test the instrument's detection capabilities, please don't rely too much on the results of so-called "air tests'" i.e., checking out the distance that a detector will detect various small and large targets with nothing but air between the searchcoil and target. Of course, you'll probably want to determine a detector's sensitivity for yourself in such a test. If so, try to measure detection distance with a small coin like a penny. Don't use a silver dollar! The smaller coin is a better test target. If a detector will pick up a penny to a good distance, it will surely detect a silver dollar to an even greater one.

Let me point out, however, that the new computerized detectors have made "air tests" completely invalid.

Remember that microprocessor-controlled circuitry enables a detector to analyze simultaneously all soil conditions as well as the target(s) beneath its searchcoil. Thus, computerized detectors with microprocessor controls, when properly designed, can sometimes detect objects at greater distances (depths) in the ground than in the air! It's a fact.

Selection Checkpoints

When selecting a metal detector, here are a few specific points to consider:

• **Portability.**

– When not in use, the equipment may be quickly and easily disassembled, without tools, for storage in a protective case.

• **Ease of Operation.**

– The equipment should be lightweight and engineered for comfortable use over extended periods of time. Remember, however, that the lightest equipment may not be sufficiently durable.

– The equipment should have only the controls and functions necessary to do the job intended – one-touch, preferably.

– Unnecessary controls and functions require extra circuitry which can degrade reliability.

– Extra controls and functions can also confuse an operator, especially one who uses the equipment just occasionally. Improper adjustment or improper use, if only temporarily, can decrease the effectiveness of a search...and make a hunt less enjoyable.

– The equipment must have certain controls and functions to be effective.

1. Circuit or means to check the batteries.

2. Push button or automatic controls to switch easily between different hunting modes (All Metal and Discriminate, for example).

3. Circuitry that automatically eliminates (ground balances) the effects of iron minerals in the soil and/or ocean salt, if you are a beachcomber.

4. Headphone jack for this essential accessory.

5. Compatibility with different sizes and types of searchcoils. No matter what you are told, one "standard"

searchcoil will not be sufficient as you gain expertise. Make certain your detector will accept other sizes and types...and that they are available!
- Access to batteries (if not rechargeable) should be easy. Are the batteries readily available and reasonably priced?
• **Capability.**
- The detector should be capable of performing, with good efficiency, all the tasks you intend for it to perform, even if this task is only finding coins.
- Necessary searchcoils (see above) and other accessories should be standard equipment or available for optional purchase.
• **Depth Detection.**
- When evaluating a metal detector, depth detection – the ability to detect an object at a given distance – is sometimes the only point a purchaser considers. True, this is vitally important. But, a quality detector should also have excellent sensitivity, mechanical and electrical stability, plus the ability to operate at great efficiency over *any type of mineralized ground.* And, it must be easy for you to use. Without all these characteristics, you may have an inadequate metal detector – despite all its bells and whistles...and its great performance in an air test.
- When evaluating sensitivity, test different types of objects. Some instruments are more sensitive to iron, some are less sensitive to coins.
• **Stability**
- No detector, regardless of features, is worthy unless it is electronically stable and not subject to erroneous signals from...
    1. Changes in battery voltage.
    2. Minor temperature changes in circuit components.
    3. Current leakage on printed circuit boards because of moisture.
    4. Poor quality components.
    5. Poorly designed searchcoils.
- Mechanical stability is the ability of the detector to

produce no erroneous signals or changes in control adjustments because of normal scanning movement of the detector. Such problems can be caused by...

1. Movement of the searchcoil connector.
2. Movement of improperly secured internal wiring and connectors.
3. Movement of improperly secured batteries.
4. Movement of the printed circuit board caused by flexing of the detector housing when the detector is lifted or moved by its handle.
5. Flexing of the searchcoil as it is moved back and forth over the ground.
6. Movement of internal searchcoil components when the searchcoil is bumped against an object, such as a large rock or tree trunk.

The most sensitive equipment may not have the stability to be effective.

• **Durability** is important because a metal detector will often be used many hours in rugged environments. Since electronic circuits can be expected to be functional for many years, a strong mechanical package is important. Points to consider are...

– All structural components should be strong enough to prevent excessive flexing. Flexing can cause metal fatigue and breakage and also can be a source of mechanical instability.

Over

This versatile one-touch computerized metal detector is suitable for finding every kind of metallic treasure in any type of soil or location.

Facing

Just press the **POWER** touchpad on one of these modern detectors and they are instantly ready to find treasure without any other adjustments.

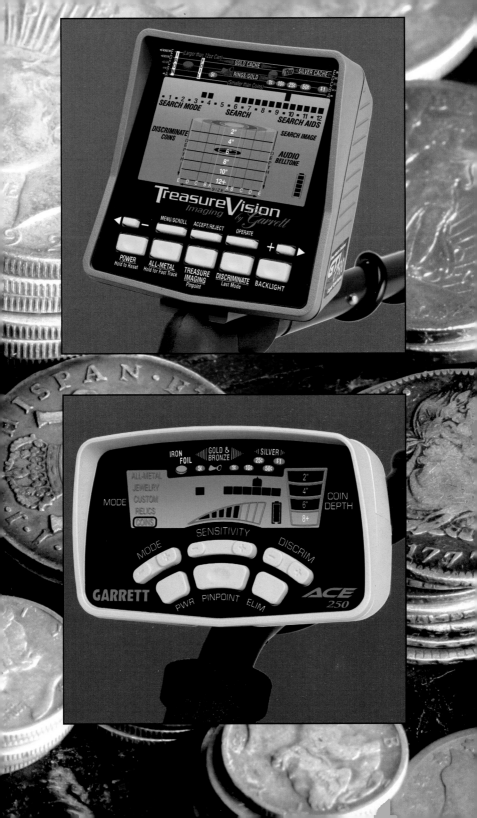

- Rivets, screws and other fastening devices must do their job dependably to prevent loosening of the mechanical package after use.

- Plastic parts should be properly designed and manufactured from high quality materials that prevent breakage, warping, melting and cracking from heat and cold.

- Properly designed carrying cases should be available to protect the equipment during transportation and storage.

- Beware of detectors with circuitry housed in a little tin box with sharp edges that may tear your clothes or car's upholstery.

- Remember that paint on the tin box will chip off and/or wear away, making the instrument less attractive than it is in the showroom.

• **Environmental Considerations** are important in selecting a detector. Some examples of problems due to environment are...

- Moisture protection is important to enable the equipment to be used in light rain or among wet vegetation.

- Submersible searchcoils allow searches in shallow water as well as under conditions listed above.

- If the equipment is to be used under water or is to be used extensively in shallow water, a guaranteed seal is absolutely necessary.

Over

Some modern one-touch detectors are so light and easy to handle that they can be used for hours and hours of searching without causing fatigue.

Facing

Certain detectors are designed primarily for specific types of hunting like this detector which offers several features that enhance its ability for gold prospecting.

Evaluation Summation

When evaluating a specific detector, here is a summary of things to look for...questions you *should* ask...

• Is the detector easy to operate? How much "adjustment" is actually necessary? In other words, is it *really* a one- touch detector?

• Is it truly a computerized instrument with microprocessor controls?

• Is the detector too heavy? Now, it may feel just fine the first time you pick it up, but decide how it will feel after you swing it several hours. Believe me, when you're on the track of treasure, the hours fly by. And, you will not be satisfied with a detector that forces you to stop hunting simply because its weight has cramped up your muscles.

• Are the instrument and its components well protected for storage, transportation and use?

• Is the detector easily assembled and are the batteries and all controls readily accessible and properly located?

• Is the equipment designed so that weight is always properly balanced?

• Is the equipment constructed with strength and durability? Look for areas that are mechanically weak and flex easily. Look for controls, meters or other items that protrude and which could be broken off. Are there sufficient fastening devices, locking nuts, etc., to keep the handle and stems from working loose?

• Is plastic used properly in the equipment? Are the searchcoils made of heavy gauge ABS for long wear and abrasion resistance? Are the searchcoils solid and filled with urethane foam for mechanical stability and long life? Is the plastic stem or stem extension made of strong materials that will not be expected to crack or break?

• Are desired operational features such as a battery check, detection depth (sensitivity) control, discrimination, ground balance and earphone jack included?

• Are desired accessory searchcoils available? Can all searchcoils be submerged?

• Are controls clearly marked? Is the instruction manual adequate, yet easy to understand?
• Is the equipment designed to do the jobs intended? Is it suitable for the operating environments in which it will be used?

Bench Test

Bench test the equipment indoors. Be sure the searchcoil is not on a metal table or near metal table supports or any other kind of metal.

- Turn the equipment on, regulate audio level, if necessary, and listen for a smooth sound.

- Listen to the sound and watch the LCD or meter indications. The sound and visual display should remain reasonably constant. If the detector is not already at room temperature, a small change may be expected due to the temperature stabilization of the circuit components and the searchcoil.

- Check the detection depth (distance) and sensitivity to a representative group of targets, i.e. coins, guns, knives, etc. If the detector has more than one operating mode, check them all.

- Check sound for loudness and tone quality.

Field Test

Take the equipment outside, away from metal in walls, floors, furniture, etc., and test for mechanical stability. Turn the detector on and set the audio threshold, if necessary, before making the following tests...

- Grasp the searchcoil with one hand, and squeeze and flex the coil. Normally the sound will change, the less the better, but it must return immediately to the starting point when the coil is released. No pops or crackles should be heard. Be sure the wire is wrapped lightly around the stem and you do not change the angle of the coil on the stem during the test. Either of these can cause a faulty test. Also, be sure to remove your rings and watch before making the test.

- Take the detector and bump it from all sides with your hand. No pops or crackles should be heard. The batteries should not jar loose.

51

- While holding the detector by the handle, lightly bump the searchcoil against a large rock or wall. Audio and visual indicators should not change. - While holding the detector by the handle, raise the searchcoil above your head and lower to two feet off the ground. The sound should not change significantly. - In an area with grass or vegetation more than three inches high, moisten the vegetation with a hose. Now test the Faraday shielding of the coil. Movement of the searchcoil through the vegetation should produce no, or very minor, audio responses. - Check balance, ease of operation, sound level, detection depth (by searching for representative targets you have buried), mechanical and electrical stability.

Choosing the *right* detector for you can be a major factor in your enjoyment and appreciation of treasure hunting. If you're not happy with the instrument you're using, you're not going to get all the pleasure possible out of this great hobby.

And, what a tragedy that would be!

For this reason I implore you to select carefully. Be as honest as you can about how you will use your detector and then select one that you believe to be just right for you!

Finding Treasure

And, that chapter heading should also read; "Especially if it's a one-touch computerized instrument! They're the most modern and the easiest to use, but this chapter will explain clearly how you can find treasure with any detector!

Did you skip Chapter 2? If so, I hope that you'll take the time to read it soon because it will help you to become a better metal detector operator...thus, a better treasure hunter. Read just the last sentence of the chapter to understand what I mean.

Now, let's learn how to find treasure with a metal detector! My good friend Charles Garrett has stated firmly his belief that as long as it performs basic functions, a poorly built detector will produce more in the hands of an experienced operator than a high quality detector will in the hands of a person who does not understand the instrument or know how to use it. I concur.

While a most important factor in successful detector operation is the expertise and ability of the operator, complete understanding of the detector is vital.

And, you can certainly believe that the detector is important also. There will be no comparison between the finds of two experts hunting the same area...one with an old detector with which he or she is absolutely familiar and the other with a modern one-touch computerized detector with which he has become proficient.

The new instrument with its microprocessor controls will hunt the pants off even the best of the old detectors. I've proved it for myself!

Still, detectors being sold today vary so widely in quality. They are not all computerized one-touch instruments. Some will barely detect a coin one inch deep, while computerized instruments will detect that same coin at extreme depths in the same soil. So, if are determined to use an older detector, make certain that it is a high quality instrument from a respected manufacturer. Then you should learn how to use it well by following instructions in your owner's manual and this and other books.

But, if you're just starting out in the hobby or if it's time for you to buy a new instrument, I urge you to select a computerized one-touch detector...even if it costs a little more. You'll be glad you did when you find yourself discovering treasures that others have passed over!

This chapter then is for all metal detector operators...especially those relatively new to the hobby. It contains practical methods, tips and procedures recommended to every treasure hunter. The success you ultimately obtain, however, with any kind of metal detector will be in direct proportion to the amount of time and study that you devote to the hobby. And, you will be more successful with a modern one-touch detector. No matter how good some of the older detectors were (and still are) they can't match the depth and sensitivity of the new computerized instruments.

With any detector, however, the first instruction is the same: *Read your instruction manual!* Carefully study the operator's manual that accompanied your detector. In fact, Charles Garrett recommends that you examine this manual *before* you purchase a detector. If the manufacturer has "skimped" on providing instructions and advice, you might find yourself shorted in other areas of an instrument.

On the other hand, an extremely detailed manual that you find hard to understand could well indicate a detector that's going to prove just as complicated...one that will be difficult to learn how to use. New one-touch computerized and microprocessor-controlled detectors are *simple to use*, not difficult.

Getting Started

Assuming that you have read this book carefully and made a thorough study of the metal detector market to select the best instrument for you, the next step is to make up your mind that you are going to learn how to use this detector properly, regardless of the effort it takes. Never deviate from your decision! A detector will remove the blindfold and permit you to "see" coins, jewelry and other hidden valuables. But you have to trust your detector. You have to learn the correct methods of operating it. You have to learn its idiosyncrasies. You have to learn what makes it tick! In other words...

Learn your metal detector!

Getting hands-on instructions from the dealer from whom you purchased your new detector is the ideal first step for the beginner. Learn all you can from your dealer, then – after you have studied your instruction manual (and audio/video tapes) thoroughly – go into the field with a notebook and carefully write down all questions you have or any problems that have arisen. Return to the dealer for your answers. Don't neglect this vital first step! If the dealer can't answer your questions, write or call the manufacturer!

When you begin your home study, please don't make the mistake of immediately assembling the detector and running outside to begin looking for treasure. First, read your instruction manual...not once, but several times. The first time through, read it from front to back without stopping. Pay no attention to your new detector, but simply read its instruction manual. If video or audio instruction tapes are available for your detector, watch or listen to these several times. Then, assemble your instrument according to the instructions on the tapes and in the manual. Take time to do it right.

With a one-touch detector you're now ready to hunt for treasure.

And, that's what you should do! Modern detectors have many capabilities beyond that available with a single touch. But, it's the touch of a single control that let's you find treasure with a modern detector, so let's go find some.

Don't worry – at least at first – about what you are finding. As you put miles behind your searchcoil, you will find yourself getting better and better with your detector. You will become more at ease in using it, and there will be fewer and fewer "problems" that bother you. The quantity of found items will be growing at an accelerated rate. Although your learning and training period and even on down through the years, you must develop persistence. *Never give up!* Persistence, Persistence, **Persistence!** These are the key words for any successful operator.

Hold the detector with the searchcoil about three feet off the ground. Turn the detector on, lower the searchcoil to a height of about two inches above the ground and begin scanning.

When the sound increases and/or an indication is shown on the LCD panel or meter, a target is buried in the ground below the searchcoil.

When a treasure hunter is scanning his searchcoil over the ground or in the water, a detector reports information on targets through increases or decreases in audible volume (universal on all detectors); graphic information presented on LCD meters (sometimes reported in a numerical "code") or meter deflections.

Remember that acceptable objects cause the audio or visual indicators to increase in amplitude while unacceptable objects cause the indicators to decrease. LCDs and meter indicators can provide additional information concerning the possible "value" of targets. Some of the new LCD's can indicate just what you've discovered.

Techniques of scanning for treasure with a metal detector are many and varied. Here are some simple recommendations:

• Keep the searchcoil level as you scan and always scan slowly and methodically; scan the searchcoil from side to side and in a straight line in front of you.

• Do not scan the searchcoil in an arc unless the arc width is narrow (about two feet) or unless you are scanning extremely slowly. The straight-line scan method allows you to cover

more ground width in each sweep and permits you to keep the searchcoil level throughout each sweep. This method reduces skipping and helps you overlap more uniformly.
• Overlap by advancing the searchcoil as much as 50% of the coil's diameter at the end of each sweep path. Occasionally scan an area from a different angle. Do not raise the searchcoil above scanning level at the end of each sweep. When the searchcoil begins to reach the extremes of each sweep, you will find yourself rotating your upper body to stretch out for an even wider sweep. This gives the double benefit of scanning a wider sweep and gaining additional exercise. To insure that you completely scan any given area, use string or cord to mark scan paths three to six feet wide.
• You can learn to use a probe to locate the exact spot where coins are buried; this will help you retrieve coins with minimum damage to grass and the target.
• Always fill in your hole after you dig a target; holes are not only unsightly, but they can be dangerous to people walking in the area. Perhaps it might be you! Before filling a hole, however, be sure to check it again with your detector to make certain you have recovered everything in and around it. It's embarrassing to have someone recover a target from a hole you originally dug. I know; it's happened to me!
• Run-down batteries are by far the single most common source of detector "failure;" be sure to check your batteries before venturing out, and carry spare batteries whenever you are searching.
During the learning phase with your own detector, keep in mind that you should work smarter, not harder. Each time you receive a signal – before you dig – try to guess what the target is, what size it is, its shape and its depth. Analyze the audio and/or meter signals. Say to yourself, "This is a coin," or "This is a bottlecap. It is about three inches deep." Then pay careful attention when you dig the object. Try to determine exactly how deep it is and how it was lying in the ground.
Did you guess right? Great! If not, try to determine why. The more you do this, the greater your success will be. You

will quickly learn how to use and actually "read" your instrument and understand everything it is telling you.

As you scan the searchcoil over the ground, scan at a rate of about one foot per second. Don't get in a hurry, and don't try to cover an acre in 10 minutes. Always remember that what you are looking for is buried just below the sweep you are now making with your searchcoil. It's not across the field.

After you've become comfortable with your one-touch detector and learned how easy it is to find treasure with it, you will want to learn more about this detector and its capabilities. Although you really never have to do more than press a single control to find treasure with the new one-touch detectors, you'll probably want to become familiar with all of your instrument's controls. You'll want to operate it in all of the various modes and functions to learn exactly what it will do for you.

So, it's back to the Owner's Manual. You can skip the parts that concern assembly and searching, but read the rest of it carefully. You'll want to learn how to regulate the sound threshold. Follow instructions carefully to set the volume control to a minimum threshold level. If silent operation is desired, always make certain that such operation is just below an audible level. Many of us never use silent audio since it is possible to overlook "fringe" signals and miss targets.

The instruction manual and tape(s) should guide you through all of these adjustments which you can make through the bench-testing process. Lay your detector on a wooden bench or table. Do not use a table with metal legs and braces because the metal could interfere with your testing. Begin with the part of your instruction manual that describes detection of metal. Go through the procedure! If your detector is equipped with a sensitivity or detection depth control, test the detector at several levels. Test the instrument with various metal targets. Make the adjustments discussed in the manual or video that let you accomplish different objectives with the detector. Try as many of these variations with different targets on the bench as possible.

Discrimination

After you have used your detector for several hours, you can begin to test its discrimination capabilities. Read about it in your owner's manual. But, whatever you do, don't use too much discrimination...just enough to eliminate from detection the junk you may have been digging. Do not try to set the controls to eliminate pulltabs. That can come later when you know more about your detector and only when you feel such discrimination is absolutely necessary.

If you haven't started using headphones, now is the time to do so. You'll learn how important they really are. You'll dig coins that you couldn't detect just by listening to a detector's speaker. You'll hear sounds you didn't hear before. Headphones may get hot and the cord may get in your way but the rewards will make it all worthwhile.

After you have even more experience and are beginning to get comfortable with your detector, it's time to go back over the same areas you searched before you learned how to use your machine. You'll surprised at the quantity of coins and other objects you missed. In fact, each time you come back to these places you'll find more coins and other treasures, especially at greater depths.

Always remember that well designed detectors are not complicated or difficult to learn to use. When you begin using controls other than the "one-touch," remember to keep the Detection Depth (Sensitivity) control turned to a low level. Whenever you begin hearing erratic sounds, it's often because you've turned it too high. Before you blame your detector or the high mineral content of the soil, turn down your depth setting. Turning down this setting also lets you work in more areas.

Scan with the searchcoil about two inches above the ground and scan at a moderate speed. Even in areas with large amounts of "junk" metal, which are very difficult to work, reduced detection depth and moderate scanning speed let you hear individual target signals rather than just a jumbled mass of sounds.

Success stories are written every day. A lot of treasure is being found and a lot of treasure is waiting to be found where you live. Detectors are not magic wands, but when used correctly they will locate buried and concealed treasure. Use a high quality detector and keep your faith in it. Have patience and continue using your instrument until you have it mastered. Success will be yours!

Make Your Own Test Plot

One of the first things many new detector owner do is to bury a few coins to see how deeply they can be detected. The usual result...*disappointment.* You see, newly buried coins are quite difficult to detect. The longer an object has been buried, the easier it can be detected. Not only is a "barrier" to electromagnetic field penetration created when a coin is first buried, but no "halo effect" has been developed. As time passes, coins become more closely associated, electrically, with surrounding earth materials and the molecules of metal begin to leave and move out into the surrounding soil. Also, it is theorized that in some cases (especially in salt water) the coin's surface becomes a better conductor. In certain areas it is believed that coins buried for some time can be detected at twice the depth of coins that have just been buried.

You should construct your own test plot to help you learn the capabilities of your detector. First of all, select the area for it and scan the area thoroughly with no discrimination so that you can remove all metal from the ground. Select targets such as various coins, a bottlecap, a nail and a pulltab. Select also a pint jar filled with scrap copper and/or aluminum metal, a long object such as a foot-long pipe and a large object such as a gallon can. Bury all these objects in rows about three feet apart and make a map showing where each item is buried. Be sure to note its depth.

Bury pennies at varying depths, beginning at one inch. Continue, with the deepest buried about six inches deep. Bury one at about two inches but stand it on edge. Bury a penny at about two inches with a bottlecap about four inches off to one side. Bury the bottlecap, nail and pulltab separately about two inches deep. Bury the jar at twelve inches to the top of its lid. Bury the pipe horizontally three or four inches deep. Bury the gallon can with the lid two feet below the surface.

The purpose of the buried coins is to familiarize you with the sound of money. If you can't detect the deeper coins, don't worry. After a while, you'll be able to detect them quickly. If you can detect everything in your test plot, rebury some items deeper. The penny buried next to the bottle cap can give you experience in Super Sniping with a smaller searchcoil and will help you learn to distinguish individual objects. The jar and gallon can will help you learn to recognize "dull" sounds of large, deeply buried objects. The pipe will help you learn to contour. Check the targets with and without headphones. You'll be amazed at the difference headphones make.

The test plot is important. Don't neglect it. From time to time expand it, rebury the targets deeper and experiment with new ones. Your test plot is important because your success in scanning over it will be a measure of how well you are progressing and how well you have learned your equipment. Remember, however, that you must make an accurate map and keep it up to date when you change and/or add to your test plot.

Miscellaneous Tips

When searching areas adjacent to wire fences, metal buildings, metal parking meter posts, etc., reduce detection depth and scan the searchcoil parallel to the structure. This lets you get as close to it as possible.

Coins lying in the ground at an angle may be missed on one searchcoil pass but detected when the searchcoil approaches from a different angle. If your detector has a volume control, keep it set at maximum. Don't confuse volume control with audio (threshold) control. You should use earphones that have individual earphone volume adjustment and set each one to suit yourself.

If you are working on the beach, set discrimination at about bottlecap rejection. A slight amount of adjusting may be necessary but you can set the detector to ignore salt water.

Pulse Induction detectors and others designed for beach hunting ignore salt water automatically.

Use your common sense. *Think* your way through perplexing situations. Remember, success comes from detector expertise, research, patience, enthusiasm and using common sense.

Don't expect to find tons of treasure every time you go out! In fact, there may be times when you don't find anything. But the hobby's real joy and the reward of detecting is never knowing what you'll dig up next!

The Treasures You Can Find

The first successful treasure recovery in which a metal detector was used occurred in 1945. The story actually began in 1846 when an unkempt and silent man came to Boston and was given a lonely job as keeper of the Bug Light on an outer island in the harbor. According to waterfront legend, this man – the King of Calf Island – had been one of the pirates who ravaged the West Indies during the early 19th century. The "King" died without ever discussing his former life.

Some 20 years later a man claiming to be the brother of the deceased lighthouse keeper spent weeks probing with long steel rods in the sands of storm-swept Great Brewster Island. He was said to be searching for a map that gave the key to a great treasure his late brother had buried.

More than half a century later Peg-leg Nuskey passed this tale on to a Boston writer, Edward Rowe Snow. Shortly afterward – in the best tradition of treasure hunting tales – Nuskey was found dead under an overturned dory with its towline around his neck. But, he had already talked to the right man!

Snow, a burly descendant of New England sailing masters, had been treasure hunting unsuccessfully for 20 years. Now, only World War II would halt his search for gold that was buried by the King of Calf Island. Snow returned from the war, however, armed with a new tool that was to revolutionize treasure hunting. It was a surplus military mine detector.

Beneath the floor of a deserted shack on Great Brewster, he unearthed a 17th-century book written in Italian. He brought this book to the Boston Public Library where one of the librarians noticed a pattern of pinholes on one of the pages. The pattern formed a simple code message which informed him that the King of Calf Island had buried his treasure on Strong Island, off Cape Cod.

Snow hastened to the island, armed with his military detector and digging equipment. Five times he received strong readings from the detector and dug to find the buried hulks of old vessels. The sixth signal truly led him to the jackpot.

He dug and found a small encrusted copper pot full of tarnished old coins from Peru, Mexico, Portugal, Spain and England. At the time they were valued at only $1,900, but today they would be worth many times that amount.

Thus was the first metal detector treasure found. Since then, wealth almost too vast to measure has been found all over the world through the proper use of metal detectors. And, these treasures have been found by amateur hobbyists as well as professional treasure hunters.

Are any of these discoveries simply "lucky finds?" Fat chance! Oh, maybe a few of them resulted from blind luck, but more than 99% of all treasure success stories begin with a goal, supported by considerable research, and then require hard work — sometimes long years of it. In short, the successful treasure hunter — be he (or she or they) amateur or professional — decides what treasure he wants to find and then goes after it.

The treasures that a metal detector can find are varied indeed, for this scientific instrument — when used properly — will detect any object made of metal.

Success in attaining any treasures, however, demands...

- Adequate knowledge and
- The right equipment.

The professional understands this. The novice may have to learn it the hard way!

You must first gain knowledge of your treasure. This book will give you a head start, but you will want to follow up with more research, such as that described in Chapter 7.

You will need much knowledge before you can truly know which equipment you will need. Books such as this are an important first step for the treasure hunter in learning about the hobby and the correct equipment with which to pursue it. As I have urged elsewhere in this book and will continue to stress, you should try to study books that deal with *modern* equipment and techniques and not learn about detectors that are already obsolete. Oh, you'll read some fine and colorful stories in the older guidebooks, some of them written by me! Such stories can be lots of fun. But, just remember that modern detectors are many times more capable than older detectors. And, those instruments whose praises are being sung so lovingly and delightfully are *obsolete.*

Get the Right Equipment

Once you know what sort of treasure you want to look for and how you want to go after it, you'll be able to select the *right* equipment. Please let us emphasize the importance of using the right kind of detector wherever and whatever you are hunting. Chapter 3 of this book described modern detectors in detail, and I urge your close attention to it. Newcomers to the hobby, especially, will learn so much. Old-timers can

Modern one-touch detectors have opened the door to new vistas of treasure hunting with their ability to locate so many objects that were passed over before.

test the strength of their own opinions and may be surprised at how much they learn as well. The chapter you are now reading is designed to describe briefly the various kinds of treasure hunting with the following chapter reviewing in the simplest possible terms the kinds of metal detectors you can buy for each type of hunting. We urge all metal detector hobbyists to read these discussions (and, all the rest of this book) carefully.

Before even *thinking* about a detector, let's review the various types of treasure hunting;

Coin hunting is simply finding and retrieving lost coins. Countless millions of coins have been lost and await recovery by the metal detector hobbyist. Thousands of Indianhead and Wheat pennies, Buffalo nickels, Barber dimes, Liberty and Washington quarters, Liberty Walking half-dollars, silver dollars, early colonial coins, gold coins and many other types are being recovered every day. People are losing far more coins today than all the coin hunters combined are finding! Coins are lost everywhere people go, and coins are being found everywhere people have been. Coin hunting is one of the most active family hobbies in America.

The person not familiar with this hobby finds it difficult to believe that coins can be found. "Who loses coins?" they ask. "Surely, there are not enough lost coins to make it worthwhile to buy a metal detector or spend time looking for them!" Charles Garrett has said many times that "any active and experienced coin hunter can find five thousand coins each year." He points out that this is only an average of 100 coins found each weekend for 50 weeks...a reasonable and attainable goal.

And, don't make the mistake of believing there are no coins to be found where you live. If you don't have the experience now, you soon will gain the knowledge to convince yourself that coins are truly found everywhere. The first place every person should start searching is right in his own backyard before branching out from there. Many people erroneously believe there is nothing in their areas worth searching for.

The truth is, all the good coin hunting sites will never be cleaned out.

Exploring a ghost town is a popular and rewarding hobby which includes a number of activities. In ghost towns you may discover old coins, perhaps a buried treasure cache, relics or antiques dating back to the earliest settlers, or lost items from only yesterday. Any place people have gathered will produce relics and coins. There are thousands of abandoned town sites, old forts, homesteads and farmhouse locations. The list is endless. Finding a place to search will never be your problem! Finding the time needed to pursue and enjoy your hobby is often more of a challenge. You will need a good metal detector since most surface items have already been picked up and those remaining will lie below the surface.

Gold and other treasures have been found in some of the most unlikely places imaginable in ghost towns. Four old whiskey bottles full of gold dust were discovered in a dry well. Several hundred rare gold coins from the early 1800s were found in a hollowed-out bannister in an old dance hall. A New Mexico merchant had used a five-gallon counterweight to hold spools of rope against the ceiling of his shop. Apparently his customers never suspected that the counterbalance contained over 50 pounds of gold. A solid gold cuspidor painted green was discovered in the ruins of an old saloon in Arizona and a cache of gold and silver coins was found under the 400-pound anvil of an old blacksmith shop in Texas.

For those interested in older artifacts and treasure there are hundreds of abandoned Spanish missions and settlements scattered all over the Southwest. Because many of these sites were abandoned in haste, usually because of Indian uprisings, they very possibly might hold a large caches of treasure. Caution: many of these settlement have been declared protected historical sites by various governmental bodies. Check with the proper authorities before you start searching to assure that you don't end up on jail or have to pay a fine!

The story is told of a straw-encased bottle filled with 773 dimes found with a metal detector over the doorway of an old shack near Maitland, FL. All the coins were dated prior to 1918. There were 46 of the rare 1916-D's, worth more than $100 each, two 1895-O's, worth more than $50, and 10 1904-S's, worth more than $10 apiece. The numismatic value of the other coins brought the total value of the cache to over $5,000, with today's valuation many times more than that amount. The most significant aspect of the find, however, is that when the coins were hidden they were probably worth little more than their face value of $77.30. In other words, they were probably not hidden by a wealthy person but rather, as the modest shack would indicate, by someone relatively poor. This bears out the old cliche that, "treasure is where you find it."

Cache hunting is seeking money or valuables that have been put away or cached by someone, the little old lady's "hard times" coins she buried in a jar in the garden 50 or 100 years ago, the old man's "bank" jar he kept hidden in the bottom of a fence post hole or, the washtub filled with gold coins. These are all "caches!" There are many, many thousands of these treasures waiting for the detector operator who seeks them out. Buried only a few inches deep or at arm's length below ground surface, they will stay buried forever if they are not dug up by the treasure hunter. These treasures can be found anywhere...in an old chicken coop, halfway between the well and a tree, between two trees, in the ground under the horse stall, in the walls of houses and barns, etc.

Find Battlefield Relics

Collecting and studying *battlefield relics* constitutes an interesting pastime for many people. Of course, the great war in this country was the Civil War, and values placed on artifacts and other items from this time are often astronomical. Simple buttons from Union and Confederate uniforms have been sold at open and private auctions for as much as $1,000. Buckles, a favorite item with most collectors, are highly sought and often demand prices beginning as low as $25 for common buckles in poor condition to more than $2,000 for the more rare or ornate ones. Detecting and digging up battlefield relics brings history so close that the hobbyist can visualize it in the making.

The numerous battle and skirmish sites of the eastern and western campaigns and naval operations abound in relics and artifacts valued by war buffs and professional collectors. All types of weapons or instruments of the war are being located by persistent metal detector operators. There are many "known" battle areas in the country, however, protected by state and federal governments. These areas, rightfully so, are protected and strictly "off limits" to all metal detector operators.

Some of the most spectacular treasure discoveries have been made on the *beaches* of the east cost of Florida. In 1715 a convoy of 12 treasure-laden galleons, their holds crammed with treasure from the New World, were bound for Spain when a devastating hurricane destroyed the entire fleet. Must of the treasure was thrown immediately onto the shore where it was promptly covered by sand. Now, the Spaniards made an effort at the time to recover their treasure from the wrecks and they were somewhat successful, but only with that small part which still lay offshore in shallow water. The bulk which had been cast onto the beach or was lying in deeper water remained out of their reach and was presumed lost forever. Over the centuries more treasure from these wrecks was blown and washed ashore with each storm. Since Kip Wagner found a few coins in 1948 and borrowed a war- surplus mine detector to locate more, millions of dollars in treasure and artifacts from these wrecks has been discovered.

Beaches all over the world continue to be one of the most popular places to search for lost coins and jewelry as well as the treasures from the past...for, where people congregate and play, they will inevitably lose some of their valuable possessions. On some beaches there are roped-off areas designed for swimming. Search these places first! Strike up a conversation with the lifeguard or concession stand operators. It may be that the swimming areas of bygone days were located elsewhere on the beach. You would certainly want to search those sites. Also, lifeguards may know where rings and valuables are reported to have been lost.

Try working along the water's edge at both low and high tides as both could be profitable. You will encounter much less trash near the water, but remember, some very valuable coins and jewelry have been found back away from the beach in the heavy traffic areas. There are thousands of swimming beaches no longer used. Visit your library and do a little research to locate these resort and health spa swimming areas where much treasure awaits discovery.

The most important and useful tool of the rockhound (besides his rock hammer and patience) can be a metal detector. If it is properly understood and operated, its use can be very rewarding and interesting, but it should not be used as the ultimate answer to the positive identification of all detectable specimens. The metal detector should be used as an accessory to the rockhound's field equipment, which will aid in locating conductive metallic specimens that the human eye cannot distinguish or identify. Check known samples and become acquainted with the metal detector. You cannot see inside an ore specimen but a good quality modern detector can.

For our purposes, "metal" is defined as any metallic sub-stance of a conductive nature in sufficient quantity to disturb the electromagnetic field of the searchcoil. If your detector responds to a target as "metallic," collect it for future inspection; it contains conductive metal in some form. If the detector responds as "mineral," it means only that the specimen contains more iron mineral than it does metal in a detectable form. In just a few minutes you might find some high-grade metallic sample that has been passed over for years by fellow rockhounds.

When searching for high grade ore specimens, pay close attention to old mine tailings. You may find that a "worked out" area isn't so barren after all. Certain gems, such as the thunder-egg, have a covering of outside magnetic iron. Some forms of jade and even garnet respond to a good detector.

NOTE: Ore sampling can only be accomplished with a detector that is designed for prospecting and is correctly calibrated to give exacting ore sample identification. To learn about, select and correctly use calibrated instruments, read the new book Roy Lagal wrote, *Gold Panning is Easy,* published by Ram Publishing Company.

The Pocket Probe metal detector is the rockhound's perfect field companion.

Laws of Treasure Hunting

While this book does not attempt to give legal advice, you need to become aware that there are laws applicable to various treasure hunting situations. Each state has its own laws concerning where you can hunt for treasure and whether you may keep treasure when it is found. You should learn these laws.

Most treasure hunters operate under the old premise "finders keepers, losers weepers," but such is not the case at all. One of the most important concepts that you must always remember is that all land in the United States is owned by someone – an individual, corporation, company, historical society, university, or by the local, state or federal government. This fact doesn't necessarily work against the treasure hunter; it simply means that he should first learn if treasure hunting is permissible on the property he wants to explore and when required, get the permission from the owner. It's always best to get this permission in writing – especially if the treasure you seek is a significant one.

All states have laws against trespassing. If a sign says, "Keep Out," do just that. It is always best to seek permission. With the proper attitude and a true explanation of your purpose, you will be surprised at the cooperation you will receive from most landowners. The majority of them will be curious enough about your metal detector and what you hope to find, to agree to let you search. Offer to split, giving them 25% (or less) of all you find and they will be more willing. If large amounts of treasure are believed to be hidden or buried on another's property, a properly drawn, legal agreement is a *must!* Such an agreement between both you and all landowners (husband and wife, etc.) will eliminate any later disagreements which might otherwise arise.

In most cases, public property is open to you. Do not destroy the grass or leave trash or holes. Most park superintendents know that conscientious coin hunters pick up trash and leave the grounds in better shape than they found them. All treasure hunters must become aware of their responsibility to protect the property of others and to keep public property fit for all. Persons who destroy property, dig large holes and leave them unfilled, or tear down buildings in search of valuables, should not to be called treasure hunters—but, more properly, looters and scavengers.

All treasure that you find must be declared as income during the year in which you receive a monetary gain from that treasure. If you find $1,000 in coins, which you spend at once because they have no numismatic value, then you must declare the face value of those coins in the current year's income tax report. If, however, you discover a valuable coin—or, say, an antique pistol—you do not make a declaration until you sell the item(s) and then only for the amount you received. If you decide to donate some of your finds to historical societies or museums, you may be able to deduct the fair market price of the items as charitable contributions. Simply stated, the tax laws require you to declare all income from treasure hunting.

You may be allowed to deduct some or all of your expenses but you must have good records. You are advised to check with a tax accountant, especially if you plan to become a full-time treasure hunter. An accountant will advise you as to what type records you are required to keep.

Join a Club!

There are approximately 350 treasure hunting clubs in the United States with a total of over 500 clubs located throughout the world. Why not join one and take an active part? Clubs are an invaluable source of information. You can learn about metal detectors and treasure hunting from those who are active in the field. You will meet people, share their success stories, and perhaps gain a few hunting partners. You will be encouraged by found treasure, and you can swap some of your treasure and build up your collection.

The hobby and sport of metal detecting has been kept clean and dignified by people who care about their hobby, themselves and their fellow men. Most detector owners go out of their way to protect a most rewarding and enjoyable hobby and to share their enjoyment with others. Keeping the hobby clean takes the effort and dedication of everyone...not just a few. So, as you go about enjoying your leisure, or perhaps full-time activity, be professional! Be worthy of your calling!

Metal Detectors You Can Use

This chapter contains a basic selection guide to help you choose the correct, or optimum detector for the type hunting you intend to do. Various detector characteristics, including ground balance and discrimination for the type of searching you will be doing, are discussed. Basically, any discussion of detectors is divided into three primary categories:

• Treasure Hunting for coins, caches and relics;
• Beach and Underwater Hunting;
• Gold Hunting.

One-touch computerized detectors are available for just about any type of treasure hunting you desire.

There are numerous books written which describe the various facets of metal detecting in much greater detail than space permits here. (On to the treasure locations!) To improve your expertise with the instrument and to learn how to become more efficient in all phases of detector use you may want to read some of these books on the hobby.

Your selection and purchase of a metal detector ought to have the same careful consideration that goes with anything you buy. Shopping has become very much a part of life, and you must depend upon yourself to make the right choice. The more clearly you understand what you want, the more likely you are to be correct in your choice. Choosing a metal detector should take no less time and consideration than buying any other valuable and expensive item. Buying the correct instrument depends both on whether you understand all the important facts about the different types and what your requirements really are.

This was all discussed in Chapter 3. Now, the preceding chapter listed most of the facets of metal detector usage, and I will now recommend the type instrument or instruments and searchcoils to use. Operational aspects are described so that you can compare the features and capabilities of the various brands and types. This information is designed to recommend a specific type of detector. Instructions on using that detector will be found in Chapter 4.

Coin Hunting

Charles Garrett recognizes that every detector his company manufactures will be used, at least part of the time, to hunt coins...and, many detectors will be used for nothing else!

Thus, he believes (and, I agree) that every detector should be manufactured with coin hunting in mind. Now, whenever we discuss coin hunting, please understand that we also include the search for miscellaneous jewelry, such as rings, earrings and the like.

Discrimination control is a must for coin hunting detectors. Also, the instruments must be ground balanced. Most of the modern coin hunting detectors, including some of the one-touch instruments, feature automatic ground balance. Progressive manufacturers have made remarkable advancements in automatic ground balance and their detectors, therefore, are highly acceptable.

Of course, you should Ideally have your choice between Automatic and Manual Ground Balancing. Locating the maximum number and deepest targets will always require an All Metal mode, while the Discriminate mode, featured on detectors with automatic ground balance, can eliminate digging many junk targets.

Round searchcoils eight to nine inches in diameter have traditionally been preferred for coin hunting. This size is lightweight and has good depth detection and scanning width. Something new, however, has come into the picture...the new elliptical searchcoils. These newly designed coils provide good scanning width and have proved especially effective in areas where trash metal targets abound.

For deeper penetration, use the 10 or 12-inch sizes. Pinpointing will be a little more difficult with larger searchcoils, but you can expect to get deeper coins. For operation in tight places adjacent to sidewalks, metal buildings and fences, and for Super-Sniping, use a three-inch to four-inch diameter searchcoil.

Cache or Money Hunting

Ground balancing is essential in searching for deep caches. And, ideally, you should also choose a *manual-adjust* instrument that is capable of using a large searchcoil and a two-box searchcoil designed especially for deep targets. This two-box coil, such as Garrett's Bloodhound Depth Multiplier, should be used whenever possible, because it detects deeply and ignores small objects like nails, etc.

When you're hunting a deep cache, you're not looking for small objects; so, you can forget small coils. A 10-inch size might be good, but a 12-inch size would be even better. When using large searchcoils, an armrest or hipmount configuration is recommended.

Relic Hunting

Relic hunting calls for the same type of equipment that cache hunting requires. You definitely need large searchcoils. You may need a good hipmount configuration, but you will absolutely require headphones. Most relic hunters do not use any form of discrimination because they don't want to take the chance of missing valuable iron relics. Some use a small amount of discrimination only when searching for brass and lead objects.

Ghost Town Searching

If you are outdoors and looking for coins, rings and jewelry, an automatic ground balanced type with good discrimination will give the best results. Since most ghost towns contain many junk metal targets, discrimination will be important. Oftentimes, a great amount of junk may necessitate your reducing the detection depth of your detector. The one-touch computerized detector is ideal for casual ghost town searching.

If you are searching for ghost town relics or money caches, however, a manual-adjust instrument with a genuine All Metal detection mode is better. It would be best to use the largest searchcoil you have available. Large money caches may be quite deep, so you should consider using the Bloodhound Depth Multiplier attachment. This multiplies the depth capability of your detector, producing great depth on objects larger than quart size while almost completely ignoring nails and other small metal trash.

Indoors, the same rules apply in ghost towns as in all other forms of indoor searching.

Beachcombing

Several good new detectors have been developed primarily for beach hunting. These instruments feature automatic ground balance and offer excellent discrimination capabilities. Another type of detector recommended for use when searching ocean beaches is a pulse induction type with discrimination. To search fresh water beaches, all types of detectors are more or less suitable—though, many fresh-water lakes have a high saline content that makes the pulse induction detector more desirable.

Manual-Adjust detectors cannot ignore both salt water and black magnetic sand simultaneously, but Pulse Induction detectors can. Automatic Ground Balancing types can be adjusted to ignore salt water and magnetic sand simultaneously.

There is a phenomenon that causes Pulse Induction detectors to detect coins and rings extremely deep in salt water. Consequently, immediately after they were first placed on the market, they became a favorite among beach coin hunters — especially those who search ocean beaches.

When hunting on any beach, be sure to wear headphones for maximum depth detection and to eliminate not only the sounds of surf but that of people.

You'll want to make certain that your searchcoils are submersible when hunting near the surf. Also, you must be careful not to lay down your detector too near the water when digging a target or for any other reason. More than one beach hunter has had a day spoiled by an errant wave that washed up over his detector. It only takes a splash to create real trouble!

Underwater Detectors

There is a basic mechanical configuration designed primarily for underwater searching. This type detector has the searchcoil, handle and stem permanently attached to a short stem. The stem is too short to use above water, but accessories are available for converting short-stem underwater units to the long-stem arrangement for use on the beach, in the surf or anywhere else. The only detectors now manufactured with a guaranteed seal for underwater use are pulse induction instruments, which are ideally suited for ocean beach hunting.

Headphones are essential for maximum sensitivity and depth. Some underwater detectors use meters and lights. Indicator lights are not as sensitive as meter indicators, which are very sensitive but are difficult to watch at all times and, in all but clear water, become difficult to see.

Gold Hunting

The recommended type detector for gold hunting will have excellent ground balance and precise calibrated discrimination. The ideal type is an instrument with a true All Metal mode that permits manually adjusted ground balancing. Get one that has been proven in the field because not all detectors are the same. Some are more versatile and sensitive than others and some are more capable of operating over highly mineralized ground.

You should select a model that has a wide range of searchcoils from which to choose. Selection of the right searchcoil depends, to a great extent, upon you. How well you have mastered your detector and how well you apply your experiences and observations will in large measure determine your success.

The Bloodhound Depth Multiplier attachment will give you multiplied depth on large ore veins, even those containing iron ore. In fact, iron ore, when in association with gold and silver, can enhance the detection characteristics of veins.

The author works with a modern underwater metal detector to adapt it for use in exceptional depths as part of a submarine.

Research

I f you are going to be successful at finding buried treasures, you should first make certain that any cache you seek is not just a myth. If its existence falls in the realm of a legend, you should undertake a thorough research project to determine if there is really any basis for the legend. If you fail to accomplish this, forget about that particular cache and go after one of the thousands you are sure of. These too should be properly researched to increase your chances of success.

Years ago when I first became interested in sunken and buried treasures, I made the same mistake that most beginners make. The numerous books on the subject made exciting reading – telling of intact galleons with chests of treasure crammed in their holds and pirate caches on almost every island or beach in this hemisphere. Dozens of *Authentic Treasure Charts* noted the locations of hundreds of buried and sunken hoards "containing millions in treasure." Like many of my associates at the time, I had to learn the hard way.

After spending three exciting and profitable years working shipwrecks and land sites in Yucatan, Mexico, I decided to expand my operations throughout the nearby Caribbean area. I used the available literature and "charts" to select 100

Only after proper research did Charles Garrett, Monty Moncrief, Bill Fulleton and Roy Lagal (from left) pursue an Indian cache on this Washington mountain.

different wreck locations and 150 buried treasure sites. Then, I set off to track them down.

Fifteen months later, after exploring from the Gulf of Honduras to the San Blas Islands off Panama, and from Trinidad to the Bahamas, diving and digging on almost every island, rock and reef in between (so it seemed), I had only located two of the 100 wrecks – and neither contained anything of interest – and not a single buried treasure.

These results were not surprising, as I was to learn after completing three years of original research in dozens of European and American archives and other depositories. Most of the 100 "authentic wrecks" had never even existed and those that did either sank in other areas or were lost without any treasure. For the 150 "authentic buried treasure" locations, the picture was even more heartbreaking. I was unable to find proof that even a single one of them had ever existed! All of this "authentic" information was merely the creation of imaginative authors of the books I used as my primary sources.

Actually, any modern book on the subject of lost treasures must be considered a secondary source and should be used only in combination with data from an earlier date. Whenever possible, the modern treasure hunter should trace any treasure that interests him to a primary source such as an original document, contemporary newspaper account or other type of documentation. Just remember that anyone knowing the exact location of a hidden hoard of wealth could scarcely be expected to write about it in a treasure magazine or book. He's going to go after it himself! Second sources are nothing more than sketchy information that can lead to the recovery of a treasure only if you research the initial clues.

Contrary to popular belief, proper research can be done by anyone who can read and write, and it need not necessarily be expensive.

The idea of researching the locations of buried treasure prompts two basic questions from skeptics:

– Why did people bury treasure?

Why didn't they dig the treasure up for themselves instead of leaving it buried?

The answers to both questions are both simple and almost obvious.

- People buried treasure to keep it out of the hands of others or to prevent others from knowing that they possessed it.

- They failed to recover the treasure for themselves because they died before the opportunity arose or the lost the locations of their hidden hoards.

Consider the buried treasures of Colonial America...because banks were rare and not available to most people, they kept their money buried somewhere on their property. Even if colonists hid their valuables in their homes, when the cry was sounded that Indians were attacking or that the British were coming, they quickly buried their treasures. In some cases colonists survived attacks but because their property may have been burned to the ground, they were unable to locate their possessions. If they were unfortunate enough to be killed and the attackers failed to find their hidden caches, the treasures remained buried. And, some still are!

During the Civil War people in the South buried their treasures not only to keep them out of the hands of the enemy but also to avoid having to donate them to the Confederate Treasury for the war effort. Even before the war there was always the chance of a slave uprising or Indian attack and the only safe "bank" available was a hole in the ground.

On the Western Frontier, as it progressed from the Allegheny Mountains to the Pacific Ocean, there were many more cutthroats who preyed on the hapless pioneers than there were in settled areas "back East." Every possible means, therefore, had to be taken to protect one's wealth. Indian attacks threatened early Spanish missionaries and settlers as well as the tens of thousands of westward-bound gold-seekers and settlers.

Prospectors faced being bushwhacked at work or while traveling to town for supplies. They were understandably reluctant to advertise a big strike by arriving in a town toting a large sack of gleaming nuggets.

When outlaws robbed stage coaches or wagon trains, they were generally forced to dispose temporarily of their heavy loot in order to escape a posse. Even gamblers who were lucky at the card table had to be wary of robbers, and they too often buried their winnings. Soldiers stationed in hundreds of forts had the same problem. Since they couldn't send their pay—whether silver or gold coins—through the mails to their families, they were forced to find a hole in the ground. Many shop or saloon keepers who did not have sturdy safes faced the same problem of finding hiding places for their profits.

So, buried treasures are waiting to be found. There can be no question about that. The next step is to show how to undertake the necessary research to locate them.

Determining the best area to research depends on a number of factors, especially how much money and time you have available. For example, a treasure hunter who can travel to certain areas of the West may search for a lost gold mine or treasure near the ruins of an abandoned ghost town. This person has more chances of striking it rich in a big way that someone who is limited to a search of his hometown picnic grounds for modern coins and jewelry.

So, first of all, select *your* treasure site. Thousands are listed in the next 250 pages of this book. Like many authors writing on the subject of buried treasure, I was limited by space to giving only a very brief description of each site. And, in most cases I could give only a general location, except for known historical sites such as Indian ruins, battlefields, old forts, ghost towns, abandoned mines, etc. It would take a multitude of lifetimes to authenticate and pinpoint every buried treasure cache – and even then would be impossible. As I stated earlier, no one in his right mind would publish a book indicating the exact location of a buried treasure worth millions of dollars.

Most maps of buried treasures are mass produced and sold for $1 to $5. The best use for these is for decorating your family den or study. The "X" that indicates a specific treasure location usually denotes an area of many square miles; the description of each site is vague; and the value of the treasure is grossly exaggerated.

Other types of charts and maps, however, are important research tools for today's treasure hunter. In fact, before you begin any original research for a particular treasure in a specific location, you should secure as many maps and charts of the area as possible. They can prove as valuable a tool as your trusty one-touch detector, and you may be surprised at the different types of essential information they contain.

The best topographical maps for treasure hunting purposes are those in the "seven-and-one-half-minute" series, with a scale of 1 to 24,000. Each of these maps covers an area of approximately 60 square miles. These maps can be obtained from the U. S. Geological Survey. Information on them can be obtained at any Government bookstore or by writing the Superintendent of Documents, Government Printing Office, Washington, DC. You should request information about all maps of areas you are interested in which deal with geology, army, transportation, historic sites, Indian reservations, mines and abandoned settlements.

The Bureau of Land Management, Department of the Interior, Washington, DC, sells a large series of charts called "Public Land Maps," which are updated periodically. They are invaluable for determining whether or not your potential site is situated on private land or public domain, especially valuable information for persons prospecting for gems or minerals. The United States Forest Service and the National Park Service also publish and distribute maps showing all lands under their jurisdiction.

Many states also have geological survey departments and other agencies that produce and distribute excellent maps that have proven to be invaluable for treasure hunters. Some states have maps dating back more than 100 years showing the exact locations of mines and mining settlements. Many historical societies sell maps showing the historical sites in their areas. Regular road maps usually show the locations of historical sites and in many cases even abandoned settlements. Another method of locating abandoned settlements is to obtain access to copies of all old maps of a given area. By matching them to a modern chart you will notice that certain place names no longer appear on the modern maps. You can safely assume that the settlement no longer is populated and has become a ghost town.

Old charts are harder to come by but they can be studied or copies obtained from state archives and libraries and from the Map Division of the Library of Congress in Washington, DC. They are especially useful for locating sites that are no longer on modern maps such as ghost towns, lost mines, old forts and battlefields. Sometimes you may see interesting names on these old maps such as Golden Rock, Money Hill, Treasure Point or Robber's Bluff. These generally are associated with lost treasures. Old geographical dictionaries or atlases are also very useful and contain valuable data.

In some cases a treasure and its probably location can be traced back to its origin through painstaking detective work from original documentation covering the event. In others this is impossible to accomplish – either nothing was written about the buried cache at the time or the documents have been lost over the years. This latter reason applies especially to information about shipwrecks. Documents carrying shipwreck news back to Europe or elsewhere were in many cases lost because the ships carrying the news were themselves lost.

Then there is the problem of the European depositories. Hundreds of thousands of documents that did reach Europe are lying uncatalogued in various archives and not accessible to researchers. In addition, the Great Fire of London in 1666 destroyed the majority of documents dealing with England's American Colonies prior to this date. The same fate has befallen many of the old records in this country. The British burned the Capitol in Washington in 1814, and almost every major city that existed in the United States during the Revolutionary periods has suffered major fires and other disasters. The result was the loss of incalculable numbers of original documents — many of which dealt with buried treasures, shipwrecks or related subjects.

Old newspapers are a good source of information for shipwreck locations and just about every other type of treasure site. One must remember, however, that the press of yesteryear was no different from that of today...newsworthy events were covered and written for public consumption and to help sell newspapers. They were not written with the intention of aiding someone to find a lost treasure — decades or centuries later! If you will take this into consideration and try to verify anything you read about in an old newspaper with other more reliable sources, they can be helpful.

Most major newspapers are now preserved on microfilm and they are generally located in state archives, state and university libraries and state historical societies, in addition to the newspapers themselves — if they are still published. Local librarians can generally direct you to copies or microfilms of old newspapers.

In the absence of documents on the subject, newspapers are *the* most authoritative source on outlaws and their caches in the Old West. Old newspaper are also good sources for learning where treasures were discovered in the past. Such stories might lead one to finding more of the same treasure or another cache in the same area. The old newspapers also contain a great deal of information about lost or abandoned gold and silver mines. Often their stories contain enough clues to enable someone to find the mine again — especially if information from other sources is also used.

Old books are a good source of information, particularly if they contain footnotes or references to where the author has obtained his information. This can lead you directly to original documentation. During the gold rush days many guide books were published and sold (sometimes at high prices) to help Easterners locate gold fields and teach them how to mine gold. Of course, the intent here was for promoters to make money selling books, but their information can be valuable when used correctly. In fact, collectors today pay in excess of $1,000 for such books whose value to the treasure hunter is their reports of campsite locations on the trails traveled by gold seekers. Such locations are veritable gold mines themselves since the old prospectors not only lost valuables here but might have hidden a bag of dust and not recovered it for one reason or another.

Although newspapers and books can provide you with a great deal of information, always try to obtain more about your particular treasure by looking up original documents. Valuable documentation can be found in the National Archives; Library of Congress, Manuscript Section; the Historical Sections of the Departments of Defense, the Interior, Justice and Agriculture. On the state government level documentation can be found in the state archives, state libraries, state universities, historical societies, secretary of states' archives, state treasurers' archives, state land offices' archives and state prison records. On a county level documents may be found in the archives of the county attorneys, clerks, surveyors, assessors and sheriffs, as well as historical societies, In city governments old records can be found in the files or archives of mayors, city clerks, city engineers, libraries, city museums, police departments, street commissions and utilities offices. Private libraries and museums as well as private records of attorneys, bankers, businessmen, doctors and auctioneers can also furnish clues to finding a treasure.

Relic hunters often rely of contemporary descriptions of skirmishes and battles. Instead of complaining about the major battlefields being closed to metal detectors because they are now state parks or monuments or the like, these resourceful individual seek out locations of the less important engagements. Many outstanding finds have been made at such sites which are quite easy to locate from old battlefield accounts.

Obviously, you must be familiar with the treasure you're seeking before you can search for further documentation of it. And, it will usually be time consuming as you encounter one dead-end street after another. Still, many treasure hunters consider the hours and days spent in research as rewarding as those spent in the field.

Historical societies have been helpful to treasure hunters in more than one way. In every state they have been responsible for erecting thousands of historical markers showing the exact locations where historical events took place or where settlements once stood. They are especially helpful in pinpointing battlefields when no earthworks or other fortifications have survived. Also, they reveal the locations of campsites along the trails used by travelers of yesteryear, as well as those frequented by the cowboys on their long cattle drives.

If you are after a treasure buried in relatively recent times, you can in some cases go beyond the printed source and make personal inquiries of persons still alive who may be able to help you. People may even be of assistance when you are looking for older treasure. Legends are passed from generation to generation...unfortunately, with gross exaggerations.

Remember, always, to seek documentation that is as close to the time of the original event as possible.

Good hunting!

List of Sites

S everal factors must be weighed when you investigate any site from the following locations where treasure and artifacts may be found. Although my research clearly indicates that a treasure was lost or buried here, it does not mean that the treasure necessarily *still remains*. It may have already been found – with the discovery kept secret.

Plus, my research data may have been inaccurate. The treasure may *never* have been there. Locations of outlaw hoards were usually based on outlaw testimony; maybe they lied. The same holds true for mine locations. Miners who discovered, but later couldn't return to, valuable mines may have given incorrect locations to keep their bonanzas secret.

Many treasures were hidden along the banks of streams, whose courses change over the years. And, what was once on a riverbank may now be deep beneath a man-made lake.

What's each treasure worth? Values I give are based on that at the time it was lost or hidden, but current worth is far more. So, here's buried treasure you can find. Obey all laws, and search to your heart's content. May your finds be big ones!

HAPPY TREASURE HUNTING!

ALABAMA

The ghost town of Arberchoochee is located off County 46, Cleburne Co. During the past century it was a booming gold mining town before being abandoned around 1900.

The site of Fort Mims is off State 59, four miles west of Tensaw, Baldwin Co. This wooden stockade was built in 1813 by early settlers with about 100 houses around it. It was attacked soon after being built, and all but 36 of the 500 whites inside the fort were massacred by the Creek Indians, who burnt the fort and houses to the ground. This incident started the Creek War (1813–1814).

Moundsville National Historic Park is located seventeen miles south of Tuscaloosa on State

69. This is the site of a great Indian metropolis that flourished between 1000 and 1500 AD. Outside of the park are a number of mounds where the public is permitted to dig for relics.

The ruins of Fort Tombigbee are located on the Tombigbee River, just off U.S. 11, near Epes, Sumter Co. The French built the fort in 1735 during the Chicksaw War. It was taken over by the British in 1783, renamed Fort York, and then abandoned by them five years later. Soon after the Spanish built Fort Confederation on the same site, but left the area in 1797 when it was seized by Americans. After it was abandoned in 1803, it fell into ruins.

The site of Fort Toulouse is located at the head of the Alabama River near Wetumpka, Montgomery Co. The French built the fort in 1717 and surrendered it to the British in 1763, who held it until the end of the Revolution. Americans rebuilt the fort in 1814 but used it only a short while before abandoning it. Today only the ruins of the powder magazine remain. Close by is the site of a prehistoric Indian village and numerous mounds.

The ruins of the McGillivray Plantation are located near County 47, four miles north of Wetumpka, Elmore Co. The plantation, which dates from the second half of the eighteenth century, was destroyed during an Indian attack. A hoard of silverware and some gold coins are supposed to be buried on the site.

The abandoned town of Demopolis is on the Tombigbee River near the intersection of U.S. 43 and 80, Marengo Co. Near the present town of Demopolis at a place now called White Bluff, a band of exiled followers of Napoleon Bonaparte founded a colony named Demopolis around 1810. But it was a failure and they abandoned the site several years later. Between 1830 and 1860 a number of rich plantations were also started in the area and the ruins of most of them still remain.

The site of Fort Mitchell is on the Chattahoochee River, off State 165, right across the river from Fort Benning, Russell Co. It was built in 1813 and used as a post for trading with the Creek Indians. Sometime after 1840 it was abandoned and only the foundations are now visible.

The town of Fort Payne is at the intersection of U.S. 11 and I-59, De Kalb Co. It was founded in 1890 and was a boom town for a few years as the result of false claims about coal and iron ore being discovered in the area. Ruins of many buildings dating from that period remain. In 1898 the owner of half the town, a John Willismith, died; he is alleged to have buried over $100,000 in gold, which has never been found, on one of his many pieces of property.

Horsehope Bend Park is on State 49 about twelve miles north of Dadeville, Tallapoosa Co. On 27 March 1814 General Andrew Jackson won a decisive victory over the Creek Nation which ended the Creek War. More than 900 Indians were slain here.

The ghost town of Old Cahaba is on State 22 about fourteen miles southwest of Selma, Dallas Co. This town was built on the ruins of an old Indian village around 1750 and served as the first state capital from 1819 to 1826. During the Civil War it was used as a Confederate base and prison. As a result of several floods and a bad fire, it was abandoned around 1870. Only a few chimneys and columns can be seen today sticking up above the dense brush.

The lost site of Fort St. Stephens is on the Tombigbee River near U.S. 43 and County 34, Washington Co. About two miles north of the present village of this name, the fort was built by the Spanish in 1789, taken over by Americans in 1795, abandoned soon after, and its location lost.

Selma was a vital Confederate army depot. On April 2, 1865 the Federal Army won a decisive victory here, then plundered and burnt the town to the ground. Today the ruins of many of the old buildings destroyed at that time are still visible.

Talladega is on U.S. 231A, about twenty miles east of Birmingham, Talladega Co. First settled in 1800, the town was the scene of a big victory by Andrew Jackson's Tennessee volunteers over the Creek Indians on November 9, 1813. The site on which the battle was fought is still unspoiled.

The lost site of Fort Louis de la Mobile was located about 39 miles up river from present Mobile, about three miles east of Calvert on U.S. 43, Washington Co. This community was settled about 1704 by the French, abandoned in 1760, and no traces remain.

Fort Morgan stands on Mobile Point about twenty miles west of Gulf Shores on State 180, facing the east end of Dauphin Island, Baldwin Co. The Spaniards under Tristan de Luna y Arellano built a fort on this same site and used it for a short time during 1559. A fleet of thirteen ships had sailed from Vera Cruz this same year to plant a colony at Pensacola, but while at anchor in Mobile Bay they were struck by a hurricane. Seven ships were cast up on the beach and another flung into a grove of trees about 300 yards inland on the east side of the bay. The survivors from this disaster were picked up about six months later and taken back to Mexico. During the War of 1812 a wooden stockade named Fort Bowyer was built on the site but it was destroyed by a storm in 1819 and the present fort built over its ruins in 1833. One of the fiercest naval actions of the Civil War was fought off-coast from this fort on August 5, 1864. Two weeks later it was captured by Union troops. Treasure and artifacts may be found on the beach near this fort as the American merchantman, **Margaret Ann,** coming from New York, was wrecked here on September 25, 1822.

Dauphin Island is located at the entrance to Mobile Bay. In 1702 the Frenchman Jean Baptiste le Moyne founded a colony somewhere on this island of which no trace remains today. He named it Massacre Island because of the large number of bleached human bones found on its beaches. During the Civil War two forts were built on the island, Fort Gaines on the eastern tip and Fort Morgan (not to be confused with the above fort of the same name) on the opposite side. On the beaches at the eastern end of the island might be found items from two wrecks, the British **H.M.S. Hermes,** of twenty guns, lost on September 15, 1814; and the American merchantman **Mississippi,** which ran aground on June 20, 1821.

Mobile was founded in 1702 by the French and was the seat of the French government in the Louisiana Province until 1720 when the seat was transferred to Biloxi. In 1711 the French built Fort Condé, which was renamed Fort Charlotte when the British took it over in 1783. In 1780 a Spanish force under Bernardo de Galvez captured it and held it briefly. The site of the fort, of which no traces remain, is on Church St. in the city. Across the bay from Mobile, on the eastern approach to the city at a place now called Spanish Fort, the Spaniards built a large stone fort in 1780. But it was destroyed several years later by an explosion in its magazine.

During the Civil War a treasure estimated at around $200,000 was supposedly buried by a Henry Nunez who operated a ferry on the Perdido River. The site is near where U.S. 90 now crosses the river, which is about sixteen miles northwest of Pensacola. The treasure lies near the ruins of his house on the Alabama side of the river.

Approximately four miles north of **Athens,** Limestone Co. and about a half mile from a prominent stream crossing, two huge metal boxes containing over $100,000 in gold and silver were dumped into a bog by Confederate troops to prevent their seizure by Union soldiers in 1865.

Many tales are told in and around **Birmingham** about a lost treasure in gold valued at close to $1,000,000. The money was destined for the Confederate treasury in Richmond, Virginia, in 1862. It was buried and not recovered, but the precise location and sufficient details are lacking to warrant searching for it.

Near the town of **Bay Minette,** Baldwin Co., there are numerous legends about the Spaniards having buried an enormous treasure of gold bars around 1780 while being pursued by hostile Indians.

The pirate Jean Lafitte is rumored to have buried about $80,000 in gold coins on a beach in present **Bayou la Batre,** south of Mobile.

ALASKA

Anaktuvuk Pass is located in the Endicott Mountains, the part of the Brooks Range in northern Alaska through which the Walter Hickel Highway now cuts. It is one of the few passes in these mountains and was used by prehistoric hunters during glacial times more than 25,000 years ago when Siberia was linked to Alaska by a land mass. More than 30 settlements of these early men have been identified but none have been properly investigated by archaeologists.

The town of Eagle is on the Yukon River west of Mt. Harper and near the United States-Canadian border. Located in the heart of the Yukon gold region, it first served as a fur-trading post before becoming a boomtown during the gold rushes of the 1890s. In the town and the surrounding area there are remains of hundreds of deserted dwellings, mining structures, and abandoned mine shafts.

Somewhere in the **St. Elias Mountains** near the Yellow River is a site called the Lake of the Golden Bar. It produced a great wealth of nuggets in the 1880s for three lucky prospectors who found and worked it for about five years. Late in 1884 they hid about 500 pounds of nuggets in a nearby cave. As the story goes, they were trapped in a blinding blizzard and were later eaten by grizzly bears. When their remains were found one prospector's diary mentioned the gold being buried, but the site was never found.

Fairbanks is situated in the geographic center of the state. In 1910, when gold was discovered in the area, it quickly grew from a small trading post into a boom-town. Around the outskirts of the town are remnants of many mining camps and abandoned mine shafts.

The town of Fort Yukon on the Yukon River about 140 miles northeast of Fairbanks is the oldest English-speaking settlement in the state. It was founded in 1847 as a trading post and heavily used during the gold-rush period. There are many tales of treasures being buried by miners in the area but it is very difficult to authenticate them.

Juneau is located in the Panhandle region near the Canadian border. In this area the first major gold finds were made in 1880, starting the gold stampede. A spokesman for the local historical society claims that there are remnants of over 1,000 miners' dwellings within a ten-mile radius of the city.

Kenai, about 100 miles south of Anchorage on the east shore of Cook Inlet, is one of the oldest permanent settlements in the state. The Russians built Fort St. Nicolas here in 1791 and near its ruins are the ruins of Fort Kenay, built in 1869 by the United States Army. There are ruins of many old buildings in the surrounding area, some dating back to the Russian occupation.

The Russians began exploring **Kodiak Island** in the Gulf of Alaska in 1763 and in 1784 founded a colony at Three Saints Bay. In 1792 the settlement was completely demolished by an earthquake and the ruins are still visible. The present town of Kodiak is located a few miles to the north of the ruins.

Nome, on the south shore of the Seward Peninsula, was the site of the now-legendary gold rush which began in September 1898 at Anvil Creek, about four miles north of present Nome. A tent city sprung up and extended for about fifteen miles along Nome Beach. During the next two years the mining activities spread over the entire peninsula. Each man averaged about $50 a day in gold; 1899 was the banner year in which more than $10,000,000 in gold was mined on the beaches. Amateur prospectors still work this beach during the summer months. The whole area is a paradise for treasure hunters as the remains of many dwellings abound. It is one of the best bottle-collecting sites in the hemisphere.

Ipiutak National Historic Landmark is adjacent to Point Hope, north of the Artic Circle and Bering Straits. Near the village of Point Hope are the remains of an extraordinary large Eskimo settlement which flourished about A.D. 300. The ruins of more than 800 stone houses and several cemeteries are visible.

The ghost town of Fort William H. Seward is on the neck of the Chilkat Peninsula in the southeast portion of the state. This settlement was founded in 1898 after gold was discovered in the area. Today the ruins of 85 brick buildings can still be seen and several abandoned Eskimo villages are also nearby.

Castle Hill, which overlooks the harbor of Sitka, was the first ancestral home of the Tlingit Indians. Early in the nineteenth century the Russians built a fort and settlement on this site of which few traces now remain.

The site of Old Sitka is located six miles north of Starrigavan Bay on Baranof Island. It was the main Russian settlement in Alaska when it was attacked and destroyed by the Tlingit Indians in June 1802. The ruins of many buildings are still visible.

Sitka Battlefield is roughly six miles south of the above settlement and several miles north of the present town of Sitka. In 1802 the Russians built a new settlement here and today some of the ruins can be seen. In 1804 more than 1,000 Russians defeated a force of twice that number of Tlingit Indians but a fire accidentally destroyed the settlement soon afterwards.

Skagway is at the head of the Lynn Canal, 80 miles north of Juneau. This town developed as a result of the gold strikes in the Klondike and Upper Yukon Valley in 1896. Within a year it boasted a population of over 20,000. Today less than 700 people live here and there are countless remnants of abandoned buildings and mining operations. In 1897 the steamship **Clara Nevada** sank right off this town carrying over $1,500,000 in gold, none of which was recovered.

The Tangle Lakes District, about 40 miles west of Paxson on the Denali Highway, remains as primitive today as it did when early man settled the area about 15,000 years ago. There are numerous archaeological sites in the area of which very few have been investigated properly.

Wrangell is near the mouth of the Stikine River in southeast Alaska. One of the first white settlements in the state, it was founded by Russian traders in 1834 and originally called Redoubt St. Dionysius. When the Americans moved in (about 1867), they built a larger settlement and fort, which became a boom town with the gold strikes of 1870 and 1897-1900. Remnants of hundreds of dwellings and commercial buildings are visible.

The site of New Russia is in the Tongass National Forest near the town of Yatukak under the shadow of Mt. Vancouver. The Russians established a settlement here in 1796 which was destroyed by the Tlingit Indians in 1805 and abandoned. The town, which was briefly used during the gold rushes of the 1890s, has ruins of the Russian and American occupations.

The ghost town of Forty-Mile is located near the junction of Bullion Creek and the north fork of the Forty-Mile River, 40 miles north of Fort Reliance. It flourished for about five years before being abandoned in the 1890s. In the settlement are ruins of many buildings. The Lost Sourdough Sailor's Mine is somewhere in the surrounding area.

ARIZONA

Fort Verde is an abandoned military post a few miles east of I-17 and the town of Camp Verde, Yapavai Co. During the 1870s it served as the main base for General George Crook's cavalry. Several of its stone buildings are still standing.

Montezuma's Castle is located off I-17, near Rimrock, Yapavai Co. This is the site of one of the Southwest's best preserved Indian ruins; large stone dwellings were cut into the face of a massive cliff in around 1200 and there are a number of other archaeological sites in the area.

Canyon de Chelly is off State 63 near Chinle, Apache Co. Nestled at the base of the sheer red sandstone cliffs are the ruins of several hundred dwellings of the Pueblo Indians dating between 700 and 1300 A.D. The area was settled by warlike Navajos around 1700. In 1805 a detachment of Spanish troops defeated a band of Navajos who had hidden themselves in a rock shelter now known as Massacre Cave. In 1864 Kit Carson also defeated a large band of Navajos here. Nearby are other Pueblo ruins at Monument Canyon, Black Rock, and Canyon del Muerte.

Casa Grande Monument is off State 87 about two miles north of Coolidge, Pinal Co. This four-story tower of packed walls probably served as a ceremonial structure for the Hohokam Indians who settled the area around 400 B.C. and abandoned it by 1450. Surrounding the structure are the remains of about 90 buildings built of mud and brush.

Tonto National Monument is off State 88, 28 miles northwest of Globe, Gila Co. The site contains remnants of over 100 cliff dwellings built in the mid-1300s and abandoned by 1425. The Salado Indians who lived there did extensive gold and silver mining in the area and many artifacts made of these precious metals can be found.

The Mission of San Xavier del Bac is nine miles south of Tucson via Mission Road. The first mission by this name was built by Jesuits in 1692 in the center of the Pima Indian village. The Indians revolted in 1751 and the Jesuits reportedly buried a great amount of treasure before all were massacred. The Indians also totally destroyed the mission but a new one was built in 1767 by Franciscans and is still standing.

Cactus Jack may look like a sourdough but he's a sophisticated electronic prospector who uses metal detectors to find nuggets and other Arizona treasures.

Many of America's great lost treasures are located in the lonely desert lands of Arizona and other Western states awaiting today's modern metal detector.

The ruins of Tubac Presidio are on I-19, 45 miles south of Tucson, Santa Cruz Co. The Spanish built this military post in 1752 and abandoned it in 1776. It was rebuilt and used again by Mexican troops to protect miners who had discovered rich silver deposits nearby. In 1850–1851, Mormons on their way to California used the site; in 1856 it was occupied by Texan miners. The remains of over 50 brick structures are what is left of this military post.

The ruins of the town of Fort Yuma are on the banks of the Colorado River near present Yuma, Yuma Co. For a short time around 1700, the Spanish had a mission here which was obliterated by hostile Indians. After the discovery of gold in California it became an important communications hub. Fort Yuma was built in 1850. There are other ruins of the past century in and around the present town of Yuma, including a territorial prison built in 1873 and abandoned in 1909.

Coronado National Memorial is off State 92, 30 miles west of Bisbee, Cochise Co. In 1540 the Spanish explorer Francisco Vasquezde Coronado set off from Mexico with 1350 followers in search of the fabled Seven Cities of Cibola. After a rugged five-month trek they reached this site, which turned out to be a rock-masonry village inhabited by the Zuni Indians who possessed little gold. After camping for several months in the area the expedition moved off to the east, inspired by more rumors of gold to be found. Eventually they reached Kansas. Before leaving this area they abandoned several pieces of bronze artillery and other heavy objects. Finding their campsite would produce a great wealth of valuable artifacts.

Tuzigoot National Monument is off U.S. 89A, about 33 miles southwest of Flagstaff. The site contains remnants of an extensive fortified Indian settlement on a hillside, which was constructed around 1125 A.D. and abandoned by the Sinaqua Indians in about 1450. They were gold and silver miners and produced exquisite objects from these precious metals.

Walnut Canyon Monument is on I-40, about eight miles east of Flagstaff. The remains of over 300 Sinaqua Indian cliff dwellings are built into recesses along the face of this 400-foot-deep canyon, which was occupied between the years 1065 and 1200.

Wupatki National Monument is about 45 miles northeast of Flagstaff off U.S. 89. On several mesa tops of this site are the remains of over 800 stone ruins of the Hohokam and Sinaqua Indians. These dwellings were in use between the years 1100 and 1225. Many gold and silver artifacts have been recovered on the site.

The ruins of Fort Bowie are off State 86, thirteen miles south of the town of Bowie, Pima Co. The fort was built in 1862 close to the ruins of an old stage station and abandoned in 1894.

The site of Hubbell Trading Post is one mile west of State 264, Apache Co. The post was built in 1878 to trade for fine silver jewelry and other handicrafts made by the Navajo Indians, who destroyed it around 1900. A modern trading post stands nearby.

Navajo National Monument is off State 64 about 32 miles southwest of Kayenta, Apache Co. Three of the most elaborate and largest Pueblo cliff dwellings built in 1225 and abandoned during the last century are preserved at this site. Large amounts of silver and gold jewelry have been found here.

Tumacacori National Monument is on U.S. 89 about eighteen miles north of Nogales. In 1691 the Jesuits founded a mission and settlement named San José de Tumacacori to convert the Pima Indians and it continued in use until 1848. The ruins of the church and about twenty other large stone buildings are visible.

Old Oraibi Village in the northeast corner of Arizona, is on State 264, about three miles west of the present town of Oraibi on the Hopi Indian Reservation. At the base of a mesa are ruins of more than 100 Indian houses built of stone masonry and adobe, dating back to around 1150. There are also many other archeological sites and vestiges of a Spanish mining settlement in the nearby area.

In the **Phoenix** area are traces of many Indian, Spanish, and pioneer buildings in and on the outskirts of the modern city. In Pueblo Grande City Park there is a large mound covering a Hohokam structure which dates back to about the year 900.

Pipe Spring National Monument is off US 89 about fifteen miles southwest of Fredonia and 25 miles north of the Grand Canyon. This area was settled by Mormons in 1858. In 1870 Texan miners built a fort on this spot. Ruins of several hundred nineteenth-century buildings are in the area.

Tombstone is off U.S. 80 about twenty miles northwest of Bisbee, Cochise Co. After the discovery of rich silver deposits in 1877, the town grew quickly and by 1880 it had a population of over 15,000. In the 1880s it had an unparalleled reputation for lawlessness and violence, as it attracted a large number of gunslingers, gamblers, and prostitutes, all bent on getting a share of the silver wealth. Floods forced the mines to close down in 1887 and by 1900 the town was almost completely deserted. Today fewer than 1,000 persons live there and remnants of its heyday are numerous.

The ghost town of Austerlitz is located about seven miles south of Arivaca, Santa Cruz Co. It was once a wild mining town and was abandoned by 1900.

The near-ghost town of Bluebell is located four miles west of County 69, about ten miles southeast of Prescott, Yavapai Co. Only a handful of people now live in this town, which is surrounded by the ruins of the old Bluebell Mine and the nearby silver and copper refineries.

The ghost town of Bradshaw City is located in the Bradshaw Mountains near Mt. Wasson, south of Prescott, Yavapai Co. It was once a mining city of 5,000. Nearby are the ruins of the Crown King mine.

The ghost town of Calabasa is located six miles south of Nogales on State 89, Santa Cruz Co. The Spaniards had a settlement here in the 1770s and worked nearby silver deposits, which were later taken over by Indians and Mexicans. During the Civil War it was a Confederate stronghold; the ruins of Fort Mason are nearby. By 1870 it was completely deserted.

The ghost town of Cerro Colorado is in the Quinlan Mountains about 30 miles northwest of Nogales on the Papago Indian Reservation. The town was founded because of the Heintzelman Mine nearby. In 1885 it had over 10,000 inhabitants. Today the ruins of over 800 buildings can be seen.

The ghost town of Charleston is on the banks of the San Pedro River, eight miles southwest of Tombstone, Cochise Co. Many ruins of the town and the Tombstone Mining Company remain visible.

The ghost town of Chloride is located about twenty miles northwest of Kingman and four miles west of State 93, Yuma Co. Most of the original town and several old mines are still standing.

The ghost town of Congress is near the junction of State 89 and County 60, sixteen miles north of Wickenburg, Yavapai Co. Most of the original town and the Congress Mine remains today.

The ghost town of Contention City is about two miles north of County 82, five miles north of Tombstone, Cochise Co. Few vestiges of the original town remain except for a number of mine buildings.

The ruins of Dos Cabezas are on a mountain slope near State 186, ten miles southeast of Wilcos, Cochise Co. This town existed briefly between 1878 and 1887.

The ghost town of Dusquesne is located off County 83 about nineteen miles east of Nogales, Santa Cruz Co. Once it was a riotous sin city of 1000 citizens; now only the shells of buildings remain.

The ruins of Ehrenberg are located just south of where U.S. 10 crosses the Colorado River, Yuma Co. The town was once an important mining supply center and river port.

The ghost town of Gila City is on the Gila River about 25 miles east of Yuma, Yuma Co. It was once a booming mining town of over 1000 people.

The ghost town of Jerome is on U.S. 89A near present Jerome, Yapavai Co. A rich copper mine was discovered there in 1883 and by 1929 the population was over 30,000. Today about 200 people live in the new town about a mile from the old, which was abandoned in 1952 when the mine was closed.

The ghost town of Johnson is in the Dos Cabeza Mountains off U.S. 10, near the present town of Willcox, Cochise Co. Several hundred ruined buildings are still visible in this old mining town.

The ghost town of Kofa is located 25 miles south of Quartzite and seventeen miles east of State 95, Yuma Co. Most of the town buildings are in ruins, but the buildings and tramways of the famous King of Arizona mine are well preserved.

The **ruins of the town of La Paz** are located on the Colorado River ten miles north of Ehrenberg, Yuma Co. It once had a population of over 5,000, but was destroyed by an earthquake around 1890.

The **ruins of Los Guijas** are located seven miles west of Cerro Colorado on an old dirt road in Pima Co. Very little of the town remains but the buildings of the Freenstrom Mill Refinery are still standing.

The **town of Mammoth** is on County 77 about 44 miles northeast of Tucson, Pinal Co. Today only a handful of people still live in this town but the ruins of hundreds of abandoned houses and structures of the famous Mammoth mine are visible.

The **ghost town of McMillanville** is fifteen miles northeast of Globe along State 60, Pinal Co. For 25 years after 1870 it was a very rich silver mining city; and many of its original buildings and mill structures can still be seen.

The **ghost town of Mowry** is located eighteen miles south of Patagonia on the old trail road, Santa Cruz Co. It was a rich silver- and lead-mining town and many of the original buildings are standing today.

The **town of Oatman** is on the Colorado River about seventeen miles north of Topock, Mohave Co. The town became a near ghost town in 1942 after the mines were closed. Many ruins in the town and surrounding area date back to the 1880s.

The **town of Paradise** is located in the Pedregosa Mountains about fifteen miles north of Rodeo, New Mexico, off State 80, Cochise Co. Only a few residents and a large number of dilapidated buildings remain of this lawless town of the past.

The **ghost town of Pearce** is located about five miles west of State 666 and 50 miles northwest of Douglas, Cochise Co. During the last two decades of the past century it was a booming mining town and produced over $30,000,000 in gold alone, as well as silver and other minerals. It was the headquarters of the Alvord-Stiles and other outlaw gangs.

The **ghost town of Planet** is on the Bill William River about fifteen miles northeast of Parker, Yuma Co. It was the site of the state's first copper mine, boomed briefly, and then died.

The **ghost town of Rich Hills** is located on an old mountain road about twelve miles north of Wickenburg, Yavapai Co. It was a booming gold town in the 1860s and by 1875 had been totally abandoned. Today a few buildings are still standing but there are ruins of many others as well as a very unusual cemetery.

The **town of Tubac** is 22 miles south of Tucson on State 89, Pima Co. A Spanish presidio was established here in 1752 to protect the miners; and many of its original buildings remain standing. In 1775 De Anza assembled the colonists here for the march across the mountains to found San Francisco. After American miners moved into the area in the 1860s, it was renamed Tubac. About 100 people still live in this town surrounded by rather spectacular ruins spanning two centuries.

The **ghost town of Washington** is on the Santa Cruz River about ten miles east of Nogales, Santa Cruz Co. Mining activity in the area dates back to prehistoric times. Many of the original nineteenth-century buildings and the mining tramway remain today.

The **ghost town of White Hills** is near Squaw Peak about seven miles east of State 93 in Mohave Co., the northwest corner of the state. Only a few of the buildings of this silver-mining town are still standing.

The **lost Virgin de Guadalupe Silver Mine** is in the Tumacacori Mountains just north of the San Ramon River in the vicinity of the ghost town of Tubac, Santa Cruz Co. The Spaniards worked this mine until about 1648. It was again worked in the early nineteenth century by Mexican miners.

The **lost San Pedro Mine** is located in the same area about four to six miles west of the former Tumacacori Mission site. The Spaniards also worked this silver mine until around 1648.

The **lost Opata Silver Mine** is in the same area as the San Pedro mine, only a few hours walk to the east of the above two mines. It rests in the western foothills of the San Cayetano Mountains.

The **lost Bella of Old Guevari Mine** is also in the same vicinity somewhere along the extreme southwest end of the same San Cayetano Mountains. The Jesuits who worked this mine claimed in several documents that it also produced large amounts of platinum, which was thrown away as being worthless.

The lost Gila Bend Mine is off I-8 about fifteen miles east of Gila Bend, Maricopa Co. Here the Spaniards mined large amounts of silver in the early 1700s, stopping around 1750. A large number of Indian petroglyphs cover many rocks and the walls of caves in this area.

The lost Escalante Mine is somewhere in the Santa Catalina Mountains close to Tucson, Pima Co. Called the Mine with the Iron Door, it was one of the richest silver mines worked by the Jesuits in the seventeenth century.

The lost Del Bac Mine is located in the rugged mountain chain near Tucson, Pima Co. It is about seven miles southwest of the present-day Mission of San Xavier del Bac. In the seventeenth century the Jesuits worked the mine.

Other lost silver and gold mines are reputed to be all over the state. Their approximate locations are listed here by county.

APACHE CO. The **Lost Blonde Mayo Mine** is on the east side of Altar Valley, Black Princess Mountain, in the Cerro Colorado Mountains; **the Lost Silver Monument Valley Mine** is in the vicinity of Mitchell Butte; **the Lost Reina de Espana Mine** is in the vicinity of the Canyon Chelly National Monument. **COCHISE CO.** The **Lost Apache Girl Mine** is in the Dos Cabeza Mountains on the west side of old Fort Bowie; **the Lost Skeleton Mine** is in the Pelocillo Mountains, probably in Skeleton Canyon. **COCONINO CO.** The **Lost John Lee Placer Mine** is near Vulture's Throne in Grand Canyon; **the Lost Tonto Apache Mine** is within a two-hour walk of Sedona; **the Lost Coconino Mine** is about twenty miles southwest of Flagstaff, at the extreme southwest corner of the county; **the Lost Deadman Mine** is southwest of Cameron; **the Lost Morgan Mine** is several hours south of Flagstaff. **GREENLEE CO.** The **Lost Black Burro Mine** is northeast of Clifton, at the junction of the Blue and San Francisco Rivers. **GILA CO.** The **Lost Sander's Mine** is on the north slope of the Sierra Anchas Mountains, about ten miles from the head of Coon Creek; **the Lost Apache Mine** is in Tonto Basin on the north slope of Mount Ord. **MARICOPA CO.** The **Lost Lord Duppa Mine** is near Wickenburg; **the Lost Pick Mine** is 25 miles northwest of Fort McDowell in Bronco Canyon; **the Lost Squaw Hollow Mine** is in Squaw Hollow about 40 miles northeast of Phoenix. **MOHAVE CO.** The **Lost Nugget Mine** is near Wikieup. **PIMA CO.** The **Lost Cerro Colorado Mine** is northeast of Arivaca on the south slope of the Cerro Chiquita Mountains; **the Lost Cienega Bender's Mine** is about 30 miles southeast of Tucson near the old stage station of Cienega; **the Lost Fortuna Mine** is several hours east of Tucson; **the Lost Carreta Canyon Mine** is in the foothills of the Tascosa Mountains, near Arivaca; **the Lost Escalante Mine** is northeast of Tucson, on the south bank of the Canada del Oro River, in the Catalina Mountains; **the Lost Esmeralda Mine** is about a three-hour hike east of Tucson; **the Lost Orphan Mine** is near Tule Tank, in the Cabeza Prieta Mountains; **the Lost Papago Gold Mine** is within a five-mile radius of the town of Ajo; **the Lost Spoon Gold Mine** is in the mountains between Arivaca and Tucson; **the Lost Waggoner's Mine** is on the south slope of La Barge Canyon, between Miner's Needle and Weaver's Point, in the Superstition Mountains. **PINAL CO.** The **Lost Coyotero Mine** is near the north end of Toto Basin on the Mogollon Rim. **SAN CARLOS CO.** The **Lost Soldier's Mine** is between Needle and East Boulder Canyons. **SANTA CRUZ CO.** The **Lost Doc Throne's Mine** is high in the White Mountains; **the Lost Don Miguel Peralta Mine** is close to La Barge Creek, La Barge Canyon, in the Superstition Mountains; **the Lost La Purisima Concepcion Mine** is about fifteen miles southwest of Tumacacori Mission, near Cerro Ruido, in the El Pajarito Mountains; **the Lost Major Peoples' Mine** is southeast of Congress Junction in the hills near the Hassayampa River. **YAVAPAI CO.** The **Lost Geronimo Gold Mine** is between Parkinsville and Jerome, close to the Verde River, in Sycamore Canyon; **the Lost Organ Grinder Mine** is west of Prescott, on Cottonwood Creek, in Peoples Canyon; **the Lost Apache Gold Mine** is in Sycamore Canyon between Parkinsville and Jerome; **the Lost Nigger Ben's Mine** is east of Congress Junction, at the foot of Antelope Peak; **the Lost Squaw Hollow Mine** is near Camp Creek. **YUMA CO.** The **Lost Bicuner Gold Mine** is near Squaw Creek, in the Laguna Mountains; **the Lost Belle McKeever Mine** is near the western extremity of the Granite Mountains; **the Lost Trigos Silver Mine** is near the foot of Clip Mountain, in the Trigos Mountains; **the Lost Castle Dome Mine** is on the Colorado River between Ehrenberg and the old King Arizona Mine; **the Lost John Nummel's Mine** is on the Colorado River between Yuma Wash and Norton's Landing; **the Lost Squaw Mine** is between Phoenix and Yuma; **the Lost Rancho De La Yumas Mine** is on the east bank of the Colorado River, about 40 miles north of Yuma; **the Lost Six-Shooter Mine** is on the Bill Williams River between Quartzite and the ghost town of Planet, about fifteen miles northeast of Parker; **the Lost Sopori Mine** is near the foothills of Black Princess Peak in the Cerro Colorado Mountains; **the Lost Lead Mine** is near the extreme north end of the Harguahala Mountains.

A large number of **old abandoned gold, silver, and lead mines** are located all over the state. These are arranged by counties:

COCHISE CO. The **Dos Cabezos Mine** is in the Cabezos Mountains, eighteen miles southeast of Wilcox; **the Gleeson Mine** is twenty miles east of Tucson; **the Golden Rule Mine** is east of Dragon Pass; **the Hill-Top Mine** is northwest of Portal in the Chiricahua Mountains; **the Lavender Mine** is southeast of Bisbee; **the Middlemarch Mine** is five miles southwest of Pearce; **the Paradise Mine** is eight miles northwest of Portal in the Chiricahua Mountains; **the Pearce Mine** is near Sulphur Springs; **the Prospect Mine** is on Turkey Creek on the east side of the San Pedro Valley; **the Pyramid Mine** is 75 miles southeast of Tombstone; **the Reef Mine** is in the Huachuca Mountains, eight miles west of Hereford; **the Roberts Mine** is twenty miles southeast of Wilcox. **GILA CO.** The **Arizona Commercial Mine** is five miles north of Globe; **the Black Warrior Mine** is seven miles northwest of Globe; **the Boston Mine** and the **Iron Cap Mine** are on Copper Hill, five miles north of Globe; **the Crowley Mine** is in the Apache Mountains; **the Julius Mine** is nine miles east of Globe in the Quartzite Mountains; **the Black Morris Mine** is twenty miles north of Globe; **the McMillen Mine** is 22 miles northeast of Globe; **the Nugget Mine** is three miles north of Richmond Basin; **the Oxbow Mine** is between Roosevelt and Payson; **the Pioneer Mine** is on the west bank of Silver Creek in the Pinal Mountains; **the Silver Nugget Mine** is fourteen miles north of Globe; **the Superior Mine** is on Copper Hill, four miles north of Globe. **GREENLEE CO.** The **Ash Creek Mines** are on Ash Creek, near Hardy; **the Metcalf Mine** is on Chase Creek, eight miles east of Metcalf; **the Oro Gold Mine** is on the San Francisco River, four miles east of Clifton. **MARICOPA CO.** The **Easter Mine** is near the outskirts of Easter; **the Judson Mine** is near Edith. **MOHAVE CO.** The **American Flag Mine** is on the west side of the Hualpai Mountains; **the Climax Mine** is six miles south of Haulpai Landing in Virginia Canyon; **the Cyclopic Mine** is northwest of Kingman; **the Diamond Joe Mine** is on the Big Sandy River; **the German Mine** is four miles southeast of Oatman; **the Golconda Mine** is in the Cerbat Mountains; **the Gold Basin Mine** is in Haulpai Wash, 40 miles north of Kingman; **the Greenwood Mine** is near Greenwood City; **the Hardyville Mine** is near Bullhead City; **the Horn Silver Mine** is seven miles northeast of Boulder Inn Station; **the King Tut Mine** is on Lake Mead, fourteen miles south of Pierce Ferry Landing; **the McCracken Mine** is southwest of Wickieup; **the Mineral Park Mine** is near Chloride; **the Mohave Mine,** the **Signal Mine,** and the **White Hills Mine** are just outside of Needles, California; **the Oatman Mine** is near Bullhead City; **the Oro Plata Mine** is four miles south of Mineral Park; **the Pope Mine** is nine miles northeast of Boulder Inn Station; **the Prosperity Mine** is six miles south of Mineral Park; **the Secret Mine** is in the Black Mountains, sixteen miles east of the Colorado River; **the Stockton Hill Mine** is on the northeast slope of the Cerbat Mountains, eight miles southeast of Mineral Park; **PIMA CO.** The **Bates Well Mine** is fourteen miles south of Ajo; **the Cerro Colorado Mine** and the **Heintzeman Mine** are 42 miles south of Tucson; **the Dowling Mine** is in the Ajo Valley at the south end of the Sonoita Mountains; **the Esperanza Mine** is west of Sahiarita; **the Gunsight Mine** is near the western edge of the Papago Indian Reservation; **the Horseshoe Mine** is on the south end of the Quyotoa Mountains; **the Mammoth Mine** is 30 miles west of Marana; **the Mineral Hill Mine** is on the Nogales-Tucson Road; **the Old Boot Mine** is 28 miles west of Marana; **the Olive Mine** is west of Santa Cruz; **the Rosemont Mines** are in Furnace Gulch in the Santa Rita Mountains; **the San Xavier Mine** is on the Santa Cruz River; **the Silver Bell Mine** is 35 miles west of Marana; **the Vekol Mine** is on the west side of the Cimarron Mountains. **PINAL CO. The American Flag Mine** is in the Catalina Mountains, near Oracle; **the Reynert Mine** is ten miles southwest of Superior; **the Schultz Mine** is ten miles northeast of Oracle; **the Silver King Mine** is near Pinal City. **SANTA CRUZ CO. The Austerlitz Mine** is on Arivaca-Pena Lake; **the Duquesne Mine** is on the east side of the Patagonia Mountains, sixteen miles northeast of Nogales; **the French Mine** is twenty miles northeast of Nogales; **the Luttrell Mine** is near Lochiel; **the Oro Blanco Mine** is nine miles southeast of Arivaca; **the Salero Mine** is near the foot of Salero Peak in the Santa Rita Mountains; **the Washington Mine** is near Washington on the east side of the Patagonia Mountains. **YAPAVAI CO. The Bluebell Mine** is six miles west of Mayer; **the Chaparral Mine** is west of Humboldt; **the Congress Mine** is five miles north of Congress Junction; **the Crown King Mine** is in the Bradshaw Mountains, eleven miles from Cornville; **the Goodwin Mine** is on Turkey Creek, near Prescott; **the Iron King Mine** is just outside of Walker; **the Jersey Lily Mine** is 24 miles south of Prescott; **the Placeritas Mine** is on the northeast end of the Weaver Mountains, eight miles east of Peoples' Valley; **the Richinber Mine** is on the Aqua Fria River, five miles east of Bumblebee Station; **the Senator Mine** is near the head of the Hassayampa River; **the Tip Top Mine** is on Castle Creek near Kirbyville. **YUMA CO. The Castle Dome Mine** is in the Castle Dome Mountains, 34 miles north of Yuma; **the Fortuna Mine** is on the north side of Sheep Mountain, 24 miles southeast of Yuma; **the Kofa Mine** is 30 miles south of Quartzsite; **the La Paz Mine** is six miles east of Ehrenberg.

In 1929 three miners accidentally stumbled across 700 gold bars southeast of **Ajo** and close to the United States-Mexican border, Pima Co. The last surviving partner died in 1963 without revealing the secret location. Since that time it has been established that the bars they found were only a small part of a larger hoard being carried to Mexico in 1648 by the Jesuits who were attacked by Indians and forced to bury all of their treasure. Somewhere in the same area they are known to have buried another two thousand gold and between four and five thousand silver bars. Only one of the priests survived the attack, and when he returned to the area a year later he was unable to locate any of the treasure.

Silver bullion worth over $150,000 from the famed **Cerro Colorado Mine** is reported to be hidden in a cave on the slopes between the Cerro Chiquito and Cerro Colorado Mountains.

There is a legend that a tunnel leads from under the ruins of the **Tumacacori Mission** on the west bank of the Santa Cruz River, about twenty miles north of Nogales via U.S. 19, for about half a mile to the river bank, and that a great treasure is hidden inside the tunnel.

The Lost Carretta Canyon Treasure, also known as the **Ajo Treasure,** is supposed to be located along the old Carretta Road which connected the Tumacacori Mission with the Mexican town of Sonoyta in the state of Sonora. The treasure is said to consist of church vessels and gold and silver bullion worth over $2 million.

The Lost Arivaca Treasure is alleged to be located in a cave in the Baboquivari Mountains near Arivaca. Sometime around 1880 a Papago Indian accidentally found this treasure consisting of hundreds of gold and silver bars which had been secreted in the cave by Spanish Jesuits sometime during the late seventeenth century. The Indian used a few of the bars to purchase supplies from a nearby trading post, then nothing more was ever seen of him. He did tell where the bars had come from but only gave a rough position of the cave.

The Blackgown's Treasure is hidden "in the third little mountain to the southwest of Tubac Presidio, from a point slightly to the west of Tubac." This would put it in the Sierrita Mountains about ten to fifteen miles north of Arivaca, Santa Cruz Co. The treasure is said to consist of gold statues, chalices, bars, and a store of nuggets and gold dust that was hidden by Spanish missionaries in the eighteenth century. While searching for this treasure several years ago, a hunter from Tucson investigating an abandoned mining shack in the area found two large tin cans full of gold nuggets valued at over $20,000.

The Guadalupe Treasure is one of the most famous and most sought after in the state. According to the story, after the Jesuits were expelled from the New World colonies in 1767 they took with them more than two thousand mules loaded with silver ore and more than two hundred mules with gold bars and nuggets. When they were about four miles southwest of the Tumacacori Mission they got word that a large band of Indians was rushing to intercept them.

Supposedly they hid all of the treasure in an abandoned mine before fleeing towards Mexico. The tale is very intriguing but no one has ever explained why the Jesuits never came back to recover the treasure, if they really ever buried it.

Gold valued at over $100,000 which was robbed from a Wells Fargo shipment in 1865, is alleged to be buried near the small town of **Vail,** about 17 miles southeast of Tucson on U.S. 10, Santa Cruz Co.

Somewhere in Pontano Canyon near the **Old La Cienega Pony Express Station,** between Tucson and Benson, Santa Cruz Co. the Cienega Brothers, notorious nineteenth-century bandits, are alleged to have buried $75,000 in gold coins taken from an army paywagon.

On the site of the **Guevavi Mission** in the San Cayetano Mountains, near Calabasas and northeast of Nogales, Spanish priests are supposed to have buried a great hoard of gold church treasures and also several hundred gold bars.

Just west of the town of **Patagonia** on County 82, about twenty miles northeast of Nogales, a cache of gold coins is said to have been buried in or around the ruins of a prospector's adobe home.

Treasure is supposedly hidden in the ruins of the old **San Bernardino Hacienda** located on Robber's Roost, just south of Tombstone. In 1967 a treasure hunter found an iron kettle containing about 20 pounds of gold nuggets buried near this site.

A large cache of gold nuggets and dust is said to be buried near the **Buckhorn Ranch** in a cave in the Rincon Mountains, several miles north of Mescal on U.S. 10, Cochise Co.

Spanish missionaries are alleged to have buried a large treasure in gold on a ledge of a steep hill and covered it with tons of rocks. The site is along the old trail leading south from the **San Xavier del Bac Mission,** which is eight miles north of Patagonia, Santa Cruz Co.

The Lost Treasure of Fort Huachuca, which reportedly consists of hundreds of gold bars weighing 50 pounds each, is worth more than $60 million. It is believed to have been buried in Huachuca Canyon, on the Fort Huachuca Military Reservation about midway between Bisbee and Nogales, by a Mexican bandit named Juan Estrada. In 1941, Robert Jones, who was stationed on the base, claims to have fallen into a hole and found the great treasure and after taking only a few of the bars, he covered the hole and kept quiet about the discovery. In 1959 he received permission from the United States government to recover the treasure but was not able to relocate the site despite the use of good search and excavation equipment.

An army payroll worth over $100,000 in gold is alleged to have been buried in the vicinity of the **Cienega Stage Station** on the Butterfield State Trail between Silver City and Tucson, Pima Co.

The La Esmeralda Church Treasure consisting of several tons of gold bars and church ornaments is reported to be buried in a cave about six miles southwest of the old San Xavier del Bac Mission, along one of the south ridges of the Santa Catalina Mountains, Santa Cruz Co.

According to legend, the Mexican bandit Bonita buried about $22 million in gold and silver bullion on the southwest slopes of **Mt. Graham** at a place now called Meadows of Gold, about 30 miles southwest of Safford, Graham Co. Nearby is the small town of Bonita, named after the bandit.

In the Winchester Mountains, northeast of **Willcox,** Cochise Co. a cache of gold dust and silver coins was supposed to have been hidden by Apaches after they attacked a wagon train near the stage station at Mountain Springs.

The outlaw Black Jack Ketchum is alleged to have buried a large treasure in a cave in **Wild Cat Canyon,** in the Chiricahua Mountains, about 40 miles north of Bisbee, Cochise Co.

The American outlaws Zwing Hunt and Billy Grounds supposedly buried about $3 million in booty, stolen in Mexico, in a cave in **Skelton Canyon,** in the Davis Mountains, Cochise Co.

A prospector named Tom Watson hid a sackful of gold nuggets behind a waterfall in a small cave on the **Tanner Trail** between the Colorado River and the town of Cibola, Yuma Co. and was unable to relocate the site later.

Around 1710 some Spaniards found a very rich gold mine in **Sycamore Canyon** just off the Verde River north of Cottonwood, Yapavai Co. They loaded their burros with several hundred pounds of gold and then were attacked by Apaches who killed all but two of them. The Apaches covered the entrance to the mine and the Spaniards were unable to relocate it.

In the town of **Cottonwood** on State 89A, Yapavai Co., two miners named Marvin and Dreher were known to have hidden many bottles full of gold dust in the 1890s. Three of these bottles were found by a young boy digging for fishing worms in 1961.

In 1865 prospector Jim White, who was braving the Colorado River in a raft, claimed to have found a cave containing what many believe to be ancient Aztec treasure of Montezuma. The cave is supposed to be near the ruins of an old Indian settlement on the south bank of the river in the Lower Granite Gorge of the Grand Canyon, about three miles east of **Pierce Ferry,** in the northwest corner of the state. After reaching civilization delirious from weeks of hunger and hardships, White reported seeing thousands upon thousands of golden idols and other objects. Since that time many persons have unsuccessfully searched for the site, which is supposed to contain one of the greatest treasures in the United States.

During the 1880s a large dam was built in a gorge of the Hassayampa River near **Wagoner** to provide water for placer gold mining. During a cloudburst it collapsed and washed away a mining camp. The safes in the assay office and Main Chance Saloon contained large amounts of gold which were lost under tons of mud.

The site of **Fort Mohave** is close to Mohave Springs, about twenty miles east of Lake Havasu City, Mohave Co. The fort was burnt in 1861 to keep it from falling in the hands of the Confederates, rebuilt in 1863, and used until 1890. Under the ruins of the carpenter shop on the north side of the fort, a large cache of gold nuggets is alleged to be buried.

In 1891 two miners buried about $75,000 in gold nuggets under a toadstool-shaped rock near a small spring on the east side of **Bronco Canyon,** about 30 miles northwest of Fort McDowell, Maricopa Co., and were unable to relocate the site at a later date.

The Lost Treasure of Telegraph Pass is said to consist of about $50,000 in gold and jewelry placed in a iron kettle. It was buried in 1870 close to Telegraph Pass, in a level campsite with a small butte on the east side, below Montezuma's Head on the southern end of the Estrella Mountains, Yapavai Co.

There is another buried treasure tale about $1 to $2 million in gold bars being buried in a cave near **Montezuma's Head.**

Around 1880 some Indians are alleged to have buried about one thousand pistols and rifles in the mountains to the west of **Santa Rosa Wash,** between Casa Grande and Santa Rosa, on the Papago Indian Reservation, Pima Co.

In a cave on the east side of the **Estrella Mountains,** south of Butterfly Peak, is a deep box canyon running east and west about midway between the Peak and a stone out-cropping named Montezuma's Head; a cache of some 50 gold bars and 30 bags of nuggets is alleged to be hidden.

Many treasure hunters have searched for the fabled **Sunlit Cave Treasure** which supposedly consists of several tons of Spanish gold bullion. The cave is located on the Arizona side of the Colorado River about fifteen to twenty miles south of Ehrenberg, Yuma Co.

In 1875 a prospector named William Rood is alleged to have buried several chests of gold coins on or near the **Rancho de los Yumas,** on the east bank of the Colorado River about 40 miles north of Yuma, Yuma Co. About $1,000 in twenty-dollar gold pieces was found in 1897, but the main hoard has not been found.

The Lost Laguna Treasure is said to consist of about 50 pounds of gold nuggets and is located near the present site of the Laguna Dam, between the Colorado River and Laguna Mountains, Mohave Co. Indians ambushed and killed a group of miners and threw their bodies and the gold into a gorge in the hills.

During the 1850s a man named Lincoln is alleged to have buried about $80,000 in gold and silver coins near the **Yuma Crossing** on the east banks of the Colorado River near the present city of Yuma.

In the late nineteenth century the Alvord gang is supposed to have buried about $60,000 in gold bullion somewhere along the old trail between **Willcox** and **Cochise Co.**

ARKANSAS

Arkansas Post National Memorial is off State 1 and 169, eight miles southeast of Gillett, Arkansas Co. In this area in 1686, the French explorer Henri de Tonti built two forts and founded a settlement of which no traces now remain. In 1752 the French built another fort in the same area; this too has vanished. Then in 1762 the Spaniards built Fort San Carlos III on the site and some remnants of it are still visible. After the Louisiana Purchase was made in 1803 and the Spaniards abandoned the area, Americans moved in and founded a town called Arkansas Post. It became one of the most important towns in the state. The Confederates built Fort Hindman near the town and in January 1863 it was besieged by Union troops. Then a Federal fleet under Admiral David Porter sailed up the Arkansas River forced the fort to surrender. Before the Union troops departed they demolished the fort. Soon after the town went into a steep decline and today there is only a small village on the site. However, in the general area there are remains of hundreds of old buildings.

Poison Spring Battlefield is off State 24 about eighteen miles northwest of Camden, Quachita Co. As a result of a victory here on April 18, 1864, the Confederates stopped the Union invasion of Texas and caused the fleeing Union troops to abandon some 200 wagons full of supplies and war materials.

Eureka Springs, Carroll Co. is one of the oldest health resorts in the Ozark regions. In a two-square-mile area of the present town can be seen the vestiges of many old buildings of the old town, totally destroyed by fire in 1883.

Fayetteville Battlefield is on the outskirts of Fayetteville, Washington Co. On April 18, 1863 the Confederates won an important victory and the fleeing Union troops dumped a great deal of arms and munitions in a nearby creek.

Prairie Grove Battlefield is on U.S. 62 about ten miles southwest of Fayetteville, Washington Co. A 65-acre park now covers only the heart of the area where the Union troops won a battle on December 7, 1862. Outside the park a number of earthworks can still be seen.

Mark's Hill Battlefield is off State 8 about ten miles southeast of Fordyce, Dallas Co. On March 25, 1864 the Confederates won a battle and captured 240 wagonloads of supplies and prisoners.

The site of Fort Smith is at Belle Point in the town of Fort Smith, Crawford Co. The first fort of this name was built here in 1817 as one of the first United States forts in the Louisiana Territory. It was abandoned in 1839 and only the foundations are still visible. The Army built another Fort Smith nearby in 1839 which served as a hospital during the Civil War. Very few traces of it are still visible.

Ten-Mile House is on State 5, ten miles south of Little Rock, Pulaski Co. The structure, which is still standing, was built around 1822 and served as an inn on the Old Southwest Trail. In 1863 it was used as a headquarters for Federal troops. A number of buried treasure tales are associated with this building.

Jacksonport State Park is on State 69, three miles northwest of Newport, Jackson Co. Jacksonport was a very prosperous town on the banks of the White River, founded in 1833 and abandoned in 1872. Today only the courthouse of this town is still standing but there are remnants of several hundred other houses.

Pea Ridge Military Park is near U.S. 62 about eleven miles northeast of Rogeres, Benton Co. This site is located just south of the Missouri border. On March 7-8, 1862 a major battle was won by Union troops which resulted in Missouri falling into the Union camp. Many trenches and earthworks can be seen here.

Jenkin's Ferry Battlefield is on State 46 about twelve miles southwest of Sheridan, Grant Co. An indecisive battle was fought here on April 30, 1864, with heavy losses on both sides.

The ghost town of Old Washington is on State 4 about nine miles northwest of Hope, Hempstead Co. This town was famous as being the place in which the Bowie knife was invented; the blacksmith shop in which thousands were made still stands. Near this shop a treasure hunter recently unearthed a cache of several hundred Bowie knives in a very good state of preservation. The ruins of many other buildings dating back to the 1820s are intact in the deserted town.

The ghost town of Butterfield is off State 270, five miles west of Malvern, Hot Springs Co. Many of the original early nineteenth-century buildings are still standing.

The ghost town of Cadron is on the Arkansas River, about four miles west of Conway, Faulkner Co. The town was founded in 1814 and once rivaled Little Rock in size and importance. Today there are only a few ruins in a grove of cedar trees.

The ghost town of Camp is located about fourteen miles west of Mammoth Springs, Sharp Co. Founded in 1870, it was first called Indian Camp; by 1900 it had been abandoned. Today the ruins of only a few buildings are still visible.

The ghost town of Chalk Bluff is on the St. Francis River about one mile from St. Francis on State 62, Clay Co. It was founded in 1842 and abandoned by 1880. The ruins of a Confederate fort stand near the abandoned settlement.

The ghost town of Champagnolle Landing is on the Quachita River, off State 167, 3 miles east of Calion, Union Co. It was founded in 1818 as Scarsborough Landing, changed to Union Courthouse in 1840, then assumed its last name in 1844. Until the railroad bypassed it, the town had been a thriving riverport and a wealthy commercial center. In the ruins of the town's old bank a treasure hunter recently located four leather bags containing about $500 in silver coins dating in the early 1900s.

The ghost town of Davidsonville is off State 63 about six miles northeast of Powhatan, Lawrence Co. It was founded in 1815, abandoned during a yellow fever epidemic, and never resettled. Vestiges of several hundred buildings can still be seen.

The ruins of the town of Dwight are located on the west bank of Illinois Bayou, off State 64 near Russelville, Pope Co. The town was founded in 1822 and abandoned soon after the Civil War. Only the foundations of a few brick houses are still visible.

The ghost town of Golden City is off County 23 about four miles south of Booneville, Yell Co. Founded in 1886, it became a booming gold-mining center after some mines were salted; it had a life-span of less than two years. Many of the original buildings are still standing.

The ruins of Hopefield Settlement are located on the Mississippi River about two miles north of State 70, across the river from Memphis, St. Francis Co. It was founded in 1797; now there are only a few foundations of houses.

The ghost town of Kirby is near the junction of State 70 and County 27, about 90 miles west of Little Rock, Pike Co. It was a mining town supporting the nearby mercury mines and abandoned after the mines closed in 1903.

The ghost town of Napoleon is located at the junction of the Arkansas and Mississippi Rivers near Rosedale, Desha Co. It was founded in 1820 and became an important shipping town before being abandoned because of a great flood in 1874. More than $400,000 in gold bullion and coinage was lost during this flood when a river steamer sank near this town.

The small settlement of Norfold is at the junction of the White and North Fork Rivers, about fourteen miles south of Mountain Home, Baxter Co. It was once a booming river town of 8,500 inhabitants. Today less than a third that number live in the town, which is surrounded by many deserted nineteenth-century buildings.

The ghost town of Old Austin is on County 27, about one mile from Austin and 27 miles northeast of Little Rock, White Co. Founded in 1821 and abandoned before 1870, it now stands hidden in a grove of trees.

The ghost town of Ravenden Springs is located six miles east of Imboden on State 62-63, Lawrence Co. It was a booming health resort in the Ozarks until being abandoned in 1910 and now is a deserted cluster of hotels and health spas.

The ruins of Rondo are located two miles north and three miles east of Texarkana, Texas, off U.S. 30 and close to Mandeville, Miller Co. Only the stone church of this town is still standing but there are numerous foundations of buildings in the area and a cemetery.

The ghost town of Wittsburg is on the St. Francis River about two miles south of Levesque, off State 64, Cross Co. The French settled there in 1739 and built Fort Bienville. Later the town became a riverport known as Strong's Point and was renamed while serving as the county

113

seat during the 1860s. Only about ten buildings from the nineteenth century are still standing and no traces of the French settlement remain.

The Lost Diamond Mine is somewhere to the east of Murfreesboro in Pike Co.

The Lost William Flynn's Diggings is also east of Murfreesboro in Washington Co.

A lost gold mine is located in the vicinity of the Caddo River, just south of Norman, Montgomery Co.

The Lost Pig Pen Bottoms Gold Mine is located in the vicinity of Lockesburg, Sevier Co.

The Lost Field of Silver Mine is in the vicinity of Quachita, Dallas Co.

The Lost Spanish Silver Mine is on Pilot's Knob near Batavia in Boone Co.

The Lost Tabor Silver Mine is within a five-mile radius of Tomahawk, Searcy Co.

The Lost Sugar Cave Silver Mine is within a three-mile radius of Eureka Springs, Carroll Co.

The Lost Fred Conley Gold Mine is about seven to ten miles northwest of Eureka Springs, Carroll Co.

Several lost silver mines are located along the White River in the Ozark Mountains in the northern section of the state.

The Lost White Mountain Silver Mine is in the area of Hurricane Creek, Crawford Co.

A lost silver mine is located somewhere in the Poteau Range on the east end of Judy Mountain, Scott Co.

The Lost Caddo Indian Gold Mine is in Caddo Gap, south of Norman, Montgomery Co.

The Lost La Harpe Gold Mine is near the Arkansas River near Morrillton, Conway Co.

The Twin Springs Treasure, according to legend, consists of about $1 million in gold bars buried during the Civil War near Wickes, Polk Co.

The Spanish explorer Hernando De Soto is said to have buried a cache of gold which was taken from Indians along the Quachita River near **Arkedelphia,** Clark Co.

In the early 1800s a bandit named John Murral is alleged to have buried two different treasures on **Stuart's Island** near Lake Village on the north edge of Lake Chicot, Chicot Co.

During the Civil War a Union gunboat sank on the White River near **Claredon,** Monroe Co., carrying $150,000 in gold coins. Two years later it was recovered by a John Crittenhouse. When the Federal government demanded it, he hid it in a cave near Claredon and died soon afterwards.

The Madre Vena Treasure is supposed to consist of $110 million in silver and gold bullion, located near Pineville, Izard Co.

During the Civil War three Indians are said to have buried two iron pots of silver and gold coins in a sink hole beside the old wagon trail near **Bee Creek** in the northern part of Boone Co.

The Falls of Coweta Treasure is alleged to consist of a cache of more than one thousand twenty-dollar gold pieces buried by a rich trader in 1876 near Short Creek, Boone Co.

About midway between **Huntsville** and **Hindsville,** off County 68, are the ruins of a farm that was owned by a Jim Hawkins around the turn of the century. On his deathbed Hawkins revealed that he had secreted numerous treasure caches on his property but refused to give the exact locations. Right after World War II, treasure hunters found $11,000 in gold coins in an iron box in the hearth of his mill house and another $8,000 in gold coins in his yard. More treasure is believed still to be on his property.

In the Ozarks, about five miles southeast of **Sulphur Springs,** Benton Co., about $3 million in Spanish gold is reported to be buried on a farm now owned by Elias Dunbar.

On County 45, several miles east of **Fayetteville,** Washington Co. is the William Flynn farm. In 1897, Flynn's grandfather is alleged to have buried a hoard of gold coins then valued at $115,000, which has never been found.

According to legend, Jesse James buried about $32,000 in gold in the **Brushy Mountains** between Hot Springs and Plainview, Perry Co. The loot was robbed from the Hot Springs Stagecoach in 1877.

During the 1880s many outlaws used **Big Rock,** about eight miles east of Little Rock, Pulaski Co., as their base and are alleged to have concealed numerous treasures in the area. Several small caches have been found in recent years by treasure hunters using metal detectors, but more is believed to remain in the area.

A wealthy merchant named Hen Wesson hid his accumulated fortune of some 40 years on the west bank of the Arkansas River, near U.S. 40, about five miles southwest of **Conway,** Faulkner Co.

Cherokee Indians are said to have stored a huge cache of silver bullion and other ill-gotten plunder in a cave in the **Norristown Mountains,** about one mile southwest of Russellville, Pope Co. Three miles from the site the remains of an Indian settlement are visible.

During the Civil War the Hermann Family buried five large ceramic jugs of gold coins in separate locations on their farm at **Dutch Mills,** a few miles southwest of Fayetteville, Washington Co. After the war they were able to locate only three of the jugs.

CALIFORNIA

The Mission of San Luis Obispo is still standing in the town of this same name located about 80 miles northwest of Santa Barbara, San Luis Obispo Co. The mission was founded in 1772 and a Spanish settlement was built up around it. Around 1840, when news arrived that John Charles Fremont was coming to the area, the Padres quickly hid a great deal of church plate in a cave near Bishop's Peak. Some of these objects were centuries old at that time. Apparently the priests concealed some treasure in the mission as well, because in 1900 when the mission was being rebuilt, workmen discovered six large silver bars hidden under the floor of the chapel.

Two successive fires in **San Francisco** during June 1850 caused property damages of over $3 million. The following year another fire on May 3 destroyed more than 2500 buildings in the city with property damage of more than $12 million. The Great San Francisco Fire took place on April 18, 1906 and resulted in 600 dead, 300,000 homeless and property losses of over $400 million. During the month of July 1850 more than 500 ships were deserted and left to rot along the waterfront as sailors fled to the gold fields. Treasure hunters have been making good finds in recent years in the sections of the town where these fires occurred and also in the waterfront area where valuable objects from old ships have come to rest.

The Manila Galleon, San Agustin was sailing between the Philippines and Acapulco in 1599 when it was grounded and wrecked. Documents state that this occurred in the vicinity of San Francisco. In recent years large amounts of Chinese porcelain, of which the ship was carrying thousands of pieces, have been found on Montara Beach south of the city. Many other items from this wreck can probably be found on this beach with the use of metal detectors.

The Capitana, or flagship, of a small squadron commanded by General Juan de Velasco, sent from Peru to search for Dutch pirates in 1600, was wrecked on the beach in the vicinity of the point of land in the Cabrillo National Monument at the entrance to San Diego Harbor. In 1973 several Spanish silver coins from this period were found on the beach in the area.

Just a few miles outside of the Mother Lode town of **Mariposa,** Mariposa Co., lies a rotting leather pouch containing 300 octagon-shaped fifty-dollar gold slugs, now worth more than $100,000 on the collector's market. Early in the 1850s, Joseph Marre, a county tax collector, was caught in a cloudburst while on the job. He hid the money for safekeeping but was drowned before he could return for it.

The ruins of the Mount Ophir Mint are located in the outskirts of Mariposa, Mariposa County. It was built in 1850 by John L. Moffat, part-owner of a mine and assaying firm in San Francisco. Here in February 1851 he coined the first fifty-dollar hexagonal gold coins, which are extremely valuable in today's numismatic market. Several of his workmen are alleged to have buried large numbers of these coins on the premises.

The town of Old Auburn is on I-80, 35 miles northeast of Sacramento, Nevada Co. It was founded as a gold-mining camp in 1848 and after the gold-rush days was an important railroad center. Many of the original buildings still stand on the outskirts of the town.

The ghost town of Bodie is seven miles south of Bridgeport, Mono Co. The town was founded in 1858 when gold was discovered in the area and within a few years it had a population of over 10,000. During the boom years the local mines yielded $400,000 a month. A total of over $100 million in gold was removed before the town was abandoned. Today about 170 of the original buildings are still standing.

Coloma National Landmark is on State 49, seven miles northwest of Placerville, El Dorado Co. The site is near Sutter's Mill where the first gold strike was made in 1848. Coloma became a town overnight when more than 80,000 flocked to the gold fields that year. The ruins of many dwellings dot the surrounding area.

The town of Colombia is on State 49, four miles north of Sonora, Calaveras Co. It is situated in the heart of the Mother Lode country at the foothills of the Sierra Nevada and within a month of the discovery of gold nearby in 1850 more than 5,000 prospectors swarmed in and founded the town. During the next 30 years some $87 million in gold was extracted from placer deposits in the area. Part of the town burned down in 1857 and only a handful of people still live there among the many deserted nineteenth-century buildings.

The ghost town of Skiddo is off State 190 about ten miles east of Emigrant Junction in Death Valley. During the 1880s it was a main borax-mining town but was abandoned sometime before 1900.

The site of Fort Humboldt is on U.S. 101 near Eureka, Humboldt Co. It was built in 1853 to protect settlers from hostile Indians. Ulysses Grant served as commander for its first two years of operation. The fort was abandoned in 1870.

Fort Ross National Landmark is on State 1 about thirteen miles north of Jenner, Del Monte Co. In 1812 Russian fur traders settled here, erecting a wooden stockade and trading post on the site, and used it for the next 29 years until selling it to Americans. Most of the original buildings are still standing.

The ruins of Fort Tejon are on U.S. 99 in Grapevine Canyon, 36 miles south of Bakersfield. It was built by the United States.Army in 1852 to protect the strategic pass in the Tehachapi Mountain Range. Near the ruins of the fort are remains of an unidentified ghost town of the past century.

The ruins of the San José de Guadalupe Mission are on State 238 near Fremont, Alameda Co. The mission and settlement was established in 1797, but completely destroyed during an earthquake in 1868 and never rebuilt.

The San Antonio de Padua Mission is on U.S. 101, twenty miles southwest of King City, Monterey Co. It was established in 1771 by Padre Junipero Serra, fell into ruin about 1820, but has been restored recently. Several treasures are believed to be buried on the premises.

Lava Beds National Monument is on State 139 about 60 miles north of Alturas, Modoc Co. White settlers began moving into this area around 1870 and built a stockade on the site for protection from hostile Indians. In 1873 a bloody battle was fought on the site between the Indians and United States Cavalry, in which 500 persons on both sides were killed.

Old Los Angeles was originally named El Pueblo de Nuestra Señora la Reina de Los Angeles when founded by Spaniards in 1781. On a number of vacant lots and in a park in this section of the present city many vestiges of the original stone buildings can be seen. A number of interesting artifacts have been found here by treasure hunters in recent years.

The Rio San Gabriel Battlefield is located near the intersection of Bluff Road and Washington Blvd. in the Los Angeles suburb of Montebello. During the Mexican War, in January 1847, United States troops fought and routed a Mexican force on this site.

The ruins of the San Gabriel Archangel Mission are located in the town of San Gabriel, Los Angeles Co. It was founded in 1771 and for 50 years served as the only outpost of civilization west of the vast California desert. The original mission and other buildings were destroyed by an earthquake in the 1850s. Now a reconstruction of the church stands on the site, surrounded by the ruins of the original buildings.

The New Almaden Mine is located on County G8, four miles south of San Jose, Santa Clara Co. The mine, which is one of the four major sources for mercury in the world, was opened in 1845 and became indispensible during the gold-rush days for processing the precious metal. There are numerous old ruins surrounding the present mining operation.

116

San Juan Bautista State Park is on U.S. 101, about three miles east of San Juan Bautista, Benito Co. A mission was founded here in 1797 and a large Spanish settlement built up around it. A number of the original structures are still standing and many ruins dot the area. About ten miles southeast of this site on the San Juan Canyon Road is Fremont Peak, where Captain John C. Fremont and his American soldiers defied the Mexicans by building a wooden fort in 1846, of which no traces remain.

The ruins of the San Juan Capistrano Mission are located in the town of this same name, San Diego Co. The mission was founded in 1776 and a very large and elaborate stone church was completed in 1806. In 1812 a severe earthquake struck, causing the structure to come crashing down on the congregation. It was never rebuilt.

San Luis Rey Mission is on Mission Road, four miles east of Oceanside, San Diego Co. It was known as the "King of the Missions" after being established in 1798. For many years it was the home of more than three thousand Indians until being abandoned in 1834. It was restored and is now being used as a seminary. Ruins of many of the Indian dwellings can be seen.

San Pasquel Battlefield Park is located eight miles southeast of Escondido, San Diego Co. A major battle occurred here on December 6, 1846 between Spanish Californios and United States Army troops. Both sides suffered heavy losses in this indecisive engagement.

The site of San Rafael Archangel Mission is in present-day San Rafael, Marin Co. It was established in 1817 and consisted of more than twenty large stone buildings, including a monastery and hospital. No traces of the original site remain; only a reconstructed chapel now marks the site.

The site of the Santa Barbara Presidio is located in the city of Santa Barbara. Only the mission church remains to mark the site. It was established in 1782 and four years later a large town stood on the site, but no traces of it remain today.

The site of Santa Clara Mission is in the present city of Santa Clara, Santa Clara Co. It was founded in 1777 and in use for at least 50 years until being destroyed by hostile Indians. At that time a few of the surviving padres fled for Mexico after burying a considerable amount of treasure on the site. A replica of the church now marks the spot.

The site of Santa Cruz Mission is in present Santa Cruz, Santa Cruz Co. It was established in 1781 but finally abandoned after being completely destroyed by earthquakes in 1840 and 1857. Today a half-size replica of the church stands on the site.

The ghost town of Shasta is on State 299 about six miles west of Redding, Shasta Co. After gold was discovered in the area in 1849 the town was born. Since the wagon road ended here and the Oregon pack trail began at this point, the town soon became the "Queen City of the North." The town was abandoned after the gold deposits were exhausted, but today many of the original buildings are still standing.

Santa Ynez Mission is off U.S. 101 near Solvang, Santa Barbara Co. It was established in 1804 and then completely destroyed by Indians during an uprising in 1824. Only the chapel has been restored, though vestiges of many other buildings can be seen.

Weaverville Joss Park is on U.S. 299 in present Weaverville, Trinity Co. During the gold-rush days thousands of Chinese arriving to strike it rich settled in this town. The ruins of many of their homes are visible in this park.

Old Monterey Town in the present city of Monterey was first settled by Spaniards in 1770. It quickly became the most important Spanish settlement in the state. A number of the early buildings have survived and ruins of others have been preserved in a park covering the central portion of the original settlement.

The site of Fort Sutter is located on the fork of the American and Sacramento Rivers in Sacramento. It was built in 1839 to protect newly arrived settlers. By 1890 all traces of it had disappeared when a new fort by the same name was built on the site. The original fort served as a refuge for weary miners during the gold-rush days, many of whom are alleged to have buried gold in the area.

The site of San Diego de Alcala Mission is on Presidio Hill in Mission Valley in what is now called Old Town San Diego. It was founded in 1769 by Padre Junipero Serra, then was

Over
Early day miners and dredgers took millions of dollars of gold from California, yet today's metal detectors can find nuggets in the tailings they left behind.

Facing
Seashores of America such as this tourist spot in South Carolina often provide lovely—and profitable—locations for beachcombing treasure hunters.

Over

Metal detectors provide electronic "eyes" that can look beneath the ground to find coins and other valuable objects that are made of metal.

Facing

Abandoned mines in California's Sierra Nevada Range and other Western mountains often contain gold nuggets and othere valuable treasures abandoned and fell into ruins within a few years. Another mission building standing today was built on the same site. A fire in 1872 caused great destruction to the settlement which had been built up around the mission; however modern buildings have obliterated all traces of these ruins.

San Diego Presidio was located on a hill overlooking the Pacific in the heart of downtown San Diego. The site was settled by the Spaniards in 1769 but by 1835 all of the original structures had fallen into ruin. In 1838 Fort Stockton was built on the site by Americans. Today only remnants of the fort's ramparts are still visible.

Angel Island State Park in San Francisco Bay was the site of a Spanish settlement built in 1775, of which no traces are visible today. During the 1870s it was used as a prison for Arizona Indians and in 1892 it became the Quarantine and Immigration Station for San Francisco.

The site of Castillo de San Joaquin is on White Cliff near the Golden Gate Bridge in San Francisco. The Spaniards built this large stone fort in 1794 but it was completely demolished by United States Army engineers in 1863 when they built Fort Point, which still stands.

Presidio National Historic Landmark, on U.S. 101 and I-480 at the entrance to San Francisco Bay, is one of the oldest and largest military reservations in the nation. It was established in 1776 by the Spaniards to protect the city and port and has served as a military post ever since. Of the numerous original buildings, only the Spanish commandante's house remains today.

The ghost town of Ballarat is on a dirt road leading to Death Valley, 48 miles northeast of Ridgecrest, Kern Co. A few of the original buildings and many ruins remain.

The ghost town of Bend City is near the Owens River, four miles east of Independence, Inyo Co. The ruins of about twenty buildings can still be seen of this deserted mining town.

The ghost town of Bettysburg, also known as Elizabethtown, is a few miles outside of the present town of Quincy, Plumas Co. The ruins of over three hundred buildings can still be seen. Many other ghost towns are in the immediate vicinity.

The ghost town of Bidwell Bar is on a dirt road about nine miles east of Oroville, Butte Co. It was once a booming mining town and county seat; today only one building is still standing but hundreds of others in ruins are visible.

The ghost town of Bodie is about twenty miles east of State 395 and the same distance north of Mono Lake, Mono Co. It was one of the roughest, toughest boom towns of the West and has been immortalized in hundreds of Western stories. Most of the town is in ruins with the exception of a saloon and the assayer's shop.

The ghost town of Calico is in the Calico Mountains about four miles northwest of Yermo, San Bernardino Co. It was once a prosperous silver-mining town of four thousand inhabitants and is now being restored.

The ruins of Cerro Gordo Mine are located about three miles north of Keeler, Inyo Co. This mine produced over $25 million in gold, silver, lead, and zinc before being abandoned. The ruins of the mine and the foundations of the camp buildings are visible.

The ghost town of Claraville is in the Sequoia National Forest about 23 miles southeast of Bodfish. It had a life of less than five years as a rip-roaring gold boomtown in the 1860s. None of the original buildings remain.

The ruins of Coarse Gold are located 36 miles northwest of Fresno on County 41, Madera Co. Only the foundations of a few buildings and some rusted mining machinery remain.

The ghost town of Dale is about fifteen miles east of the town of 29 Palms on the north edge of Joshua Tree National Monument. Many of the original buildings are still well preserved and standing.

The ghost town of Havilah is near Breckenridge Mountain about seven miles south of Bodfish, Kern Co. It was a thriving mining town and county seat until being abandoned around 1870.

The ghost town of Hawkinsville is a bit west of U.S. 5 and about two miles north of Yreka, Siskiyou Co. It was once a mining town with a main street stretching for three miles along Yreka Creek. Today only a few buildings are still standing.

Ghost towns along County Highway 49. Starting from the town of Sattley located about 45 miles northwest of Lake Tahoe, Sierra Co. and following this highway down to the town of Mariposa, Mariposa Co., which covers an area of about 174 miles, one can literally see a continuous string of deserted ghost towns which were booming during the gold-rush days. The names of many have been forgotten but the ruins of more than 10,000 old buildings dot both sides of this long stretch of highway.

The ruins of Iowa Hill are located about fifteen miles east of Colfax, Placer Co. In its heyday the mines around this town were one of the main producers of gold in the area. Numerous other mining camps are in the vicinity.

The ghost town of Jacumba is located about 70 miles east of San Diego, south of U.S. 8, close to the Mexican border, Imperial Co. It was founded in 1852 and served as a health resort until the 1930s. Many of the present-century buildings are still erect.

The ruins of Kearsage are east of the Sequoia National Park, near Kearsage Peak, along the Union Pacific Railroad, Inyo Co. Only the foundations of a few buildings remain of this mining center.

The ruins of Kernville, originally named Whiskey Flats, are on the Kern River about ten miles north of Isabella, Kern Co. Foundations of many buildings and rusting mining equipment are visible.

The ghost town of Kingston is on the Lower Kings River near Hardwick, Kings Co. Several buildings of this mining town are still standing.

The town of Laport is in the Sierra Nevada Mountains about ten miles northwest of Downieville, Plumas Co. Only a few people still live in this old mining town, in which many old buildings are still standing. The ruins of many others dot the area.

The ghost town of Lundy is on the shore of Lundy Lake in the center of Modoc Co. Some of the old buildings are still standing in this mining town, but most of the town has been inundated by the lake water.

The ruins of Ogilby are located fifteen miles west on State 80 and four miles north of Winterhaven in the southeastern corner of the state, Imperial Co. From 1879 to 1918 it was a mining boomtown. Today only the railroad station is still there.

The ghost town of Tumco is six and a half miles up the railroad tracks from Ogilby. It also was a booming mining town during the same period with three thousand residents and four saloons. Many of its buildings are standing.

The town of Olema is on State 1 about 30 miles north of San Francisco. Only a few dozen people still live in this town, which has a large number of late nineteenth-century buildings still intact. The ruins of limestone kilns can be found a bit to the south.

The Town of Onion Valley is about twelve miles north of Downiesville, Sierra Co. A few people still live in this town which had more than 1500 residents during the last three decades of the past century. The ruins of many buildings are visible.

The ghost town of Panamint is on a desert road, four miles east of Ballarat and 52 miles northeast of Ridgecrest, Inyo Co. It was famous as a most notorious mining camp and today numerous ruined buildings, the old smelter, and the tramway remain.

The ruins of Picacho are located on the west bank of the Colorado River about 25 miles north of Yuma, Arizona and Winterhaven, Imperial Co. The ruins of more than two hundred buildings dot the area. The Picacho Mine is located on a dirt road about six miles from the town and at one time over two thousand men were employed here. The ruins of the mill, smelter, and many buildings remain in the mine area.

The ghost town of Purisima is located four miles south of Half Moon Bay on the Pacific, San Mateo Co. About 25 deserted buildings can be seen in the cypress tree forest.

The ruins of Quartzburg are on the Kern River about nine miles north of Isabela, Kern Co. Only the remains of a few walls and stone chimneys mark its location.

The ruins of Rich Bar are located on County 24 between Oroville and Quincy, Butte Co. It was a prosperous gold mining boomtown during the 1850s, but today consists only of the foundations of a few buildings and the cemetery.

The ghost town of Rough and Ready is near the intersection of County 20 and 49, near the town of Grass Valley, Nevada Co. It was a gold-mining boomtown in the 1850s. About 40 of the original buildings are still standing.

The ghost town of Scott Bar is three miles south of U.S. 5 and a bit east of Yreka, Siskiyou Co. A few of the mines in the area are being worked today by small groups of weekend prospectors. Many of the town's original buildings are still standing.

The ruins of Tioga, originally named Bernetville, are located a few miles south of the ghost town of Lundy, Modoc Co. It was a busy mining town in the 1870s and 1880s and completely abandoned by 1892. Many ruins and mine shafts dot the area.

The ghost town of Traver is located off State 99 about eighteen miles north of Tulare, Tulare Co. Before the turn of the century it was a prosperous agricultural town of a thousand residents. Today only a number of windmills and abandoned buildings can be seen.

The town of White River, originally named Tailholt, is 22 miles southeast of Porterville on Balance Rock Road. It was a large placer gold mining supply town in the 1850s, but only a few people still live there today. Many old buildings are still standing.

The following is a list of names and approximate locations of lost gold and silver mines in the state, by counties: **CALAVERAS CO. Lost Golden Caverns Mine** is near the lower end of French Gulch, near Columbia; **Lost Yankee Hill Mine** in the vicinity of Columbia. **DEL NORTE CO. Lost Cabin Mine** is near the mouth of the Klamath River, south of Crescent City. **IMPERIAL CO. The Lost Black Butte Mine** is east of Ogilby, on Black Butte slope in the Cargo Mountains; **Lost Hank Brandt's Mine** is in the Superstition Mountains, 18 miles northwest of El Centro; **Lost Bullring Mine** is in Mule Spring Canyon of the Black Hills. **INYO CO. Lost Alec Ramy's Mine** is on the south base of Dry Mountain of the Last Chance Mountain Range; **Lost Burro Mine** is in Lost Burro Gap, Death Valley; **Lost Gunsight Mine** is at the lower end of Butte Valley in the Panamint Mountains; **Lost Skiddo Mine** is near the west side of Emigrant Pass. **KERN CO. Lost Carry-Cart Mine** is in Mountain Spring Canyon of the Argus Mountains; **Lost Frazier Mountain Mine** is somewhere in a tunnel near Chucapate Park; **Lost Chance Mine** is two to six miles north of the White River; **Lost Goler Diggings** is in Goler Canyon, 32 miles north of Mojave. **KINGS CO. Lost Mexican Mine** is in the mountains about 60 miles northeast of Visalia. **LASSEN CO. Lost Captain Dick Mine** is in the Warner Mountains, northeast of Eagleville between Owl Creek and Pine Valley. **MARIPOSA CO. Lost Aqua Fria Mine** is on the outskirts of Aqua Fria; **Cave of Escondido Mine** is on the Merced River near Bagby; **Lost Frenchman Flat Gold Mine** is in the vicinity of French Mills, near a ghost town on a small creek; **Lost Sierra Rica Mine** is 3 to 5 miles from Midpines; **Lost Whispering Pines Gold Mine** is within a 5 mile radius of Midpines. **MONO CO. Lost Bodie Mine** is near Bridgeport; **Lost Dogtown Mine** is within a 3 mile radius of Bridgeport. **PLACER CO. Lost Iowa Hill Mine** is near the head of the East Fork of the American River. **SAN BERNARDINO CO. Lost Black Magic Mine** is near Owl Hot Springs; **Lost Chuckawalla Wilson Mine** is in the Providence Mountains near Mitchell State Park; **Lost Arch Diggings** is 25 miles north of Rice at the north end of Turtle Mountains; **Lost Lee Mine** is in the San Bernardino Mountains north of Old Woman's Well; **Lost New Deal Mine** is near Owl Hot Springs; **Lost Sheephole Mountain Mine** is near Amboy in the northwest end of the Sheep Hole Mountains; **Lost Van Duzen Canyon Mine** is in Holcomb Valley between Gold Mountain and Bertha Peak. **SAN JOAQUIN CO. Lost Nigger Hill Mine** is near Mokelumme Hill on the north bank of San Antonio Creek. **SHASTA CO. Lost Humbug Creek Mine** is near Redding on the western side of Humbug Mountain; **Lost Waterfall Mine** is on Bear Creek, in Bear Canyon, near Linwood. **SISKIYOU CO. Lost Frenchman Mine** is on the Indian River near Happy Camp. **TOULUMME CO. Lost Big Oak Flat Mine** is near Big Oak Flat on the north side of Yosemite Road. **YUBA CO. Lost Frenchman Mine** is on Grizzly Hill, Frenchman's Canyon, near Nevada City.

The following is a list of names and locations of abandoned gold and silver and gem stone mines in the state by counties: **BUTTE CO. Bader Mine,** one and a half miles east of Magalia; **Black Diamond Mine,** off Ponderosa Way Road, north of De Sabla; **Blue Hog Mine,** five miles north of Magalia; **Bumble Bee Mine,** between Oroville and Oregon City; **Emma Mine,** north of Nimshew Cemetery; **Era Mine,** near Dry Creek; **Guamer Mine** on Dry Creek; **Genie Mine,** one mile north of Magalia; **Golden Nugget Mine,** on the west slope above the West Branch of the Feather River; **Indian Springs Mine,** near De Sabla; **Lucky John Mine,** two miles north of Paradise; **Lucratia Mine,** north of Sawmill Peak; **Madre de Oro Mine,** south of Ponderosa Way Road, near Paradise; **Magalia Mine,** near Magalia Camp; **Mineral Slide Mine,** three miles southeast of Magalia; **Old Utah Mine,** north of Empire Creek; **Oro Fino Mine,** on Butte Creek, near De Sabla; **Princess-Cory Mine,** two and a half miles northeast of Magalia; **Royal Drift Mine,** near Ponderosa Way Road and the near forks of Butte Creek; **Steifer Mine,** near Magalia Camp. **INYO CO. Albertoli Mine,** in Black Canyon, east of Bishop; **Amargosa Mine,** two miles from Salt Spring; **American Mine,** at the foot of Ibex Peak, Ibex Hills; **Argus Sterling Mine,** twelve miles south of Darwin; **Arro Gordo Mine,** nine miles northeast of Keeler; **Ashford Mine,** in Death Valley, six miles northeast of Ashford Junction; **Big Four Mine,** seven miles north of Panamint Springs; **Big Silver Mine,** in Daisy Canyon; **Bunker Hill Mine,** twelve miles north of Willow Creek; **Burgess Mine,** outside Lone Pine; **Cerro Gordo Mine,** six miles east of Keeler; **Columbia Mine,** three miles north of Tecopa Pass; **Crystal Spring Mine,** two miles north of Crystal Spring; **Darwin Mine,** a few miles northeast of Darwin; **Defense Mine,** 6 miles west of Ash Hill Road, Panamint Springs; **Desert Hound Mine,** in Death Valley, six miles northeast of Ashford Junction; **Eclipse Mine,** in the Ibex Hills, five miles off State 127; **El Conejo Mine,** in the Etcheron Valley, six miles west of Howard Ranch; **Eureka Gold Mine,** in the Eureka Valley, in Cowhorn Valley; **Gladstone Mine,** in the Ibex Hills, five miles off State 127; **Golden Lady Mine,** four miles west of Ash Hill Road, Panamint Springs; **Grandview Mine,** ten miles east of Bishop; **Grant Mine,** four miles northwest of Ibex Pass; **Gray Eagle Mine,** near Bishop, in Black Canyon; **Ibex Mine,** five miles west of Ibex Springs; **Keane Wonder Gold Mine,** four miles southwest of Chloride City; **Keeler Mine,** on Ulida Flat, in Death Valley; **Lee Mines,** in Santa Rosa Hills, 6 miles north of County 190; **Lemoigne Mine,** in Lemoigne Canyon, Cottonwood Mountains; **Lone Indian Mine,** on Willow Creek, Cowhorn Valley; **Lotus Mine,** 3 miles west of Sourdough Springs; **Mammoth Mine,** near Darwin, two miles south of Mariposa Spring; **Mexican Mine,** on South Fork River, ten miles east of Bishop; **Minnietta Mine,** three miles west of Ash Hill Road, Panamint Springs; **Modoc Mine,** three and a half miles north of Ash Hill Road, Panamint Springs; **Mohawk Mine,** two miles south of Homewood Creek; **Mollie Gibson Mine,** three miles west of Payson Westgard Pass; **Montezuma Mine,** four miles northeast of Tenemaha Reservoir; **Morningstar Mine,** nine miles northeast of Keeler; **Noonday Mine,** three miles north of Tecopa Pass; **Orondo Mine,** two miles north of Homewood Creek; **Onyx Gold Mine,** in Shepard Canyon, ten miles west of Ballarat; **Paddy Pride Mine,** in Ibex Hills, five miles off State 127; **Poleta Mine,** four miles east of Bishop; **Porter Mine,** nine miles east of Ballerat; **Radcliff Mine,** four miles southeast of Ballarat; **Rusty Pick Mine,** in Ibex Hills; **Ruth Mine,** two miles south of Homewood Creek; **Sally Ann Mine,** on Ulida Flat, Racetrack Valley, Death Valley; **Santa Rosa Mines,** five miles west of Santa Rosa Flat Road, in Santa Rosa Hills; Silver Dollar Mine, nine miles south of Darwin; **Star of the West Mine,** near Trona; **Silverspoon Mine,** two miles south of Trona; **Stockwell Mine,** five miles northeast of Valley Wells; **Surprise Mine,** four miles south of Ash Hill Road, Panamint Springs; **Tee Mine,** in Santa Rosa Hills; **Thorndyke Mine,** nine miles south of Ballarat; **Ubenheba Mine,** six miles west of Lost Burro Gap; **Vega Mine,** in Keynot Canyon; **White Swan Mine,** five miles east of County 190, in Santa Rosa Hills; **Wonder Mine,** seven miles west of Ibex Pass; **World Beater Mine,** eight miles southeast of Ballarat; **Yaney Mine,** on the outskirts of Bishop. **KERN CO. Amalia Mine,** six miles south of Jawbone Well; **Apache Mine,** just outside Garlock; **Bobtail Mine,** eight miles south of Johave; **Bond Buyer Mine,** outside Saltdale; **Bright Star Mine,** seven miles north of Claraville; **Cactus Mine,** five miles south of Willow Springs; **Copper Basin Mine,** near Last Chance Well; **Digger Pine Mine,** two miles east of Davis Guard Spring; **Don Levy Mine,** five miles south of Claraville; **Elephant Eagle Mine,** eight miles south of Mohave; **Glen Olive Mine,** nine miles southeast of Bodfish; **Gold Bug Mine,** seven miles south of Ridgerest; **Gold Peak Cowboy Mine,** three miles south of Loraine; **Golden Queen Mine,** nine miles south of Mohave; **Gwynne Mine,** near Claraville; **Hi-Peak Mine,** near Athel; **Iconoclast Mine,** 9 miles south of Claraville; **Indian Creek Mine,** two miles southeast of Loraine; **Jeanette Grant Mine,** ten miles south of Lake Isabella; **Joe Walker Mine,** two miles east of Yates Hot Springs; **Laurel Mine,** 8 miles south of Lake Isabella; **Lonely Camp Mine,** four miles south of Ridgerest; **Lone Star Mine,** six miles north of Claraville; **Long Tom Mine,** eight miles south of Granite Station; **Mohawk Buddy Mine,** one mile east of Hoffman Well; **Mammoth Eureka Mine,** one mile east of Soda Springs; **Oakley Mine,** near Saltdale; **Opal Mine,** three miles north of Saltdale; **Posomine Mine,** in the Pine Mountains; **Prospect Mine,** near Last Chance Well; **Rademacker Mine,** seven miles south of Ridgerest; **San Antonio Mine,** near Alpha Spring; **Seismatite Mine,** seven miles north of Saltdale; **Skyline Mine,** six miles south of Jawbone Well; **Smith Mine,** near Garlock; **Tropico Mine,** five miles east of Willow Springs; **Tungsten Chief Mine,** eight miles south of Havilah; **Valley View Mine,** six miles southeast of Bodfish; **Waterhole Mine,** two miles east of Claraville; **White Rock Mine,** near Jawbone Well; **White Star Mine,** six miles south of Ridgerest; **Yellow Aster Mine,** three miles west of Randsburg; **Zenda Mine,** four miles southwest of Loraine. **LASSEN CO. Big Ben Mine,** near Big Bend, in Lassen National Forest; **Bunker Hill Mine,** near Big Bend, Lassen National Forest; **Evening Star Mine,** near Big Bend, Lassen National Forest; **Hornet Mine,** on Stoney Creek, Lassen National Forest; **Surcease Mine,** near Big Bend, Lassen National Forest; **Treasure Hill Mine,** near Big Bend, Lassen National Forest. **LOS ANGELES CO. Gillete Mine,** on Bear Canyon. **MONO CO. Black Rock Mine,** near Benton, Casa Diablo Mountain; **Casa Diablo Mine,** near Benton, Casa Diablo Mountain; **Mono Piute Rainbow Mine,** on Piute Creek in Sacramento Canyon; **Pumice Mine,** near Benton, Casa Diablo Mountains; **Sacramento Mine,** on Piute Creek, Sacramento Canyon; **Sierra Vista Mine,** five miles south of Moran Spring. **PLUMAS CO. Carlysie Mine,** in Plumas National Forest; **Gold Bank Mine,** near old Forbestown, Plumas National Forest; **Horseshow Mine,** near Junction House; **Midas Mine,** in Plumas National Forest; **Southern Cross Mine,** on east side of Coon Ravine, on the South Fork of the Feather River; **Walker Mine,** five miles southeast of Genesee. **SAN BERNARDINO CO. Amargosa Mines,** five miles south of Soda Lake; **Black Magic Mine,** four miles north of Owl Spring; **Monarch Mine,** four miles north of Ibex Spring, Ibex Pass; **Morehouse Mine,** three miles northeast of Ibex Spring, Ibex Pass; **New Deal Mine,** two miles north of Owl Hole Spring; **Waterman Mine,** four miles north of Barstow. **SHASTA CO. Walker Mine,** five miles west of Buckeye; **Yankee John Mine,** ten miles southwest of Redding. **TULARE CO. Big Silver Mine,** two miles south of Saltworks; **Burgess Mine,** seven miles east of Pine Station, Mt. Whitney. **VENTURA CO. Castac Mine,** near Buck Creek Guard Station; **Coquina Mine,** in Chino Canyon; **Frazier Mine,** near Lincoln Air Park; **Hess Mine,** near Lockwood; **Sibert Mine,** near Lincoln Air Park; **Hess Mine,** near Lockwood; **Tapo Gillibrand Mine,** in Gillibrand Canyon. **YUBA CO. Bootjack Mine,** near Oroville; **Golden Princess Mine,** eight miles northeast of Oroville; **Fancy John Mine,** eleven miles west of Oroville.

In 1894 one of the workmen of the San Francisco Mint robbed about 290 pounds in gold bullion and buried it in the vicinity of **Shelter Cove,** Humboldt Co.

In 1876 robbers made off with $123,000 in gold bullion from a stagecoach and are alleged to have buried it in the vicinity of **Myrtletowne,** a small village about 8 miles east of Eureka, Humboldt Co.

In July 1928 the Willow Creek Post Office was robbed of $28,000 in gold coins and the bandits buried the loot in **New River Canyon,** at the mouth of New River, near Eureka Humboldt Co.

Gold and silver Spanish coins dating between 1804 and 1809 have been found on the beaches on the south and north side of the **Mattole River,** south of Eureka, Humboldt Co. They are probably being washed in from a shipwreck offshore.

The bandit, Rattlesnake Dick, and his gang of cutthroats are said to have buried $106,000 in gold which they netted from two stagecoach robberies at the western foot of **Mt. Shasta,** Siskiyou Co.

Bandits are supposed to have buried $128,000 in gold coins from a robbery near the town of **Weed,** Siskiyou Co.

About a two-hour hike south of Mt. Shasta, a chap named Adam Lingaard discovered in

1850 the **Lost Lake of Gold.** This was a dry lake bed covered with gold nuggets encompassing an area of several square miles. He carried over 100 pounds of the nuggets more than 40 miles to the nearest settlement and then failed to find the site again.

The Treasure of Castle Crags, consisting of $210,000 in gold bullion, is alleged to be hidden in the vicinity of Dunsmuir, Siskiyou Co.

According to legend, the bandit, George Skinner, buried $35,000 in gold bullion in 1856 on the western slopes of **Trinity Mountain,** near Horse Lake, Lassen Co.

Around 1860 two miners were attacked and killed by Indians, who were later captured and hanged, but not before telling that they had thrown about $40,000 in raw gold taken from the miners, into a pit near **Hall City Cave,** a few miles west of Weaverville, in the Klamath Range, Trinity Co. The white men were not able to find the gold and it is possible that the Indians lied about the location.

Three copper chests were filled with raw gold, valued at over $100,000, by a prospector named "Big Jim" Fisher in the 1890s. He is alleged to have buried the chests somewhere on the banks of Canyon Creek, a tributary of the Trinity River near **Fisher Gulch** (named after him), above the Canyon Creek Bridge, about twenty miles northwest of Weaverville, Trinity Co.

A prospector is said to have buried ten stone bottles filled with gold dust and a leather pouch of gold coins on the banks of a creek in the **Big Flat area** on the Trinity River, nine miles west of Helena, Trinity Co.

In 1892 the Ruggles Brothers robbed a stagecoach and made off with over $75,000 in gold bullion which they buried somewhere on **Red Bluff,** located near Redding on U.S. 5, Shasta Co. They were captured and hanged without revealing the location, other than the fact that it was inside a cave.

A prospector is known to have buried about $25,000 in gold nuggets somewhere along the banks of the Middle Creek, five miles upstream from **Redding,** Shasta Co. In this same area at a place called Ruggle's Boy Gulch about $10,000 in gold was buried from a holdup in the 1890s.

Fort Roop, a stopping place for settlers on the Lassen Trail, is on the outskirts of Susanville, Lassen Co. Many artifacts discarded by the persons camping here can probably be found in the area.

Around the turn of the century a Henry Gordier was murdered by robbers who tried to force him to reveal the location of a large cache of gold dust and nuggets. These were known to be buried on his ranch, which was on **Baxter Creek,** close to Janesville (County 36) on the north side of Honey Lake, Lassen Co.

In 1830 a Peter Lassen died after having buried a large fortune in gold on his ranch near the confluence of **Deer Creek** and the **Sacramento River,** Tehama Co.

In the 1850s a prospector named Charles Sterling died after burying over $25,000 in gold dust packed into liquor bottles on the banks of a slough at **French Crossing** on Butte Creek, Colusa Co.

Bandits buried over $65,000 in gold coins, contained in a safe, in **Russian Gulch,** a bit north of Mendocino on State 1, Mendocino Co.

In 1888 more than $20,000 in gold coins were buried by bandits near the summit of the **Calistoga-Middletown State Route** (now County Road 29), a few miles north of the Sonoma County line. The robbers were hanged before being able to retrieve their loot.

In 1884 a J. William Wilcox died after burying more than $50,000 in gold coins somewhere on his homesite on **Andrus Island,** located on the Sacramento River opposite the town of Rio Vista, Solano Co.

The Saddlemaker's Treasure is said to consist of over $100,000 in gold coins and bullion that a leathersmith buried in the vicinity of a stone-tanning vat. The treasure lies near Santa Teresa Spring, on the Santa Teresa Ranch in the Santa Clara Valley, several miles south of San Jose, Santa Clara Co. The leathersmith took the exact location to the grave with him.

During the Bear Flag Revolt a man named J. H. Pickett buried a hoard of gold coins valued at over $75,000 in his **San Agustino Rancho** near Santa Cruz, just west of State 1, Santa Cruz Co.

In 1875 a large iron safe containing $780,000 in gold was robbed in Monterey from a rich Chinese merchant named Tom Sing. With a posse hot on their trail the bandits were forced to bury the loot somewhere along the banks of the Salinas River about midway between **Chualar** and **Gonzales,** both on U.S. 101, San Benito Co. They were caught and hanged without revealing the exact location.

The Mexican bandit Tiburcio Vasquez is known to have hidden over $500,000 in gold specie and bullion in 1875 shortly before being killed in an attempted robbery, somewhere in the **Pinnacles National Monument** near the Monterey-San Benito County lines.

In the 1890s a Jim Savage operated a trading post on the Merced River's south fork several miles from **Coarsegold,** Merced Co. He was shot to death in a gun battle. It was common knowledge that he had secreted a large flour barrel full of gold nuggets which he had been gathering for many years from nearby placer deposits.

In 1897 the small steamer **Mollie Stevens** sank in **Owens Lake,** located on the east side of the Sierra Nevada Range in Death Valley, Inyo Co. It was carrying over $200,000 in gold and silver ore at the time and none of it was recovered.

About eight miles north of Jayhawker Spring in **Death Valley,** Inyo Co., near a chalklike cliff in a narrow canyon, some settlers who were attacked by bandits in the 1880s are known to have buried about $16,000 in gold coins. They failed to find the gold when they returned after a heavy wind storm several days later.

There is a legend that an ancient Indian burial cave is located in the **Coso Range** in the China Lake region, Inyo Co., which contains a large number of mummies wearing necklaces of gold nuggets. Several Indian burial mounds in the same general area did produce necklaces of this type when dug up by prospectors in the past century.

In the late 1800s a prospector buried a six-foot-long drainpipe full of gold nuggets in the tiny village of **Glennville,** in the Grenhorn Mountains, Kern Co.

Around 1890 a large band of renegade Indians buried gold, silver, weapons, and everything they possessed with their dead when an epidemic struck and killed most of them. The burial site is north of the Kern River on **Greenhorn Mountain** near the Davis Ranger Station on the banks of Freeman Gulch.

In 1873 four bandits robbed a stage of over $50,000 and buried it in several different caches at their Robber's Roost hideout near **Ridgecrest,** Kern Co. A marker now indicates the exact site of the hideout. They were all killed by soldiers without revealing the location of the loot. In 1957 a treasure hunter found some $12,000 in gold coins and there is believed to be much more in the area.

Several miles north of Robber's Roost, about half a mile from **Freeman Junction,** buried in the wash below the ruins of the stage station, is a strongbox containing $25,000 in gold together with the remains of the stagecoach caught in a flash flood.

Mexican bandits buried about $40,000 in gold in the immediate area of **Vasquez Rocks,** one mile southwest of Freeman Raymond's old stage station located just off County 14, 30 miles north of Mojave, Kern Co. Before dying Freeman Raymond, who was a wealthy businessman and stage station operator, is known to have buried his accumulated fortune of about $80,000 in gold in a wash just south of his stage station.

In the area of the **Toltec Mine** between Baker, California and Searchlight, Nevada, on the California side of the border about ten miles south of County 68, turquoise that was valued at $200,000 in 1903 was buried by a prospector named G. Simmons who never told the location of the stones.

Near the mouth of Cachuma Creek, near **Solvang,** on State 264, Santa Barbara Co., Mexican miners are known to have buried several caches of raw gold in the 1800s and supposedly never dug them up again.

The Candle Holder Treasure, said to consist of one and a half million dollars in gold and silver coins is alleged to be buried in the vicinity of Solvang, Santa Barbara Co.

In a canyon near the top of **San Marcos Pass,** on the north side of Lake Cachuma, Santa Barbara Co. three different treasures are alleged to be buried. One was a Wells Fargo strongbox containing $30,000 in gold hidden by a bandit who was killed before he could return to dig it up. Another is in the apple orchard on the Pat Kinevan Ranch and is supposed to consist of several hundred octagonal fifty-dollar gold pieces. The last is an unknown amount of loot buried by stagecoach robbers at a spot known as Slippery Rock.

The bandit Three-Fingered Jack is supposed to have buried about $20,000 in gold among four pine trees in **Murrieta Canyon,** close to Wheeler Hot Springs, Kern Co.

At the foot of a tall butte that stands alone on the desert about three miles due east of **Mojave** (State 14) near the old Borax wagon train road, Kern Co., treasure hunters have been finding many sixteenth-century Spanish artifacts such as weapons, armor, cooking utensils, and even a few coins.

In the ghost town of **Calico** located on U.S. 15 a few miles east of Barstow, Mojave Co. a large gold bar worth over $250,000 is buried near three cottonwood trees. It was robbed from the assayer's office in Barstow and the robber was hanged soon after without revealing the exact location.

In 1853 a lone bandit robbed a stagecoach of about $65,000 in gold and buried it near the peak of the **Santa Susanna Pass,** Los Angeles Co. He died from bullet wounds suffered in the holdup and the loot was never located.

In the outskirts of the **Cahuenga Pass,** opposite the Hollywood Bowl in Los Angeles, a cache of about $400,000 in treasure is alleged to have been buried by Mexicans. It was to be used to purchase arms during the revolt of the Mexican peons during the reign of Maximillian during the 1860s. A landslide covered the site before it could be recovered.

About $30,000 in gold taken from a Wells Fargo robbery in 1853 is alleged to be buried in an oak grove about three miles east of the old **Rincon Stage Station,** and southeast of the junction of the East Fort and San Gabriel Rivers, a bit north of Azuza, Los Angeles Co.

There is said to be about $30,000 in gold bullion buried on the old **Irvine Ranch,** near present Irvine, off U.S. 5, Orange Co.

Don Tiburcio Tapia, the founder of the Cucamonga Ranch located near the eastern side of Pomona, a bit north of U.S. 605, Orange Co., and his son Ramon, are alleged to have buried two steel caskets containing 3125 Spanish gold coins each, at the site of **Arroyo Seco** on the ranch. Many have searched for this treasure unsuccessfully.

Gold was mined on **Santa Catalina Island** during the 1850s and 1860s and the ruins of a number of miner's dwellings can still be seen. A treasure hunter several years ago found two leather pouches containing over fifteen pounds of gold dust beneath the fireplace in one of these ruins.

Two Mexican bandits named Chavez and Murrieta reportedly secreted about $212,000 in gold near an oak tree at the head of **Rawson Canyon** on an old Spanish ranch, a few miles west of Hemet, Riverside Co.

During an Indian attack on a wagon train, a substantial amount of gold nuggets was buried in the lower reaches of the **Borrego Valley,** about 5 miles northeast of Carrizozo, Riverside Co.

Two oxcarts loaded with Spanish golden church treasures are alleged to have been concealed in a tunnel of a rich silver mine, which was then sealed off, in the area of the **Santa Maria Valley,** near Escondido, 28 miles north of San Diego via U.S. 15, San Diego Co.

Another large cache of Spanish treasure is alleged to be buried in a cavern in the **Poway Valley,** located on County S4 about fifteen miles northeast of downtown San Diego. The Spaniards hid the valuables during an attack by hostile Indians and later were unable to locate the site again.

In 1876 two bandits held up the stagecoach at **Vallecitos,** located off County S2, about 40 miles east of San Diego, San Diego Co., and buried the $60,000 in gold about a mile to the north of the station before being killed by a posse.

Other bandits are known to have buried a strongbox containing $65,000 in gold along the old **Butterfield State Route** between the ruins of the old stage station at Carrizo and the restored stage station at Vallecitos, San Diego Co.

About three miles northeast of the Vallecitos stage station is a site called **Treasure Canyon.** Numerous legends are told about different treasures being buried there. The most plausible one concerns a prospector who buried two kettles full of gold nuggets near the base of the highest tree in the area.

The ruins of the Mission San Pedro y San Pablo de Bicuner are located on the California side of the Colorado River between the All-American Canal and Laguna Dam. Prior to an Indian attack in 1871, the padres are alleged to have concealed a great amount of treasure on the premises, after which they were killed and the mission destroyed.

The bandit Three-Fingered Jack is supposed to have buried a strongbox containing 250 pounds of gold nuggets on the riverbank of the Feather River a few miles south of **Paradise,** Butte Co.

Several different treasure caches are alleged to be buried near the **Mountaineer Roadhouse,** which was a notorious outlaw hideout in the mid-nineteenth century, located on the Folsom Road about three miles from Auburn, 36 miles northeast of Sacramento, Placer Co.

An Indian burial grounds is located on **Ceremonial Ridge** near the town of Murphys, Calaveras Co. Large amounts of gold artifacts were buried in these graves with the bodies.

In 1854 bandits got about $600,000 in newly minted gold coins by attacking a wagon hauling it from the mint in Columbia. The gold was buried in a cave near the village of **Twainharte,** Toulumme Co. The bandits were killed several days later in a gun battle with a posse.

A rich Chinese merchant named Wah Chang, who lived in **Coulterville,** Mariposa Co., hid about $75,000 in raw gold on his premises for a large number of miners. But he was murdered the night before he was supposed to have shipped the gold to the refinery and was never able to disclose the location. The ruins of his store and house remain in this town.

COLORADO

The ruins of Bent's Old Fort are located on State 194, eight miles east of La Junta, Otero Co. It was built by traders in 1823 at this strategic location along the Santa Fe Trail on the north bank of the Arkansas River, and a settlement grew up around it. During the Mexican War (1846–1848) it served as military base for the American conquest of New Mexico. The fort and settlement were abandoned in 1849 and then reinhabited in 1861 and used as the main stagecoach stop between Dodge City and Santa Fe.

Central City is on State 279, Gilpin Co. The town was founded in 1859 as a result of the state's first important gold discovery, which brought in hoards of prospectors. Within a year the town of tents and log cabins was called "the richest square mile in the world." A beautiful community of elegant buildings was soon constructed but all traces of them disappeared because of a fire which leveled the town in 1874. Today several hundred Victorian buildings, built after the fire, still stand in this near ghost town, which has a population of less than 200.

Chimney Rock is on U.S. 160 about two miles east of the Piedra River, Archuleta Co. There are Indian ruins on a high mesa here dating back some thousand years. The area was used as an important camp site by settlers and prospectors passing through and remains of makeshift cabins surround it.

Cripple Creek on State 67, Teller Co. The town was founded when gold was discovered here in 1891, and between that date and 1961, when the last mine closed in the area, more than $500 million was mined. Most of the original town was leveled in a great fire in 1906. Fewer than 500 people now live in this town that held over 25,000 at the turn of the century.

The restored Fort Garland stands on the edge of the town of Fort Garland off U.S. 160 about 25 miles east of Alamosa, Alamosa Co. It was built in 1858 by Army troops and was used for the next 25 years to protect settlers from the Ute Indians.

Georgetown-Silver Plume District is on I-70, Clear Creek Co. This region produced more than $90 million in gold and silver between 1859 and 1939. Until the great silver strike at Leadville in 1878 Georgetown was the largest silver camp in the state. It is the only major mining town in the Southwest never to have been ravaged by fire. Both towns still retain much of their boomtown atmosphere, containing hundreds of deserted buildings of the past century.

Hovenweep National Monument is located at the southwest corner of the state, Montezuma Co. Take U.S. 160 to Pleasant View, then drive on the dirt road for about 27 miles. There are hundreds of Indian ruins here that were settled from 400 until 1300, when a long drought forced the Indians to abandon the area.

Leadville is on U.S. 24 and State 91, Lake Co. The town was founded as a result of a big gold discovery in 1860. Later it served as the silver capital of the state, the area producing about $136 million in silver between 1879 and 1889. After silver prices collapsed in 1893 miners went back to extracting gold until around 1900. Many original structures have survived and there are ruins of many others.

The Lowry Ruins are on U.S. 160, nine miles west of Pleasant View, Montezuma Co. These massive stone ruins were used by the Indians between 1075 and 1200 and then abandoned until a settler named Lowry with his companions lived here during the 1850s and 1860s. There are also remains of other settler buildings.

Mesa Verde National Park is about ten miles southeast of Cortez on U.S. 160, Montezuma Co. This park contains hundreds of spectacular cliff dwellings and pueblos inhabited by the Indians between about 100 and 1270.

The site of Pikes Stockade is near U.S. 285 and State 136, about twenty miles south of Alamosa, Alamosa Co. A replica of the stockade now stands near where the original was. It was built on the Conejos River in 1807 by United States Army troops; they were later captured by Mexicans who burned down the stockade.

The ruins of Fort Vasquez are on U.S. 85, one mile south of Platteville, Weld Co. Built by mountain men in 1835 as a base for trade with the Indians along the South Platte River, problems with the Indians caused its abandonment in 1842 and it fell into ruins.

The site of Fort Pueblo is near the outskirts of present Pueblo on U.S. 50, Pueblo Co. This area was an ancient crossroads of Indian trails. The fort was built in 1842 by fur traders and later occupied by Mexicans, all of whom were massacred by Indians in 1854. It gradually fell into ruins; its adobe bricks may have been used to build the present town of Pueblo which grew as a result of the 1859 gold rush.

Silverton is on U.S. 550, San Juan Co. In the 1880s important silver discoveries caused the town to prosper. A few mines still operate in the area. Very few buildings have survived of the original town but there are ruins of many in the present town of about 500 people.

Telluride is on State 145, Ouray Co. It was founded when gold was discovered in 1875; the most famous mine in the area was the Smuggler Mine where miners found a vein that assayed at $1,200 a ton. The town became one of the most important in the state after the railroad reached it in 1890. Most of the original buildings were lost in several fires that destroyed the town. Today about 600 people still live there working a few mines.

Ute Mountain District is east of State 66 and south of Durango, La Plata Co. A number of spectacular cliff dwellings and abandoned mining camps are here, along with the ruins of log cabins.

The ghost town of Altona is off State 36 about 9 miles north of Boulder, Boulder Co. It boomed briefly in the late nineteenth century because of mining in the surrounding area. Today only a few of the original buildings are still standing.

The city of Boulder was incorporated in 1871 as a result of many gold and silver mines being found in the area, many of which are still being worked today. The modern city has obliterated all traces of the original buildings but there are ruins of many mining camps and mines in the surrounding hills.

The ghost town of Ashcroft is on a dirt road about nine miles northwest of Aspen on State 82, Pitkin Co. A large number of the original buildings from the second half of the past century are still standing in this well-preserved ghost town.

The town of California Gulch is two miles south of Leadville on State 24, Lake Co. It was founded when gold was discovered in 1860 and was originally named Oro City. By the end of its first year there was a population of 5,000, but by 1870 after more than $5 million in gold had been extracted from the gulch, the town was almost completely deserted. A few people are still living in a few of the original buildings but most of the others are in ruins.

The ruins of Columbine are located a bit west of Mt. Farwell and can be reached by a dirt road 32 miles northwest of Steamboat Springs, Rout Co. The town was a mining supply center during the past century.

133

The ghost town of Crystal is located six miles east of Marble (State 133) on a treacherous road suitable only for hiking or horseback, near the Schofield Pass, Gunnison Co. A few of the original buildings still stand but the majority are in ruins. Nearby are several abandoned mines.

The ghost town of Eldora is reached via a dirt road running west about three miles south of Nederland on County 72, Boulder Co. It was a gold boomtown for about twenty years in the late nineteenth century and today about 40 buildings still remain.

The ghost town of Gillet is about six miles northwest of Cripple Creek, Teller Co. It was famous as a resort town for the gold miners and even boasted a large race track. Many of the original nineteenth-century buildings are still standing.

The Gold Hill Area is located between Boulder and Nederland connected by State 119. There are four ghost towns in this ten-mile stretch—Crisman, Gold Hill, Salina and Sunshine—and all contain many standing buildings and the ruins of hundreds of others.

The ruins of Gold Park are located about 10 miles south of the Mount of Holy Cross marker on State 24 on the northern fringes of the White River National Forest, Eagle Co. Very few traces remain of this gold boomtown.

The ghost town of Gothic is located eight miles west of Crest Butte (State 135), near the Kebler Pass, Gunnison Co. Many of the original buildings have survived and the ruins of others can also be seen.

The ruins of Granite are about a mile north of Otero reservoir, on State 24 about sixteen miles north of Buena Vista, Chaffee Co. It was founded in 1859 because of the gold activities at nearby Kelly's Bay and Cache Creek. By 1865 more than 4,000 people lived in the town. Today there are ruins of more than 500 buildings in the area.

The ghost town of Hamilton is located opposite another ghost town named Tarryall across Tarryall Creek near Lake George, Gunnison Co. Both towns were founded in 1859 because of gold found in and around the creek. By 1870 both were completely deserted. They can only be reached on horseback or on foot.

The ruins of Hancock and Romley are about a mile apart, a few miles north of County 162, between Mt. Antero and Mt. Princeton, Chaffee Co. In a stream cutting through both ghost towns a modern prospector found over twenty pounds of gold nuggets in only a week of panning.

The ghost town of Independence is a bit north of County 82, on the west side of Independence Pass, about fifteen miles east of Aspen, Pitkin Co. At one time this mining town had over 2000 residents. More than 100 of the late nineteenth-century buildings are still standing.

The ghost town of Ilse is located on the west bank of a stream about 23 miles south of Canon City, Fremont Co., and is accessible only on horseback or on foot. During its heyday it boasted a population of over 3000 persons. The ruins of several mining camps are nearby.

The four towns of Julesburg are located in the northeast corner of the state, Sedgwick Co. Three ghost towns named Julesburg are located within a two-mile radius of the present town on State 138, which is now flourishing.

The ghost town of Kokomo is located near Fremont Pass, off State 91, about nineteen miles north of Leadville, Summit Co. There are more than twenty abandoned gold mines within a ten-mile radius of this site.

The ghost town of Marble is located about 12 miles southeast of Redstone, Gunnison Co. (State 133) via a very difficult road. The marble for the Lincoln Memorial and Unknown Soldier came from this area. Part of the town's standing buildings were destroyed by a flood in 1941.

The ruins of Newett are located about a mile southwest of Trout Creek Pass on State 285, about ten miles northeast of Buena Vista, Chaffee Co. Only concrete and stone foundations remain of the original buildings. Some treasure was found in this area in recent years.

The ghost town of Ohio is located nine miles northeast of Parlin on State 40, Gunnison Co. Two other towns are in the same vicinity: **Quartz** fourteen miles north of Parlin and **Tincup** ten miles further north of Quartz.

The ghost town of Portland on State 550, about 33 miles south of Montrose, Ouray Co. was established in 1883 as a future railroad town. However the railroad never came and it was abandoned.

The ruins of Primero are about a mile north of Segundo on County 96, Custer Co. Only walls and foundations of a few houses can be seen.

The ghost town of Quidera is eight miles east of Silver Cliff on County 96, Custer Co. There are many abandoned mines in the area.

The ghost town of Rosita is nine miles southeast of Westcliffe and three miles south of County 96, Custer Co. Among the many buildings still standing are three churches, a brewery, a creamery, and a cheese factory. One mile south of town is an old cemetery.

The ruins of an old Spanish fort are located seven miles south of Badito and ten miles north of La Veta (County 12), Huerfano Co. The fort was built in 1819 to protect miners from hostile Indians and was abandoned by 1850.

The ruins of Teller are located twenty miles east of Rand, Gunnison Co. and accessible only by packhorse. Founded in 1879 because of a rich silver strike, a year later it boasted 2000 residents; but it was soon after abandoned because of the difficulty of getting in supplies.

The ghost town of Ward is 29 miles northwest of Central City (County 279), Gilpin Co. It was a gold-mining boomtown until the gold was exhausted and the miners moved on. About 100 buildings are still standing.

The ghost town of Whitepine is about 34 miles east of Gunnison, and ten miles north of Sargents (State 50), on the Continental Divide, Gunnison Co. It was once a boomtown of 3,000 residents. Nearby are the ghost towns of North Star and Tomichi, also a number of abandoned gold and silver mines.

The ghost town of White River is located on the White River about twenty miles west of Meeker and two miles south of County 64, Rio Blanco Co. This old cow town once had more than 20 saloons.

The ghost town of Tarryall stands opposite its rival town of Hamilton, near Lake George, Gunnison Co. In 1861 a John Parson started a mint and made two-dollar-and-fifty-cent and five-dollar gold coins, which are extremely valuable today. The ruins of his mint are still there and should be searched thoroughly for any of these rare coins.

The Lost Brush Creek Mine is within view of the Mountain of the Holy Cross and the Taylor Range, Eagle Co.

The Lost Spanish Peaks Mine is in a canyon at the foot of Spanish Peaks Mountain, Huerfano Co.

The Reynolds bandit cache, estimated to be about $100,000 in gold, is allegedly buried somewhere in Hardcart Gulch, in Hall Valley, Park Co. The bandits accumulated it from holding up stagecoaches and terrorizing miners around the South Park mining camp.

Abandoned mines—Colorado has more than 300 abandoned gold and silver mines, too great a number to cover in this book. The University of Colorado has published a book entitled **Stampede to Timberline** by Muriel S. Wolfe, which lists all of these mines and gives a good history and other background material about them.

A lost platinum mine is located north of Dinosaur National Monument in the northwest corner of the state very close to the Utah-Wyoming border. The terrain is very rugged and several streams are in the area. A prospector found and lost the location about 30 years ago.

The Will Bunch outlaw gang allegedly hid about $50,000 in gold nuggets and coins near the village of **Brown's Hole,** Moffat Co. Other treasures are also believed to exist in the area.

The Butch Cassidy gang supposedly buried over $100,000 in bank robbery loot in a cave near **Wild Mountain in the Dinosaur National Monument,** Moffat Co.

Outlaws are alleged to have buried about $60,000 in gold at Robber's Roost, on the east side of **Horsetooth Reservoir,** a few miles west of the city of Fort Collins, Larimer Co.

In the vicinity of **Grand Lake in the Rocky Mountain National Park,** about 30 miles north of Boulder, a prospector is said to have hidden about $40,000 in gold coins. The money is in a dutch oven located among the ruins of a mining camp on a bluff that overlooks the juncture of two streams.

Several caches of gold coins are known to have been hidden during the 1930s in and around the settlement of **Jamestown,** about ten miles northwest of Boulder. In 1968 a pot containing about $10,000 worth of gold coins was found by a farmer plowing his fields near Jamestown.

During the 1860s the Jim Reynold's outlaw gang supposedly buried gold and silver coins valued at $175,000 in the vicinity of the junction of the South Platte River and Hardcart Creek, located in the **Pine National Forest.**

Jesse James and his gang are alleged to have buried about $50,000 in gold and silver coins at their hideout in **Half Moon Gulch,** about two miles south of Leadville, Lake Co.

The Spanish Princess Treasure is supposed to consist of a hoard of gold ore and coins worth $100,000. It is buried in the area of Mt. Princeton, south of Rainbow Lake, Chaffee Co.

The ghost town of Red Mountain is located near Red Mountain Pass, off U.S. 550, thirteen miles south of Ouray, Ouray Co. A miner is known to have hidden about 500 pounds in gold nuggets in a well in this town. Another prospector mentioned on his deathbed that he had buried about $50,000 in gold bullion under one of the town's three saloons.

The ghost town of Howardsville is on County 110, about five miles northeast of Silverton, San Juan Co. About 50 of the original buildings are still standing and several abandoned mines are in the area.

Creede area ghost towns. The town of Creede is on the Rio Grande River and County 149 in the northern part of Mineral Co. Within a ten-mile radius there are eight ghost towns: Amethyst, Antelope Springs, Bachelor, North Creede, San Juan City, Spar City, Sunnyside, and Weaver. All were flourishing mining centers in the past century and all were abandoned by 1900.

The ghost town of Stumptown is four miles east of Leadville, Lake Co. Only about twenty buildings are still standing here.

The ghost town of Gladstone is eight miles north of Silverton near Red Mountain Pass, San Juan Co. About 100 buildings still exist in different states of deterioration.

The ruins of Middletown are on the west side of the Continental Divide about seven miles east of Silverton, San Juan Co.

The ruins of Animas Forks are along the Continental Divide about thirteen miles northeast of Silverton, San Juan Co.

Around 1855 the Ute Indians are alleged to have robbed ten sacks of gold bullion and coins from returning California miners. They dumped the loot in a shallow ravine on the west side of the **Piedra River** near its junction with Stolstemier River, with Chimney Rock bearing northeast. This location would be a few miles south of State 160 in the western part of Archuleta Co.

In 1860 Charles Baker and his party of prospectors supposedly buried a large cache of gold dust and nuggets on the Animas River about five miles south of **Durango,** La Plata Co. After the Civil War they returned to find their buried cache but were unable to locate their markers or the treasure.

Somewhere on **Treasure Mountain,** so called because of the cache believed to have been buried by some Frenchmen, more than $3 million in gold bullion was hidden in 1790. The site is three to four miles from the top of Wolf Creek Pass, near Summitville, in the southeast corner of Mineral Co.

The Purgatoire Canyon Treasure is alleged to consist of about $12 million in gold which Spaniards buried in the sixteenth century after taking it from Indians. The site is supposed to be near the ghost town of Higbie, about twenty miles southwest of Las Animas (State 50), Otero Co. on the Purgatoire River. Some early Spanish armor was found in a cave nearby in Vogel Canyon.

CONNECTICUT

Bridgeport in Fairfield County, called Newfield during the Revolutionary War, was the scene of a number of skirmishes. The most notable site is Grovers Hill Fort where a gun emplacement stood to protect the harbor. Old ruins are in the surrounding countryside.

On **Compo Beach,** Long Island Sound, between Norwalk and Bridgeport, a force of 2,000 British and Tory raiders landed on April 25, 1777. They embarked here three days later after burning Danbury, fighting their way through a blocking position at Ridgefield, and launching a vigorous spoiling attack from Campos Hill to permit their safe withdrawal.

Danbury was first settled in 1684 and good waterpower made it an important manufacturing center during the colonial days. It became an important supply depot for the patriot forces in the Revolution, and consequently became the object of a devasting enemy raid in April 1777. The enemy burned about twenty homes, twice that number of barns and storehouses, and destroyed military provisions and supplies.

Fairfield, in Fairfield County. Just east of the present settled area of Fairfield is the site of a famous battle that took place in 1637 in which the colonists defeated the Pequot Indians in the last major stand of this war. The town was founded here in 1638 and prospered until it was virtually destroyed in July 1779 by a British force: 83 homes, 54 barns, 47 storehouses, twó schools, two churches, and the courthouse were all burnt to the ground.

Fort Griswold State Park is located in the town of Groton, New London County. The sites of two forts are located here, both at the mouth of the Thames River—Fort Trumbull on the west side and Fort Griswold on Groton Heights. Both were destroyed by British led by Benedict Arnold during his raid on September 6, 1781.

Greens Farms, on Long Island Sound, Westport Township, in Fairfield County was an early colonial settlement. It was totally destroyed—more than 200 buildings were burnt—on July 9, 1779 by a force led by Governor William Tyron.

Guilford on Long Island Sound in New Haven County was first settled by English puritans in 1639. Today only three buildings from the colonial period have survived.

Hartford was first settled by the Dutch in 1633 and then settled a few years later by Englishmen. The town played a major role in colonial and Federalist politics. None of the seventeenth-century buildings has survived. The old town square, laid out in 1637, is now called City Hall Square.

Litchfield was founded in 1719 and is still a tiny village. Although no fighting took place here during the Revolution, it was an important communications hub and military depot for the Continental Army. Many of the old homes are still preserved.

Middletown in Middlesex County was founded in 1650 but no traces of the early settlement remain today.

Mystic in New London County. Although the 37-acre Mystic Seaport Village recreates a coastal village of the nineteenth century, when famous clipper ships were built here, no traces of the early colonial settlement can be seen today.

Newgate Prison and Granby Copper Mines are located between Granby and East Granby, about one mile north of Newgate Road. The mines were first opened in 1707 and coins minted there, called "Granby coppers," became common currency after 1737. By 1773 the mines, no longer productive, were converted to Connecticut's main prison, Newgate, which was used until 1827. During the Revolutionary War it was used to incarcerate Tories and British.

Farmington on the Farmington River, Hartford Co. was first settled in 1640. During the next 50 years the town was destroyed three times by Indians. Today a few colonial buildings are still standing and numerous ruins of others are visible.

The site of **The Battle of the Great Plains** is on State 12, about three miles north of Norwich, New London Co. One of the bloodiest battles in Indian history took place here in 1743 between the Mohegans, who were friends of the white men, and the Miantonomohs, and more than 2,000 were killed on both sides.

Old Wethersfield Historic District is located in Wethersfield, Hartford Co. It is one of the most picturesque and historical villages in New England. Many buildings dating back to the eighteenth century still stand and numerous ruins remain in the surrounding area.

Norwich is located at the head of the Thames River, New London Co. The town was founded in 1659 and became an important port during the eighteenth century. Very few traces of its colonial past remain visible today. In 1634 a major battle was fought between rival Indian tribes at a site marked with a plaque about three miles north of the present city. Some

137

A father and son prove that hunting for buried treasure
can be a family affair as they display treasures found
in the beautiful wooded hills of Connecticut.

While hunting for treasure, hobbyists can gain a greater appreciation of nature's beauty, whether in New England or anywhere else in America.

ruins of **Fort Shantok** are visible in the Fort Shantok State Park located off State 32 about four miles south of the city. The fort was built around 1670 by Mohegan Indians who were allied to the white settlers in the area. Numerous battles between Indians took place at the fort and surrounding area. Only its foundation is still visible.

New Haven was settled by English puritans in 1637 and by 1750 it was one of the main seaports in New England. During the Revolution a number of skirmishes were fought in the area and markers indicate the exact sites. Along the water-front area many colonial artifacts are found by treasure hunters.

New London, at the mouth of the Thames River on Long Island Sound, was settled in 1646. Of the original settlement only the Old Town Mill and the cemetery have survived. During a British raid led by Benedict Arnold on September 6, 1781, more than 150 buildings were burnt to the ground. Vestiges of numerous shipwrecks can be seen on several beaches near the port. A few of these might date from a hurricane on October 19, 1770 in which over twenty ships were smashed to pieces on the beaches. In 1812 the merchantman **Osprey** was wrecked during a gale on Pleasure Beach south of the city. In 1816 the Spanish merchantman **Anion** was run aground on Goshen Point, also south of the city.

Norwalk is a seaport in Fairfield Co. at the mouth of the Norwalk River. It was founded in 1651 but the original town was burnt to the ground by British raiders led by Governor Tyron on July 11, 1779. Few traces of the colonial period are visible today. Offshore a few miles is Sheffield Island on which are a few ruins of colonial buildings. There are a number of tales about pirate treasure being buried here.

Putnam Memorial State Park is just north of Redding, Fairfield Co. This was the encampment site for several Continental brigades under General Israel Putnam during the severe winter of 1778–1779. Ruins of some of their barracks and some wells exist today.

Ridgefield Battlefield is about fifteen miles south of Danbury on State 7, Fairfield Co. It was here that a force of Continental soldiers and the local militia tried to intercept the 2,000 British and Tory raiders under Governor William Tyron after they destroyed Danbury. The Patriots were badly defeated. Some of the original earthworks are still visible.

There are countless tales of pirates burying treasures near the coast and on the offshore islands of this state. According to a number of books on the subject of **Captain Kidd,** he is reported to have buried loot at the following places: at Milford, New Haven Co.; on Charles Islands, off Milford (a few old coins have been found on the beaches there); on Pilot Island, off Norwalk, Fairfield Co.; on Sheffield Island, off Norwalk; on Money Island, off Norwalk; near Middletown, Middlesex Co.; on another Money Island, in the Thimble Island group off Stoney Brook; on Conanicut Island; near Old Lyme, New London Co.; on Clarke's Island in the Connecticut River; and on Kelsey Point of Middlesex Co. If all of these alleged sites are authentic, Captain Kidd must have been a very busy pirate to have amassed such great amounts of treasure.

The pirate **Blackbeard** is alleged to have buried a large treasure in the vicinity of **Brooklyn,** Windham Co. However, despite the fact that many persons have searched for this treasure, there is no sound evidence that Blackbeard ever appeared in this area during his days of blood and plunder.

Many treasure hunters have also searched for an alleged $2 million in gold coins buried during the Revolution but there is no authentic information which supports the tale. The treasure was supposed to consist of coins specially minted for Washington's Army. These were buried during a Tory and Indian attack by some Patriots who were killed in the skirmish. The site is alleged to be about one mile north of **East Granby** off State 202, in the vicinity of a tavern once owned by a Captain Lemuel Bates, in Hartford Co.

Large numbers of English silver and gold coins from the late 1700s have been found after storms on the beach at **Madison,** located several miles south of the Number 61 exit off the Connecticut Turnpike, New Haven Co. During a bad storm in the 1950s local residents claim that on the same beach, vestiges of an old sailing ship were uncovered, which is probably the source for the coins.

In 1758 during the French and Indian War, the residents of **Windham,** near Willamantic, had to flee for their lives and buried their treasures before leaving. The town was burnt to the ground and many of the treasures never recovered.

DELAWARE

Fort Delaware State Park is on Pea Patch Island off present Delaware City on the Delaware River, New Castle Co. A fort was built here in 1848 and then replaced by a larger fort in 1860. Union troops were garrisoned here. It soon became known as the "Andersonville of the North," as it served as one of the main Federal prisons during the last few years of the war, quartering as many as 12,000 Confederate prisoners at the close of the war. Vestiges of many of the prisoners' wooden barracks still can be seen around the fort.

Island Field Site is near South Bowers on U.S. 113, Kent Co. The site contains many graves and remnants of an Indian village which flourished between 600 and 1000.

The site of Zwaanendael is located near the crossroads of King's highway and Savannah Road near present Lewes, Sussex Co. Dutch settlers founded a town here in 1629 after purchasing the land from Indians who had a village on the site. To protect the town with its large brick buildings and wooden homes, the Dutch built a wooden palisade. In 1632 additional colonists arrived, but when they found that all the first settlers had been massacred by Indians, they departed. The Dutch began the settlement again in 1655 and again abandoned it at some unknown date later in the century. Today there are no traces of the site.

Odessa on U.S. 13, New Castle Co., was first named Appoquinimink after the creek where it was built by English settlers around 1700. The original town was destroyed by Indians around 1725 and another built on the site was renamed Odessa. Many colonial buildings still stand in the present town and vestiges of many others are in the area.

Brandywine Village Historic District is located in the present city of Wilmington. Many of its early colonial buildings have survived. The town was founded by the Dutch around 1670, later on passed into the hands of Swedes, and finally was colonized by the English. Remnants of many ruins are still visible near Christina and Brandywine Creeks. The site where Fort Christina once stood at the foot of the present 7th Street is now occupied by a modern building.

Cooch's Bridge is on State 281 about half a mile from its junction with State 72 and about a mile south of Newark, New Castle Co. Delaware's only Revolutionary battle occurred here when American forces fought an unsuccessful delaying action against the superior British army.

Dover was founded in 1683 and has been the state capital since 1777. Many colonial buildings still stand in the city and many ruins of others are scattered over the surrounding farm lands.

New Castle is on the west bank of the Delaware River, a bit south of Wilmington. It was founded by the Dutch in 1651, captured by Swedes in 1654, retaken by the Dutch the following year, and then settled by the English in 1664. It was the state capital from 1704 until the Revolution. Many colonial buildings are still standing in the town and remains of several old ships can be seen along the river bank south of the town.

There are numerous tales about pirate treasures buried in the vicinity of **New Castle.** In 1699 a band of pirates bringing treasure from Madagascar are alleged to have buried one hoard in a deep well near the town jail and another one in the area of Taylor's Bridge.

Blackbeard the pirate is said to have buried a treasure on the banks of **Blackbird Creek** near Blackbird, on State 10, New Castle Co.

According to legend, pirate James Gillian, a member of Captain Kidd's crew, hid a treasure on tiny **Kelley Island** located in Delaware Bay off Bombay Hook National Wildlife Refuge. Somewhere in the area of the Refuge Captain Kidd is also alleged to have buried a treasure. Old coins have been found on the nearby beaches but they probably came from offshore shipwrecks.

The **Patty Cannon Treasure** is alleged to consist of about $100,000 in gold and silver coins buried in the vicinity of Laurel, Co. 24, Sussex Co.

At **Silver Hill,** several miles south of Milford, Sussex Co., a wealthy eighteenth-century planter is said to have buried a large hoard of silver bullion and coins, giving the spot its name.

Reedy Island is on the Delaware River about five miles south of Delaware City. Over the centuries numerous ships have been wrecked on this island making it one of the best treasure-hunting spots in the state. Large numbers of Spanish coins dating from the 1750s have been found after storms. They probably come from the British merchantman **Pusey,** commanded by Captain Good, which was sailing between Jamaica and Wilmington, carrying about 100,000 pounds sterling in Spanish coinage when she was wrecked during a gale in 1757. In 1775 the English merchantman **Endeavor** commanded by Captain Caldwell caught fire and was deliberately run onto the island to save her crew. Vestiges of her burnt hull can still be seen off the southern tip of the island.

Lewes is a seaport a few miles west of Cape Henlopen settled by the Dutch in 1631 and severely damaged during a British bombardment in 1813. In 1798 the British warship **H.M.S. De Braak** sank near this port carrying a large amount of silver and gold specie and bullion. Over the years there have been many tales about large numbers of coins being washed ashore from this wreck onto the nearby beaches.

Cape Henlopen has had more than a fair share of shipwrecks over the centuries, so its beaches are an excellent spot for finding treasure and artifacts. During the eighteenth and nineteenth centuries more than 50 ships were wrecked on this jutting headland. Among the most interesting ones are the English merchantman **Cornelia,** wrecked in 1757 carrying more than 300,000 pounds sterling in gold and silver specie; the Spanish merchantman **Santa Rosalea,** wrecked in 1788 with more than 500,000 pesos in silver bullion and specie aboard; and the American merchantman, **Adeline,** wrecked in 1824 while carrying over $200,000 in gold coins.

In 1973 a bulldozer operator uncovered a hoard of more than 2,000 silver Spanish coins dating between 1780 and 1795 in the village of **Harrington** on State 13, Kent Co. It is believed to have been one of several buried in the area by a rich merchant-farmer in 1798.

On the south end of **Rehoboth Beach** facing the Atlantic Ocean, Sussex Co., gold coins periodically come ashore during strong northeast storms. They are believed to be from the British frigate **The Faithful Stewart,** which was wrecked there in 1785 carrying 240,000 pounds of sterling in gold coins.

DISTRICT OF COLUMBIA

Fort de Russy is located near Oregon Avenue and Military Road in Rock Creek Park. This was one of the forts built during the Civil War to protect the city against a Confederate advance.

The ruins of **Fort Dupont** are located off Alabama Avenue near the southeast entrance to Fort Dupont Park. It was built in 1861 to defend the capital; plans are underway to rebuild it soon.

Fort Lesley J. McNair is located at the corner of 4th and "P" Streets in the Southwest section of the city. Since 1791 there have been military operations on this site overlooking the Anacostia and Potomac Rivers. The fort is now being used as the National War College.

Fort Stevens, on 13th Street between Piney Branch Road and Rittenhouse Street, NW, was built in 1861. On July 11-12, 1864, Union troops held the fort against an attack by the Confederates in a very bloody battle.

Georgetown Historic District was first settled in 1665 but didn't become a town until 1789. Most of the buildings now standing were constructed after 1800 but remnants of earlier homes can be found in park areas and empty lots.

A cache of about $25,000 in gold and silver coins is alleged to be buried under the house once occupied by the Commandant of the United States Marine Corps, near **8th and "I" Streets.**

FLORIDA

De Soto National Memorial is a 25-acre park located in Bradenton, Manatee Co. This site is believed to be the landing place where in 1539 the Spanish explorer Hernando de Soto and his 600 men prepared to set off on their 4,000-mile trek after gold throughout the Southeast. Several Spanish weapons and a suit of chain mail were discovered here around 1920, lending some substance to the legend.

The ruins of **Bulow Plantation** are off State S-5A, 9 miles southeast of Bunnell, Flagler Co. In the 1820s this was one of the largest and richest plantations in the state. During the Second Seminole War in 1836 it was used as headquarters of Federal troops. Today remnants of the original mansion, slave quarters, a springhouse, sugar mills, and several wells can still be seen.

Dade Battlefield is on State 476, just west of U.S. 301 near Bushnell, Sumter Co. On December 28, 1835 a large band of Seminole Indians ambushed and massacred more than 100 Federal soldiers on this site. Recently a number of weapons and other objects were located by treasure hunters.

Cedar Key on the west coast of the state, Levy Co. was once a bustling Gulf Coast port. During the Civil War it was widely used by Confederate blockade runners until it was captured by Union troops in 1862 and remained in their hands for the duration of the war. A large number of nineteenth-century buildings still survive and there are ruins of many others, especially along the waterfront area.

Crystal River State Park on U.S. 19, two miles west of Crystal River, Citrus Co. The archaeological site was settled by Indians between 200 B.C. and 1400 A.D., and although no digging is permitted in the park, scuba divers have been finding many artifacts in the river touching the site.

The ruins of **Yulee Sugar Mills** are on State 490 near Old Homosassa, Citrus Co. The Yulee Plantation was started in 1851 and then destroyed by Union troops in 1864. Today only traces of the sugar mill are visible; the remains of the mansion and other buildings are now overgrown by dense vegetation.

Fort Jefferson is located on the largest of the Dry Tortuga Islands, 68 miles west of Key West. This fort was the largest built by the United States Army between Maine and Texas in the nineteenth century. Construction was begun in 1846 and took 30 years to complete. During the Civil War it was garrisoned by Union troops. After 1865 it was used for a short time as a prison, until it fell into ruin, a result of several big fires and hurricanes. Today a limited amount of restoration work is being done on it. In the moat surrounding the fort many artifacts have been found by archaeologists working for the National Park Services. On this and the six other islands nearby are vestiges of many shipwrecks cast onto the beaches during storms. There are also camps used by survivors and salvors. Bottle collectors claim this area is one of the most productive in the state.

The original site of Fort Caroline was washed away in 1880 when the St. Johns River was deepened. It stood about ten miles east of Jacksonville and had been built in 1564 by French Huguenots led by René de Laudonnière. On August 28, 1565 just as the settlers were about to abandon the place and sail for home, Jean Ribault arrived there with supplies and more people. Soon afterwards, the Spaniards attacked and massacred most of the people in the fort.

Alligator Bridge on Alligator Creek, east of Callahan in Nassau County was the site of a Revolutionary War battle between troops of the Georgia militia led by Col. Elijah Clark and British regulars supported by Tories and Indians.

Cowford is on the north side of the St. Johns River around the west end of the I-95 bridge in Jacksonville. Here the British had their headquarters during the Revolutionary War; a skirmish with Patriots occurred in 1777.

Fort St. Marks is located at the junction of the Wakulla and St. Marks Rivers, near the

145

village of St. Marks, Wakulla County. During the British occupation of Florida, 1763-1783, it was an important Indian trading post. The Spaniards took it over in 1783, naming it San Marcos de Apalache. The fort was captured in 1818 by General Andrew Jackson during the Seminole campaign and was held by the Confederates during the Civil War. During the periods around 1565 and 1763 the Spaniards had constructed three wooden forts in the general area; the stonework for the 1763 Spanish fort still stands in a heavily wooded tract near Fort St. Marks.

Fort Tonyn Site in Nassau County is less than a mile east of the spot where U.S. 1 crosses the south bank of St. Mary's River. A wooden fort was built here in 1776 and fell into disuse after the Revolutionary War. On the same site Fort Pickering was built in 1812, and like its predecessor, no traces are visible today.

Natural Bridge Battlefield is located off U.S. 319, six miles east of Woodville, Leon Co. The Confederate Army won an important battle on this site on March 6, 1865. Battle trenches and graves of soldiers from both sides are still visible.

Fort Clinch stands on the north end of Amelia Island on State A1A, three miles north of Fernandina Beach, Nassau Co. Construction on the fort, begun in 1847, was not even completed when it was seized by Confederate forces in 1861 and retaken the following year by Union troops.

The Fort Gadsden Historic Site is situated on Prospect Bluff on the east bank of the Apalachicola River, six miles southwest of Sumatra, Franklin Co. This site contains the earthworks and trenches of two forts. The first, known as British or Negro Fort, was erected by the British in 1812 and then abandoned in 1815. After this it was used by Indians and their Negro allies who preyed on shipping and raided settlements along the river. An American force captured and demolished the fort in July 1816. Then in 1818 the American Fort Gadsden was built nearby but abandoned in 1821 and fell into ruin.

The site of Yellow Bluff Fort is one mile south of Jacksonville on State 105 overlooking the St. Johns River. Confederate troops built a large triangular earthworks here in 1862 and fought off a major Union naval attack the same year. Some traces of the earthworks are still visible.

Okeechobee Battlefield is on U.S. 441, four miles south of Okeechobee, on the banks of the northern end of Lake Okeechobee. A key battle of the Second Seminole War occurred here on Christmas Day, 1837, when Federal troops soundly defeated a band of Seminole and Mikasuki Indians.

Olustee Battlefield is on U.S. 90, two miles east of Olustee, Baker Co. The most important Civil War battle in Florida was won here by the Confederates on February 20, 1865 and the Union troops were forced to withdraw leaving behind a great deal of equipment.

Sawpit Bluff is at the mouth of the Nassau River, Duval Co. It was a thriving plantation at the time of the Revolutionary War and served as a base for the Patriot forces. Several years ago a treasure hunter discovered several hundred intact wine bottles on the site and a small bronze cannon dated 1767.

St. George Island is located at the mouth of the St. Johns River off Jacksonville, Duval Co. In the 1580s the Spaniards built the Mission of San Juan del Puerto on this island but it was destroyed by the British in 1702 and no traces of it remain today. In 1736 the British built Fort St. George in the center of the island but demolished it four years later when they abandoned the area; only its foundation can still be seen. Around 1770 a number of large plantations were established on the island and some of their ruins are still visible.

Around 1570 the Spaniards built a large wooden fort at Cape Canaveral to be used as a refuge for the survivors of the many shipwrecks on this coast. It was destroyed by Indians after they massacred the whole garrison in 1583 and no traces of it remain. There are a number of prominent Indian mounds in this vicinity. In these mounds and hidden on other sites, amateur archaeologists have found hundreds of Spanish silver and gold coins, which the Indians apparently found on the beaches or robbed from shipwreck survivors.

St. Augustine was Spain's northernmost outpost in the New World. Ponce de Leon landed here in 1513 and then Spaniards, under the leadership of Pedro Menendez de Aviles settled the site in 1565. They built a fort named San Mateo a few miles south of present St. Augustine but in April 1568, in retaliation for the massacre at Fort Caroline, the French attacked this settlement and burnt the fort and all of the houses after killing most of the Spaniards. The site of this first settlement and fort has not been located. The colony was then reestablished in present St. Augustine and Fort San Marcos was built. The present fort called Castillo de San Marcos because of its great size and strength, was built on this site over the remains of nine other wooden, earthen, and stone forts. In 1586 Francis Drake attacked and destroyed the town and fort. It was reconstructed between 1672 and 1696. British raiders burnt the town to the ground in 1702 but failed to capture the castillo, nor did they take it when they again burnt the town during the War of Jenkin's Ear in 1740. St. Augustine passed into the hands of the British in 1763; they held it until 1783, then turned it back over to the Spanish. In 1821 the town became a part of the United States. During the Seminole Wars the castillo was used as a prison and during the Civil War it was occupied by both Confederate and Union troops. The whole area is a gold mine of artifacts dating back to the mid-sixteenth century and there are many unspoiled areas where traces of old building foundations are visible. Many artifacts can be found along the river banks during very low tides and after storms.

The ruins of Fort Matanzas are located on tiny Rattlesnake Island at the mouth of Matanzas Inlet, near State A1A, fourteen miles south of St. Augustine, St. Johns Co. About 300 unfortunate French colonists were shipwrecked near this island in 1565. After building some shelters here they were attacked by Spaniards from St. Augustine who massacred every single one. Four years later the Spaniards built a wooden fort on the island. In 1740 they replaced it with a larger stone structure, which fell into ruin after being abandoned in 1821 when the Spaniards left the area.

Pensacola is believed to have been visited by Ponce de Leon in 1513 and Panfilo de Narvaez in 1528 and used as a base by De Soto while exploring the interior in 1539-1542. But the Spaniards did not establish a permanent settlement at the present city until 1696, when they built Fort San Carlos, which was destroyed in 1812 and replaced by Fort Barrancas. During 1719 there was a great deal of fighting in the town and it changed hands three times, only to be burnt to the ground by the French. Spain regained control of it in 1723 but the colonists decided to found a new settlement on the west end of Santa Rosa Island, which lies off the mouth of the port. In 1559 on this same site the Spaniards under Tristan de Luna had a short-lived settlement of which no traces remain. A hurricane destroyed this second colony on the island in 1752 so the Spaniards moved back across the harbor and rebuilt Pensacola, which was ceded to England in 1763. In 1781 the Spaniards laid siege to the town and severely damaged it before retaking it. During the War of 1812 the British recaptured the town after a fierce bombardment but they were expelled in 1814 by Andrew Jackson who turned the town back over to the Spaniards. Then in 1818 during the First Seminole War Andrew Jackson seized the town and held it for a year before giving it back to the Spaniards. It was finally ceded to the United States in 1821. During the Civil War Fort Pickens was built on the east end of Santa Rosa Island and it still stands today. Very few traces of the city's interesting historic past remain, but metal detector addicts have found many interesting artifacts.

In 1769 the British established the first port of entry in the present state of Florida at **St. Mary's Island,** located at the mouth of the St. Mary's River which is the boundary between Florida and Georgia. There are many remains of eighteenth- and nineteenth-century houses, plantations, and farm sites on this island and the surrounding area that should produce a great array of interesting artifacts.

In 1562 the French built **Fort Charles** about six miles south of Matanzas Inlet, but very little is known about the history of this fort or exactly where it is situated. In 1664, British commander William Hilton who was exploring the east coast of Florida mentions visiting the ruins of this fort.

There were a number of Spanish plantations on **Amelia Island** during the seventeenth century and around 1750 a settlement was established. In 1817 an Englishman named Sir Gregor MacGregor, who was serving in the Revolutionary Army of Venezuela captured the island from the Spanish. It was recaptured by American forces, returned to the Spaniards and then ceded to the United States in 1821 after which it became an important shipping center. In

1862 it was captured from the Confederates by Union troops. There are numerous ruins all over the islands and vestiges of many shipwrecks on the beaches. On the south end of the island near Franklintown many silver Spanish coins from the early 1800s can be found on the beaches after storms.

Indian Key, located several hundred yards off the west end of Upper Matacumbe Key in the Florida Keys, has a fabulous past and is one of the choice treasure-hunting spots in the state. It was used for centuries by the Calusa and Matacumbe Indians as a fishing camp and remnants of their occupation are seen in their pottery and other artifacts. Around 1550 a large French ship was lost near this island. About 400 survivors made it ashore only to be massacred by the Indians. During the Spanish colonial periods hundreds of ships were lost in the Florida Keys and this island served as the main salvage camp for the Spaniards. A number of greedy salvors are known to have hidden hoards on the island, which they may not have dug up again. Around 1810 American wreckers settled here and the island became prosperous. During the Seminole Wars the United States Navy used nearby Tea Table Key as a base. In 1840 the Indians lured the Navy away while Seminoles, led by Chief Chikika, attacked and killed almost every person on the island and burnt most of the buildings. A number of rich wreckers are known to have had hoards buried on the island when this occurred.

The Florida Keys are one of the most exciting and productive treasure-hunting areas in this hemisphere. Because of the great number of ships lost in this area over the centuries there are more buried treasures, and concealed coins, and other objects washed ashore from the wrecks than anywhere else in the nation. Rarely a month passes that some cache of treasure isn't found in the area. In recent years most of the finds have been made accidentally during intensive construction and development activities in the Keys.

Most of the caches buried on these Keys were hidden by shipwreck survivors; in some cases they were lost at sea before being able to come back for their hoards, in others they came back and were unable to find where they had hidden the treasure. Most of the keys were also used by the salvors sent to recover the treasure and cargo; and many of these men grabbed an extra bonus by concealing some of the loot they recovered—a nest egg for their old age.

Records indicate that during the efforts to salvage the 21 ships lost in a 1733 hurricane, more than 500,000 pesos were robbed by the salvors and concealed in various locations in the keys. Many of these hidden caches were found but many are still unrecovered, for hoards of buried 1733-period coins are constantly turning up today. In the past year three large caches of gold and silver coins were found on Key Largo. Around 1930 a laborer digging a ditch unearthed a treasure then valued at $300,000, which consisted of silver and gold specie and bullion from one of the 1733 wrecks. On Grassy Key in 1936 a fisherman dug up over $25,000 in gold coins, a gold candlestick, and a diamond ring—all of which came from one of the 1733 wrecks. Many of the "conchs," as the old-time residents of the keys are called, know a number of areas where coins come ashore during storms and they have been working these beaches for years. One of the better-known sites is called "Treasure Beach," located on U.S. 1 around the middle of Lower Matacumbe Key. Offshore about a quarter of a mile lies one of the 1733 wrecks and large numbers of valuable "Pillar Dollars" and other items wash ashore from it. While constructing a marina at the western tip of this key a few years ago, the wooden remains of an old wreck were uncovered causing a stampede of treasure hunters to the area. Within a week they recovered several thousand silver and gold coins dating from the mid-seventeenth century, many exquisite pieces of jewelry, and other objects.

The swampy **Florida Everglades** is known to be the depository of numerous buried treasures. One of the most interesting treasure caches, since it is well documented, occurred near the end of the Civil War. A Confederate paymaster being pursued by Union troops buried a million-dollar payroll—$200,000 in gold coins and the rest in paper currency. He left this clue: "Chased by the enemy, we buried our payroll at a point in the Everglades at a junction of two creeks, where the land rises like a camel's back. The money is buried in the west hump of the rise." The area is somewhere between Alligator Alley and State 41 near the Seminole Indian Reservation in Hendry Co.

Among the many pirates who are alleged to have buried loot around the state, there are more stories about **Billy Bowlegs** than any other cutthroat. During the early 1800s he is alleged to have buried about $5 million in gold and silver coins near Franklin, Franklin Co. Another well publicized tale has him burying $3 million in a secret cavern below Pensacola's Fort San Carlos. Other alleged sites of his buried treasures are on the north side of Santa Rosa Island, at Bald Point in Apalachee Bay, and on Dog Island, off Carrabelle, Franklin Co.

Another well-known pirate who is alleged to have buried numerous treasures in over fifteen sites in the state was José Gaspar, better known as **Gasparilla,** who preyed on shipping in the Gulf of Mexico between 1784 and 1821. His main base was on Upper Captiva Island located off Fort Myers. In 1953 a treasure hunter dug up a chest containing gold and silver coins valued at $17,000. More recently, two sets of leg irons were discovered, lending some credence to the tale that he kept women prisoners on the island for the amusement of his bloodthirsty followers. During the period when he prowled the seas, he and his crew took more than $5 million in plunder, so there certainly is a great deal more to be found.

Near Cross City, on State 19/98, Dixie Co. lie eight barrels of money hidden by two Bahamian traders just before they were hanged by Andrew Jackson for selling arms and inciting the Seminole Indians. The treasure was buried near the junction of two streams near the northern edge of the present town.

Another of **Billy Bowlegs'** alleged treasures is buried near the mouth of a small river that empties into Choctawatchee Bay, north of Fort Walton Beach, Walton Co. Four large brass-bound chests contain more than $5 million in gold and silver bullion and specie, as well as some church treasure.

Around 1825 a pirate named **Copeland** is alleged to have buried three kegs of treasure at Money Bayou (so named because of this treasure), south of State 98 and west of Apalachicola, Gulf Co.

During the Second Seminole War a party of Indians being pursued by Andrew Jackson's soldiers are known to have hidden seven horse-loads of gold and silver coins near **Neal's Landing,** a few miles southwest of Fernandina Beach, close to the Georgia state line, Nassau Co. The place where the treasure is believed to be hidden is now called Money Pond by the local residents because the whole area is very swampy.

There are three different tales of Civil War treasure being buried on the **Steinhatchee River** which empties into Dead Man Bay, Taylor Co. An unidentified blockade runner being chased by a Union gunboat supposedly was deliberately sunk at the mouth of the river. After the gunboat left the area the Confederates are alleged to have raised more than $500,000 in silver bullion from the wreck and buried it close by. While trekking across the state they were killed by Indians. How anyone learned of the incident if they were all killed has never been revealed.

A second tale concerns another blockade runner which was hiding near the mouth of the river when a Union gunboat appeared. In this case the crew quickly went ashore and buried about $140,000 in gold coins before being captured. After the war they returned to claim the money, but were unable to find it because a flood had obliterated their markers on the river bank.

The third story concerns some Union soldiers who also buried a large cache of gold coins about five miles up the river. They took this money during the Federal capture of Cedar Key and several other Confederate strongholds in the area and then concealed it rather than turn it over to their superiors.

The pirate **Jean Lafitte** is alleged to have buried a large amount of booty near three large oak trees at Fowler's Bluff, near Chiefland, about fifteen miles up the Suwannee River, Levy Co.

A pirate vessel carrying over $5 million in gold and silver coins lies in the mouth of the Suwannee River a bit north of Big Bradford Island in 25 feet of water. In 1953 about $625,000 of this treasure was recovered in the nets of a fishing smack. By the time the nets were hauled in and the treasure discovered, the fishermen had been dragging for several hours so the exact site is not known.

Along the swampy coast between the mouth of the Suwannee River and Cedar Key, a United States Naval vessel carrying exactly $5 million in gold bullion to be paid to Spain for the purchase of Florida was cast ashore during a hurricane in 1820. No traces of the crew or treasure was found but wreckage from the ship was seen on the beaches in this area. The heavy gold bullion most likely sank beneath the sand on the beaches or in the marsh area behind it.

During the Seminole Wars a wealthy plantation owner is known to have buried a chest of gold coins and family silver on **Bumblebee Island** in Waccasassa Bay, Levy Co. He was killed by Indians and so the location of the treasure is a mystery.

The northern end of **Amelia Island,** north of Fernandina Beach, Nassau Co. was a notorious pirates' lair for many years, used by many such as Blackbeard. There are tales of much pirate treasure being buried in the area. Stede Bonnet is alleged to have buried a great deal of church plate near present Fort Clinch; Blackbeard is alleged to have buried several chests in the area; and Luis Avery hastily buried his booty near the southern end of the island when an American warship appeared to capture him. In 1788 two Negro slaves testified that they assisted several pirates bury two large chests of treasure in a patch of palmettos about one and a half miles from the south end of the island, about 200 paces back from the beach. They escaped from the pirates during a drinking bout and made their way to St. Augustine where they told this tale. Spanish soldiers were sent to the island and drove the pirates off, but were unable to find the treasure. During the 1930s several small hoards of gold doubloons were accidentally discovered in this general area.

In the vicinity of **Mayport,** near Jacksonville, Duval Co. an English ship was wrecked in 1784 and the survivors buried four chests of gold coins. Two days later they reached St. Augustine where the Spaniards accused them of being spies and hanged them.

A rich merchant named Richard Crowe died in 1894 in **St. Augustine.** In his will he mentioned burying $60,000 in gold coins somewhere on his property. The locals dug up his land, but the treasure was not found.

While being pursued by several vessels, Gasparilla the pirate went ashore on **Anastasia Island,** near St. Augustine and buried a chest containing $50,000 in gold coins not far from a large oak tree. When he returned a few months later a hurricane had devastated the area and he could not relocate the spot.

During the Seminole Wars a large treasure of gold coins and family silver was buried by a Spaniard known only as Don Felipe on his plantation two miles northwest of **Ocala,** Marion Co. He was killed by the Indians and his plantation destroyed.

In the 1720s a band of Spaniards buried a chest of silver coins within 300 paces of **Ponce de Leon Springs** while being pursued by hostile Indians. The site is seven miles north of Deland, Volusia Co.

Several miles northeast of the **Ponce de Leon Springs,** on the east side of State 17, the ruins of a Spanish sugar mill can be seen. It was destroyed by Seminole Indians who massacred everyone living on the plantation. All of the 20 or so buildings were also burnt to the ground. The owner of the plantation was very wealthy and it is believed that he had a considerable treasure buried in or near the mansion.

There is a well known tale about an iron chest of pirate treasure that lies at the bottom of a pool formed by a cold-water spring near **Ponce de Leon Springs,** Volusia Co. Efforts to recover it with a dragline were made in the 1890s and again in 1927. Because of a swift current and strong suction divers cannot go after the chest. On occasions the chest has been pushed near the surface; the last time this occurred was in 1939 when the event was heralded in the world press.

Another mysterious chest lies in a very swampy area between the Atlantic Ocean and Indian River on the outer bank close to State A1A, eight miles south of **Vero Beach,** Indian River Co. Since 1907 when the chest was first sighted, it has appeared on numerous occasions during the dry season and has actually been seen by many. It has also been the cause of great frustration to many treasure hunters and the bankruptcy of more than a few. Quicksand surrounds the area where the chest lies, making its recovery extremely precarious. Draglines and other more ingenious methods of securing the chest have all failed. In January 1974 when the chest popped up again, a treasure hunter in a helicopter tried dragging a grappling hook to catch the chest but the downdraft from the huge blades forced it to sink once again. Offshore nearby lie the hulks of several old shipwrecks; the chest may have been cast ashore from one of them or buried by survivors.

Around 1550 a band of Ais Indians massacred a number of survivors from a Spanish shipwreck and buried a large cache of gold coins and jewelry at **Turtle Mound,** seven miles south of Coronado Beach, near New Smyrna, Volusia Co.

Two longboats carrying pirate loot are alleged to be buried on the banks of **Sweetwater Creek** near Rocky Point on the east side of Tampa Bay and close to the International Airport, Pinellas Co.

Several different pirates are alleged to have buried treasures on **Mullet Key** near the mouth of Tampa Bay. Gold and silver coins have been found on the beaches of this island by treasure hunters with metal detectors, but the coins probably were washed ashore from shipwrecks.

Large numbers of Spanish silver coins dating from the early 1800s are constantly being found on the south shore of **Honeymoon Island** and at the northern end of Caladesia Island. Both are located in the Gulf of Mexico a bit north of Clearwater.

There are alleged to be several treasures in the vicinity of the **Courtney Campell Causeway** which connects Tampa and Clearwater across Tampa Bay. A wealthy farmer is said to have buried a treasure chest at Pierce's Bluff in the center of a triangle formed by three oak trees on the top of the bluff. A bit north of the western end of the causeway is a place called Copper's Point, which was an eighteenth-century pirate haunt. Numerous markings on various rocks in the area may be clues to buried hoards.

Seminole Indians are supposed to have buried seven casks of gold and silver coins, payment to them as treaty indemnity money, on **Big Island,** located on the western side of Tampa Bay.

During the War of 1812 the British are said to have buried a paychest on the small key where the **Vinoy Park Hotel** now stands in St. Petersburg.

Christmas Island near the mouth of Tampa Bay is also associated with many treasure tales; in fact, large numbers of old coins have been found on its beaches. Gasparilla is known to have been based here on occasions and is alleged to have buried some treasures. In the 1920s a bank robber is known to have hidden about $50,000 in paper currency on the island. He died in prison before returning for the loot. During the prohibition Christmas Island was used by rum runners and several hoards of loot were allegedly to be buried by them.

Large numbers of gold and silver Spanish coins being found on the beach resulted in **Treasure Island** being so named. It is located on State 699 a bit west of St. Petersburg.

At **Pinellas Point** in St. Petersburg several chests of Spanish silver and gold coins were dug up during the 1930s and more is believed to be concealed in the immediate area. Gold coins also washed ashore on the beach at this point.

Right after a hurricane struck in 1921 large amounts of treasure were found on the beach on **Shell Island** near Cabbage Key, which is close by St. Petersburg.

After a hurricane in 1955 many chests were sighted in the water just offshore the **Pass A Grille Beach,** which is west of St. Petersburg. Sand covered the site before divers reached the area. Since this area was once covered by land that eventually was eroded away, the chests were probably buried ashore years back. Gold and silver Spanish coins have been found on the beach here in recent years.

Another of the pirate Gasparilla's haunts was **Gasparilla Island** off Charlotte Harbor, north of Fort Myers. Ruins of various old dwellings are still visible in the dense bush, but none of the $30 million, which he is alleged to have hidden in various caches, has yet been found by the thousands of treasure hunters who have combed this island over the years.

During the 1700s a pirate named Castor used **Egmont Key** off Tampa Bay as a base. He is said to have buried some of his plunder on the island before being captured and beheaded by the Spaniards.

In 1824 the pirate **Miguel Guerra** was chased up the Manatee River near Bradenton by an American gunboat and was run aground at **Rocky Bluff.** The pirates got ashore with a large chest which they buried nearby before being killed in a land skirmish with their pursuers. The pirate vessel was sunk by gunfire; only later did it become known that she carried several tons of silver bullion under her ballast.

The John Ashley gang allegedly buried about $25,000 in bank loot in the vicinity of **St. Lucie Inlet,** St. Lucie Co.

The pirate Bocilla is alleged to have buried treasure on **Bokeelia Key,** north of Pine Island in Charlotte Harbor, west of Fort Myers.

The Ashley gang, which operated in Florida between 1915 and 1926, made their headquarters near **Canal Point** on the southern tip of Lake Okeechobee. Legend says that they buried numerous hoards of loot in the area, including $110,000 in gold from their last bank robbery.

About a mile north of Fort Lauderdale at **Hillsboro Rocks,** many Spanish silver coins from the late sixteenth century wash ashore during strong northeast storms. In 1967 a fisherman accidentally found a beautiful jewel-studded sword handle, which he sold for $15,000.

On Key Biscayne off Miami, right in the area where ex-president Richard Nixon had his house, large numbers of gold and silver Spanish coins from the mid-eighteenth century plus fragments of Chinese porcelain wash ashore during rough weather.

The Cape Canaveral area is another of the choice treasure-hunting spots in the state. Countless ships were wrecked on this jutting point and plenty of treasure made its way ashore, with the help of nature or man. Indians were living on a high hummock here in 1556 when a treasure-laden galleon was wrecked nearby. They salvaged over a million pesos in treasure—it is believed that in the area, the Indians buried that treasure and others over the years. Many Spanish coins and other artifacts have been found in Indian middens and mounds in the area.

On both sides of the inlet at **St. Augustine** is another lucrative area of beach. To enter this port, one had to cross a very dangerous sand bar. During the sixteenth through eighteenth centuries more than 75 ships were wrecked on this bar and broke up; their contents were strewn about the ocean floor and eventually cast up on nearby beaches. Treasure hunters have been successful in finding coins in this area for many years.

GEORGIA

Andersonville National Historic Site is on State 49, one mile east of Andersonville, Sumter Co. This is the site of the notorious Andersonville prison where nearly 13,000 Union prisoners died between February 1864 and April 1865. Remains of the stockade, surrounding fortifications, and vestiges of many buildings are still standing.

Grant Park Sites. In this park in downtown Atlanta the famous Battle of Atlanta was fought on July 22, 1864 and won by Union troops under General Sherman. Some 4,000 Union and 8,000 Confederates lost their lives in this battle. After sacking the city the Union troops burnt most it down to the ground before beginning their destructive march to the sea. Many earthworks, entrenchments, and gun emplacements are still there, as well as Old Fort Walker built early in 1864.

Kolomoki Mounds Park is off U.S. 27 about six miles north of Blakely, Early Co. During the twelfth and thirteenth centuries this area was one of the largest and most important population centers in North America. In this 1200-acre park many large mounds cover ruins of the great city that stood here. A number of burial grounds are located here also.

Etowah Mounds Park is three miles south of Cartersville off State 113, Bartow Co. Etowah was a large, fortified Indian town which flourished between 1000 and 1500. A number of high mounds now cover the remains of the temples and other buildings of this site.

Columbus Historic District in Columbus, Chattahoochee Co. was founded as a trading post in 1828 and was one of the last frontier towns of the thirteen original colonies. A number of bloody battles with Indians took place here and the early settlement was burnt down several times. Today over 600 structures dating from around 1850 and later still stand and many artifacts can be found in the gardens and vacant lots surrounding them.

Jekyll Island in Brunswick County was first a hunting and fishing ground of the Guale Indians, then a Spanish stronghold and pirate base from 1566 to 1732 when Georgia was founded as an English colony. The Spaniards burnt their settlement before departing for

Florida. The English settled on the island in 1742 and ruins of some of their buildings can still be found.

Kettle Creek Battlefield, near the village of Tyrone in Wilkes Co. is the site of the Revolutionary War battle that took place on February 14, 1779. A Patriot force of 300 under Andrew Pickens defeated a Tory force of 700 commanded by the notorious bushwhacker Colonel Boyd.

Kennesaw Mountain Battlefield Park is off U.S. 41, two miles north of Marietta, Cobb Co. The park preserves the site of several battles and skirmishes fought here in June 1864 when Sherman was pushing his armies from Chattanooga towards Atlanta. Heavy losses were suffered on both sides. A number of large cannon and other weapons were thrown into the creek that cuts through the park as the Confederates fled towards Atlanta.

Mulberry Grove Plantation, located on GA 21, about ten miles north of Savannah on the Savannah River in Chatham County was one of the most important plantations built during the Revolution. The plantation house was destroyed by Sherman's troops late in 1864 or early 1865 and later rebuilt, but destroyed by a storm in the early 1900s and abandoned.

Sunbury Site and Fort Morris, about eleven miles east of Midway on the Midway River in Liberty County, is the site of an abandoned town that had 496 houses, three large public squares, five wharves, and a fort. It was founded in 1758; during the Revolutionary War a number of battles were fought in the area. After hurricanes inflicted grave damages in 1804 and 1824 the inhabitants moved elsewhere. By 1850 it was completely deserted and now is hidden in a pine forest.

Augusta was settled by the British in 1735 and Fort Augusta was built the following year, but a trading post had been established there at a much earlier date. On the eve of the Revolution it was the most heavily settled area in Georgia and the most important trading center in the southeast. The British occupied the place in January 1779, but were forced to withdraw back to Savannah after two weeks. During the British occupation of Savannah Augusta served as Georgia's temporary capital.

Brier Creek Battlefield, located at the junction of Brier Creek and the Savannah River in Screven County, was the site of a major Revolutionary War battle between Patriot militia commanded by General Benjamin Lincoln and the British under General Prevost.

Cherokee Ford at the mouth of Rocky Creek, about a mile north of where State Road 72 crosses the Savannah River, was the site of a major skirmish between Patriot and British forces in February 1779.

The town of Darien is situated between U.S. 17 and I-95, McIntosh Co. Because of its location, Darien was of great strategic importance from the earliest colonial days until the end of the Revolution. It was built in the center of the Altamaha River delta, which served as a natural barrier between the English and Spanish colonies in North America. The site of Fort King George, built in 1721 and abandoned in 1733, is located about a mile east of present Darien. Ruins of a Spanish settlement can be seen between the site of the fort and the present town. Scots built a Fort Darien in 1736 in the area but its location is not known.

The ghost town of New Ebenezer is on the Savannah River near where State 275 dead ends, Effingham Co. It was settled in 1736 by Salzburg Lutherans who built the first rice mills in the nation and started the culture of silk. The British used the town as a staging area during the Revolution before taking Augusta and Charleston. Then they totally destroyed the town, which fell into ruin and is now hidden in a thick forest.

Ocmulgee National Monument is located on the south side of Macon, Bibb Co. The park contains a large number of mounds covering the remains of huge structures built by the Mississippian Indians around 900. There are also numerous other mounds located outside of the park area.

At the mouth of the Satilla River, opposite the northern end of Little Cumberland Island, Camden Co., the Spaniards had a short-lived settlement during the early 1700s but no traces of it have yet been found.

All over **St. Simon's Island** are numerous traces of the pre-Colombian and colonial periods. The Spaniards had a settlement and mission there prior to the arrival of the English in 1736, when they began construction on Fort Frederica, now in ruins. The Spaniards attacked the English settlement in 1742 and a bloody battle was fought at Christ Church. The remainder of the fleeing raiders were annihilated at Bloody Marsh—both sites are well marked. An accidental fire burnt the first English town to the ground in 1758, but it was rebuilt. Most of the English moved elsewhere after 1763 and the foundations of many of their homes and later dwellings dot the island. French silver ecu coins can be found on the beach on the southern end of the island.

The site of Midway is off U.S. 17 and I-95, Liberty Co. It was settled by religious dissenters from South Carolina in 1754 and then totally destroyed by Tories in 1755. Another town called Midway was built several miles away, but it too was burnt to the ground by Sherman's soldiers in 1864. The present town is located halfway between the ruins of the above two. About 150 residents live in this near-ghost town, which has many abandoned buildings built after the Civil War. A large number of weapons were thrown into a well on the outskirts of the present town at the end of the Civil War.

Fort McAllister is on State 67, ten miles east of Richmond Hill and fifteen miles south of Savannah, Chatham Co. This massive Confederate earthwork was begun in 1861 and two years later it successfully resisted a devastating bombardment from iron-clad Union ships. The fort was captured by Sherman's troops in December 1864 and partially destroyed at the time. There are numerous ruins on nearby McAllister Plantation.

Fort Pulaski is located on Cockspur Island at the mouth of the Savannah River, about seventeen miles east of Savannah, Chatham Co. It was constructed in 1829 and 1849 and was considered impregnable, that is, until Union troops assaulted it with new rifled cannon and captured it in April 1862. Vestiges of many old wrecks can be seen on the island's beaches.

The Spanish **Mission of Santa Catalina de Gualé** was built in 1620 and abandoned in 1686 as a result of numerous raids made by the English from the Carolinas. It stood somewhere on St. Catherine's Island located about 25 miles south of Savannah, but no traces remain. The ruins of several eighteenth-century plantations can be seen in the same area.

Savannah was founded in 1733 as the state's first permanent white settlement and became one of the most important commercial seaports in the nation. Hundreds of colonial buildings have survived in a remarkable state of preservation but the majority of them date from after 1816, the last time the city was burnt down. The British captured the city in December 1778 and while attempting to recapture it in October of the following year more than 1,000 Patriots were killed. The sites of the various battles and skirmishes are well-marked in this picturesque city. The city was accidentally burnt down twice—in 1796 and 1816.

Tybee Island at the mouth of the Savannah River off U.S. 80 is famous as being the base for numerous pirates and privateers over the centuries. A number of treasures are believed to be buried there. Coins and other artifacts have been found on the beaches but they were probably washed ashore from the many ships lost in the area.

The site of Fort Jackson, about three miles east of the city, can be reached via the Island Expressway. The fort has been used for the defense of Savannah since a wooden fort was built there in 1734. It was replaced by a larger mud-and-wood fort in 1798; then in 1809 was constructed the stone fort which still stands today. It was used by the Confederates during the Civil War and a number of battles were fought in the area.

Savannah Beach and other beaches on both sides of the entrance to this port are good sources of treasure and other artifacts which have been washed ashore from shipwrecks. During the colonial period at least 50 large vessels of various nationalities were wrecked along these beaches; a number of them were carrying considerable amounts of treasure. On the seaward side of Daufuskie Island, large numbers of American twenty-dollar gold pieces and also English nineteenth-century silver coins can be found after storms.

A large treasure of gold bullion is believed to be concealed in or near the ruins of an old stage station in the vicinity of where State 201 crosses Cahulla Creek, at the northwest corner of the **Chattahoochee National Forest,** Whitfield Co. The site is about fifteen miles southeast of Chattanooga, Tenn.

Cherokee Indians are alleged to have hidden about 1,000 bars of gold in a cave on **Rocky**

Face Mountain, near Varnell on Co. 2, Whitfield Co. This area was a well-worked gold mining area long before the white settlers arrived; then they too began mining gold. The bullion was robbed from a wagon carrying it to the Dahlonega Mint.

A slave trader is alleged to have buried about $20,000 in gold coins on or near the old **Malachi homestead,** one mile northeast of Subligna on Co. 201 in the Chattahoochee National Forest.

The Lost Old Billy Chambles Gold Mine is in the vicinity of Beaver Ruin Creek, off Co. 23, three miles north of Swanee Creek, Gwinnett Co.

A large cache of gold bars is reported to be hidden in a cave near a waterfall on the Coosawattee River to the east of the bridge near Fort Coosawattee in the vicinity of **Carter's Quarter** (State 441), Murray Co.

A lost Indian silver mine is somewhere in the vicinity of the mouth of Flat Creek near the Coosawattee River, Gilmer Co.

Within a few miles of the above site, close to the confluence of the Scarecorn and Talking Rock Creeks, the Indians are known to have had a gold smelter. Around the time the white settlers began moving into the area they buried a number of gold caches.

In the vicinity of **Rock Creek Lake,** located between Suches and Gaddiston, Union Co., the Cherokee Indians are known to have hidden countless treasures in caves which they sealed to prevent the whites from finding them. This occurred when they were driven off their lands and forced to resettle elsewhere.

Dahlonega in Lumpkin Co. was first settled in 1833 after a number of big gold strikes were made. A mint even operated here between 1831 and 1861 to coin the great amount of gold extracted from the surrounding mines. The coins from this mint are very valuable and some of the rarer ones are worth in the neighborhood of $50,000 each. There are many tales about gold being buried in and around this sleepy town, which has only 2,000 residents today. Vestiges of many old buildings are visible in and around the town.

The Lost Settler Silver Mine is located within a five-mile radius of Robertstown, Co. 17, White Co.

A cache of about $40,000 is reported to have been buried in White Co. by a pioneer trader, about midway between **Nacoochee and Robertstown,** a distance of three miles. The man hid his money on his homestead before going on a long trip, died while he was away, and his family was unable to locate it.

The Lost Indian Gold Mine and the **Lost Hunter Gold Mine** are both located in the vicinity of Unicoi Gap, Habersham Co.

One of the last strongholds of the Cherokee Indians was on **Fishtrap Mountain,** five miles northeast of Lakemont, Rabun Co. Before being driven out of the area by white settlers, the Indians are known to have concealed many treasures in caves on this mountain. In 1937 a group of Boy Scouts found over 100 pounds of gold ore while exploring a cave here.

In a grove of trees on the **Lindale Mills** property several miles south of Rome, west of State 411, Floyd Co., $600,000 in gold bullion is reported to be hidden.

On the **Felton Farm** near Cartersville, on State 41, Bartow Co., a chest containing around $50,000 in gold and silver coins was buried near the barn. The building burned down in the 1930s, obliterating the markers denoting the site.

Cherokee Indians reportedly hid several iron chests of gold bullion in **White Bubbling Springs,** in the foothills of Oak Mountain, twelve miles north of Canton, Cherokee Co.

Many scuba divers have unsuccessfully searched for some 200 pounds of raw gold which was flung into the **Etowah River, near Canton,** by an Indian woman as she was forcibly being removed from her ancestral homeland.

Another rich hoard of Cherokee raw gold is known to be hidden near the **Shallow Rock Creek Bridge** near Canton, Cherokee Co.

On a farm that was owned by F. R. Groover, located between **Silver City and Frogtown,** west of State 19, Forsyth Co., two boys found a pot of raw gold in 1932. It was one of eight known to have been buried in the same general area by Cherokee Indians.

In 1851 a lumberman named Mr. Ledbetter hid about $40,000 of valuable Dahlonega Mint

Deserted Southern homesteads are popular with treasure hunters because of their potential, both inside and outside the house itself.

Modern metal detectors are easy to use yet, can hunt deeply and ignore metallic trash to find just those valuables that have been lost or abandoned.

gold coins in the basement of his home near **Free Home,** Co. 20, Cherokee Co. He was killed when his house and mill burnt down. About 50 years later his son found the will which mentioned the coins. Months of digging produced only sore hands and backs.

When Sherman's troops reached the vicinity of **Dahlonega** in 1864, the local residents entrusted about $3 million in gold from the town's two banks and merchants' safes to clergyman named Guy Rivers for safekeeping. With the help of several slaves he concealed it in one of two places: either in a cave (called Guy Rivers Cave), which is now flooded, on the Josephine Mine property; or somewhere on Rocky Etowah River Bluff. He died of a heart attack soon after and the slaves who concealed the money could not be found.

A Civil War cache of gold coins and family silver is known to be buried on the old **Brock homesite** about four miles northeast of Clermont, near the crossroad from Gainesville to Cleveland in the Chattahoochee National Forest.

In the vicinity of the horse pen on the **Dionysis Chenault Plantation,** a hoard of about $200,000 in gold was buried during the Civil War. Its owner died before telling the location of the money. The plantation is on County 44, about twelve miles northeast of Washington, Wilkes Co.

The Confederate President Jefferson Davis met with his cabinet for the last time in May 1865 in **Washington, Wilkes Co.** At the time there was more than $10 million in gold bullion and specie in the Confederate treasury. Most of it was buried in different hoards all over the surrounding area to prevent it from falling in Yankee hands. Several large hoards of Confederate paper currency has been found in the area, but to date, the gold is still missing.

A plantation owner named Jeremiah Griffin is known to have hidden a cache of over $100,000 in gold in the banks of a small creek, about two miles south of the **Little River,** McDuffie Co. He died in an accident in 1847.

According to a legend there is about $1 million in gold hidden in the vicinity of the **Williams, Jones, Ferguson house,** located at the corner of Liberty and Washington Streets in Milledgeville, which was the old state capital, in Baldwin Co.

During the Civil War a leather mail pouch containing over $100,000 in gold coins was said to have been hidden. It was concealed 300 yards northeast of the **Nashville, Chattanooga, and St. Louis Railroad tracks,** in a hollow near a spring on the Cobb County side of the Chattahoochee River, a short distance from the old Marietta Road, near Marietta.

An estimated $6 million in gold, silver, jewelry, and other loot, which Union soldiers sacked from Atlanta, is hidden in the vicinity of **Lithonia** on U.S. 20, about ten miles east of Atlanta. The soldiers who robbed this treasure and then buried it were caught soon after. Their superiors hanged them without their revealing the location of the great treasure hoard.

About a dozen wooden kegs containing $400,000 in gold coins, which were to be a payment from the United States to some Indians for the purchase of a great tract of land, is alleged to be buried near the ruins of a log cabin on the Chattahoochee River and old **McIntosh Trail,** about five miles southwest of Whitesburg, State 27A, Carroll Co.

A cache of about $100,000 in gold and silver coins is supposed to be buried on the old **Lipscombe Plantation,** located about eight miles north of La Grange between the west bank of the Chattahoochee River and Alabama state line, Troup Co.

A cache of gold and silver coins is alleged to be hidden under a large pile of rocks on the **Layfield Plantation** near the top of Pine Mountain, about two miles south of Warm Springs, off County 85W, Meriwether Co.

After the Union troops captured **Columbus** in 1865 they threw more than 60 large Confederate cannon into the Chattahoochee River near the old steamboat piers. On the collector's market today these cannon are worth around $5,000 each.

In the 1860s a farmer named Whitney buried two chests containing about $150,000 in gold on his farm. The site of the farm is now inside the **Fort Benning Army Base.** In the 1920s an army officer found one of these chests in an old ravine near Outpost #1; the other is still waiting to be discovered.

In 1901, there was a dredging operation to clear a section of the Chattahoochee River, which cuts through the **Fort Benning Army Base.** During the dredging, a large hoard of silver dollars was recovered from a sunken riverboat. On the river bank in the same area, a soldier in 1962 found a large ceramic jug of more silver dollars.

In the 1760s, French explorers from New Orleans are reported to have hidden about 2700 pounds of pure silver ore near the forks of the **Okapilco and Mule Creeks** in Brooks Co.

Prior to the arrival of Sherman's army in **Savannah** the citizens in great panic hid all valuables. Because of the great destruction that the city suffered at the hands of the Yankee invader, many of the treasures could not be found afterwards. It has been estimated that over $15 million in treasure and personal property remains hidden from this sad episode of American history. A number of professional treasure hunters operate in the city searching for these lost treasures, in many cases, hired by relatives of the original property owners.

Shortly before the arrival of the Union troops in 1865 it is well documented that about $2 million in gold and silver coins were hidden somewhere in the vicinity of **Kingsland,** Camden Co. A thorough job of historical research should better pinpoint the location of the money.

HAWAII

Captain Cook Memorial is across Kealakekua Bay from Napoopoo Village on the Island of Hawaii. A monument here was built on the spot where the British explorer Captain James Cook was slain in a battle with the Hawaiians in January 1779. Weapons and other European artifacts might be found in the area.

City of Refuge National Park is at Honaunau on the Island of Hawaii. The park, situated on a lava bed overlooking the Pacific Ocean, is surrounded by a great stone wall built around 1550. It consists of the ruins of temples, palace grounds, royal fishponds, and other structures used by the kings and high priests of the islands.

Puukphola Heiau Landmark is southwest of Kawahae off State 26 on the Island of Hawaii. The remains of a great stone temple built in 1791 by King Kamehameha stands on this site.

Cook Landing Site is at Waimea Bay, two miles southwest of State 50 on the southwest corner of the Island of Kauai. This is where Captain Cook, the first known European to set foot on the Hawaiian Islands, made a campsite in 1778 of which no traces now remain.

The ruins of an old Russian Fort are off State 20 about 200 yards southwest of Waimea Bridge on the Island of Kauai. This hexagonal stone fort, built in 1817 by Russians under the German Dr. Georg Anton Scheffer, served as a trading post.

Wailua Archaeological Complex is located at the mouth of the Wailua River on the Island of Kauai. These Polynesian ruins consist of four temples and numerous other dwellings, as well as a sacred rock where human sacrifices were made.

Iwao Stream is in the Iao Valley, three miles west of Wailuku on State 32, on the Island of Maui. The battle of Kepaniwai was fought here in 1790 and the invading army of Kamehameha the Great slaughtered most of the Maui warriors and dumped the bodies into this stream, which turned red from all the blood.

Lahina Historic Landmark is on State 30 on the Island of Maui. These ruins served as the capital of the islands until 1845 and are best known as being the center of the American whaling industry that flourished in the Pacific from 1840 to 1865. There are numerous ruins here, including a prison that held disorderly whalers.

Pilanihaie Heiau Landmark is four miles north of Hana at the mouth of Honomaele Gulch on the Island of Maui. These sixteenth-century ruins, constructed by Piilani, the great chief of the Maui, measure 340 by 425 feet. The landmark is the largest religious center in the island.

Mission Houses and Kawaiahao Church are located at the corner of King and Kawaiahao Streets in Honolulu on the Island of Oahu. These ruins, the first wooden buildings made in the islands, were built in 1821 by Protestant missionaries from New England.

Nuuanu-Pali is seven miles from Honolulu via Pali Highway on the Island of Oahu. This towering cliff was the scene of a bloody battle fought in 1795, in which Kamehameha the Great defeated warriors of the Oahuans and consolidated his control of all the islands. Many of the defeated warriors committed suicide by leaping over this cliff.

In 1823 some pirates are alleged to have hidden six chests of treasure near some walls of fitted stone at the top of the hill at **Kaena Point** on the Island of Oahu.

A cache of unknown origin and description called the **Cave of Kings Treasure** is alleged to be hidden on Ford Island off Oahu.

A large hoard of gold called the **Keakauailau Treasure** is reported to be buried near the head of Manoa Stream, high in the Koolau Range above Honolulu.

A hoard of five-sided gold coins, minted by the old Hawaiian monarchy and worth between $100,000 and $150,000, is alleged to be buried in a cave in the **Aina Moana State Park** near Waikiki Beach on Oahu.

Many ancient stone artifacts have been found around the big cinder beds and lava beds near the **Makena fishing village,** below the Haleakala Volcano on the Island of Maui.

An English pirate named Captain Cavendish is supposed to have buried a huge treasure of gold and silver at **Palemano Point** on the Island of Hawaii.

In 1818, the pirate Captain Turner is alleged to have buried a large number of chests containing gold and silver coins and church treasure in some caves on the north side of **Kealakakua Bay** on the Island of Hawaii.

The ghost town of Hoopuloa is located on the southwest coast of the Island of Hawaii.

Large numbers of seventeenth-century Chinese bronze coins are found after rough weather on **Maili Beach** on the western side of Oahu Island. They are probably being washed ashore from a vessel sunk nearby.

IDAHO

Mud Lake is located 30 miles northwest of Idaho Falls and about 60 miles north of Pocatello, Jefferson Co. In 1865 the notorious Guiness and Updike gang robbed a Wells Fargo stagecoach of more than $180,000 in gold bullion. With a posse hot on their trail they were seen throwing all of the booty into this deep lake. In 1901 an amateur treasure hunter using a makeshift grab-bucket discovered three of the twenty-pound gold bars. The remainder is still awaiting discovery on the muddy lake bottom.

City of Rocks Landmark is on State 77 near Almo, Cassia Co. While traveling across the continent on the California Trail tens of thousands of pioneers stopped and camped at this site and many inscribed their names and dates on the surrounding rocks. Many items which they discarded or lost are buried under the windswept sands on this site.

The ruins of the Cataldo Mission are on U.S. 10 about twenty miles east of Coeur D'Alene, Kootenai Co. It was built by Jesuit missionaries in 1848 and used for about 25 years before being destroyed by Indians, who massacred all of the priests. It is the oldest building in the state and some church treasure is believed to be buried on the site.

The ghost town of Idaho City is on State 21 about 40 miles northeast of Boise, Boise Co. It was founded in 1862 after gold was discovered in the area. Within a year it became a boomtown of over 40,000 residents and soon after the metropolis served as the first capital of the Idaho Territory. The town contains the ruins of hundreds of buildings.

Nez Perce Historical Park is on U.S. 12 about ten miles east of Lewiston, Lewis Co. The park contains more than 25 Nez Perce Indian villages as well as abandoned towns built by missionaries, miners, traders, and soldiers. Among the most interesting are: **Fort Lapwai** built in 1862 by the United States Army and destroyed by the Indians soon after; the **White Bird Battlefield,** where the Indians defeated a contingent of United States Cavalry in June 1877— the first engagement of the Nez Perce War; the **Clearwater Battlefield** where the Cavalry routed the Indians in July 1877; and the **ghost town of Pierce,** which sprang up in 1860 as a result of the first major gold discovery in the state.

The site of Fort Hall is located at "the Bottoms" of the Snake River near the junction of the Oregon and California Trails, about eleven miles north of Pocstello, Bingham Co. The fort was built in 1834 by American fur traders and sold two years later to the British Hudson Bay Company. It was very important during the westward migration and served as the main communication and supply center for the gold mines of Montana and Idaho. The United States Army took control of the fort in 1846 but it and several hundred buildings in the surrounding community were destroyed during a flood in 1863. A large safe containing several hundred pounds of gold dust and nuggets was lost when the assayer's shop was swept into the raging river waters.

The **ghost town of Albion** is located about fourteen miles southeast of Burley on County 77, Cassia Co. It was a mining boomtown and once the county seat on the main road to Utah. About 50 of the old buildings still stand.

The **ghost town of Bonanza** is eight miles north of State 93 in the Yankee Fork District, Custer Co. It was established in 1877 as a gold mining supply center and boasted nine saloons two years later. In the vicinity are the remains of ten gold mines and numerous mining camp sites. Only a few of the town's original buildings are still standing.

The **ghost town of Clayton** is 24 miles west of Missoula, Montana near the White Sand River and Lolo Pass, Clearwater Co. In the surrounding mountain range within a ten-mile radius are five other ghost towns: **Aetna, Bonanza** (not to be confused with the above Bonanza), **Crystal, Custer,** and **Bay Horse.** All of these towns were gold-mining centers during the second half of the nineteenth-century and they contain many standing buildings and ruins of hundreds more.

The **ghost town of Cuprum** is located 39 miles northwest of Council (on State 95), south of Hells Canyon, Adams Co. Only the main hotel is still standing in this town, but the ruins of over 70 buildings can be seen. In 1968, a treasure hunter found in the ruins of a saloon a cache of over 800 silver dollars from the 1880s.

The **ghost town of Galena** is located close to Galena Peak in the Sawtooth National Forest, 36 miles northwest of Hailey (State 93), Camas Co. Only a few of the original buildings are still standing in this gold mining boomtown.

The **ghost town of Gem** is four miles northeast of Wallace (U.S. 90) and about ten miles west of Cooper Pass, Shoshone Co. The ghost towns of **Eagle, Pritchard, Murray,** and **Burke** are located in the same general area. All were gold mining centers and were abandoned by 1890.

The **ghost town of Centerville** is about 30 miles northeast of Boise on the Grimes River, Boise Co. In the same area there are four other ghost towns: **Old Centerville, Pioneersville, Placerville,** and **Quartzburg.** Since all were gold-mining centers, there are numerous abandoned mines in the area.

The **ghost town of Kingston** is seven miles west of Kellog on State 10, Shoshone Co. Nearby are three other unidentified ghost towns, all in complete ruins. Kingston has over 100 standing buildings.

The **ruins of Leesburg** are on the Panther River about fifteen miles west of Salmon (State 93), Lemhi Co. Nearby are the ghost towns of **Shoup** and **Cobalt;** all three were gold-mining centers and have ruins of many buildings.

The **ghost town of Mount Idaho** is on the Clearwater River about three miles east of Grangeville (State 95), Idaho Co. Stories of several caches of buried gold dust and nuggets are associated with this dead boomtown.

The **ghost town of Silver City** is high in the mountains near the Jordan River, 24 miles east of Jordan Valley, Oregon and 22 miles southwest of Murphy, Owyhee Co. Many of the original buildings of this town, including a hotel, courthouse, and several saloons are still standing. Nearby are the ghost towns of **De Lamar** nine miles to the west, and **Dewey** five miles to the south. The ruins of **Triangle** are also on the Jordan River about 20 miles to the south.

The **ghost town of Spalding** is nine miles east of Lewiston (State 95) in the Nez Perce National Historical Park, Lewis Co. It was settled in 1836 and destroyed by a fire in 1847, rebuilt and flourished until about 1875.

The **ghost town of Springton** is located on the rim of Snake River Gorge just west of Hansen Bridge near U.S. 80N, Jerome Co. Only two buildings are still standing; the rest were destroyed by a fire during the last century.

The **Lost Sly Meadows Gold Mine** is in the vicinity of Sly Meadows on the Bond Creek west fork of the St. Joe River, Benewah Co.

The **Lost Swim Gold Mine** is on Moley Creek above Robinson's Bar, south of the ghost town of Bonanza on the Salmon River, Chalis Co.

The **Lost Rock Bandit Cache** consists of $75,000 in gold bullion robbed from a stagecoach by the infamous Plummer gang and buried a short distance above the town of Spencer in Beaver Canyon, Clark Co.

The **Lost Indian Post Office Mine** is believed to be one of the richest ever found and lost in the state. It is located by the Indian Post Office cairn near Cayuse Junction, Clearwater Co.

One of the largest and best-documented treasure losses in the state occurred on November 12, 1889 when the steamer barge **Kootenai** sank in 75 feet of water about 300 feet offshore of McDonald's Point in Lake Coeur D'Alene. She was carrying 140 tons of gold ore and 685 pounds of gold bullion. Most of the ore was recovered with the use of grab-buckets but the bullion was not recovered and believed to lie hidden under about twenty feet of mud on the lake bottom.

The **Lost Bill Rhodes Mine** is located near Grave Peak, in Lolo National Forest, Idaho Co.

The **Lost Isaac Gold Mine** is located in the vicinity of Coolwater Ridge near Indian Springs on Coolwater Mountain, between the Locksa and Selway Rivers, Idaho Co.

The **Lost Rusted Wheelbarrow Mine** is somewhere in the Thatuna Hills of the Moscow Mountain Range, Latah Co.

The **Lost Breen Gold Diggings** is on the east side of Lake Hayden, on the western edge of the Coeur d'Alene National Forest, Kootenai Co.

The **Lost Cleveland Gold Mine** is near Wallace Creek, twelve miles from the town of Salmon and eight miles west of the Salmon River, Lemhi Co.

During the seventeenth and eighteenth centuries the Spaniards had a very rich silver mine in the vicinity of **Eddiville,** about ten miles south of Coeur d'Alene, Kootenai Co. Indians tired of being used as slaves revolted and killed all of the Spanish overseers. They dumped the bodies along with several years' accumulation of silver bullion into the mine shaft and then sealed it off.

A cache of gold bullion worth around $1 million is hidden in or near the town of **Pierce City,** Co. 11, Clearwater Co. It was hidden by Ling Kee Nam, the head of the Tong and spokesman for the large Chinese population in this mining town. He and his henchmen were lynched in 1885.

The **ghost town of Moose City** is on Moose Creek in the Bitterroot Mountain Range, nine miles from the Montana border, Clearwater Co. Two unidentified lost gold mines are also in the area.

The **Lost Chinese Mercury Mine** was about halfway up the southwest side of Ruby Mountain, several miles south of the town of Warren and a bit west of the Salmon River, Idaho Co. In the ruins of a stone cabin near the mine some Chinese hid over three tons of liquid mercury in iron flasks.

During the 1890s a gold prospector accidentally found a large number of diamonds—enough to fill two bushels, he claimed—on the banks of **Goose Creek near Rock Flat,** between McCall and New Meadows, Adams Co. He buried most of them in the same area but a flood destroyed his markers and he was unable to locate the buried diamonds or the spot where he had first found them. A diamond that he had kept in his knapsack he sold for $1,000; later it was resold by a merchant for $25,000, a fantastic price in those days for an uncut diamond. It must have been enormous to command such a high price in New York.

A cache of gold ore valued at $300,000 was hidden near **Dry Digging Ridge** in the Pioneer Mining Area north of Warren, Idaho Co.

The **Lost Squawman Gold Mine** is in the heavily wooded mountains about 25 miles northeast of Shoup in the northern section of Lemhi Co. Two Nez Perce Indians stumbled across this abandoned Spanish gold mine around 1885 and brought out rich samples of high grade ore, but they were unable to find the mine again.

About $25,000 in gold bullion that was robbed from a stagecoach by bandits in 1864 is hidden on the banks of **Camas Creek** about one mile north of Camas on U.S. 51, Jefferson Co.

Stagecoach robbers got away with about $75,000 in gold bullion and then buried it in some high rocks near **Robbers Gulch** along the Salmon River, about five miles southwest of White Bird, Valley Co.

The owner of the **Twin Springs Ranch,** who died in 1897, revealed on his death bed that he had buried over $100,000 in Californian gold coins near his house. The money was never discovered. The ranch is on the east fork of the Battle River in the southwest corner of the state, Owyhee Co.

Workers from the Hahn Smelter on the outskirts of **Leadore,** Lemhi Co. were known to steal large amounts of gold and to have buried various caches in the immediate vicinity of the smelter. In 1936 about 50 pounds of gold bullion was found buried two feet deep and about 200 yards north of the smelter.

The ghost town of Gibbonsville is on the North Fork of the Salmon River about fifteen miles south of Lost Trail Pass, near Co. 43, Lehmi Co.

A large iron strongbox containing $90,000 in gold coins was hidden on the banks of Grimes Creek, about halfway between Grimes Pass and the **ghost town of Crouch,** approximately 30 miles north of Boise, Boise Co.

A strongbox containing about $50,000 in gold coins was lost or hidden about six miles up the Boise River from **Boise.** It was robbed from a stagecoach but the bandit died soon after from gunshot wounds and was found without the loot or his horse.

A substantial treasure is known to have been buried in a cave around Rocky Canyon a few miles north of **Boise** by a Dave Levy, one of the most successful prospectors and saloon keepers in the state. When he died, it was estimated that he had accumulated a fortune of over $1 million.

Somewhere in the vicinity of **Kuna Cave,** about 25 miles southwest of Boise, Ada Co., a bandit buried $30,000 in silver and gold coins from a stagecoach holdup. He died from gunshot wounds received during the holdup and his body was found at the entrance to this cave; no coins were on his body.

The ghost town of Loon Creek is a few miles north of Stanley Basin in the Sawtooth Mountains, Custer Co. Several miles to the west is the ghost town of **Oro Grande,** which was one of the richest gold placer deposits areas in the state until the diggings petered out.

The Lost Swimm's Gold Mine is located near Robinson Bar in the Salmon River Mountains, Custer Co.

Outlaws buried about $75,000 in gold bullion somewhere in the area of the Shoshone Ice Field between a point known as the Cottonwoods on Big Woods River and Magic Reservoir, Lincoln Co.

In the crater of the **Moon National Monument** in Blaine and Butte Counties, several treasures are reported to have been buried. Between 1867 and 1895, three different bandits robbed stagecoaches and supposedly buried their loot in caves on the inside of the crater. In another instance, a large cache of gold bullion is alleged to be concealed among some large brick volcanic rocks about one mile east of State 93A on the northwestern edge of the park.

During the 1870s a lone bandit robbed a Custer Mine wagon of several thousand dollars in gold bullion and then buried the bars on **Root Hog Divide,** two miles east of old Butte State Station in Butte City, Co. 88, Butte Co.

In 1897 bandits robbed $215,000 in gold bullion from a pack train en route from Blackfoot to Arco and then hid the loot in a cave about two miles northeast of **Acros,** State 93A, Butte Co. They were apprehended and hanged but their plunder was never found.

Members of the Plummer gang are said to have hidden $75,000 in gold coins on the east side of the railroad tracks near the "Y" in **Beaver Canyon** near Holdup Rock, a few miles north of Spencer, U.S. 15, Clark Co.

On the north shore of Buffalo Creek, about eight miles southeast of **Kilgore,** County A2, Fremont Co., in the northwestern corner of the Targhee Forest, a large cache of gold bullion worth around $2 million was robbed by renegade Indians in the 1880s and buried in this area. About two hours after the robbery, they were killed by United States Cavalry soldiers but they had already disposed of the two wagonloads of gold bars. The empty wagons were later found in a deep ravine.

An outlaw named Blackburn died soon after robbing five mule loads of rich gold ore. He buried his take somewhere in the forest near **Henry Fork** on the south side of Buffalo Creek, near Co. 84 in the northern extremity of Fremont Co.

In 1869 bandits robbed and buried about 300 pounds of raw gold beneath **Sentinel Rocks** near the junction of Big and Kelly Canyons, near Kelly's Gulch, a few miles north of Rigby, Booneville Co.

The notorious Plummer gang is alleged to have concealed about $500,000 in gold bullion in a natural cave-like room behind a waterfall on the **Snake River,** about two miles southwest of the American Falls Reservoir, Power Co.

Outlaws are said to have hidden about $40,000 in newly minted gold coins, still in their original wrappers, in a metal box which they buried on **Rye Flats,** two miles south of Riddle, Co. 51, Owyhee Co.

In 1930 a sheepherder found a streak of "odd looking sand," which turned out to be platinum. Later he tried to find the sand again, but could not. The area was somewhere in the vicinity of the town of **Rupert,** U.S. 80N, Minidoka Co.

A lone bandit robbed $150,000 in gold bullion and then concealed it in an abandoned mine shaft near the City of Rocks formation, located about twelve miles southeast of **Oakley,** Co. 27, Cassia Co. He died in jail before being able to retrieve his cache.

In the middle of the triangle made by the **City of Rocks,** the town of **Almo** (County 77), and **Cache Peak,** bandit Jim Looney took over $100,000 in gold bullion from the Boise-Kelton stagecoach in 1876. He buried the loot in this area before being killed in a barroom gun fight.

The ghost town of Bridgeport is two and a half miles northwest of Preston on State 91, Franklin Co. Seven saloons and over 100 old buildings are still standing in this town.

Bandits are alleged to have buried about $110,000 in gold coins and bullion in the vicinity of **Portneuf Canyon,** a few miles south of Pocatello, U.S. 15, Bannock Co.

ILLINOIS

In the **Cave-in-the-Rock State Park** off Co. 1, near Elizabethtown, Hardin Co. a number of treasures are known to be buried. In the early 1800s it served as a hideout for notorious robbers. Several small caches of coins have been found in recent years.

Black Hawk State Park is located off U.S. 67 and State 2 near Rock Island, Rock Island Co. The site contains vestiges of the main villages of the Sauk and Fox Nations. During the 1820s the Indians won numerous battles over white settlers in the area but they were soundly defeated in 1832 and their villages burnt to the ground.

The ruins of Bishop Hill are located two miles north of present Bishop Hill, off U.S. 34, Henry Co. The original town was settled by Swedish religious dissenters in 1846 and abandoned in 1862. Only a few brick chimneys are still visible.

The town of Galena is on State 20, Jo Daviess Co. At one time during the nineteenth century, Galena was an important riverboat town and the richest in the state. The status of the town declined when the Mississippi changed course and left the town two miles away from the river's edge. Many old abandoned buildings and ruins remain.

The town of Nauvoo on Co. 96, Hancock Co. now has a population of around 1,000, but back in 1844 it had over 20,000 residents and was an important Mississippi riverboat town. From 1839 until 1846 it was the headquarters of the Church of the Latter Day Saints and the principal Mormon settlement. After rioters from surrounding settlements burnt down their great temple, the Mormons were expelled and began their westward migration. From 1849 until 1858 the town was occupied by Icarians, a communistic sect of Frenchmen and Germans, who were also forced to vacate the town because of their religious beliefs. Only a few of the mid-nineteenth-century buildings are standing, but there are ruins of many others.

Cahokia Mounds State Park is on the Mississippi River about five miles east of East St. Louis on U.S. 40, St. Clair Co. It was an important settlement in prehistoric times and a number of massive Indian mounds can be seen. It was also the first European settlement in the state, founded by Frenchmen in 1699; however none of their buildings are in existence now.

The Chicago Area—Chicago Portage is located at the western end of Portage Road at the junction of Portage Creek and the Des Plaines River in downtown Chicago. It served as a natural artery connecting the water routes from the St. Lawrence River and the Great Lakes system with the Mississippi Valley. Although the Chicago Portage was widely used by French explorers and traders from 1673 onwards, there are no traces of any of the wooden buildings they constructed. The French had another small settlement that stood at the north end of Damen Avenue Bridge at 26th Street, but this too has disappeared. In 1685 the French built a fort at the junction of the North Branch and Chicago River, of which only the foundations of several buildings still remain. Around 1690 a French mission stood on the North Branch near Foster Avenue in the suburb of Bowmanville but today it is completely gone. The British built **Fort Dearborn** in 1803 but it was burnt down in 1812 by Indians, rebuilt in 1816, and then consumed by the Great Fire of 1871. It stood on the present site of the Stone Container Building at 360 North Michigan Avenue; some artifacts were found when this structure was constructed. The site where the Indians massacred a large number of white settlers in 1812 is at Calumet Avenue and 18th Street. An Indian trading post and portage site stood at the spot where U.S. 34 and Harlem Avenue intersect in southwest Chicago. During the Great Chicago Fire in 1871 the city suffered over $400 million in property damages with 17,500 buildings destroyed, 100,000 homeless, and 300 dead. On August 1, 1894 another tremendous fire caused over $30 million in property damages.

Fort Checagou was a French settlement founded by Sieur de la Salle in 1679. It stood somewhere along the east bank of the Illinois River near the present city of Peoria.

The ruins of Fort de Chartres are on the Mississippi River between Fort Kaskaskia State Park and Cahokia, Randolph Co. It was one of the first French settlements in this part of the country. The first wooden stockade was erected in 1709, followed by a wooden fort in 1720, and then a large stone fort in 1735 named Fort de Chartres. It was ceded to the British in 1763 and renamed **Fort Cavendish** but because the river was eating away the fort's outer walls, it was abandoned in 1772.

The ruins of Prairie du Rocher are located four miles east of Fort de Chartres. This village of 700 Frenchmen was founded in 1721; today one can see vestiges of about 40 buildings.

Fort Kaskaskia State Park is on the Mississippi River below the mouth of the Kaskaskia River, near Chester, Randolph Co. The French built this fort in 1736 and used it until the end of the Colonial Wars in 1763 when they demolished it. The French had a settlement also named Kaskaskia on the west bank of the Kaskaskia River about six miles from the Mississippi, which has since shifted its bed and eaten away at the site of this settlement. It had about 80 well-built stone homes and other structures of wood.

The French also had three other settlements—**Ste. Anne, St. Philipe, and Bellefontaine**—located between Kaskaskia and St. Louis, Missouri. They were abandoned in 1763 when Britain gained control of this area and nothing is left of them today.

The Lost Old Fort. The French had another unnamed fort prior to 1763 somewhere on a bluff on the Kaskaskia River about six miles from the Mississippi and very close to the settlement of Kaskaskia.

The site of Fort Massac is on the Ohio River about two miles east of the town of Metropolis near U.S. 45, Massac Co. The French built it in 1757, later renamed it **Fort Ascension,** and abandoned it in 1763. In 1796 the Americans built another **Fort Massac** on the same site; both forts have since been completely destroyed.

Kankakee River State Park is on State 102, about 8 miles northwest of Kankakee, Kankakee Co. It was an important French settlement and portage center which connected the Ohio and Mississippi Rivers with the Great Lakes. No traces remain.

The site of Fort St. Louis is off State 71, about five miles east of La Salle, located in Starved Rock State Park. It was built by the French explorer La Salle in 1682 and abandoned about five years later. The name Starved Rock dates from 1769 when a band of Illinois Indians took refuge there to escape Indian enemies and died from thirst and starvation.

Matthiessen State Park is located off State 178 about seven miles southeast of La Salle. It was an important prehistoric Indian settlement and contains many caves, some of which were used by early French explorers.

Prior to the arrival of white settlers, the area surrounding **Galena,** Jo Daviess Co., was an important Indian silver-mining center; a number of lost silver mines are in the area.

A large hoard of gold coins is alleged to have been buried on the **Abbot farm** near Fulton, about a half mile from the Mississippi River, off Co. 136, Whiteside Co.

The famous author John M. Hoffman is alleged to have buried a large fortune in gold and silver coins and jewelry in or near his house in **Chicago** before his death in 1928. He distrusted banks and was worth several million dollars when he died.

According to legend, a large number of gangsters buried hoards in or around their homes in the **Chicago** area. During the Depression a number of hoards were uncovered on property owned by racketeers in the Cicero area.

A Frenchman named Tonti is alleged to have buried a cache of gold coins valued at $100,000 in the immediate vicinity of **Starved Rock** on the Illinois River between La Salle and Ottawa, Ottawa Co. He was a paymaster for the French during the French and Indian Wars.

Gangster Sam Anatuna is known to have buried a metal box containing about $400,000 in paper currency near **State 66** a few miles south of Braidwood, Will Co.

During Prohibition days a Mafia gangster named Vito Giannola operated a still on his farm near **Horseshoe Lake,** Granite City, Madison Co. Before being killed in a gang war he is said to have buried twelve waterproof lunch buckets full of money on this farm.

In the early nineteenth century there was a stockade named **John Hill's Fort** about six blocks south of the present court house in Carlyle, Clinton Co. Before he died in 1833, John Hill buried a large hoard of gold coins in or around this fort.

A train robber named Larson is known to have buried a large number of gold and silver coins in the vicinity of **Centralia,** Marion Co.

An officer of the 1778 George Rogers Clark Expedition is known to have buried about $3,500 in silver coins on the west bank of the Mississippi River, in the vicinity of **Chester,** County 150, Randolph Co.

After robbing a stagecoach in 1809 the bandits buried $44,000 in gold coins in the vicinity of **Chester,** Randolph Co.

The Cave in the Rock Treasure is reported to consist of about $200,000 in gold and silver coins. It is hidden in a cave near the west bank of the Ohio River, near the village of Cave in the Rock, County 91, Hardin Co. After heavy rains some gold and silver coins have been found along the river bank.

Along the west bank of the Ohio River near **Golconda,** County 146, Pope Co. hundreds of American silver dollars from the late 1800s are found after the flood waters recede each year. The coins probably are washed in from a riverboat lost in the area.

INDIANA

Angel Mounds Historic Park is off State 662 about five miles east of Evansville, Vanderburgh Co. The park contains the largest group of prehistoric Indian mounds in the state. A city of over 1,000 flourished here during the fifteenth century.

New Harmony Historic District is on the Wabash River in the present town of this name, Posey Co. It was the site of two ambitious but short-lived nineteenth-century experiments in communal living. In 1815 it was settled by Lutherans and abandoned by them in 1825. Welsh and Scots moved in soon after, but they too abandoned the site two years later. Today about 35 of the original buildings still stand.

The site of Pigeon Roost stands on U.S. 31, a bit south of Underwood, Scott Co. The place was settled in 1809, but three years later all of the inhabitants were massacred by marauding Shawnees and the settlement burnt down. All of the victims were buried in a mass grave.

The site of Fort Miami is near the confluence of the Maumee, St. Joseph and St. Marys Rivers in the present city of Fort Wayne. It was built by the French sometime before 1712 and was part of the network linking the Great Lakes with the Mississippi Valley. A settlement stood around the fort until it was ceded to the British in 1761. No traces now remain.

The site of Fort Wayne is located close to the above fort. It was built in 1794; a number of major battles were fought in and around it. All traces of it have been covered by the modern city.

The site of Fort Quiatenon is located at the bend of the Wabash River about four miles below Lafayette, Tippecanoe Co. It was built by the French in 1719 and taken over by the British in 1761, at which time the French had a settlement of several hundred homes. The fort and town were destroyed by United States troops in 1791.

Tippecanoe Battlefield State Park is on State 25 about four miles southwest of Lafayette, Tippecanoe Co. A famous battle was fought here between United States and British troops in 1811. One can still see some of the breastworks and trenches.

An unnamed settlement founded shortly after the Revolution and abandoned several decades later stood somewhere in Spring Mill State Park, near Mitchell, Lawrence Co. A frontier trading post dating about 1815 has been discovered in the same area and is now being restored.

The city of Vincennes is on the Wabash River, Knox Co. The French built a military post here in 1731 and a large settlement grew up around it. The place was ceded to the British in 1764; they took it over in 1777, renaming it Fort Sackville. In 1779 a major battle took place and the Americans won, renaming the place **Fort Henry.** Many settlers soon moved into Fort Henry, which served as the capital of the Indiana Territory from 1800 to 1813. There are still vestiges of a number of the French and British buildings.

One of the best-documented buried treasures in this state is hidden in the vicinity of **Marshfield,** near the Illinois state line, Warren Co. In 1828 four bandits robbed a passenger train of some $80,000 in gold bullion, as well as a large amount of coins and paper currency. Several days later the empty safe was found near Marshfield and the bandits were caught and hanged without revealing its hiding spot.

Another well-documented buried treasure is hidden somewhere between **Rockford and Seymour,** near State 31A, Jackson Co. In 1868 the Reno Brothers hid a safe containing $80,000 in loot from a train robbery before fleeing to Canada with a posse after them.

Somewhere along the shores of Lake Michigan, in the vicinity of **Michigan City,** Laport Co., henchmen of the gangster Al Capone hid some 2,000 cases of whiskey in a cave, probably now worth around $300,000, before being gunned down. The entrance to the cave was sealed off with the use of explosives.

During the 1920s the hoodlum Jim Colosimo from Chicago is reported to have buried a cache of diamonds worth millions on the outskirts of **Crown Point,** County 8, Lake Co.

In 1923 a gangster named Jim Genna buried a large amount of money in a steel box in a pasture under a rock pile near the intersection of State 6 and 331 near **Bremen,** Marshall Co. A gangster who was with him described the hiding spot as being about a mile and a half down a dirt road off State 6. FBI agents searched for the cache unsuccessfully for weeks; many others have also looked, to no avail.

During the Prohibition a racketeer concealed a large amount of money along the banks of the Wabash River between **Berne and Geneva,** where State 27 crosses the river, Adams Co.

On a farm on the outskirts of **Terre Haute** near State 42, Vigo Co., around $95,000 in paper currency and some gold coins were hidden during the 1920s by a bank employee who embezzled the money and committed suicide soon after burying it.

The notorious John Dillinger is known to have buried several caches of loot on his father's ten-acre farm near **Mooresville,** County 67, Morgan Co. According to the FBI, who spent considerable effort without finding any of the money, there is close to $600,000 buried on the farm.

Around 1810 Indians buried a large quantity of gold bullion and a number of figurines in a cave on the **Rocky McBride Bluff,** overlooking the White River, just north of Shoals, State 150, Martin Co.

In May 1868 the Reno Brothers robbed a train of $98,000 in gold and silver coins, and buried it somewhere in **Rockford,** Jackson Co., the home base of the gang.

During the Civil War the Confederate general, John Morgan, is alleged to have buried about $5,000 in gold coins near County 441, just south of **Vincennes,** in the George Rogers Clark Historical Park, Knox Co.

The Harris farmhouse is located at the mouth of a hollow, three miles northeast of Madison on the Ohio River, Jefferson Co. The site is now called the Bear Farm. Prior to and during the Civil War it was used as a headquarters for smuggling slaves out of the South. A number of gold coin caches are believed to be hidden on the premises.

In the early 1800s river pirates operated out of a cave in a bluff overlooking the Ohio River a few miles south of **Mt. Vernon,** Posey Co. They are alleged to have concealed several hoards of treasure in this general area.

IOWA

Mormon Trail Park off State 189, is about two miles southeast of Bridgewater, Adair Co. A segment of the old wagon route used by the Mormons in 1846 on their journey to Utah is preserved in this park. Here they had a camp site and established a temporary medical center of which no traces have survived.

Pilot Rock is off U.S. 59 just south of Cherokee, Cherokee Co. This giant glacier boulder marks the site of an encampment used by the Sioux Indians over the years. Later thousands of pioneers headed westward along several trails that pass close to this rock.

The site of Fort Defiance is on State 245 about a mile southwest of Esthersville, Emmet Co. The fort was built in 1862 to protect the settlers from the warlike Sioux Indians, abandoned early in 1864, and fell into ruin. A cavalry unit was stationed there during the short period it was used.

The ruins of Fort Atkinson are on State 24 just north of the town of the same name, Allamakee Co. The fort was built in 1832 and garrisoned by U.S. Army troops, but it was abandoned in 1848 and fell into ruin.

The site of Fort Dodge is close to the junction of U.S. 20 and 169, near the city of Fort Dodge, Webster Co. It was built in 1850 as a garrison for the United States 6th Infantry Dragoons to protect the settlers in the area from the Sioux Indians and abandoned only three years later, falling into ruins. A replica fort is built about a mile from the site of the original.

Effigy Mounds National Monument is on State 76, three miles north of Marquette, Clayton Co. This archaeological park contains over 200 mounds which cover the remains of an Indian settlement which flourished around 1000.

The site of Fort Peterson is on a farm on the outskirts of the present village of Peterson, Winnebago Co. Very little is known about this fort except that it was built in 1857 as protection against the Sioux Indians. No traces of it remain today.

The ghost town of Burris City is located on the north bank of the Iowa River at its junction with the Missouri River, about two miles north of Toolesboro, County 99, Louisa Co. It was a riverboat boomtown until being destroyed in a flood. About 70 buildings are still standing.

The ghost town of Galland, also known as Nashville, is located three miles east of Montrose and twelve miles north of Keokuk on Lake Shore Drive, Lee Co. It was another riverboat town on the Mississippi, founded in 1830 and abandoned by 1900.

The ghost town of Hauntown is on the west bank of the Mississippi River five miles south of Sabula, County 64 and State 67, Jackson Co. It is one of the best places to search for old bottles as the main industry of this nineteenth-century town was making whiskey. A number of houses and distillery buildings still stand.

The ruins of Elk River are located near the outskirts of Almost, State 67, Jackson Co., about ten miles south of Hauntown. It served as an outlaw hangout during the Civil War and was burnt down soon afterwards.

A ghost Icarian community is located four and a half miles northeast of Corning, County 148 and 186, Adams Co. Several old buildings are still standing in this community which was founded in 1858.

The ghost town of Iowa Phalanx is on the Des Moines River about sixteen miles northwest of Oskaloosa, Mahaska Co. It was a short-lived settlement founded in 1845 by an obscure religious sect.

The ghost town of Kossuth is on State 61 about two miles east of Mediapolis, Des Moines Co. More than 300 buildings of the late nineteenth century still remain in this town.

The ghost town of Preparation is in Preparation Canyon State Park, nineteen miles north of the junction of State 75 and County 183, near Mondamin, Pottawattamie Co. In this former Mormon settlement, only two houses are still standing.

The ghost town of River Sioux is opposite **Malta,** another ghost town on the Sioux River, about 24 miles north of Missouri Valley on State 75, Pottawattamie Co. Both towns prospered for only about a decade around the middle of the last century.

The ruins of Sandusky are located off Lake Shore Drive about five miles north of Keokuk, Lee Co. It was established as a trading post on the Mississippi River and destroyed by a flood some time after 1820.

The ruins of Talmage are on the Thompson River on State 34 about thirteen miles east of Creston, Union Co. Talmage was another short-lived Mormon settlement during the mid-nineteenth century.

The ghost town of Vandalia is located about seventeen and a half miles east on County 163 from Des Moines and then four and a half miles south on a dirt road, Marion Co. It flourished as an agricultural center during the second half of the 1800s and then was abandoned.

Numerous river pirate treasures are reported to be hidden in **Stone Park** overlooking the bend in the Missouri River in Sioux City, Woodbury Co. A hoard of several hundred American silver dollars was found by a park worker in 1957.

In 1866 two riverboats carrying cargoes of mercury and whiskey sank on the Missouri River northeast of **Blair,** Nebraska. Three flasks of the mercury were found on the river bank just south of Horseshoe Lake on the Iowa side of the river in 1956 and a great deal more of this valuable commodity is believed to be concealed under the muddy river bank in the same area. Occasionally some of the whiskey bottles are also washed ashore here.

The outlaw Jesse James buried $35,000 in gold coins on a farm near Weston on County 191, a few miles north of **Council Bluffs,** Pottawattamie Co.

A prominent merchant is known to have concealed over $75,000 in gold coins near the west bank of the Nishnabotua River about a mile north of **Shenandoah,** State 59, Page Co.

The notorious Burrow gang buried $65,000 in gold coins near **Redfield,** State 6, Dallas Co.

During the 1930s Bonnie and Clyde are alleged to have buried a sizable amount of loot at their camp in a wooden area overlooking the Racoon River, about three miles north of **Dexter,** State 6, Dallas Co.

A band of outlaws known as the Banditti of the Plains had their headquarters near the mouth of the Boone River, about two miles north of **Stratford,** County 175, Hamilton Co. Before being killed in a battle with lawmen, they allegedly buried all of their ill-gotten money in an Indian mound surrounded by a thicket of trees close to where the John Lott Monument now stands.

In 1877 gold was discovered on the Iowa River about seven miles north of **Eldora,** County 175, Hardon Co., and a number of prospectors are known to have hidden gold nuggets in the area.

About $25,000 in gold nuggets sealed in ceramic jars was buried about a mile north of the cemetery near **Eddyville** on the Des Moines River, County 137, Monroe Co., by three prospectors returning from the Black Hills in 1878.

Early in the 1800s the Indian chief Black Hawk and a number of his warriors buried much gold on the northern side of the Des Moines River in the northwestern corner of **Davis County.** The site of one large cache is known to be in Section 11, Township 70, Range 12 of this county.

Early in the 1800s Indians are reported to have buried a large amount of gold near a log cabin owned by a settler named Bonnifield located near **Fairfield,** State 34, Jefferson Co.

During an Indian attack, an Army paymaster buried $7,000 in gold coins close to **Fort Atkinson,** located near Decorah, County 9, Winneshiek Co. He was killed before he could tell anyone where the payroll was hidden.

Another larger Army payroll is alleged to be buried along **Miner's Creek,** near Guttenburg on the Mississippi River, State 52, Clayton Co.

A lead miner named Tom Kelly is known to have concealed a great deal of gold and silver coins on **Kelly's Bluff,** towering above Second and Bludd Streets in downtown Dubuque. During the 1830s he amassed a small fortune and was considered an eccentric old man until he mentioned his hidden hoards on his deathbed. In 1867 a jar containing $1,200 in gold coins was found, in 1871 two hoards of $10,000 and $1,800 were discovered, and in 1914 another $4,000 was found. It is believed that there is still another $100,000 or more buried on the bluff.

During the 1880s Mississippi River pirates buried their plunder in a cave near the southern side of **Bellevue,** State 52, Jackson Co., before being lynched by angry vigilantes.

A horse thief hid about $40,000 in gold coins along the banks of the Mississippi River, a few miles north of **Sabula,** where the State 64 bridge crosses the river into Wisconsin, Jackson Co.

A wealthy merchant buried an iron pot full of gold coins and stock certificates in what is known as **River Front Park** in Clinton on the Mississippi River, Clinton Co.

The wealthy Ives brothers buried several hoards of money and stock certificates on their farm near **Sunbury,** a few miles north of U.S. 80, Cedar Co. In 1935 relatives of theirs found $200,000 in paper money but the rest is still waiting to be found.

In a swampy, deserted, five-acre area near a creek that enters the Mississippi River at **Buffalo,** a tiny village southwest of Davenport on County 22, Cott Co., robbers buried about $50,000 in gold coins from a train holdup.

At **Burris City** located on the north side of the Iowa River where it enters the Mississippi River, Louisa Co., river pirates are known to have hidden several different treasures. In 1960 a treasure hunter found a large hoard of California-minted gold coins near the base of a large tree.

The Indian Chief Black Hawk is alleged to have buried about $50,000 in gold coins in the hills near **Denmark,** County 103, Lee Co.

KANSAS

Dodge City on the Arkansas River, Ford Co. was formerly a frontier town and cattle-shipping center. During the 1870s and 1880s it was known as the wickedest little city in America; many outlaws ended their days being buried on Boot Hill. Very few traces of the original city, which was founded in 1772, still remain but the area should prove to be a treasure hunter's paradise on account of all the old weapons and other Wild West memorabilia waiting to be found.

The Santa Fe Trail, which was one of the most traveled byways of America between 1820 and 1880, cut across the southern portion of this state. Countless markers indicate the various camp sites used by the westward-bound pioneers, also the scenes of Indian raids.

Fort Larned is on U.S. 156 a bit west of Larned, Pawnee Co. During the 1860s and 1870s this well-preserved fort was the main guardian of the Kansas segment of the Santa Fe Trail and the principal base in the state for all wars fought with the Indians. A number of old ruins dot the area.

Fort Scott is on U.S. 54 near the town of this name, Bourbon Co. The fort was constructed in 1842 and continued in use until 1873 when it was abandoned. Today many of the original buildings of the fort's interior are still well preserved.

The Hollenberg Pony Express Station is six miles north of U.S. 36 near Hanover, Washington Co. It was built in 1857 on the heavily traveled Oregon-California Trail and also

172

served as a way station for travelers. The original building still stands and there are vestiges of other ruined buildings around it.

Fort Hays still stands on old U.S. 40 south of the town of Hays, Ellis Co. It was built in 1865 to afford protection for travelers, settlers, and construction gangs on the Union Pacific Railroad. Both Buffalo Bill Cody and General George A. Custer served at this post. A number of battles were fought here with Indians before the fort was abandoned in 1889.

Some remnants of the **Shawnee Methodist Mission** built in 1830 can still be seen in downtown Kansas City. Both the Santa Fe and Oregon trails ran right through this mission, which was one of the largest in the Midwest before 1900.

A marker located about four miles west of Lyons, Ellsworth Co. indicates the site of one of the largest villages of the **"Kingdom of Quivira,"** visited by the Spanish explorer Francisco Vasquez de Coronado during the summer of 1541 in his quest for wealth. Around 1890 a large number of artifacts dating from this period were found in a cornfield and are now on display in the Lyon's Court House. Other artifacts were also found several years ago in the same area.

The site of the original **village of Osawatomie** is located in a park in the present town of this name in Miami Co. The community was destroyed by a large band of proslavery raiders in August 1856 and another settlement soon sprang up around the ruins.

Pawnee Rock Memorial Park is off U.S. 56 near the town of Pawnee Rock, Pawnee Co. This bold, projecting cliff of red rock was one of the most distinctive features along the Kansas segment of the Santa Fe Trail. Because the rocks afforded the Indians with an excellent place to hide before attacking wagon trains, it was also a most dangerous spot in the trail.

The ruins of Abram are located about three miles southeast of Lincoln, County 14, Lincoln Co. Only the foundations of about 25 brick buildings remain.

The ghost town of Albany is located two miles east of Sabetha on County 236, Brown Co. It was an important center for the Underground Railroad during the Civil War and was burnt down in 1865 by Confederate raiders. A new town sprang up on the site but was abandoned by 1890.

The ghost town of Big Timber is located five miles northeast of Randolph, State 77, Pottawattomie Co., on the western side of Turtle Creek Reservoir. It was an important agricultural center until around 1900 when it was abandoned after a plague killed most of the residents. In the same general area are the ghost towns of **Spring Lake, Bellegarde,** and **Olsburg.**

The ruins of Central City are located eight miles southwest of Garnett, State 59, Anderson Co. Only the ruins of a church, parsonage, an old hotel, and several farmhouses are left in this settlement, which once had over 5,000 residents.

The ghost town of Chikaskia is located on the Chikaskia River about six miles north of Caldwell, near the Oklahoma state line, State 81, Summer Co. In the same general area are the ghost towns of **Alton, Aurellville, Hessel,** and **Rome.**

The ghost town of Fredericksburg is located seven miles south of the state line near Alma, Nebraska, off State 183, Phillips Co. Nearby about three miles west of Prairie Dog Creek is another ghost town called **Woodruff.**

The ghost town of Hollidaysburg is located on the Arkansas River, about three miles west of Syracuse, State 50, Hamilton Co. Before the coming of the railroads, it was a stage station and camping ground for westward-bound settlers.

The ghost town of Iowa Point was on the Missouri River, but is now set about a mile back from it, six miles north of Highland, State 36, Doniphan Co. It was once a booming town of 3,000 residents until the river changed its course and meandered to the east.

The ghost town of Limestone is on the Little Blue River about midway between Hollenburg and Hanover, Washington Co. Only a few of the nineteenth-century buildings are still standing.

The ghost town of Queen City is on the north side of the Arkansas River about four miles north of Haven, County 96, Reno Co. Once an important riverboat town, only ten saloons and about 100 other wooden buildings are left today. A tycoon is known to have buried about $60,000 in gold coins underneath one of the saloons before he died in 1876.

Kansas and the Plains States offer a host of opportunities with promising sites where treasure is waiting to be found by a modern metal detector.

174

Many veteran treasure hunters insist that "your own front yard" is the place where a hobbyist should begin searching for lost valuables.

The **ruins of Ravanna** are located about nine miles northwest of Kalvesta, State 156, Dickinson Co. Just a mile to the east are the **ruins of Beersheba,** which was an unsuccessful Jewish farm community in the 1880s.

The **ghost town of Richfield** is located near the junction of County 27 with the North Fork of the Cimarron River, Morton Co. During its heyday around 1850 it had about 1500 residents.

The **ghost town of Silver City** is five miles southwest of Yates Center, State 54 and 75, Woodson Co. It was founded in the 1850s as a result of false silver discoveries which brought several thousand prospectors into the area for a few months. In the area are many deserted mine shafts.

On a farm a few miles south of **Republican** on the Republican River, near the outskirts of a Shawnee Indian village ruin, Republic Co., several sizable hoards of gold coins were hidden by illegal liquor makers during the first few decades of this century. In one case a large cask of gold coins was thrown into a deep well when a sheriff's posse arrived to destroy a still operation.

During World War II a workman accidentally discovered a ceramic jar full of gold coins at a lumber yard in **Blue Rapids,** State 77, Marshall Co. Research indicates that this was only one of about twelve such caches buried in this same area by the original owner of the lumber yard, who died in 1904.

Before being killed by Indians, two miners returning from the California gold fields buried two buckskin bags full of gold dust on the Blue River near **Marysville,** State 77, Marshall Co.

Two other California miners heading back to Massachusetts are also said to have buried a large number of gold nuggets on the east bank of the old Nemaha River channel, about one and a half miles north of **Seneca,** State 36, Nemaha Co.

During the 1860s another returning California prospector carrying about 20 pounds of gold nuggets drowned while trying to ford Harris Creek on the old **G. W. Potts farm,** near Oneida, Nemaha Co.

In 1891 a G. G. Fox was digging a site for a new ice house when he discovered a large iron box full of Spanish and French seventeenth-century gold and silver coins. Many of his neighbors saw the hoard, then valued at around $25,000, before he died several weeks later. It is believed that he reburied the treasure somewhere on his farm near **Highland** in Donaphan Co.

The paddle-wheel steamboat **Francis X. Aubrey** carrying over $500,000 in gold and silver specie and bullion sank in the vicinity of Leavenworth, on the Missouri River, Leavenworth Co. Coins are found on the beach off the **Leavenworth National Cemetery** and are believed to be coming ashore from this wreck.

Somewhere on the campus of the University of Kansas near **Lawrence,** Douglas Co., an army payroll of $195,000 in gold and silver was buried in great haste by four United States Army soldiers who were being chased by outlaws. Only one officer survived the outlaw attack. Though he knew the general area, he could not find the payroll because heavy rains had obliterated all traces of their diggings.

During the late 1800s an eccentric millionaire named Ernest Valeton de Boissière hid a large fortune in gold coins in or near his mansion in **Silksville,** Franklin Co.

A prospector returning from California concealed about $85,000 in gold coins in an abandoned well near the outskirts of **Richmond,** State 59, Franklin Co. He was killed soon after describing the fortune to his wife, who was not able to locate it.

In 1757 a group of French explorers buried a large hoard of raw gold at the confluence of the Little Arkansas and Arkansas Rivers in downtown **Wichita.** A number of old Spanish documents mention that the Indians worked a number of gold mines in the surrounding area which have never been located.

During the 1870s, the ruthless Bender couple ran an inn, where they are alleged to have murdered and robbed their guests of an estimated $100,000. The money is concealed on their inn and farm, located about half a mile west of State 169, about seven miles north of **Cherryvale,** Montgomery Co. In 1922 a jar containing over 300 gold coins was found on the site but a much greater amount is awaiting discovery.

Right after the Civil War members of Quantrill's Raiders are known to have stashed their sizable individual treasures near **Baxter Springs,** State 66 and 166 in Cherokee Co., the southeast corner of the state. Many of these men were killed in other raids and never came back for their money.

During the late nineteenth century, a rich merchant named Peter Robidoux hid a number of treasure caches along the banks of the Smoky Hill River, near **Wallace,** State 40, Wallace Co. In the 1930s a young boy discovered one of these hoards, about 500 twenty-dollar gold double eagles.

Spaniards are supposed to have buried about $400,000 in gold bullion on the banks of the Solomon River near **Morland,** County 85, Graham Co.

At the turn of the century a rich merchant and tavern owner, Tom Daly, had amassed a fortune in the neighborhood of $200,000 in gold. Shortly before he died he is known to have concealed all of it somewhere near the peak of the 2000-foot **Round Mountain** a few miles south of Ellis, State 247, Ellis Co. Around the same time a cowboy won $6,000 in gold and buried it among some rocks near a corral about one mile east of Ellis. When he sobered up he was unable to find his gambling winnings.

In 1870 bandits robbed a $22,000 payroll from the Wells Fargo office in Ellis. Before the bandits were caught and hanged, they buried their plunder near **Big Creek,** two miles south of the town.

In the **Point of Rocks State Park,** eight miles north of Elkhart on County 27, Morton Co., several outlaw treasures are known to have been buried. The area was used as a bandit headquarters for almost 75 years and many relics, guns, and coins have been found in recent years.

About four miles northwest of **Dodge City** near St. Mary of the Plains College, Ford Co., is a cave where several different bandits hid money before a landslide sealed it closed.

At a point on the Arkansas River about five miles west of **Dodge City** Indians attacked and almost wiped out an entire train of Mexicans on the Santa Fe Trail in the early 1800s. The Indians are alleged to have buried about $500,000 in gold and silver bars which were being carried to Independence for the purchase of arms and munitions by an insurgent general. A rise in the river level after several days of rains obliterated the signs marking the burial site and the survivors were unable to relocate the treasure.

In the same general area, only two to three miles further west along the river and **Santa Fe Trail,** another wagon train was attacked by Indians in 1853 and a chest containing 4,000 Spanish silver dollars was buried and not found again.

A bandit known as Ugly Harry is supposed to have buried a Wells Fargo Express Company chest containing a large amount of gold dust and nuggets. The treasure is somewhere within a 200-yard radius of old **Fort Dodge,** a few miles east of present Dodge City.

A returning California miner buried a buckskin bag containing about $50,000 in gold coins on the banks of a stream about a half mile west of **Offerle,** State 50, Edwards Co. He was badly wounded during an Indian attack and before dying told some friends about his cache.

The Big Basin Treasure reportedly consists of $200,000 in gold coins and bars buried in the vicinity of St. Jacobs Well and Big Basin Monument, about twelve miles northwest of Ashland, State 160, Clark Co.

Fort Leavenworth was built in 1827 as a base for military units patrolling the Santa Fe trade route. A permanent settlement was established here in 1825 when the Santa Fe Trail began being used by many settlers heading westward.

The ghost town of Rome is near State 77 west of Milford Reservoir, Riley Co. It was founded in 1867 as a cow town and before long had a population of 2,000 residents. But by 1890 it was completely abandoned and today very little of it remains.

The ghost town of Greenwood City is located between Eureka and Lake Eureka in the center of Greenwood Co. It was founded in 1870 and although it lasted only for four years, Greenwood City was one of the wildest towns in the state and rivaled Dodge City and Abilene as having the largest number of resident outlaws. When the railroad missed the town by three miles it just folded up.

The **ghost town of Juaniata** was located about twelve miles west of Greenwood City on the Fall River, Riley Co. The settlement, also known as Dyers Town, was abandoned after about a decade. Today many of the original buildings are standing including several churches, a hotel, post office, and eighteen saloons.

The **ghost town of Moneka** is located about three miles southeast of Mound City (many Indian mounds are located here) on County 7 and 52, Linn Co. The town lasted from 1857 through 1871 and never had more than 200 residents.

The **ghost town of Paris** is located two miles west of Farlinville (County 7), Linn Co. It was founded in 1857 and abandoned by 1864 after being burned down.

The **ruins of Oread** are located near the eastern edge of John Redmond Reservoir near State 75, Coffee Co. The town existed only briefly around the mid-1800s and very few of its ruins can be seen today.

The **ghost town of Sumner** is on the Missouri River at a place early French explorers used and called "le gran detour." A person wrote in 1911: "Three miles south of Atchison, in Atchinson County, is Sumner, a dead city that boasted 3,000 residents and whose streets once were filled with the clamor of busy traffic and echoed to the tread of thousands of mules and oxen that in pioneer days of the Great West transported the products of the East across the Great American Desert to the Rocky Mountains." In 1860 a tornado totally destroyed the city and it was never rebuilt. At the time a large number of persons concealed valuables and treasure that they were unable to locate after the disaster.

The **site of Fort Belmont** is about a quarter mile northwest of Belmont, not far from the Eureka-Humboldt Road, Woodson Co. This oval-shaped wooden fort stood on the banks of Sandy Creek and was built around 1850; nothing more is known about it.

In the late nineteenth century, the two flourishing towns of **Clarksburg** and **Godfrey** were located in the middle of Bourbon Co., a bit west of the Fort Scott National Historical Site. Today their exact locations have been lost. They were coal-mining towns with populations of several thousands each and it is a real mystery how they could have disappeared without a trace. In the southeast corner of the same county a town named **Midland** suffered a like fate.

KENTUCKY

The **site of Camp Charity** is on U.S. 62 about ten miles east of Bardstown, Nelson Co. This was the encampment site used by Confederate General John Hunt Morgan to train the troops for his Second Kentucky Cavalry, known as Morgan's Raiders. These soldiers sacked and destroyed a number of towns in Kentucky, Ohio, and Indiana in 1861–1863.

Belmont Battlefield Park is on State 80 just outside Columbus, Hickman Co. This 177-acre park on a bluff overlooking the Mississippi River was a strongly fortified Civil War post called the Confederacy's "Gibraltar of the West." More than 140 cannon were placed there but no major battles were ever fought before the Rebels were forced to evacuate the site in February 1862.

Big Bone Lick State Park on State 338 is 26 miles southwest of Covington, Kenton Co. The 175-acre park contains extensive remains of many different types of prehistoric animals, including mastodons, mammoths, elephants, and saber-toothed tigers that came to this area during the last Ice Age.

West High Street Historic District is located in Lexington. A number of original structures built when the city was founded in 1779 still stand. During the Civil War the city changed hands three times and many buildings were destroyed as a result of the fighting.

The **site where Fort Nelson** stood is located in downtown Louisville near the corner of 7th and Main Streets. The wooden fort was built in 1781–1782 several years after the city was first settled. An earlier fort of the same name had been built on Corn Island opposite the city, but this island is now under the waters of the river.

Perrysville Battlefield is just off U.S. 68 and 150, two miles north of Perrysville, Boyle Co. The battle which was fought here on October 8, 1862 was one of the bloodiest of the Civil

War; over 44,000 men fought and more than 7,500 casualties were suffered on both sides. A park covers only 30 acres of the battlefield which encompassed an area ten times this size. The fallen were buried in unmarked graves scattered over the terrain.

Richmond Battlefield is on U.S. 25, just south of Richmond, Madison Co. A major battle took place here on August 29-30, 1862 between 7,000 Union and 12,000 Confederate troops who suffered heavy losses on both sides.

Fort Jefferson on the Mississippi River near Wickliffe in Ballard County was built by the Americans under George Rogers Clark in 1779. The following year it withstood six days of attack by British-led Indians, but in June 1781 it was abandoned as being untendable. No traces remain.

Harrodsburg Site is located near Lexington and Warwick Streets, in present Harrodsburg, Mercer County. It is the site of the state's first permanent settlement, founded in 1774 by frontiersmen from Pennsylvania. The first settlers were hoping to find the rich silver mines that Indians claimed were in the area, but the mines were never found. A fort built in 1777 withstood several fierce Indian attacks in 1778.

Falls of the Ohio is a point on the Ohio River which is interrupted by falls and rapids. It is close to the present city of Louisville, where in 1763 a settlement was founded; but in 1773 the town was moved a short distance away and its name changed to Louisville. A spit of land above the falls called Corn Island, since eroded away by the river, was the site of George Rogers Clark's fortified campsite during the summer of 1778.

Sportman's Hill is on U.S. 150 about nine miles southeast of Sanford, near Crab Orchard in Lincoln County. In this area are the remains of many homes built by early frontiersmen in the last three decades of the 1700s. One of them has survived—the William Whitley House, built in 1787 and believed to be the oldest brick residence west of the Alleghenies.

Blue Licks Battlefield is located in an 100-acre park near the U.S. 68 crossing of the Licking River, near the village of Blue Lick Springs, Nicolas Co. On August 19, 1782 the Tories and Indians inflicted a devastating loss on a band of Patriot frontiersmen, led by Daniel Boone, who lost his son in the battle.

The site of Fort Boonesborough is marked on U.S. 227 about nine miles north of Richmond, Madison Co. Daniel Boone and his frontiersmen built a wooden fort on this site in 1776 because of increased hostilities with the Indians. Settlers soon began arriving and a town began to flourish. In 1778 it withstood a fierce Indian attack. Soon afterward, the settlers moved on to other areas and today no trace of the fort or settlement exists.

The site of Fredericktown was located about six miles northwest of Fort Boonesborough and should not be confused with a present town in Kentucky with this same name. The earlier Fredericktown was another frontier settlement founded about 1776 that withstood fierce Indian attacks in 1778 and 1779. Settlers abandoned it to search for better farming country.

Cumberland Gap National Park located off U.S. 25E, near Middlesboro, Bell Co., is a natural passage in the Cumberland Mountains. Through the Gap runs the Wilderness Road, which was widely used by early settlers in their westward migrations. It was first discovered in 1750 and during the next 50 years a number of small settlements sprang up in the general area—none of which exists today. The Gap was also the scene of many Indian attacks upon the settlers. About two miles of the Wilderness Road can be clearly seen in the park, as well as several Civil War fortifications, and the ruins of an early iron furnace. In the areas where the settlers camped are numbers of artifacts.

In the vicinity of **Russelville,** Logan Co., lies a treasure concealed by the Jesse James gang in 1868. They robbed a Russelville bank of about $50,000 in gold coins, and with a posse hot on their trail they hastily buried the money on the outskirts of the town.

In the 1930s a rich merchant named James Langstaff buried gold coins valued at $75,000 on the premises of his hardware store in **Paducah,** McCracken Co.

On the south bank of the Ohio River at **West Paducah,** opposite Metropolis, Illinois, McCracken Co., many American silver coins of the late nineteenth century have been found along the banks of the river. They are probably being washed ashore from a riverboat wrecked nearby.

During the spring, low waters one can see the remains of a nineteenth-century paddle-wheel steamer along the south river bank of the Ohio River at **Todd,** County 387, Rittenden Co. Large numbers of bottles and other artifacts have been found on the site in recent years.

Vestiges of another large river boat can be seen along the bend of the Ohio River about a half mile east of **Henderson,** County 1, Henderson Co. American gold and silver coins from the 1880s have been found among the wreckage above the river bank in a marshy area.

Harpe's Head on the Natchez Trace near Tilden, County 56, Webster Co., is named after the outlaw Micajoh Harpe who buried about $300,000 in gold coins in this area.

On Harpe's Head Road, about ten miles south of Henderson, Henderson Co., the Harpe brothers are alleged to have buried another treasure of gold coins in a cave above a stream.

In 1888 a sack containing about $3,000 in gold coins was buried in the vicinity of **Pilot Rock,** near Apex, County 189, in the northeast corner of Christian Co.

A rich farmer named Roger Barrell is alleged to have buried about $200,000 in gold coins on his farm near **Steff,** State 62, Grayson Co.

In his diary, gambler Anthony Caccoma, who died in 1940, recorded burying a number of caches around the town of **Horse Cave,** County 218, Hart Co. One cache of $3,200 was found east of the town around the foundations of an old house.

Somewhere in the vicinity of **Covington,** on the Ohio River, opposite Cincinnati, Kenton Co., a Prohibition bootleg king is said to have buried about $4 million in gold coins and paper currency.

During the Civil War a William Pettit buried his accumulated fortune of about $80,000 in gold coins somewhere on his 2,000-acre farm, about three miles south of **Lexington,** Yette Co.

After raiding a number of white settlements in the 1820s, a band of Cherokee Indians hid a large treasure of gold coins and family silver near **Winchester,** County 627, Clark Co.

Somewhere along the Little Laurel River in the **Levi Jackson Wilderness State Park** near London, U.S. 75, Laurel Co., Indians in 1784 attacked a group of pioneers known as the McNitt party and killed most of them. Prior to the attack the pioneers buried all of their valuables and the survivors were unable to find most.

A lost silver mine is located in the vicinity of Red River Gorge on the south side of Daniel Boone National Forest, Wolfe Co.

About $500,000 in silver bars and a lost silver mine are supposed to be in the vicinity of **Pottsville Gorge** on either Lower or Upper Devil's Creek, near Campton, County 15, Wolfe Co.

A lost Indian silver mine is located in the vicinity of Greenup on the Ohio River, State 23, Greenup Co.

In 1881 wealthy trader and farmer Jack Neal is said to have buried about $200,000 in silver and gold coins in an orchard on his farm. The land is located in the mountains to the east of **Hueysville,** about five miles west of Pikesville, Pike Co.

Silver bullion and ore worth about $150,000 are believed to have been buried by miner John Swift in a cave on **Pine Mountain,** on the northern side of Fishtrap Lake, Pike Co.

In the vicinity of **Kings Creek,** County 160, Letcher Co., in the Pine Mountain Range, are several lost Indian silver and gold mines. Indians were working them as late as 1810 before they were driven out of the area.

During the Civil War a Union paymaster being pursued by Confederate troops is said to have thrown about $3 million in silver and gold bars into the Big Sandy River near **Pinesville,** State 25E, Bell Co. In the 1920s a number of silver bars were found in this area by fishermen.

LOUISIANA

The ruins of Fort Livingston are located on the southern end of Grand Terre Isle, about one mile across Barataria Pass from Grand Isle and can be reached only by boat. The fort was occupied by both Union and Confederate troops during the Civil War. Remnants of various shipwrecks can be seen on the beaches at low tide and treasure hunters have reported finding large numbers of Spanish silver and gold coins dating from 1802–1809 in the vicinity of the fort ruins.

Mansfield Battle State Park is on U.S. 84 and State 175, four miles south of Mansfield, De Soto Pa. The park covers only 44 acres of a much larger battlefield where the South won its last victory of the Civil War. On April 8, 1864 some 15,000 Confederates defeated a Union force of over 40,000 men. There are numerous remnants of earthworks and entrenchments.

The site where Fort Jesup stood is on State 6, six miles north of Many, Sabine Pa. This fort, which was built in 1822, was the most southwesterly military outpost in the United States until 1846. In 1845 the United States Army grouped here for the invasion of Mexico and the liberation of Texas under General Zachary Taylor. The following year the fort was abandoned and fell into ruin. Only one of the original buildings still stands.

The Marksville National Park is located on a bluff overlooking the Old River, off State 1, near Marksville, Avoyelles Pa. The park contains remnants of an ancient fortified Indian village which flourished between 300 and 600, including a number of burial mounds and earthen embankments that surrounded the village.

The site where the first Fort St. Jean Baptiste de Natchitoches stood is near the corner of Jefferson and New Second Streets, in the town of Natchitoches, Natchitoches Pa. In 1714 the French built this fort on the banks of the Cane River so they could fight off the Spanish and marauding Indians. Because of floods during the years 1735–1737, they abandoned the fort and built another about 200 yards to the west on a site now occupied by the American Cemetery. This they used until 1749 when they left the area. No traces of either fort remain.

Jackson Square Park in Vieux Carré section of present New Orleans, originally called the Place d'Armes, was used as a parade ground for many years by the different nationalities that occupied the city. Old coins, clay pipes, and other artifacts have been found here in recent years.

The site of Fort de la Boulaye was off State 39 about a mile north of Phoenix, near the mouth of the Mississippi River. This wooden fort, also known as **Fort Iberville,** was built by the French in 1700 but in 1704 hostile Indians forced them to abandon the site. It soon fell into ruins and no traces remain today.

Fort Pike is on U.S. 90, about 30 miles east of New Orleans, Orleans Pa. It was built between 1819 and 1828 to guard Rigolets Pass, one of the waterways leading into New Orleans. In 1861 the Confederates used the fort for a short while until it was taken over by the Federals.

The Presidio of Los Adaes site is located off State 6, about two miles northeast of Robeline, Natchitoches Pa. Originally the site covered some 40 acres; now a park occupies nine of them. The Spanish built this mission and settlement in 1717 but it was attacked and destroyed by the French in 1721. Returning soon after, the Spanish built another settlement, including a fort, on an adjoining hill. The Presidio de Nuestra Senora del Pilar de los Adaes, so they called it, was abandoned in 1773. Today there are still traces of both settlements.

Longville-Evangeline State Park covers 157 acres on State 31, about one mile north of St. Martinville, St. Martin Pa. The park is set in the heart of a region settled by a large number of French Acadians who were expelled from Nova Scotia by the British in 1755. Vestiges of many of their homes are found in the park and surrounding area.

Fort Jackson is on the west bank of the Mississippi River off State 23, about three miles south of Triumph, Plaquemines Pa. Built in 1792, it was enlarged in 1815 and again in 1861. During the Civil War the defense of New Orleans was entrusted to this fort and to **Fort St. Philip** on the east bank of the river about five miles north of Fort Jackson. Both forts saw heavy action in April 1862 when the Union Navy under Admiral David Farragut attacked and then bypassed them to capture New Orleans.

Chalmette National Historic Park is on the east bank of the Mississippi River off State 39, about ten miles southeast of New Orleans. It marks the spot where General Andrew Jackson had his stunning victory over the British on January 8, 1815; in the encounter the British lost 2000 men and the Americans only 71. The ruins of a plantation can be seen near the outskirts of the park.

Fort MaComb is on U.S. 90 about 22 miles east of New Orleans. It was built after the War of 1812 to protect the approaches to New Orleans and was used by both Confederate and Union forces during the Civil War.

Grand Isle is located at the southwest entrance to Barataria Bay and can be reached via State 1, Laforche Pa. During the first decade of the nineteenth century it was used as a base by the swashbuckling pirate brothers, Jean and Pierre Lafitte, who fought bravely for the Americans against the British. There are a number of tales about buried pirate treasure on the island and a great deal of unsuccessful searching has already been done.

Baton Rouge on the Mississippi River, one of the earliest French settlements in the Mississippi Valley, was a vital link in the chain of outposts connecting Natchez and New Orleans. The French settled the place around 1720 and held it until 1763 when it was ceded to Britain by the Treaty of Paris. Then in 1783 it was captured by Spain and exchanged hands several times until 1810, when it became a part of the United States as a result of the Louisiana Purchase. A monument stands at the center of the city on the site where the Confederates launched a bloody assault on August 5, 1862 and tried to recapture the city from the Union. During the attack a large part of the city was gutted by fire. Today only a few of the eighteenth- and nineteenth-century buildings remain.

Somewhere on the **Parlange Plantation,** near New Roads, Pointe Coupee Pa., the family that owned this property during the Civil War is reported to have buried gold and silver treasure valued at over $400,000. After concealing their valuables, the family fled for safety during a Union raid, but all were killed in a riverboat accident. The treasure is one of the most sought after in the state.

The lost site of Fort Manchac is somewhere on the Mississippi River a few miles downstream from Baton Rouge, East Baton Rouge Pa. It was built by the French around 1720 and in use as late as 1745, but the site has since been lost.

New Orleans was founded by the French in 1718 on a malarious patch of swampy ground. In 1721 the community consisted of only about 130 houses, but two years later it had become the capital of French Louisiana. The town really grew during the Revolutionary War when it served as an important supply base for the Patriots. Most of the original buildings were destroyed by a fire in 1788. During the Spanish occupation of the city between 1764 and 1803 several large forts were built. But the French demolished these in 1803 when they took over the city in order to eradicate suspected causes of yellow fever. On Lake Ponchartrain at the mouth of Bayou St. John the foundations of a Spanish fort are visible. During the War of 1812 it served to garrison Andrew Jackson's troops. Many of the old buildings were destroyed in the British attack in January 1815; still more were leveled when the city was captured by Union troops in 1862. Today most of the surviving buildings date from after the Civil War.

Islands #82 and #83, located on the Mississippi River below New Orleans, are considered two of the best treasure-hunting areas in the state because of the large numbers of gold and silver coins found on them. On March 2, 1871 the steamer **Oregon** hit an obstruction near Island #82 and sank alongside the southern tip of the island with a large loss of life and more than $300,000 in gold bullion and specie. A few days before on February 27, 1871 another steamer **John Adams** had struck the same obstacle and sank in 60 feet of water with the loss of 107 lives. The forward part of her superstructure, in which more than $500,000 in gold was being carried, floated down to Island #83 where it grounded and went to pieces. Most of the treasure being found on these islands is probably from these two steamboat wrecks.

The town of Bellwood is in the Kisatchie National Forest on State 39, about fourteen miles south of Hagewood. Today only a few people live in this community, which was a booming lumber town in the past century. In the vicinity there are other ghost towns which can only be reached by hiking.

The ghost town of Braithwaite is about twenty miles southeast of New Orleans on County 46, St. Bernard Pa. It was a prosperous industrial town until 1930; today several hundred old buildings are still standing.

The ghost town of Fairfax is on Grand Lake about four miles east of Centerville, State 90, St. Mary Pa. The French first settled here in the early eighteenth century but no traces of their homes remain. During the 1800s the town had a population of about 3,000 but their homes were wiped out by a hurricane around 1900. The buildings now standing were built in the 1920s and 1930s.

The ruins of Galvez Town are located two and a half miles south of Oak Grove and two and a half miles west of Port Vincent (County 49), on the Amite River, Livingston Pa. The town was occupied only between 1775 and 1789 by the French and a picnic ground now surrounds the ruins of about 50 stone buildings. According to local legend the pirate Jean Lafitte buried a great hoard of gold on the opposite side of the river; enormous excitement was created in 1956 when several hundred gold coins were found in the area by a farmer plowing his field.

The town of Grand Ecore is on a bluff overlooking the Red River, about midway between Clarence and Natchitoches (County 6), Natchitoches Pa. It was first settled around 1800 but by 1850 it had become the main shipping center for east Texas. In 1853 the populace was badly decimated by yellow fever and then in 1863 Federal troops sacked and destroyed most of the town. Today about 50 people still live here among the ruins of hundreds of old buildings. Nearby are the ruins of old **Fort Selden.**

The ruins of Isle Dernière, located across Terrebonnie Bay south of Houna (State 90), Terrebonne Pa., can be reached only by boat. It was used by pirates and privateers in the 1700s and numerous tales of buried treasure are associated with the site. During the first half of the nineteenth century the island was a fashionable resort for the rich of New Orleans until it was totally destroyed in September 1856 by a hurricane. Modern treasure hunters have been having good success finding nineteenth-century coins and artifacts, but none of the pirate treasure has been found yet.

Jefferson Island has been known as Cate Carlin, Miller's Island, and Orange Island. Actually it isn't even an island but rather a salt dome located nine miles west of New Iberia, State 90, St. Martin Pa. Numerous ruined settlements from the eighteenth and nineteenth centuries are in the vicinity. Legend has it that the island was one of Jean Lafitte's treasure storehouses. In 1923 a man named Daynite unearthed about $25,000 in Mexican silver coins of the early 1800s while digging a culvert.

The ruins of Niblett's Bluff are on the Sabine River about five miles west of Vinton, County 109, Calcasieu Pa. Once a prosperous river port, it became a Confederate stronghold during the Civil War until an epidemic decimated the residents. Confederate soldiers camped in the area in May 1863 and the town was completely abandoned. Only the old church is still standing but the ruins of many buildings and the Confederate breastworks remain.

The ghost town of Kernan is located ten miles north of Gillis near the intersection of County 7 and 171, Beauregard Pa. Only the church and schoolhouse are still standing in this former lumber boomtown.

Lafitte Village is located about 21 miles south of Marrero at the southern end of County 30, Lafourche Pa. Strung along the six-mile stretch between the Lafitte Post Office and Lafitte Village are several unnamed ghost towns. Lafitte Village was originally founded by pirates and used by them for over 150 years. It has been the scene of a great deal of treasure hunting—some very successful. Local tradition has it that in the general area of the cemetery where he now rests, two miles south of the town, Jean Lafitte buried $1 million in treasure.

The ruins of Lincecum are located on the Mississippi River near Dupont, Pointe Coupee Pa. It was once an important lumber town but very few of its buildings can still be seen. Local lore has it that a great amount of gold was buried in the area by returning California miners during an Indian attack in which all miners were massacred.

The town of Longville is on State 171 about fifteen miles south of De Ridder, Beauregard Pa. Founded as a lumber town in 1906, four years later it had over 2,000 residents; today fewer than 100 people live among the many old buildings still standing.

The ruins of Old Athens are located two and a half miles west of the present town of Athens, County 9, Claiborne Pa. The town was founded in 1833 but almost entirely destroyed by fire in 1849. Today only a church, two cemeteries, and the ruins of a few old buildings mark the site.

The ruins of Point Pleasant are on Bayou Bartholemew, a swampy area near Bastrop, County 139, Morehouse Pa. It was an important steamboat landing until destroyed by fire in 1875.

The three towns of Port Hudson are at the junction of Thompson Creek with the Mississippi River, about five miles west of Plains, State 61 and 65, Catahoula Pa. The original town was a river trading post dating from the early 1800s. Floods caused it to be moved at least twice, so that three different towns of the same name exist close by one another. It was a Confederate Civil War outpost until 1863. There are hundreds of ruined buildings in the area and three other ghost towns within a few miles radius: **Alto, Port Hickey,** and **Thompson's Creek.**

The town of Quebec is on the Tonsas River and State 80 about six miles west of Tallulah, Madison Pa. Quebec was a busy steamboat landing until Union troops destroyed it during the Civil War. Only 35 residents now live among the hundreds of ruined buildings.

The ghost town of Ramsey is four miles north of Covington on County 437, Tammany Pa. Only a few buildings are now standing in this once important lumber town.

The ruins of St. Maurice Landing are on the Mississippi River about six miles west of New Roads near County 1, Pointe Coupee Pa. It was a booming river town in the early 1800s; however most of it was covered by mud during flooding, so that only the ruins of a few buildings are now visible. Low tide exposes the remains of the iron passenger steamer **J. M. White** which caught fire in 1886 with the loss of 80 lives. Many artifacts have been found on her in recent years.

The ruins of Village des Chapitoles are on the west side of a levee between the town of Southport and State 90, about five miles west of New Orleans. It was built by the French in the late 1600s and should produce some very interesting early artifacts.

A farmer named Holt died in 1963; although he was known to be worth several hundred thousand dollars, he had no use for banks. It is believed that he concealed a large amount of money somewhere on his farm, located about five miles northwest of **Vivian,** County 1, Caddo Parish.

The Hubbard Treasure is alleged to consist of about $90,000 in gold buried in the vicinity of Ivan, County 160, Bossier Parish.

During the 1930s the owner of the present J. B. Hawk Plantation, located near **Athens,** County 9, Claiborne Pa., is known to have hidden a large amount of paper currency in the woods behind his home.

During the Civil War a band of Confederate refugees being pursued by Union troops buried about $20,000 in silver and gold coins at Old Camp Place, about ten miles west of **Monroe,** Quachita Pa. Two more tales about hidden treasure by another group of Confederate refugees describe burying $150,000 in the same area and a third treasure being concealed on nearby Limerick Plantation.

Around 1900 a farmer named Evans buried several large fruit jars full of ten- and twenty-dollar gold coins on his farm about three miles east of **Baskins,** County 128, Franklin Pa.

The ruins of the Frisby Plantation are located just north of County 4 about midway between Newellton and New Light, Tensas Pa. With a large number of Union troops approaching the plantation during the Civil War, Colonel Norman Frisby loaded two wagons with over $1 million in treasure, including an immense silver bell he had cast from 200 pounds of silver coins. Somewhere in the marshland south of the ruined manor house he concealed all of this treasure. He was killed soon after while trying to prevent his property from being destroyed by the Union soldiers.

The famous Red River Treasure reportedly consists of about $2 million in gold bullion buried on the banks of the Red River in the vicinity of Coushatta, State 71, Red River Pa.

A few days before the Union troops arrived and sacked the town of **Grand Ecore,** four miles north of Natchitoches, many of the town's residents buried their family treasures along the banks of the Red River. Unfortunately for them, the river overflowed destroying the markers of the hiding places. Many other caches are believed to be buried right in Grand Ecore. Most of the residents died during a yellow fever epidemic in 1853 and the sites of their buried hoards were lost. In 1852 a famous gambler concealed a chest full of gold coins in a bluff overlooking the Red River near the town. He was killed in a saloon brawl soon after. In this same general vicinity the Murrell outlaw gang are believed to have buried treasures amounting to a total of $30 million.

Natchitoches suffered severe damages during the Civil War from raids made by both sides.

186

Old people still tell of countless treasures having been buried during this period and never recovered. The two most interesting stories concern a chest of gold being buried on the old Metoyer Plantation and another large cache of gold being hidden on the Simmons House property in the city itself.

Fallen Springs Campsite is several miles east of Toleda Bend Reservoir about four miles south of Many, County 6, Sabine Pa. During the early nineteenth century it was a popular campsite along the Nolan Trace and a favorite place for bandits to attack and rob unwary travelers. Many small caches of treasure are known to be buried in the area.

In a pine forest a few miles northeast of **Winnfield,** County 156, Winn Pa., eight mule loads of Spanish gold bullion are reported to have been buried during the eighteenth century.

In the Georgetown Area on the northeastern corner of the Kisatchee National Forest, County 500, Grant Pa., are a number of alleged treasures. Various travelers under Indian attack are supposed to have buried their valuables here. During the Civil War two brass cannon filled with gold coins were dropped into nearby Lake Hull and several other treasures are alleged to have been buried on the fringes of this lake. During the Civil War over twenty large plantations in the area were destroyed; most have tales of hidden wealth associated with them.

Large numbers of Spanish silver coins have been found in Indian mounds at **Marksville** and **Bayou Manchac** about County 1, Avoyelles Pa. Nearby is the Marksville Prehistoric Indian Park.

During the Civil War the **U.S.S. Mississippi** sank off the northwest tip of **Profit Island** in the Mississippi River about twelve miles north of Baton Rouge. Treasure hunters have been finding many artifacts and coins from this wreck on the island.

A lost Indian gold mine is supposed to be on Wyndham Creek in Beauregard Pa.; nearby on the same creek near De Quincy in Calcasieu Pa. there is a **lost silver mine.**

Among the places where Jean Lafitte is alleged to have concealed treasure is in the neighborhood of **Starks,** County 12, Calcasieu Pa., about four miles east of the Sabine River.

In the same general area, except right on the river about three and a half miles east of the **Old Spanish Trail** near a grove of about 40 gum trees, Lafitte is alleged to have buried about $1 million in gold.

Another story has Lafitte burying loot near the site of the **Barbe House** on Shell Beach Drive, Contraband Bayou near Lake Charles, U.S. 10, Calcasieu Pa.

There are many tales about Jean Lafitte burying many different treasures up the Mermenteau and Calcasieu Rivers around Contraband Bayou. One of the most sought-after treasures is allegedly near a shell bank in **Lake Misere,** up the Mermenteau River, north of Cheniere Ridge, Cameron Parish

Another of Jean Lafitte's alleged treasures is now under **White Lake** north of the town of Pecan Island, Vermilion Parish.

Several large chests containing about $650,000 in gold and silver coins, the treasure of plantation owner Hippolyte Chretien, is buried somewhere on the grounds of the **Chretien Point Plantation** near Opelousas, State 190, St. Landry Parish.

Another great plantation treasure worth about a half million dollars in gold, plate, and jewels is alleged to be buried in the gardens of the **Fusilier de la Calire** mansion in Grand Coteau, State 167, St. Landry Pa. The fortune was buried during the Civil War and never recovered.

Still another and even larger plantation treasure is said to be among the ruins of the **Thibodeaux Plantation** near Breaux Bridge, County 31, St. Martin Pa. In the early nineteenth century the slaves revolted and killed all the white people on the plantation. They buried this treasure in the area before all were killed by irate white residents from the surrounding area.

During the Civil War a fortune of about $150,000 in gold coins was secreted on the **Pine Alley Plantation** near St. Martinsville, County 31, St. Martin Parish.

Numerous treasures were concealed in the vicinity of Baton Rouge during the Civil War. The best-documented one is somewhere on the **Conrad Plantation** and believed to consist of about $50,000 in gold coins, family plate, and jewelry.

During the Civil War a barge carrying about 100 iron cannon and a paychest for the Confederate Army was sunk near the mouth of the Tchefuncte River on the northern side of Lake Pontchartrain near **Madisonville,** Tammany Pa. The town of Madisonville was burnt to the ground by Union troops during the Civil War and a number of treasure caches are believed to be hidden amid the ruins of the many buildings. Just before the Union troops took New Orleans during the Civil War, some banks entrusted about $6 million in gold bullion and coins to several Confederate officers. They buried the gold somewhere on the **Walter C. Flowers Estate,** located about midway between Madisonville and Chinchuba, County 437, Tammany Pa. Within hours after burying this vast amount of treasure, all were killed in a skirmish with Union soldiers.

At least five different treasure caches are alleged to be buried on **Honey Island** on the Pearl River, near the town of Pearl River, State 59, Tammany Pa. The outlaw Calico Dick reportedly buried about two and a half million dollars in the middle of the island. The second largest cache consists of $450,000 in gold bullion buried by a Frenchman named Pierre Rameau. There must be some treasure on the island as gold and silver coins have been found in large numbers after the river floods.

Another Civil War cache of about $200,000 in silver and gold coins is alleged to be hidden among some Indian mounds near **Lutcher,** on the Mississippi River, St. James Parrish.

On the **Bonafice Plantation** on the north bank of the Mississippi River near Edgard, St. John the Baptist Pa., a cache of about $400,000 in gold bullion and coins is said to have been buried during the Civil War.

Large numbers of early-1800 French and Spanish gold and silver coins have been found on the beaches of **Lake Borgne** in the vicinity of Pte. aux Marchettes, near the eastern edge of New Orleans. The coins might be coming either from ships wrecked nearby or from several treasure caches known to be buried in the area.

An alleged treasure of $470,000 in gold, silver, and jewels is believed to be hidden in or around the perfectly preserved **Destrehan Plantation** manor house near New Orleans, which is now owned by the American Oil Company.

Countless treasures are alleged to have been buried in many of the old houses around **New Orleans.** Most of these were concealed by residents during the many enemy attacks on the city over the years. The most famous cache is supposed to consist of about $3 million in gold buried by the voodoo queen Marie Lavel before she retired in 1869. She owned many pieces of property on the shores of Lake Pontchartrain, but her treasure is believed to be hidden in her last residence at **1020 St. Ann Street.** Several other treasures are believed buried on the premises of the old New Orleans mint, including about $400,000 in gold bullion concealed by fleeing Confederate troops.

There are many tales about pirate treasures being buried on the **Chandeleur Islands** in the Gulf of Mexico, St. Bernard Pa. In 1942 a fisherman did find a cache of several thousand Spanish silver coins while digging for turtle eggs on the northernmost in this chain of islands. Coins have also been found on the beaches of nearby North and New Harbor Islands.

A pirate named Ballowe, a contemporary of Lafitte, is alleged to have buried about $260,000 in gold and silver coins in the vicinity of **Point a la Hache,** on the east side of the Mississippi River, County 39, Plaquemine Parish.

Of the many tales about Jean Lafitte burying treasure all over the state, those concerning his caches on **Grand Terre Island** located between Barataria Bay and the Gulf of Mexico are the most plausible. The pirate did use this island as base between 1803 and 1815, a period during which he captured over $7 million from the ships of many nations. The island had also been used by other eighteenth-century pirates as well as by Confederate privateers after the Union capture of New Orleans. On the island there are also ruins of several plantation manors which flourished after the Civil War and were abandoned by the early 1900s.

MAINE

The site of Fort Edgecomb is on Davis Island in the Sheepscot River, off U.S. 1 near Wiscasset, Sagadahoc Co. The fort was built in 1808 to protect the seaport of Wiscasset, at that time the most important shipping port north of Boston. No battles were fought there and today only the original blockhouse still stands.

Fort Kent is off State 11 about a mile southwest of Fort Kent, Aroostook Co. The fort was constructed in 1839 because of a border dispute with Canada but it never saw any action and was abandoned soon after. Today only the original blockhouse still remains.

Fort Halifax on U.S. 201 a mile south of the Winslow-Waterville Bridge in Kennebec County was established as an early warning post during the French and Indian War. The blockhouse built in 1754 still stands and may be the oldest in the country. The Arnold Expedition stopped here briefly in 1775.

The site of Fort Pownall is on the Penonscot River near U.S. 1 about three and a half miles from Stockton Springs. This wooden fort built in 1758 or 1759 served as an important Indian trading post. In March 1775 the British took all of its cannon and ammunitions during an attack and burnt the wooden fortifications. It was rebuilt by Patriots and destroyed when they retreated in 1779. Only the earthworks have survived.

Fort Western on the east bank of the Kennebec River just south of the City Hall in Augusta was the site of the New Plymouth Trading Post founded in 1626. A garrison dating from 1754 is now situated there and the ruins of the earlier constructions have also been built over. Very little of Fort Western can still be seen today.

Fort William State Memorial is located at the mouth of the Pemaquid River about a mile west of New Harbor. On this site a community was founded in about 1620 and achieved considerable importance. Around 1630 a stockade was built named **Fort Pemaquid** as a defense against pirates. In 1632 it was captured by the pirate Dixie Bull. In 1677 **Fort Charles,** another wooden structure, was built on the same site, but destroyed by Indians in 1689. In 1692 **Fort William Henry** was built and it was the largest and strongest stone fort in America at that time. The French attacked and totally leveled the fort in 1696. In 1729 another large stone compound, **Fort Frederick,** was built on the same site, but it was demolished by the Patriots to keep the British from using it during the Revolutionary War.

Fort Knox is on State 174 near its junction with U.S. 1, Neau Prospect, Aroostook Co. This granite fort was built in 1844 because of the border dispute with Canada, never saw any action and was garrisoned during the Civil and Spanish American Wars.

The St. Croix Island National Monument is in the St. Croix River on the Canadian border. In 1604 the French explorers Samuel de Champlain and Sieur de Monts founded the first European colony north of Florida on this site but after a disastrously bad winter the site was abandoned and the settlers moved to Port Royal, Nova Scotia. No traces of the original settlement remain.

After abandoning the colony on the St. Croix River some of the French colonists founded a new settlement on **Mount Desert Island** in Somes Sound, Hancock Co., but they were driven away by English settlers from Jamestown. The settlement has completely disappeared.

In 1607 English colonists led by Captain George Popham founded the first British settlement in New England, Popham Colony at Sabino Head, just west of Hunniwell's Point in Popham Beach State Park, about fifteen miles south of Bath, County 209, Sagadahoc Co. They first built a large, wood-revetted earthwork which they called **Fort St. George** and then constructed a church, a large storehouse, and fifteen homes for the 120 men. The colonists suffered a very harsh winter; their storehouse burned and their leader died, so they abandoned the site less than a year after it was founded. In 1775 the Patriots built **Fort Popham** at Hunniwell Point, consisting of a wooden blockhouse mounting several cannons, to be used mainly as an early warning station for British naval threats. During the Civil War another **Fort Popham** was built near the site of the former fort and it still stands today. Many early colonial and Civil War artifacts have been found on this beach area in recent years.

Near the small village of Kittery, U.S. 95, York Co., just across the state line from Portsmouth, New Hampshire, there are ruins of over 200 early colonial homes, several of which have been restored. The John Bray House built in 1662 is the oldest in the state. In 1715 **Fort Williams** was built just south of the town on State 103; on several occasions it was the scene of action against the British during the Revolution, but by 1803 no traces of it remained.

On the same site **Fort McClary** was built in 1809 and enlarged in 1844 but only the blockhouse has survived.

The Machias Bay area is located at the southeastern end of the state in Washington Co. The seaport of Machias was established as a trading post by the French and English in 1660 and in 1763 it was settled by Americans. There are many ruins of early colonial buildings in the surrounding area. In 1775 Americans built **Fort Machias** about five miles southeast of the port; during the Revolution it was used by privateers but saw no military action. About a mile to the east the Patriots also built **Fort O'Brien** in 1773, the scene of the first naval action of the Revolution on June 12, 1775 when the British routed the Patriots. It was garrisoned by the British from 1781 until 1785. During the War of 1812 Fort O'Brien was again captured by the British who burnt it down. Only the breastworks of this fort are still visible. The seaport of Machias was also haunted by many pirates, the most famous being Black Bellamy who built a wooden fort on the Machias River near the present bridge on State A1. Under his fort the pirate constructed an underground vault and kept a great deal of plunder in it, according to local legends. The fort has disappeared but the general area where it stood is known.

In the vicinity of **Whiting**, on U.S. 1, Washington Co., there are ruins of several hundred early colonial buildings dating back to the second half of the seventeenth century.

A large treasure of gold bullion and coins is supposed to have been buried by a pirate in the 1720s in the vicinity of Skowhegan Falls on the Kennebec River, at the fork of U.S. 201 and 201A, Somerset Co.

Monroe Island is a thickly wooded island on the west side of Penobscot Bay, Knox Co. Since it was used for many years as a base for privateers and rumrunners, there are reports of numerous treasures being buried on it. In 1884 the side-wheel steamer, **City of Portland,** was wrecked on the island and some of the survivors are alleged to have buried silver and gold coins.

Argy Point on the Kennebec River, off State 27, about two miles south of the Gardiner-Randolph Bridge, Kennebec Co., once had a large, flourishing shipyard that dated back to the late seventeenth century. On this same site in 1775 more than 200 bateaux were constructed for the Colonel Benedict Arnold Expedition which attacked British Canada. There are numerous ruins in this area spanning several centuries.

The path used by the Arnold Expedition from Argy Point to the Canadian Border is known as **Arnold's Trail.** Many markers indicate the campsites where 1,100 men camped each night during their two-month trek. Plenty of artifacts can be found in these areas. Part of the trail has since been covered by man-made lakes and reservoirs.

Fort George State Memorial is located in Castine on Penobscot Bay, Hancock Co. The French founded a settlement here in 1625 that they named Pentegoet, later changing it to Castine. The British acquired the site by the Treaty of 1760 but did not move in until 1779 when they began building **Fort George.** Soon after, the Patriots launched their largest amphibious operation of the Revolution. Captain Dudley Saltonstall led a force of 40 ships with 2,000 men to the fort. Just as the men began landing, an arriving British relief force totally destroyed the American flotilla; the troops ashore also suffered a resounding defeat. The British held the fort until 1783 and then took possession of it again during the War of 1812. It served as an important military center until the end of the war, when the British demolished it. Today all but the foundations of the fort are gone. However, the whole area is a favorite hunting ground for metal-detector addicts, as large numbers of artifacts are found along the beaches and in and around the present town of Castine.

A large hoard of pirate treasure is believed to be hidden on **Haskell Island,** off Harpswell Neck, Sagadahoc Co.

The pirate Edward Lowe is alleged to have buried a large Spanish treasure, taken from a rich galleon heading from Havana to Spain, on **Pond Island** in Casco Bay, Sagadahoc Co. Small caches of gold and silver Spanish coins have been found on the island over the years.

Another pirate hoard is believed to be buried on **Swan's Island** in the Kennebec River, Hancock Co.

A **lost Indian gold mine** is alleged to be located in the vicinity of Lead Mountain Ponds and Lead Mountain, Hancock Co.

Blackbeard the pirate is believed to have secreted a treasure on **Smuttynose Island** off York Co. In 1971 a treasure hunter discovered about 200 United States silver dollars from the late 1800s in a ceramic jar in the ruins of a house on the island.

A Portuguese seaman who settled in the area is reported to have hidden about $50,000 in gold and silver coins near the ruins of a late eighteenth-century tavern on the northern end of **St. John's Island** in Casco Bay. There are ruins of other colonial buildings all over this island.

The notorious Captain Kidd is reported to have no fewer than 45 buried treasures in this state. Most are located in the general vicinity of **Wiscasset,** Lincoln Co. Over the years several small caches of old silver and gold coins have been discovered in this general area.

Numerous pirate treasures are also reported to be hidden in and around the mouth of the Penobscot River in the general vicinity of **Bucksport,** U.S. 1, Hancock Co.

In 1899 a farmer actually found a hoard of about one and a half million dollars in gold coins and bullion and jewelry on **Deer Island,** Hancock Co. He only used a small part of his find and allegedly reburied the hoard somewhere on this same island when many persons began laying claim to the treasure.

Gold and silver coins have been found on the beaches near the village of **Frenchboro,** on Long Island in Jericho Bay. They probably came ashore from a shipwreck.

In 1743 the British warship **H.M.S. Astre** caught afire at the mouth of the Piscataqua River, which divides New Hampshire and Maine. The crew ran her aground at **Kittery Point,** opposite Portsmouth. She blew up, scattering debris all over the beach, including over 100,000 pounds sterling in gold and silver coins, many of which have been found over the years.

After strong northeasters many Spanish silver coins of the late 1700s can be found along the beach in the vicinity of **Fort Williams,** located a few miles south of Portland, County 77, Cumberland Co. Over the years many ships were wrecked near Fort Williams. In 1779 four American warships were run aground here to prevent their capture by the British and then set afire. Treasure hunters should be able to find coins and artifacts on the surrounding beaches, on the waterfront, and off the Portland Lighthouse.

MARYLAND

Baltimore was founded in 1729 and quickly became an important communications hub and seaport. A number of buildings from the colonial period have survived but most traces of the original town have been obliterated by the modern metropolis.

The Cresap's Fort Site near Oldtown on the Potomac River in Alleghany County appeared on many old colonial charts. It was established as a trading post in 1740 along a trail that was often used by the Indians and early settlers. George Washington spent four days here in 1748 while employed to do a survey for Lord Fairfax. Only the ruins of a stone chimney now mark this site.

The Lost Site of Fort Cumberland was on the Potomac River at Wills Creek in Alleghany County. The fort was built in 1750 and Washington served as commander for two years during the French and Indian War. But the place was never attacked and was finally abandoned in 1765. It was briefly occupied again in 1794 and this is the last we know of it. A town was laid out nearby in 1785, first called Washington Town and renamed Cumberland in 1787. It became the eastern terminus of the National Road, begun in 1811, through which many settlers passed on the way to the West. The town soon lost its importance with the coming of the railroads and the Chesapeake & Ohio Canal but still stands today. Ruins of early buildings can be found in the surrounding hills.

Fort Frederick is on the Potomac River off U.S. 40, five miles south of Clear Springs in Washington County. The stone fort was constructed in 1756 and garrisoned until 1763, the end of the colonial wars. During the Revolutionary War the Patriots used it as a prison camp. The fort was also garrisoned during the Civil War.

Wilderness treasure sites may be romantic places to hunt, but many hobbyists enjoy searching in their nearest local playground.

The light weight and excellent balance of modern metal detectors permit hobbyists to hunt for and find treasure all day with little fatigue.

Head of Elk is so called because it is at the head of the Elk River which empties into the Chesapeake Bay. In August 1777 a British military force used this site as a base for their attacks on Philadelphia and other settlements. In 1780 it was also used as a military base by the Patriots and the French. The site is a short distance south of Elkton and U.S. 40.

Port Tobacco on the Port Tobacco River in Charles County was marked on Captain John Smith's map of 1612 as the place where a number of early settlers built homes and plantations. Around the time of the Revolution the port was an important trading center, but by 1800 the harbor had silted up and the settlement faded away. No remains of this ghost town can be found today.

St. Mary's City, on the St. Mary's River in St. Mary's County was the first important city and capital of the state, founded in 1633 as a haven for persecuted English Catholics. In 1694 the seat of government was passed to Annapolis. The structures of at least 60 of its seventeenth-century brick buildings have been identified and many more are located in the surrounding forests. It is considered one of the most important undisturbed archaeological sites of seventeenth-century America. In 1639 **Governor's Castle,** a fort which covered some 3,000 square feet was built in the town but it was totally destroyed a few years later by an accidental explosion of gunpowder stored in the fort. Nothing is left of it today.

Annapolis, on the south banks of the Severn River near its mouth on the Chesapeake was called Providence when first settled by Puritans from Virginia in 1649. Later the name was changed and it was known as Anne Arundel Town until 1708. In the city are many colonial buildings and ruins with numbers of nautical relics to be found along the river banks.

Fort McHenry is three miles from the city limits of Baltimore via East Fort Avenue, strategically located at the entrance to Baltimore's inner harbor. The defenders of the fort bravely resisted a devastating 25-hour bombardment by the British in September 1814, preventing the British from capturing the city after the burning of Washington. During the bombardment over 1,800 shells, rockets, and bombs were fired against the fort, but they had little effect. It has been an active military post ever since and has recently been restored.

Greenbrier State Park is on U.S. 40, ten miles southeast of Hagerstown, Washington Co. The famous Battle of South Mountain was fought here and in the surrounding area on September 14, 1862. In the conflict 20,000 Confederate troops were led to victory by General Robert E. Lee against 25,000 Union troops under General George B. McClellan; close to 6,000 men fell dead or wounded.

Piscataway National Park is across the Potomac River from Mount Vernon, Georges Co. The site was inhabited by Archaic Indians as early as 3000 B.C., later the Piscataway Indians lived here from the fourteenth to eighteenth centuries. Fort Washington was erected on the site in 1809 as the first fortification to defend the nation's capital, but during the War of 1812 it was completely destroyed by the British. The second fort of this name was built in 1824 and still stands today.

Antietam Battlefield is northeast of Sharpsburg on State 34 and 65, Washington Co. The engagement fought here on September 16–17, 1862 was the bloodiest battle of the Civil War and the Union victory marked its turning point. During the battle 12,410 Union and 10,700 Confederate troops were killed or wounded. Today more than 200 markers show where various actions of the battle occurred. Scuba divers have recently reported finding large numbers of weapons and other artifacts from this battle in Antietam Creek.

The Hampton National Historic site is just off State 146 near Towson, Baltimore Co. This area was settled around 1770 and a number of large plantations were established. Today one can see many ruins of these plantations and other colonial buildings.

Point Lookout State Park, off Route 5 where the Potomac River empties into Chesapeake Bay, St. Marys Co., has remnants of early colonial buildings. It was the site of Camp Hoffman where more than 20,000 Confederate prisoners were detained between 1863 and 1865. Because of its inadequate medical facilities more than 3000 of them died. Treasure hunters have found many items here.

During the Civil War over $100,000 in gold coins was buried along the banks of the Monocacy River about two miles south of **Frederick,** near County 144, Frederick Co.

In 1832 a guest buried a chest containing $38,000 in gold coins and jewels in the vicinity of old **Hagan's Tavern** located about midway between Braddock and Braddock Heights on State 40, Frederick Co.

A lost Indian silver mine is located on Rattlesnake Hill near Silver Run, State 140, Carroll Co. Many attempts have been made to locate this mine, which was lost around 1800. Silver Run was so named because an early settler found about 500 pounds of silver ore while digging a well on his farm site.

Around 1800 a wealthy French merchant named Jacques Champlaine is alleged to have buried a large chest containing about $150,000 in gold coins on his farm property near **Catonsville** close to old Frederick Road just outside of Baltimore.

On the premises of the **Old Mansion Home** located in northwest Baltimore, there is supposed to be a buried treasure of gold coins worth about $65,000.

Although there is no historical proof that Captain Kidd ever visited the area, he is supposed to have buried a cache in **Druid Hill Park** in Baltimore. Many persons have searched for it unsuccessfully.

A pirate named Jake Hole is reported to have buried about $200,000 in plunder on the south bank of the Choptank River in the vicinity of **Lodgecliffe,** about three miles northwest of Cambridge, Dorchester Co.

In the vicinity of the **Old Friends Meeting House,** a mile or so east of Easton, Talbot Co., a cache of about $50,000 in gold coins was buried during the Revolution.

The notorious murderess and slave trader Patty Cannon hid several caches of gold coins valued at around $100,000 on the **Harold Smith farm** in Reliance on County 677, a few miles southeast of Federalsburg on the Sussex and Caroline County Line. Before committing suicide in 1829, she left a will where she mentioned burying the treasures. Patty Cannon also owned a tavern on the Nanticoke River near the village of Riverton, County 313, Wicomico Co., and is believed to have buried other treasures on these premises.

The Poor House Treasure is alleged to consist of about $30,000 in gold coins concealed somewhere in the ghost town of Plaindealing, located two miles east of Hurtock, County 331, Caroline Co.

According to legends, various pirates have buried plunder at an eighteenth-century building called **Cellar House,** on U.S. 113 about midway between Berlin and Snow Hill, Worchester Co.

A well-documented pirate hoard valued around $2 million lies hidden on **Assateague Island,** south of Ocean City, Worchester Co. The cache, buried in the eighteenth century by the pirate Charles Wilson, consists of ten iron-bound chests containing a huge amount of treasure pirated from a Spanish treasure galleon in the Caribbean. His directions to find the hoard are: "Ye treasure lies hidden in a clump of trees near 3 creeks lying 100 paces or more north of the 2nd inlet above Chincoteague Island [in Virginia]." This would put the site in the region of Woody Knoll on the southern end of the island close to the Virginia State line.

During the Civil War a large treasure was hidden in or near the manor house of the **Resurrection Plantation** near the tiny village of Kingston, County 413, Somerset Co.

Also during the Civil War another large treasure was hidden somewhere on the premises of the **Croissant Mansion** near California, County 235, St. Marys Co.

In 1689 the English warship **H.M.S. Deptford** was wrecked on **Cedar Island** in Chesapeake Bay. After storms, parts of the ship are exposed on the beach at the southern tip of the island.

Around the northwestern tip of **Bloodsworth Island** in the Chesapeake, large numbers of French and Dutch silver coins dating from 1765 to 1783 are found along the beaches after storms. The timbers of an old wooden sailing ship are occasionally visible in the same area at low tide.

On the western side of tiny **Holland Island,** about five miles south of Bloodsworth Island in the northern Chesapeake, fishermen have reported finding many Dutch silver and gold coins from the late 1700s. It is possible the island was named Holland because of a Dutch ship being wrecked there, or possibly because the Dutch may have had an early settlement on the island.

MASSACHUSETTS

Deerfield on County 5, Franklin Co., first settled in 1669, was the early northwest frontier of New England and the target of numerous French and Indian attacks. During King Philip's War, the Bloody Brook Massacre in 1675 caused the town to be evacuated and it remained deserted for seven years. Then in the Great Deerfield Massacre of 1704, the majority of the residents were killed by Indians and most of the town burnt down. Most of the surviving colonial buildings date from after 1750. There are several treasures from early colonial times in and around the town.

Martha's Vineyard Island was permanently settled in 1642 and the ruins of many old colonial structures dot the island. During the nineteenth century it was an important whaling center and over the centuries several hundred ships are known to have been wrecked on the island's beaches, which makes it a treasure hunters' paradise. Large numbers of English silver coins from the late 1700s are found on the beach off Edgartown Great Pond.

Nantucket Island located east of Martha's Vineyard off Cape Cod was settled by persons fleeing religious persecution on the mainland about 1650. It quickly developed into an important maritime center. By 1768 over 175 whaling ships were based here and there are numerous vestiges of old sailing ships on the beaches near Long Pond, Siaaconset, and Wauwinet. Coins and various types of maritime artifacts are found along the beaches in Nantucket Harbor, especially off the seaport itself.

New Bedford on Apponagansett Bay was founded in 1760 and quickly became an important shipping center. From 1820 until the Civil War it was the nation's main whaling port and at times over 10,000 seamen were employed in this business. Ruins of many colonial buildings can still be seen, especially around the waterfront area, where the bones of numerous old hulks stick out of the muddy sea floor.

Plymouth Rock on Plymouth Bay is the site of the first English settlement in New England, founded in 1620. Of the 102 persons who landed here, more than half died during the first winter. A full-scale replica of the settlement in 1627 can be seen on Plymouth Plantation. No traces of the original settlement remain.

Bash-Bish Falls is located near Mount Washington, in the southwest corner of the state, Berkshire Co.; the Mohegan Indians are known to have buried a number of rich treasures during the seventeenth century which they accumulated through raids on the early colonial settlements.

In 1644 the first successful ironworks in the nation was established on the Saugus River near **Lynn,** about ten miles northeast of Boston, Essex Co. If the exact site of this famous works were known, it could produce many interesting seventeenth century relics.

During a hurricane on November 12, 1714, the British warship **H.M.S. Hazard** was totally destroyed leaving no survivors when she was thrown ashore about 300 yards from the beach at **Green Harbor,** about five miles north of Gurnet Point on Plymouth Bay. She was carrying over £100,000 sterling in gold coinage at the time, most of which was lost under the sands. Over the years many finds of these coins have been made in the area but a great deal more is waiting to be found.

Stockbridge on County 102, Norfold Co., was founded in 1734. During the French and Indian War the town was raided and burnt to the ground. Prior to the attack the residents, most of whom were massacred, buried all of their valuables. The present town dates from after 1850 as most of the town was accidentally burnt down in 1849.

Old Salem, located midway between Boston and Gloucester, was settled in 1626 and soon became an important port. During both the French and Indian and Revolutionary Wars it was an important privateering base and later on gained world fame as a whaling port. Many colonial buildings have been preserved and there are ruins of many others in the surrounding area. Vestiges of old sailing ships can be seen on the nearby beaches. At Marblehead close by, treasure hunters have been finding large numbers of late eighteenth-century English and Spanish silver coins.

The lost village of Menotomy is hidden under the ground in Menotomy Rick Park, midway between Boston and Lexington. It was founded in the early 1700s and during the Revolution a number of major battles occurred in the immediate vicinity. How the large settlement disappeared without a trace is a real mystery.

In **Boston** are a large number of colonial and Revolutionary War sites with great potential for the modern treasure hunter. This is true despite the fact that the waterfront area has been altered beyond recognition, the site of the Boston Tea Party is now covered with land fill, modern buildings are erected on the famed Necks of Boston and Charleston, and the old shoreline of Cambridge has been altered by the river changing its course.

Boston Common is the same 50-acre plot that was purchased by the original colonists in 1634 from William Blackstone, the first settler of the city. Unfortunately all the stones and bricks used in the early colonial buildings that stood on the Common were fitted into many of the structures of the present city. However, treasure hunters have had great success finding colonial artifacts as well as modern coins and objects on the Commons.

Castle William was on Castle Island, now the tip of a peninsula in South Boston. It was well-fortified and was used in the defense of the harbor entrance for a period prior to the Revolution. The structure served as a refuge for the British authorities during periods of trouble and later was used to garrison British troops until they evacuated Boston. The Patriots then named the place **Fort Independence;** its first commander in 1778–1779 was Paul Revere. A new fort was built on the same site in 1801, abandoned in 1880 and is now in ruins.

Copp's Hill was one of Boston's original three hills along with Beacon Hill and Fort Hill. A windmill was built here as early as 1632; the site served as a burial ground from 1659 on; and during the battle of Bunker Hill the British bombarded Charlestown from here, accidentally setting off fires that destroyed most of the town. Vestiges of the early buildings remained until 1807 when the hill was cut down several feet to fill in Mill Pond. Boston also suffered from numerous fires over the years with the result that very few old colonial buildings survived. Yet it is still possible to find coins and artifacts of the colonial and later periods in vacant lots and other areas in the present city.

Bunker Hill Monument, the site of the famous Revolutionary battle, has had its original topography severely altered by the grading of the hills, land fills, and high-density urbanization in such a way that all the original landmarks have been obliterated. Despite these changes it is still a favorite target of treasure hunters in the Boston area and many interesting finds are constantly being made.

Cambridge Township originally contained several separate villages—Arlington, Brighton, Lexington, and Newton. It was first named New Towne but became Cambridge in 1638. The campus of Harvard University, founded in 1636, now occupies much of the original site and many colonial artifacts are discovered whenever new construction is begun in the area. The only surviving earthwork of the ten-mile network built in Cambridge and Charleston during the siege of Boston in 1775–1776 is a three-gun battery in Fort Washington Park. Cambridge Township was originally located on the riverbank, but because the river changes its course, the site is now hidden several hundred yards behind the M.I.T. campus.

Concord, founded in 1635, was one of the first two Massachusetts settlements set in from the coast; the other was Dedham. There are numerous ruins from the colonial period and earthworks from the Revolution.

In **Lexington** and its surrounding area are many traces of early colonial buildings and sites of Revolutionary skirmishes.

Minute Man National Historical Park near Lexington in Concord County contains many landmarks of the running battle that started the American Revolution on April 19, 1775. These sites are unspoiled and look very much as they did in 1775. In 1973 a treasure hunter discovered several swords and muskets from this period.

After storms many early colonial artifacts and numbers of British brass coins are found on the beach east of Orleans, State 6, on the eastern side of Cape Cod. They are believed to be coming ash re from the **Sparrow Hawk,** which was carrying settlers and supplies in 1624 when she was wrecked during a bad northeaster.

The pirate ship of the notorious Captain Black Sam Bellamy, the **Whidah,** was wrecked near

Wellfleet on the eastern side of Cape Cod during a bad storm in 1717. Only one of her crew of 102 survived. At the time the vessel was carrying over $200,000 in plunder which the pirates had taken from Spanish ships in the Caribbean. Many gold and silver coins have washed ashore from this wreck over the centuries.

Lynn Beach about twelve miles northeast of Boston is a well-known treasure-hunting area which produces large numbers of old coins and artifacts, especially during the rough winter months. Numerous ships were wrecked here over the years. One of the richest was the English merchantman **Pembroke,** lost in 1766 carrying over £200,000 sterling in silver specie.

Cape Ann, a dangerous point of land projecting into the Atlantic a few miles northeast of Gloucester, has claimed its fair share of ships. Large amounts of coins—some dating from the mid-1600s—and artifacts are found on the beaches here.

During the months of January and February 1973, when the weather was very rough, large numbers of British gold and silver coins were found on the beach at **Race Point,** the northwestern tip of Cape Cod. Treasure hunters are known to have found thousands of these coins dating from the late eighteenth century—many lying completely exposed on the beach.

An unidentified pirate buried a large chest of plunder on the banks of the Hoosic River in **Cheshire,** County 8, Berkshire Co., shortly before being hanged in 1717. While attempting to locate this hoard the following year, a farmer discovered two iron kettles full of gold coins in the same area.

During the Revolution a band of Patriots attacked a Hessian supply train and made off with several chests of gold and silver coins which they buried somewhere on **Mount Amos,** a few miles northeast of Cheshire. They were all killed in a subsequent skirmish and the payroll was never located.

After the British defeat at Sarasota in 1777, a band of British soldiers spent several months raiding and plundering settlements in the northwestern corner of Massachusetts as well as in Vermont and New York. With a large band of Patriots closing in on them, they buried three wagonloads of plunder somewhere in the hills near **Dalton,** County 9, Berkshire Co.

The Black Grocery gang is said to have buried several years' accumulation of booty on **Mount Washington,** a few miles southeast of Pittsfield, Berkshire Co.

Captain Kidd is alleged to have buried a chest full of gold and jewels near **Turner Falls** on the Connecticut River, County 2, Franklin Co.

A pirate cache of gold bullion is supposed to be buried in a cave in the area of **South Hadley,** State 5, Hampshire Co.

During the eighteenth century a privateer captain concealed a large Spanish treasure at **Harbor Pond,** several miles east of Townsend, State 119, Middlesex Co.

The Old Fort Treasure is believed to consist of about $400,000 in gold and silver coins concealed near Shirley, County 111, Middlesex Co.

A well-documented hoard of about $100,000 in gold and silver coins is buried near the site of the old **Willard Tavern** in Shirley, Middlesex Co.

During the nineteenth century the Gorrill hermit brothers buried an undisclosed amount of treasure in or around **Tenney Castle** ruins on Danny Frye's Hill in Methuen, U.S. 90, Essex Co.

A large treasure was buried on the nineteenth-century farm site of a Thomas Smith, located on the east bank of the Assabet River in **Maynard,** County 62, Middlesex Co.

During the Revolution about $175,000 in British gold sovereigns was buried under a large rock marked with an "A" along the banks of the Parker River in **Byfield,** a bit west of the Blue Star Memorial Highway in Essex Co.

In 1704 the pirate Captain John Quelch is known to have buried a large cache of gold and silver coins on **Snake Island** in the Isle of Shoals chain, off Cape Ann. Treasure hunters have found small numbers of coins on this island, but with later dates.

The ghost town of Dogtown is located a bit west of Long Beach, about midway between Gloucester and Rockport on Cape Ann, Essex Co. The town was abandoned in 1830 and the ruins of several hundred buildings are still visible in a thickly wooded area. It is one of the favorite treasure-hunting spots in the state.

In 1658 the pirate Thomas Veale is believed to have concealed several chests of plunder near **Dungeon Rock Cave** at the mouth of the Saugus River near Lynn, Essex Co. Some accounts state that the treasure was hidden inside the cave, which was sealed by an earthquake.

In 1908 a bad fire destroyed most of the city of **Chelsea** on the northern side of Boston Harbor. It was a wealthy residential area and many hidden valuables and money were lost when the homes were destroyed. In 1921 a workman found about $50,000 in gold coins and silverware in a field around a ruined building on the southern side of the city.

Large numbers of Spanish and British eighteenth-century coins can be found on the beach between **Short Beach** and **Grover's Cliff** in Withrop on the northern side of Boston Harbor. They are probably being washed ashore from one of the many ships sunk in the harbor over the centuries.

The pirate Avery is alleged to have buried a chest of valuable diamonds and gold coins on **Gallop's Island** at the center of the entrance to Boston Harbor. Coins and wreckage have been found on the beaches here, probably from numerous ships wrecked on the tiny, rocky island.

During the late 1800s a fisherman found a large chest of gold coins on **Peddocks Island** in Boston Harbor. Since then many coins have been found scattered among the rocks on the shore by modern treasure seekers.

During the construction of Fort Warren on tiny **Georges Island** at the mouth of Boston Harbor, workmen found an undisclosed number of silver coins in several ceramic jars. The island is now a favorite spot to find lead shot and iron cannon balls which date from the Revolutionary War period.

In Quincy Bay, Boston Harbor divers have been finding thousands of old bottles in areas where ships anchored over the centuries. The best area to look is around the perimeter of **Hangman Island.** Many colonial artifacts have also been found on several wrecks in the area.

Several hoards of treasure are supposed to be hidden at **Money Bluff** on Deer Island in Boston Harbor. Coins dating from the mid-nineteenth century are found on the beaches.

Pirate treasures are said to be buried on **Castle Island, Grape Island, Little and Great Brewsters Island, Hog Island, and Swans Island**—all located in Boston Harbor. Another cache of pirate treasure is supposed to be hidden on the south shore of Boston Harbor at Nantauket Beach. Many bottles from the early nineteenth century wash ashore here during storms.

In 1932 a wealthy shoe manufacturer buried several caches of gold coins around his mansion in **Brockton** on the east side of Stonehill College off County 24, Norfolk Co.

During the Revolution a wealthy merchant concealed a large cache of gold coins and jewelry near **Watson Pond** near the outskirts of Taunton, State 44, Bristol Co. He died without revealing to his family its exact location.

MICHIGAN

The town of Bay Furnace stood off State 28 in the northwest Upper Peninsula between Au Train and Munising, Marquette Co. The community was founded in 1870 and became a busy iron-making center, but seven years later the whole town burnt down and only the remains of several iron furnaces can still be seen.

Beaver Island is located in upper Lake Michigan about 35 miles west of the Straits of Mackinac. The French had several settlements on the island as early as 1600 of which no traces remain. In 1847 a band of Mormons settled here and founded the village of St. James; many of its original buildings are still standing. In 1965 a treasure hunter found a chest of Spanish silver coins dating from the late eighteenth century on uninhabited **High Island** about ten miles west of Beaver Island.

Fort Wilkins is on U.S. 41, three miles east of Copper Harbor, Marquette Co. It was built in 1844 and occupied intermittently until 1870 mainly to protect the copper miners working this area from Indian attack. The fort was recently restored.

Drummond Island is located off the eastern tip of the Upper Peninsula between North Channel and the main body of Lake Huron. Remains of Fort Drummond, built by the British in 1815 and occupied by them from that date until 1828, are located on the western end of the island. Treasure hunters have found many artifacts on the parade ground and around the ruins of various fort buildings.

Norton Mound Group Park, located two miles south of Grand Rapids, is the site of seventeen mounds on the burial grounds of the Hopewell Indians who lived in the area from about 400 B.C. to 400 A.D. Archaeologists have done a considerable amount of excavation here and have found a great wealth of material.

Detroit was of great strategic importance from its founding date of 1701. **Fort Pontchartrain,** built by the French in 1701, was a stockaded village and fort about 200 feet square. After being enlarged three times during the 1750s, the fort was a formidable place; it was taken over by the British in 1760 and renamed **Fort Detroit.** The Americans captured it in 1779. Not far from this site, the British built another fort in 1778 and named it **Fort Lernault;** this was captured by the Americans in 1796 and renamed **Fort Shelby.** During the War of 1812 the fort was recaptured by the British. In 1826 it was leveled to make way for the expanding city; its site is now occupied by the Federal Building in downtown Detroit. It was located between Griswold and Shelby Streets, just south of present Jefferson Avenue.

Fort St. Joseph. In 1686 the French built the first fort of this name near the modern town of Niles in Berrien County and used it mainly as a fur trading post. Two years later it was destroyed by fire and abandoned. The new fort was built somewhere in the present city of Port Huron in 1697 and turned over to the British in 1763. After the British had attacked the Spanish settlement on the site of St. Louis, Missouri, the Spaniards countered by attacking this fort in 1781, capturing and holding it for only 24 hours.

The Straits of Mackinac, on the western end of Lake Huron, Mackinac Island, were settled in 1671 by French Jesuit missionaries as the first mission in this part of the world. The mission was moved the following year to the mainland on the north side of the straits between Lakes Huron and Michigan, where the city of St. Ignace now stands. The fort they built was named **Fort de Buade,** then changed to **Fort Michilimackinac.** In 1698 the French abandoned the area, returned again in 1715 and built the second **Fort Michilimackinac** on the south side of the straits near Mackinaw City. This site was taken over by the British in 1761; two years later they suffered a severe Indian attack. In 1781 the British abandoned the fort and moved to Mackinac Island to begin building a new fort, which was not finished when they withdrew from the area in 1796. During the War of 1812 the British occupied the position again for a brief time. As soon as they left, it became the headquarters of the American Fur Co.

The abandoned Ropes Gold Mine is located three miles northeast of Ishpeming and the **abandoned Michigan Gold Mine** is situated two and a half miles west of this same city in Marquette Co.

Long before white men arrived, Indians were doing placer gold mining in the upper peninsula Iron Range and also on the western shores of Lake Michigan. Early white settlers also found this occupation lucrative. The best areas to find placer gold are: near Allegain in Allegain Co.; on the Antrim River in Charlevoix Co.; on the Boyne River in Emmet Co.; near the town of Walton and on the Rapid River in Kalkaska Co.; on the Little Sable and Manistee Rivers in Manistee Co.; near Howard City and Greenville in Montcalm Co.; on the Muskegon River in Newaygo Co.; near the town of Whitehall and on the White River in Oceana Co.; near Grand Haven in Ottawa Co.; near the towns of Burr Oak and Marcellus in St. Joseph Co.; and near West Summit in Wexford Co. The ruins of numerous dwellings built and used by the early white prospectors can be seen in some of the above mentioned areas.

The Lost Indian Gold Mine is located somewhere in Porcupine Mountain State Park on the upper peninsula near Silver City, County 64, Ontonagan Co. When the first white settlers reached the area the Indians were wearing necklaces of large gold nuggets and used large amounts of gold to trade for European goods.

The Lost Jack Driscoll Silver Mine is on the upper peninsula in the Huron Mountains near Ishpeming, State 41, Marquette Co.

The Lost Douglas Houghton Gold Mine is in the vicinity of Log Lake, near Champion, State 41, Marquette Co.

The ruins of the Ropes Gold Mine Camp are located about a mile north of Ishpeming. It was in operation until 1879 and produced several million dollars in gold during its last decade of operation.

In 1905 a cache of about $100,000 in Spanish gold and silver coins was found on **North Fox Island,** off Grand Traverse Bay in Lake Michigan. More treasure is alleged to be buried on the island.

After the Great Chicago Fire of 1871 a band of looters are reported to have buried several million dollars in treasure, taken from several banks, at **Cat Head Point** near Northport, County 201, Leelanau Co. Several hundred American gold coins from the mid-nineteenth century were found by a treasure hunter near Government Lighthouse, about two miles northeast of Cat Head Point.

A large cache of Spanish gold and silver coins is supposed to be buried on **Espanore Island** off the southwestern end of Drummond Island on Lake Huron, Chippewa Co. Many ruins of late seventeenth- and eighteenth-centuries buildings stand on Drummond Island. Before fleeing in 1812, General Monk, who was in command of the British garrison on Drummond Island, buried a large iron chest containing army funds near the fort on the southwest tip of the island. A cache of about $50,000 in gold coins is also alleged to be concealed at Potagannissing Bay on the northwestern end of the island.

A wealthy' farmer named Henry Dansman hid a large hoard of diamonds and silver and gold coins on his farm, which is between **Lake Augusta** and the village of **Posen,** County 65, Presque Isle Co.

About $11 million in paper currency and gold coins is known to be hidden in or around the **House of David Mansion** in Benton Harbor, State 33, Berrien Co. When the founder of the religious sect that used the property was dying he reported burying the cache but did not give a precise location.

On Bridgman Beach, located about ten miles southwest of the town of **St. Joseph** on Lake Michigan, State 94, Berrien Co., gold coins and many bottles are washed ashore during storms. They are believed to be from the Steamer **Chicora** which sank in this area in 1895, carrying a cargo of silver ingots, whiskey, and about $50,000 in gold coins.

Before Hodson Burton died in 1926 he is known to have buried a large cache of gold coins and paper currency on his farm near the outskirts of **Buchanan,** about 2 miles north of State 12 in the southeast corner of Berrien Co.

Prior to his death in 1890 a rich merchant named Ransom Dopp is known to have secreted a large fortune in or near his home which is still standing and located about 5 miles east of **Dowagiac,** County 62, Cass Co.

A rich farmer named Godfrey Watson is known to have concealed his life savings some place on his farm site located two miles north of the village of **Tecumseh,** County 50, Lenawee Co.

MINNESOTA

The ruins of Fort Ridgely are located off State 4, about seven miles south of Fairfax, Renville Co. Built adjacent to a Sioux Reservation in 1853, the fort played an important role in the Dakota War of 1862. It withstood a long Indian siege in August that year and soon afterwards the fort was abandoned and fell into ruin. Only the commissary and magazine have been restored.

Grand Portage National Monument is located off U.S. 61, 38 miles from Grand Marais, Cook County. This portage of the "great carrying place" as it was called, connected the interior waterway network of western Canada with the Great Lakes and was a principal route of explorers, missionaries, fur traders, and eighteenth-century military expeditions. Before the arrival of the white men, Indians used this nine-mile trail, which extended from the navigable waters of the Pigeon River to the western end of Lake Superior. The portage was discovered by a French explorer in 1732 and was soon being used by large numbers of French voyageurs carrying furs from the Canadian northwest to the eastern markets. From 1778 until 1803 the British Northwest Company of Montreal had their headquarters here, along with a town named Grand Portage, the first settlement in Minnesota, later abandoned. Many vestiges of the settlement and warehouses can still be seen.

Old Mendota is located at the confluence of the Minnesota and Mississippi Rivers, Hubbard Co. The tiny village is the oldest permanent settlement in the state, having been started as a trading-post village in the 1820s by the American Fur Co. Today some of the original buildings are still in existence and there are many ruins of others. Several miles away off State 5 and 55 is **Fort Snelling**, built in 1819 as the northwestern link in the chain of forts connecting the Missouri River to Lake Michigan. The fort was garrisoned until the end of the Civil War when hostilities with the local Sioux and Chippewa Indians ceased. Only the round tower has survived of the original fort.

Kathio Site Park is located on the west side of Mille Lac Lake, off U.S. 169 near Vineland, Mille Lac Co. From prehistoric times until around 1740 this site as well as numerous others around the lake was the ancestral home of the Sioux Indians. French explorers visited the area in the 1600s and in about 1700 the Chippewa Indians began encroaching on the region. In a decisive three-day battle fought in 1745 the Sioux routed the Chippewa and forced them to move into other areas.

On August 12, 1893 a devastating fire destroyed a great number of homes in **Minneapolis** and property damages were estimated at between $2 and $5 million. The ruins of some of the buildings destroyed can be seen in the eastern section of the city and they are one of the favorite treasure hunting spots in the area.

On September 1, 1894 a fire broke out in **Hinckly**, State 35, Pine Co. Spread by hurricane-force winds, it killed over 500 people and destroyed every home in the town before spreading and destroying eighteen neighboring towns. More than 2,000 buildings were burnt; there were many personal valuables among the ruins of these homes.

The ruins of Buchanan are located ten miles south of Two Rivers on Lake Superior, State 61, Lake Co. The town boomed briefly during the mid-nineteenth century and then was abandoned.

The ghost town of Concord is three miles east of West Concord on County 57, Dodge Co. When the Great Western Railroad bypassed it, the residents abandoned Concord to found the town of West Concord. Many buildings from the late 1800s are still standing.

The ghost town of Forestville is on the South Branch River about five miles south of Spring Valley, County 80, Fillmore Co. It was founded in 1855 and abandoned shortly after the Civil War. A large store and several other buildings are still standing, as well as the ruins of a school, stage station, and other buildings.

The ruins of Frontenac are located off State 61 near the town of Moose Lake, Carlton Co. It was abandoned in the 1870s when the railroads bypassed it and today in Frontenac are the ruins of about 100 old buildings.

The ruins of High Forest are located about two miles southwest of Stewartville, State 90, Olmsted Co. A large flag staff marks the community, which was abandoned before 1900.

The ghost town of Itasca is located two and a half miles north of Albert Lea, State 16, Freeborn Co. Only the old schoolhouse and several homes remain.

The ruins of La Prairie are on the Mississippi River about one mile east of Grand Rapids, State 2, Itasca Co. Only the streets of this town survive since all of the wooden buildings burnt down around 1890. Treasure hunters have found several caches of gold and silver coins in this area in recent years.

The ruins of London, about 44 miles north of Schroder in the northern section of the Superior National Forest, Cook Co., can be reached only by horseback. Several other abandoned logging camps are in the general area.

The ghost town of Lothrop, near Ten Mile Lake and Hackensack, Ottertail Co., was abandoned in 1895. When the railroad bypassed the town over 2,000 residents moved elsewhere. About 100 of the old buildings are still standing.

The ghost town of Mantorville is on the Mid Bridge River about three miles north of

Kasson, County 57, Dodge Co. A few farmers still live on the outskirts of the town. It was abandoned in the late 1800s when the Great Western Railroad bypassed it. About 200 old buildings are still standing.

The ruins of Metropolisville are located on the Cannon River two miles south of Northfield, County 3, Rice Co. The town flourished for a few years during the mid-nineteenth century but today only the foundations of a few buildings remain.

The ghost town of Nininger is on the Mississippi River about three miles west of Hastings and two miles north of County 55, Dakota Co. It had about 500 residents until being abandoned in 1860 because of the town bank going bankrupt.

The ruins of Otter Tail City are located near the mouth of the Otter Tail River at the extreme northeastern end of Otter Tail Lake, a bit south of Perham, County 78, Otter Tail Co. It was an important trading center in the mid-1800s but was abandoned around 1875; now a wheat field covers most of the ruins.

The ruins of Pelan are on the South Fork of Two Rivers, midway between Greenbush and Karlstad, County 11, Roseau Co. Only the foundations of one building and a few wooden boardwalks remain.

The town of Red Rock is on the Mississippi River between St. Paul and Hastings, State 61, Washington Co. It was an early trading center founded about 1820; today only a small number of people live among the ruins of many nineteenth-century homes.

The ghost town of Sacramento is close to Mantorville in Dodge Co. The town boomed and fell quickly after a promoter salted the banks of the nearby Zumbro River with gold dust. Only the tavern and several other buildings still stand.

The ghost town of St. Lawrence is on the Minnesota River near the outskirts of Jordan, County 169, Scott Co. It was founded in 1857 in anticipation of a land boom that never occurred and a farm now surrounds the old buildings. The former hotel is now used as a barn.

The ruins of St. Nicholas are off the southern end of Albert Lea Lake, about two miles northwest of Glenville, County 65, Freeborn Co. The first town in the county, it was once prosperous.

The ruins of Salol are located about nine miles east of Roseau, County 11 and 89, Roseau Co. It was once a prosperous lumber town and today very little of it is left.

The town of Swift, named for its rapid growth, is located seven miles northwest of Baudette on the Rainy River, County 11 and 72, Lake of the Woods Co. During the late nineteenth century, over 2,000 residents lived here, but today it is a tiny hamlet of about 50 people; the ruins of many old buildings dot the area.

The ruins of Wasioja are located about midway between Mantorville and Byron, County 57, Dodge Co. Almost all of the men from this town were killed in the Civil War, so the widows and orphans abandoned it. Today only the ruins of an old mill and church are still here.

A substantial amount of treasure has been found on the west bank of the Red River near the town of **Noyes,** opposite Pembina, North Dakota, in the northwestern extremity of the state, Kittson Co. Several riverboats carrying large amounts of treasure were lost in this area during the past century and the gold and silver coins on the riverbanks are probably being washed ashore from one or more of these wrecks.

In the 1890s some bandits are alleged to have buried a large number of gold and silver coins in the woods west of **Wadena,** State 10, Wadena Co., before being killed by a posse.

The Jesse James gang buried about $55,000 in gold coins and bullion near the **Pipestone National Monument** near Pipestone, County 30, Pipestone Co.

The outlaw Curran Brothers are said to have buried about $40,000 in bank loot on the northern edge of Mud Lake, near **Green Isle,** County 5, Sibley Co.

Before a brewery owned by a Charles Ney was burned to the ground in **Henderson,** County 19, Sibley Co., in 1924, the owner buried a large fortune in an underground vault beneath the brewery, and was unable to locate it after the fire.

An unidentified farmer concealed about $10,000 in gold coins in a grove of trees on his farm along the Minnesota River about a mile south of **Henderson,** Sibley Co.

During the Civil War a settler buried about $5,000 in gold coins near the site of the **Old**

Soldier's Home on the west side of the Mississippi River, about two miles south of Minneapolis.

During Prohibition a bootlegger buried a large amount of cash around the banks of the Mississippi River at **Lake City,** State 36, Wabasha Co. He died in a car accident before recovering the money.

During the Depression many prosperous doctors and businessmen buried large sums of money in the vicinity of **Rochester,** Olmsted Co.; in recent years many of these hoards have been unearthed by treasure hunters.

During the 1930s the Ma Barker-Karpis gang hid $100,000 in paper currency, a kidnapping ransom, in a metal box, under a fence post along the ten-mile stretch of State 52 between **Chatfield** and **Rochester,** Olmsted Co. They were unable to relocate the spot and many persons have searched for this cache ever since.

American gold and silver coins have been found in large numbers along the west bank of the Mississippi River at **La Crescent,** U.S. 90, Houston Co., opposite La Crosse, Wisconsin. The coins are probably being washed ashore from a sunken riverboat.

Before dying in 1903, a farmer named Joseph Winther buried a large cache of gold coins on his farm which borders the Blue Earth River about half a mile west of **Winnebago,** County 169, Faribault Co.

Sometime during World War II, several children playing along the banks of the Red River at **Robbin,** County 11, Kittson Co., found what they thought were "shiny rocks" about the size of apples. They took a few home and their parents discovered the rocks to be huge gold nuggets. The children were unable to locate the spot where they claimed to have seen "thousands of shiny rocks." They may have been washed ashore from a river wreck or been buried there by someone, as placer gold is not known to exist in the immediate area.

MISSISSIPPI

Natchez on the Mississippi River in Adams County was settled by the French around 1700 and had probably been colonized even earlier by the Spanish. To protect their warehouses the French built **Fort Rosalie** in 1716 with Indian labor. In 1729 the Indians revolted, killed most of the settlers, and destroyed the fort. The area came under British control in 1763; in 1778 the original fort was rebuilt and renamed **Fort Panmure.** The following year it was captured by the Spanish and changed hands several more times before being abandoned. The site of the fort is on a bluff at the foot of South Broadway in the present town.

Natchez Trace, first called the Chickasaw-Choctaw Trail during the period of French domination, is a 450-mile-long trail that connected Natchez with Nashville, Tennessee. It was used even in prehistoric times and was the most traveled road in the Old Southwest until about 1820 when the new steamboat traffic began. Most of the original road still survives and the ruins of many old buildings can be found along its entirety.

Vicksburg National Park adjoins the city of Vicksburg, Warren Co. Strategically situated on high bluffs overlooking the Mississippi River, its almost impregnable fortifications made it the key link in the Confederate defenses spread from Louisville, Kentucky to New Orleans. The Union Army failed to take the city during a land and amphibious assault in 1862 so General Ulysses S. Grant laid siege to the place. After 47 days the beleaguered city finally surrendered on July 4, 1863, splitting the Confederacy in two and giving the Union control of the Mississippi River. Today the remains of nine large forts, countless gun emplacements, and miles of breastworks can still be seen.

Champion Hill Battlefield is four miles southwest of Bolton, Hinds Co. A hotly contested battle was fought here on May 16, 1863 between 20,000 Confederates under General John C. Pemberton and 29,000 Union troops under General John A. McClernand. The hill changed hands three times before the Confederates were forced to withdraw towards Vicksburg.

Brices Cross Battlefield is off State 370, six miles west of Baldwyn, Prentiss Co. On June 10, 1864 Confederate General Nathan Bedford Forrest, with 3,500 men, won a brilliant tactical victory here over 8,100 men led by General S. D. Sturgis. Before being forced to retreat, the Union troops abandoned a large amount of supplies and also dumped several large cannon in a nearby stream.

Winterville Mount site is on State 1, five miles north of Greenville, Washington Co. The mounds were constructed between 1000 and 1300 by Indians known as the Temple Mound Builders, who were the predecessors of the Tunica, Chickasaw, and Choctaw tribes. In 1540 the Spanish explorer Hernando De Soto stopped here for several weeks in his quest for gold (of which he obtained very little).

Fort Massachusetts is south of Ship Island at the entrance of Biloxi Bay, midway between Gulfport and Biloxi. The fort was built in 1861, captured the following year by Union troops, and served as the main base for Union operations along the Gulf Coast for the remainder of the war. The fort's dungeons were used to hold many Confederate prisoners. Near Fort Massachusetts are many ruins of other buildings built and used by the Union during the war.

The ruined town of Meridian stands near the outskirts of present Meridian off U.S. 45. During the Civil War it was an important Confederate supply depot. General Sherman's troops reached the town on February 14, 1864 and totally destroyed it. As Sherman recorded it, "For five days 10,000 men worked hard and with a will in that work of destruction . . . Meridian, with its depots, store-houses, arsenals, hospitals, offices, hotels and cantonment, no longer exists."

The settlement of Fort Maurepas stood on the site of the present town of Ocean Springs on the Gulf Coast on U.S. 90, Jackson Co. This was the first permanent European settlement on the Mississippi Delta, founded by the French in 1699. In 1719 it was abandoned and the settlers moved across Biloxi Bay to found the town of Biloxi.

Grand Gulf State Park is situated on the Mississippi River about seven miles northwest of Port Gibson, Clayborne Co. The Confederates had two forts on this island just below Vicksburg. On April 29, 1863 the Southern Army withstood a fierce attack by Union gunboats unsuccessfully trying to clear the way for General Grant's army to secure a bridgehead on the eastern side of the river before attacking Vicksburg. One may still see the ruins of both forts.

Raymond Battlefield is on State 18 about three miles southwest of Raymond, Hinds Co. An inferior force of Confederates were defeated on May 12, 1863 on this site while the Union Army was preparing for the attack on Vicksburg.

Big Black River Battlefield is located off U.S. 20 midway between Smith's Station and Bovina, Hinds Co. A battle was fought here on May 17, 1863, the day before the siege of Vicksburg began, and won by the Union.

Tupelo Battlefield is on State 6 about one mile west of the intersection with U.S. 45, near Tupelo, Lee Co. The last major Civil War battle fought in this state took place on July 14–15, 1864 between 9,400 Confederate and 14,000 Union troops. In the resulting draw, both sides lost about equal numbers of men and both withdrew.

Gold coins are found along the east bank of the Mississippi River near **Black Hawk,** about 30 miles south of Natchez, in Wilkinson Co. They are believed to be coming from the steamboat **Ben Sheerod** which caught fire and sank in this area on May 8, 1837. Of its 200 passengers, 150 perished; the boat was carrying over $75,000 in gold coins at the time.

During the Civil War a Union paymaster buried about $80,000 in gold coins during a skirmish with Confederate raiders in **Holly Springs,** State 78, Marshall Co. He buried the money within sight of the town's railroad station but was killed by a Confederate bullet and the coins were never found.

Another Civil War treasure of gold and silver coins is buried in the village of **Como,** State 55, Panola Co. Some claim it was buried by a Confederate officer; others by a local rich merchant.

During the Civil War when Union troops were approaching, a physician named Dr. John Young gathered up all of his wealth and buried it in a large iron pot somewhere in the yard of his home. The house still stands on Young Street in the town of **Walter Valley,** County 315, Yalobusha Co.

When news of the 1929 market crash reached the town of **Doddsville,** County 3, Sunflower

Co., an old recluse buried about $18,000 in gold coins somewhere in the town park and then died soon after from a heart attack.

The millionaire T. P. Gore buried about $400,000 in gold coins and bars near his mansion in **Calhoun City**, County 8, Calhoun Co. He never disclosed the location of this money.

With Union troops approaching the city in 1865, the local residents filled two large wooden kegs with valuables; the Mayor concealed them somewhere along the Yalobusha River near **Greenwood**, State 82, Leflore Co. The river flooded from heavy rains before the kegs could be dug up, so the location was lost.

A pirate is alleged to have buried about $100,000 in gold coins along the Big Black River near **Mathison**, State 82, Choctaw Co. It is rather strange that he would have buried a cache so far from the sea, his normal working area.

Around 1830 Indians robbed an ox cart carrying a load of silver bars up to Louisville and are alleged to have buried the plunder near the foot of a cliff near the village of **Williams,** County 15, Choctaw Co.

Loot from a Philadelphia bank robbery in the early 1900s was wrapped in waterproof bags and dropped from a bridge over the Pearl River near the town of **Ferans Springs,** County 490, Winston Co. About $100,000 of the money was in paper currency and about $43,000 in gold coins. Police using grappling hooks were unable to locate the bags and it is feared that they sank beneath the river's muddy bottom.

After the stockmarket crash of 1929 a farmer named Zack Goforth buried his accumulated wealth of about $30,000 in gold coins in several caches on his 640-acre farm, near **Little Rock,** County 15, Newton Co. After his death in 1938 many persons searched for the money. Two boys discovered a small iron pot containing about $800 in gold coins; the rest has never been found.

In the 1920s a wealthy merchant threw about $94,000 in gold coins and jewelry into one of eleven small lakes that surround the town of **Decatur,** County 503, Newton Co., to prevent his family from inheriting the treasure after his death.

The ghost town of Arundel Springs is located at the junction of Sowashee and Okitibbee Creeks just south of Meridian, State 45, Lauderdale Co. Only the foundations of some buildings remain. The Copeland gang is alleged to have buried some of their loot among these ruins.

Before being caught and hanged, the bandit John Murrell buried about $400,000 in treasure in the vicinity of **Blakely,** just north of Vicksburg, Warren Co.

During the approach of the Union troops led by General Grant, the Pickett Family buried about $200,000 in family treasure near the manor house on their plantation on the northern edge of **Vicksburg.** Their home was destroyed during the fighting and they were unable to locate the treasure after the war.

A bandit named Joseph Hale is said to have buried about $70,000 in silver and gold coins in the vicinity of **Fayette,** County 28 and 33, Jefferson Co.

The Mason outlaw gang reportedly buried about $25,000 in gold coins in the vicinity of **Tillman,** a few miles north of Natchez, Jefferson Co.

Another story about a disappearing pot of treasure is associated with the Mason and Harpe gang. They filled a large iron pot with gold coins and bullion and dropped it into an artesian well on the **Robert Dove Farm,** a few miles south of Hamburg on the northern edge of the Homochito Forest, Franklin Co. The pot has supposedly been seen a number of times, but all attempts to recover it only drive it deeper in the quicksand-like soil.

A bandit named Sam Mason is alleged to have hidden a large treasure on the Mississippi River at a spot known as the **Devil's Punchbowl,** just south of Natchez, Adams Co. Early French and Spanish pirates are also believed to have concealed plunder on this same spot.

A cache of gold coins and jewelry is buried somewhere on the **Bond Farm** located near the eastern outskirts of Natchez, Adams Co.

During September 1850 the steamboat **Drennan White** carrying over $100,000 in gold coins was wrecked on the Mississippi River where it flows past the **Ancil Fortune Farm,** about fifteen miles south of Natchez and about four miles west of State 61, Wilkenson Co. In 1870 and 1871 it was discovered that the river had changed course and the wreck had been covered by land; a substantial number of gold coins were discovered. With modern locating and excavation equipment it should be easy to recover the rest.

The outlaw Sam Mason is alleged to have buried about $75,000 in gold and silver coins along the Natchez Trace in a cemetery at **Little Sand Creek,** near the village of Rocky Springs on the Big Black River, Claiborne Co.

Treasure was buried under the ruins of **"Chicken Willy Smith's Tavern"** near Caseville, County 550, Lincoln Co.

Indians buried several caches of gold coins, paid to them for land purchases by the United States Government, on the banks of the Bogue River about half a mile north of **Bogue,** State 51, Lincoln Co.

Legend has it that an undisclosed amount of treasure is buried on a hill along Robinwood Road near the **Cooper's Creek Bridge,** between Robinwood and Monticello, State 84, Lawrence Co.

Around $80,000 in bank robbery money was buried in a field near the town of **Prentiss,** State 13, Jefferson Davis Co.

The Copeland gang had their headquarters on Big Creek, near **Laurel,** U.S. 59, Jones Co., and are alleged to have concealed money several places in this area.

During the Civil War two barrels of gold coins and silverware were buried in a vacant lot on Broad Street in **Columbia,** State 98, Marion Co. Fires destroyed the surrounding houses and the exact hiding place could not be found after the war.

An old miser named Hiberly hid several caches of gold coins on his farm before he died in 1945. His farm is located two miles northeast of **Lumberton,** State 11, Lamar Co.

During the Civil War a farmer named Gaines buried gold and silver coins on his farm on the west side of the Chickasawhey River near **Leakesville,** County 57 and 63, Greene Co.

A French privateer named Pierre Rambeau is supposed to have buried a treasure on **Honey Island** in the Pearl River near U.S. 59, Pearl River Co.

In the early 1800s the Copeland outlaw gang concealed about $30,000 in gold coins in the **Catahoula Swamp,** where they had a campsite for several years, near Wiggins, State 49, Stone Co.

During the Civil War a large amount of gold coins and jewelry was hidden near the manor house of the **Catahoula Plantation** on the banks of Catahoula Creek about half a mile east of Picayune, State 11, Pearl River Co.

According to legend the pirate Calico Dick scuttled a small boat full of pirate plunder in a bayou about three miles south of **Pearlington,** State 90, Hancock Co.

During the Civil War about $80,000 in gold coins was buried by fleeing Confederate soldiers near the site where the **Napoleon Church** stood in a thicket of large oak trees, about 100 yards from the Pearl River near Waveland, near St. Louis Bay, Hancock Co.

In the center of the town of **Bay St. Louis,** State 90, Hancock Co., there is an early nineteenth-century structure known as the "Pirate's House"; many different tales describe treasure being buried in or around the building.

During the early 1800s the privateer Captain Dave is said to have concealed about $200,000 in treasure in an oak tree grove on an old plantation near the town of **Pass Christian,** State 90, Harrison Co.

On the beach between **Pass Christian** and **Long Beach,** fishermen have reported finding large numbers of Spanish silver coins from the late eighteenth century. Apparently they are coming ashore from a shipwreck.

During the Civil War large amounts of personal treasure were concealed in and around the vicinity of **Gulfport.** The ruins of hundreds of old plantation buildings in the area are favorite spots for many treasure hunters. In 1974 one treasure hunter located about $50,000 in silver plate and coins near the foundations of a burnt-out plantation manor. In 1975 two other treasure hunters located about $40,000 in gold coins (today's market prices) in the well on an abandoned plantation.

Ship Island located off Gulfport is another choice treasure-hunting area. Numbers of ships

Over
Beaches along the Gulf of Mexico are excellent spots for finding treasure with pulse-induction detectors whose circuitry functions effectively even in salt water.

Facing
The relatively mild winter weather of Mississippi and the Deep South permits treasure hunters to search almost every day of the year.

Over

Coins have long been a major target for metal detectors, and modern one-touch instruments continue to amaze hobbyists with their deepseeking abilities.

Facing

Caches abound in Southern states, and they come in all shapes and sizes like this small tin filled with valuable old coins.

were wrecked on the south side of this island and many coins and artifacts are found with the use of metal detectors. Recently a shrimper raised two large eighteenth-century French cannon that were resting off the western tip of the island in only 20 feet of water.

MISSOURI

St. Louis was first founded in 1764 by the French who established a trading post there. The Spanish took it over in 1770; then in 1778 they built **Fort San Carlos** on the banks of the Mississippi River. In 1780 the British attacked the town and were repelled. The French took over St. Louis soon after and it was finally ceded to the United States in 1803. No traces of any structures dating before 1803 exist, but ruins of some old buildings can be seen along the river bank. A great fire struck the city in May 1849, destroying over 400 buildings and 27 steamships. On May 27, 1896 a tornado caused 400 deaths and destroyed over 500 buildings. Along the river bank treasure hunters have discovered artifacts and fragments of the many riverboats lost in the area.

The town of Defiance was on the banks of the Missouri River but is now located about a mile northwest of the river, County 94, St. Charles Co. In and around the town are a great number of ruins, some dating back to the time of the frontiersmen. One of the few surviving buildings is called Boone House, where Daniel Boone spent his last years. Several small caches of gold coins have been found around the ruins in recent years.

At the confluence of Mississippi and Missouri Rivers, about ten miles north of **St. Louis**, the French built a wooden fort in 1773 and a small settlement sprang up around it. The place was destroyed by a flood in 1786 and today no trace of it remains.

The town of St. Charles is on the Missouri River about twenty miles northwest of St. Louis. It was settled in the late eighteenth century, became a fur trading center, and in 1821 served as the state's first capital. There are numerous ruins of early nineteenth-century buildings in the area. It is one of the state's best treasure-hunting areas for coins and interesting artifacts.

The ruins of Ste. Genevieve are located three miles southeast of the present town of this name, on the Mississippi River, County 32, Ste. Genevieve Co. The original town was founded by the French in 1735, although they are believed to have settled the area much earlier. Because of bad floods the town was abandoned in 1796 and the residents moved to the present location. There are also old ruins in the present town.

Arrow Rock is a tiny village off State 41, Marshall Co. Founded in 1829, this frontiertown on the Missouri River was already well known as one of the main starting points of the Santa Fe Trail. Traffic was so heavy by 1817 that a ferry across the river began operating and tens of thousands of pioneers passed through the town over the next 50 years. Few buildings of the original settlement still remain but there are many ruins.

Boone's Lick State Historic Site is off State 87, nineteen miles north of Bonneville, Cooper Co. One of the state's first white settlements was founded in this area before 1800 but no trace of it remains today.

Booneville is located northeast of I-70 on State 5, Cooper Co. This town was the scene of one of the first land battles of the Civil War when on June 17, 1861 Union troops defeated Missouri troops led by the pro-Confederate governor. This victory gave the North control of the Missouri River.

Lexington Battlefield is off U.S. 24 near Lexington, Lafayette Co. A very bloody Civil War engagement took place here September 18-20, 1861 which resulted in an important victory for the South. There are still ruins of buildings and hillside trenches.

Utz Site Historic Park is off State 41, twelve miles north of Marshall, Saline Co. From the early 1600s until 1728 this was the main village of the Missouri Indians, who all died of white man's diseases. Small golden figurines were found in a cave on this site in 1937.

Fort Davidson is off State 21 on the outskirts of Pilot Knob, St. Francois Co. A battle was fought here on September 27, 1864 in which the Union Army was victorious; the fort was demolished by the Union soldiers, who threw the cannon into a nearby stream.

Fort Osage, on the Missouri River on the north edge of Sibley, east of Kansas City, Jackson Co., was the first Army post west of the Mississippi, built in 1808. The fort was mainly used as a Federal Government trading post to assure the Indians of fair prices for their furs. Part of the fort has been restored.

Wilson Creek Battlefield is off U.S. 60, about twelve miles southwest of Springfield, Greene Co. A bitter battle was fought here on August 10, 1861, for control of the Missouri River.

As the Union forces approached the town of Westport near Kansas City, Jackson Co., on October 21, 1864, all the residents gave their valuables to Father Bernard J. Donnelly of the **Immaculate Conception Church** for safekeeping. He buried the treasure somewhere in the church grounds or cemetery but died of a heart attack soon after; the treasure, worth somewhere between $50,000 and $100,000, was never found. The church is still standing today.

At his farm outside of **Rushville,** State 59, Buchanan Co., Frank Black recently found more than 200 stone knives, scrapers, grinding stones, choppers, hammer stones, and projectile points of prehistoric Indians, while plowing his fields.

The ruins of Adam-Ondi-Ahman are located on the Grand River about three miles north of Gallatin (County 13), Daviess Co. The settlement was first founded as a ferry station in 1837. The following year large numbers of Mormons moved in and built more than 200 homes; but within a year they had trouble with the Gentiles and were forced to leave. Only one of the original buildings still stands.

The ghost town of Bird's Point is located at the confluence of the Ohio and Mississippi Rivers, at the foot of the Interstate Bridge on State 60, Mississippi Co. It was established as a trading post in 1800 and soon became an important river town. The town, which suffered severe damages during the Civil War, was deserted when the railroad bypassed it. Many of the old buildings are still standing.

The town of Cartersville is midway between Carthage and Joplin, off State 66, Jaspar Co. It was once a booming zinc-mining town of more than 12,000 residents but today less than one tenth that number still live here. There are hundreds of old abandoned houses and ruins of many others.

The ghost town of Danville is on the old Boone's Lick Trail about twelve and a half miles from Jonesburg. It was founded in 1834 but on October 4, 1864, after Bill Anderson and his guerillas sacked and burnt most of the town, it was abandoned. Only about twenty buildings are still standing.

The ruins of Far West are located about four and a half miles east of Kingston, State 13, Caldwell Co. Established as a Mormon refuge in December 1836, by the summer of 1838 it had a population of over 4,000. Problems developed between the Mormons and the Gentiles and the Mormons were forced to flee later this same year. When they headed for Illinois, Federal troops moved in and tore down all of their homes. Today there are only foundations.

The ghost town of Hickory Springs is on State 60 near Mountain Grove, Wright Co. It was founded in 1851 and in 1857 the Mountain Grove Seminary was established here. When the railroad bypassed the town in 1888 the town was abandoned and the residents started the new town of Mountain Grove. Many of the original buildings are still standing.

The ruins of Fort Kountz are one mile north of Cittleville, County 19, Shannon Co. This trading post was founded in 1812 and destroyed by a fire in 1897.

The ruins of Marlin City are on the Mississippi River about four miles east of Palmyra, State 24 and 61, Marion Co. It was founded in 1835 and suffered from floods in 1836, 1841, and 1851. It had been one of the principal livestock markets in the state but was abandoned after the last devastating flood. Only the ruins remain.

The ghost town of Millville is two miles south of Versailles, County 52, Morgan Co. It was a major trading center and county seat until being abandoned in 1834; and now only a few buildings are left.

The ruins of Mine La Matte, about five miles north of Fredericktown, State 67, Madison Co., mark what may have been the first town in the state. It was founded in 1715 by Sieur Antoine de la Matte Cadillac, the Governor-General of Louisiana, as a lead-mining town, and was probably abandoned around 1800. Many ruins are now concealed by a tree grove above a creek.

The **ghost town of Old Franklin** is about half a mile northwest of New Franklin on the Missouri River, County 5, close to Boone Lick, Howard Co. The town was founded in 1816 and by 1821 had become the eastern terminus of the Santa Fe Trail. Kit Carson lived here as a boy until 1826. With the establishment of other boat landings further up the Missouri River the town was abandoned by 1843.

The **ghost town of New Santa Fe**, also known as Little Santa Fe, is on the South Grand River about twenty miles south of Kansas City and six miles southeast of Hickman Mills, Cass Co. It was founded in 1851 and became a booming supply town on the Santa Fe Trail and another trail leading into Mexico. During the Border War of 1855-1856 outlaws badly destroyed most of the town. Then when the railroads bypassed the town a few years later it was abandoned. About 50 of the original buildings are still standing.

The **ruins of Nouvelle Bourbon** are on a bluff overlooking the Mississippi River near the ghost town of Ste. Genevieve, Ste. Genevieve Co. It was founded in 1783 by Baron de Carondelet, the governor of Louisiana, for a group of French Royalist refugees. By 1850 it had been abandoned.

The **ghost town of Old Lebanon** is located on the outskirts of present Lebanon, U.S. 44, Laclede Co. Only a few buildings dating back to the mid-nineteenth century still remain.

The **ghost town of Orongo** is located about ten miles north of Joplin, County 43, Jaspar Co. It was founded in 1854 because of the rich lead and zinc mines in the area, which produced over a dozen millionaires. The ruins of many of their great mansions can still be seen and several caches are believed to be hidden on their properties.

The **ruins of Rivercene** are located on the banks of the Missouri River between Rock and Booneville, State 40, Howard Co. The town was a major boat-building center, which flourished during the first 60 years of the past century.

The **town of Sligo** is located about fifteen and a half miles northeast of Salem, County 117, Dent Co. It was a bustling iron-mining town from 1875 until 1921 and had an average of 2,000 residents during that period. Today only a handful of people live among the ruins of hundreds of buildings.

The **ghost town of Sparta** is four miles south of St. Joseph, on the west side of U.S. 29, Buchanan Co. It was once a prosperous farm and trading center; now the only standing building is the church.

The **ghost town of Splitlog** is four miles northeast of Anderson, County 76, McDonald Co. It was founded in 1887 as a mining center but was abandoned only a few years later. Only a few buildings are still standing.

The **ruins of Weaucandah** are situated at the confluence of the Mississippi and Wyaconda Rivers, near La Grange, State 61, Lewis Co. It was founded as a trading post in 1794 by the Frenchman Godfrey le Sieur; by 1870 the town had been abandoned and was in ruins.

Gold coins are found on the east bank of the Missouri River near **Big Lake**, about ten miles west of Mound City, U.S. 29, Holt Co. They are believed to be coming off the steamboat **W. R. Caruthers** which was lost in the area carrying about $30,000 in gold coins.

Wreckage of another steamer can be seen about two miles south of the above site when the river is low. It is believed to be the steamer **Sultana**, which sank in 1851 carrying $65,000 in gold coins.

During the Civil War a successful doctor named Lynn Talbot buried a keg full of American gold coins somewhere on his property. He was murdered when he refused to reveal the location of the coins to robbers. His home, the "House of the Seven Gables," is located a few miles north of **Barnaad**, State 71, Nodaway Co.

In August 1865 the paddle-wheel steamer **Francis X. Aubrey** was lost on the Missouri River carrying about 500 barrels of whiskey, which today would be worth a fortune. Due to the river changing course the site of this wreck is now under a swampy area about a mile from the present river bank near **Parkville**, close to Park College on the northern outskirts of Kansas City.

The **Kaffer Treasure**, alleged to consist of a large cache of gold coins is buried in the vicinity of **Armstrong**, County 3, Howard Co.

Legend has it that a large cache of gold was hidden in or near **McDowell's Cave** near Mark

Twain's home town of Hannibal, State 61, Marion Co. There is also said to be a ton of gold hidden between Mark Twain's Cave and the banks of the Mississippi River. The gold bars are believed to have been taken from a river wreck during the Civil War and hidden by the salvors.

During the early nineteenth century a band of Indian renegades buried a large cache of gold, silver, and jewels in a cave overlooking the Lake of the Ozarks near **Warsaw**, State 65, Benton Co. A great deal of plunder, taken in numerous raids on settlements throughout the state, was buried by these Indians when they were surrounded by a large posse, which soon after killed them all.

The Lost Brooksie Silver Mine is located near the southeastern tip of the Lake of the Ozarks, near Cross Timbers, State 6565, Hickory Co. It was in operation during the Civil War and then flooded to prevent capture by the Union troops. Over the years its location was lost.

A lost gold mine is on Carpenter Creek, in the vicinity of the town of Jerico Springs, County 97, Cedar Co.

The Lost Missouri Silver Mine is near a creek in the vicinity of Louisburg, State 65, Dallas Co. Confederates sealed it off during the Civil War to prevent its capture by the Union troops.

At the site of a wagon ford on the Gasconado River on the western side of **Clark National Forest,** about seven miles west of Lynchburg, County 32, Laclede Co., a returning California miner buried about $60,000 in gold before being attacked and killed by bushwhackers.

During the land preparation for the Capehart housing project on the outskirts of **Fort Leonard Wood Military Reservation,** on the banks of the Roubidoux River, Pulaski Co., a bulldozer uncovered two large boxes containing about 4,000 silver dollars dating from the late 1800s. On the nearby Tilley Farm another treasure cache is known to be hidden.

During the Civil War, raider Quantrill is known to have buried about $10 million near a cliff overlooking the Meremac River, close to **Belle Starr's Needle,** in the Clark National Forest, Laclede Co.

Outlaw Cole Younger is alleged to have buried a large chest of silver and gold coins near the tiny village of **Alba**, about seven miles west of State 71, Jaspar Co.

Shortly before being murdered, in 1874 a wealthy cattleman buried about $100,000 somewhere on his ranch, which is located about three miles northwest of **Joplin**, Jaspar Co.

The Ford Meadow Treasure, said to consist of $75,000 in gold and silver coins, is located in Ford Meadow, near Bethpage, County 76, McDonald Co.

Since World War II, military personnel on the **Fort Crowder Army Station,** located in the southwest corner of the state near the Elk River, have found numerous caches of nineteenth-century gold and silver coins. More is probably waiting to be found in the area.

During the late eighteenth century, a band of Spanish miners are known to have hidden a large cache of gold ore and dust near the creek in **Bear Tree Hollow** near Lanagan, State 71, McDonald Co.

The Lost Spanish Gold Mine is on the Big Sugar River in the vicinity of Pineville, State 71, McDonald Co. The Spanish were working this mine in the late seventeenth and early eighteenth centuries until the mine was attacked and almost all of the men were killed. Before fleeing, the survivors hid a large cache of gold ore and an undetermined amount of refined gold bullion.

The Spanish are known to have had several gold and silver mines in the area of the **Ozark Wonder Cave,** located between Noe and Jane in the southwest corner of Missouri, near the Elk River. In this general area, according to legend, there is Madre Vena Cave where they stored several years' accumulation of gold bullion. Around 1802 most of the miners were struck by a mysterious epidemic and the majority died. The entrance to the cave was sealed off and the survivors headed for Mexico, but when several returned two years later, they were unable to locate the cave because a forest fire had altered the terrain.

Prior to the arrival of the Spanish and even during the time they were mining in the southwestern corner of Missouri, the Indians were also working silver and gold mines in the area. According to legend the Indians had a huge hoard of silver and gold. This they sealed off in a cave overlooking the White River near **Cassville**, County 37, Barry Co.

219

Indians are also reported to have concealed a great number of large silver bars in another sealed cave on the White River in the Ozark Mountains near **Eagle Rock,** County 86, Barry Co. Several Indian silver mines were on nearby Turkey Mountain.

During the Civil War some Confederate sympathizers are known to have hidden about $1 million in silver bars on or near the banks of the James River near **Galena,** County 173 and 176, Stone Co. At the end of the war they were unable to locate the cache because the river had flooded and destroyed their markers. About one mile to the east of the river is an abandoned silver mine. There are also **Lost Spanish Silver Mines** within a five-mile radius of Galena and ruins of many nineteenth-century miners' dwellings in the general area.

The famous **Lost Yokum Silver Mine** is located between the tributaries of the King and St. James Rivers, near Table Rock Lake, in the southern portion of Stone Co.

During the Civil War fleeing Confederate troops are known to have hidden a large treasure of unknown value on or near **Noble Hill,** a spot about twelve miles north of Springfield on County 13, Greene Co.

The Spanish and later the French had several gold and silver mines in the vicinity of **Springfield,** U.S. 44, Greene Co. No traces of these mines now exist, but they would be well worth searching for.

The Spanish Cave Treasure is alleged to consist of $600,000 in gold coins hidden in a cave near the Norfolk River, near Hartville, County 39, Wright Co.

Jesse James is alleged to have hidden about $100,000 in loot in a cave near **Gainesville,** State 160, Ozark Co.

Around the end of the Civil War about $35,000 in gold and silver coins were hidden in a sinkhole on a farm in **Hocomo,** State 160, Howell Co. The sinkhole flooded, preventing the owners from retrieving their cache.

Close to the tiny village of **Lanton,** County 17, Howell Co., almost on the Missouri-Arkansas border, a Civil War treasure of about $30,000 in gold coins and silverware was concealed by the Confederate raider Colonel Porter, shortly before he was ambushed and killed by Union troops.

In 1902 a farmer named Charles Boucher, shortly before his death, buried about 500 silver dollars in or near his cabin near the ponds, a mile or so south of **West Plains,** State 63, Howell Co.

Jesse James is also supposed to have buried a cache of about $100,000 in gold coins and bullion somewhere in the **Des Arc Mountains,** about eight miles east of Gad Hills, County 49, Wayne Co.

MONTANA

The ghost town of Bannack is located on a secondary road off State 278, 22 miles west of Dillon, Beaverhead Co. In July 1862 the discovery of gold in this area resulted in the founding of Bannack, the state's oldest town, and two years later it became the capital of the Montana Territory. Among the surviving structures of this lawless town is the jail; the ruins of many buildings dot the area.

The Bearpaw Mountains are off U.S. 2, sixteen miles south of Chinook, Blaine Co. One of the last battles of the Indian wars was fought here on October 5, 1877, when United States Army troops intercepted several bands of Nez Perce, including that of Chief Joseph. After a bloody battle the Indians were forced to surrender.

Big Hole Battlefield is twelve miles west of Wisdom and eighteen miles east of U.S. 93, Beaverhead Co. A fierce battle occurred here on August 9-10, 1877 between some 700 Nez Perce Indians and United States Army troops of lesser numbers. Both sides suffered heavy losses and the battle ended when both sides withdrew.

Butte was founded in 1864 when prospectors came looking for gold. During the following decade there was a silver boom here, but the real wealth is in its copper deposits, over which the present city is built. More than $2 billion in mineral wealth has come out of an area of less than five square miles here. **The Butte Historic District** in downtown Butte contains many original nineteenth-century buildings and vestiges of others.

Custer Battlefield is located fifteen miles south of Hardin on the Crow Indian Reservation, Horn Co. One of the most famous battles in American history—Custer's Last Stand also known as the Valley of the Little Big Horn—took place here on June 25-26, 1876. In this encounter, all the 225 soldiers were killed by a much larger force of Sioux and Cheyenne Indians.

The remains of Fort Benton are located on the Missouri River in the town of Fort Benton, Chouteau Co. The site first served as a campsite for Captain William Clark, then as a fur trading center. The town really began to grow after the first steamboat reached it in 1859, serving as the terminus for the busy river traffic until the railroads arrived. Today parts of the old fort, trading post, and other ruined buildings can still be seen.

The site where Fort Logan stood is about seventeen miles northwest of White Sulphur Springs, Meagher Co. A military post was built here in 1869 to protect an area containing a large number of mining camps. Remnants of the fort and other buildings can still be seen here.

The site of Fort Peck is located under the waters of Fort Peck Lake. This body of water was created when a dam was built in the 1930s near the present village of Fort Peck off State Road 24. In 1867, during the height of the fur-trading activity, a trading post, Indian agency, and fort were established here and a flourishing community soon sprung up—all is now under 20 to 30 feet of muddy water.

The site of Fort Owen is about half a mile north of the town of Stevenville on County Road 203, Ravalli Co. After the fort and village were founded in 1850 it became a very prosperous trading center and a great deal of gold was discovered in the nearby Bitteroot Range. The place was destroyed by an earthquake some time during the 1890s and very few traces of it remain today.

The village of Three Forks once stood on the Missouri River a few miles north of the present town of Three Forks, Gallatin Co. The village was settled around 1840 and about twenty years later was totally obliterated by a flood.

Virginia City is on State 287, about 55 miles southeast of Butte, Madison Co. The discovery of gold in nearby Alder Gulch led to feverish mining activity and the founding of this colorful town. From 1865 to 1875 it was the territorial capital of Montana. By 1885 the town had fallen into total ruin and was almost completely abandoned but today most of it has been reconstructed for the tourist trade. Still, vestiges of many of the old buildings can be found in the town and the surrounding hills are sprinkled with abandoned mines and miners' cabins.

Two abandoned gold mines in Beaverhead County are surrounded by many ruins and a few standing buildings. The **Alder Gulch Placer Mine** is on Alder Creek in the Beaverhead National Forest; and the **Bannack Diggings** is on Grasshopper Creek near the town of Bannack, about five miles south of County Road 278.

The ghost town of Beartown is located on the Clear Fork River midway between Drummond and Bearmouth on U.S. 90, Granite Co. It was a gold-mining boomtown during the 1860s and almost became the state capital. The notorious "Beartown Roughs," who terrorized and robbed local miners, made their home base here. Nearby is "Chinese Grade" where numerous miners are alleged to have buried their gold for safekeeping.

The ghost town of Chico is located in Emigrant Gulch where gold was discovered in 1864, which is about 25 miles southeast of Livingston, State 89, Park Co. The town only boomed for a few years until the gold was worked out and the miners left. Several dozen buildings are still standing.

The ruins of Cooperopolis are on the Musselshell River about eleven miles east of White Sulphur Springs (State 89), Meagher Co. The site can be reached only by horseback; a few ruins and abandoned mine shafts are all that now mark the town.

The ghost town of Garnet is midway between Drummond and Bearmouth about twelve miles north of U.S. 90, Granite Co. This gold-mining town enjoyed prosperity for a few years during the mid-1800s; but many of its old buildings have survived.

The town of Garniel is 26 miles north of Harlowton on State 191, Fergus Co., a few miles west of the Lewis and Clark National Forest. Now only about 100 people live here but around

1900 it had a population of several thousand. Many of its old buildings are preserved intact; as well as ruins of hundreds of others. Several old abandoned gold mines are also in the vicinity.

The ghost town of Giltedge is on the Wolf River in the vicinity of the ruins of **Fort Magannis,** about fifteen miles northeast of Lewistown, County 238, Fergus Co. During the late 1880s it was a booming gold-mining town and a place for the soldiers of nearby **Fort Magannis** to let off steam. Today many of the old buildings are still standing, but only the foundation remains of the fort. There are also the ruins of a few other brick buildings.

The town of Gold Creek is on the Clear Fork River about eight miles northwest of Garrison on State 90, Powell Co. Only a few die-hard gold miners still remain in this ghost town, where many old buildings are preserved. At one time during the late nineteenth century, more than 5,000 miners lived in this town.

The ghost town of Greenhorn Gulch is located three and a half miles northwest of Helena via a dirt road, Lewis and Clark Co. It was a rich gold-mining town in the 1880s and later was used as a railroad center. Many old buildings are still standing.

The ghost town of Hassel is five miles west of Townsend (County 287) via a dirt road, on the eastern edge of the Helena National Forest, Broadwater Co. It was a famous gold-mining center in the 1890s and many of the old structures are intact. Some mine shafts are still opened and worked occasionally by weekend miners.

The ruins of Hell Gate Ronde are located about two miles northwest of Missoula, State 10, Missoula Co. The first mercantile store in the state was founded here and by 1850 the settlement had about 2,000 residents. In 1864 six members of the Henry Plummer gang were caught and hanged in this town. They are known to have concealed a cache of gold coins and gold nuggets in or near the town just before their execution. Only the ruins of a few houses can still be seen; the remainder is covered over by thick brush.

The ghost town of Highland City is located about fifteen miles southeast of Butte between Pipestone Pass and Red Mountain, Jefferson Co. The site can be reached only by four-wheel-drive vehicles or horseback. Highland City was a rip-roaring gold center, much larger than Butte, during its heyday. There are a few intact buildings and ruins of hundreds of others lining both sides of the town's one long street. Many well known frontier characters, including Shotgun Liz, are buried in the town's cemetery.

The ghost town of Independence is between the Stillwater and Boulder Rivers, about 35 miles south of Big Timber (U.S. 90), northwest of the Custer National Forest, Grass Co. It can be reached only by horseback or hiking over very difficult terrain. Independence was a flourishing gold-mining town and in 1893 had about 500 permanent residents as well as a much larger population of miners and trappers. Three miles to the north is the old **Contact Stage Station.** There are a large number of abandoned gold mines in the surrounding area.

The ghost town of Landusky is on the western edge of the Lewis and Clark National Forest, near the southern edge of the Fort Belknap Indian Reservation, on County 376, Phillips Co. It was a rip-roaring gold-mining and cattle town perched on the side of a mountain. By 1900 only a few persons still lived here. The outlaws known as the Curry Brothers had a ranch five miles south of the town and are believed to have concealed several caches of gold on their property.

The ghost town of Louisville is on Cedar Creek Road about sixteen miles northwest of Superior (State 10) in the Bitterroot Mountain Range, Mineral Co. When gold was discovered here in 1869 by two French-Canadians, more than 10,000 persons rushed to the area within a month. This short-lived town had a life-span of less than three years before all the gold deposits were worked out and the people moved on. In this same area are three other ghost towns: **Cedar Creek, Forest City,** and **Mayville.**

The ghost town of Lump City is located about twelve miles southwest of Butte near Deer Lodge Pass and State 91, Silver Bow Co. It was a rich silver-mining town in the 1890s, but now only its schoolhouse is still standing. There are five abandoned silver mines in the area.

The ghost town of Maiden, eighteen miles northeast of Lewistown (County 191 and State 87), Fergus Co. is accessible only by horseback. It was a gold-mining center in the 1880s and 1890s but only a few buildings remain.

The ghost town of Marysville is fourteen miles northwest of Helena on the eastern edge of the Helena National Forest, Lewis and Clark Co. It can be reached by four-wheel-drive vehicles or horseback. In the late 1880s and early 1890s, the town had over 3,000 residents; today a few old sourdoughs still live in the deserted town among the many standing taverns, stores, and houses. Most of the original boardwalk on both sides of the main street has survived.

The ruins of Monarch are on the Bell River, about 50 miles southeast of Great Falls, just off State 89, on the northern edge of the Lewis and Clark National Forest, Cascade Co. It was a gold-mining center in the 1880s and 1890s.

The ghost town of Nevada is one mile west of Virginia City, County 187, Madison Co. A number of famous outlaws were tried and hanged in this boisterous gold-mining town. Several caches of gold are known to be buried here.

The ghost town of New Year is twelve miles east of Lewistown on State 87, and then a mile north, in Fergus Co. It was a rich gold-mining center of the 1880s. The famous Crystal Cave opens off the main shaft of the abandoned New Year Gold Mine. In the area are several other abandoned gold mines and ruins of small mining camps.

The ghost town of Parker is on the Missouri River about twenty miles north of Three Forks on County 187, Broadwater Co. Only a few buildings are intact. About ten miles due west is the **ghost town of Radersburg,** which has now only three buildings. Both were booming gold-mining centers during the last two decades of the 1800s.

The ghost town of Pioneer is located ten miles southeast of Garrison (State 10) in the northeastern section of the Deer Lodge National Forest, Powell Co. During the 1860s it was a thriving gold town that survived for only a few years because of the difficulty of getting supplies into the town. Today it must be reached by horseback; and many of the old buildings are standing.

The town of Ruby is located on the Ruby River, eight miles west of Virginia City on County 187, Madison Co. Only about 25 people now live here but during its heyday in the 1860s it had a population of more than 5,000. Today there are only a few old buildings; many others have been destroyed by vandals in recent years.

The ghost town of Superior is half a mile east of present day Superior, on the opposite bank of the Clark Fork River. It was founded in 1869 as a gold mining center and many of its buildings still exist. An even older town of this same name once stood about a mile further to the east at the mouth of Bear Creek, but it was destroyed by a flood and there are no traces of it. The present town of Superior is about 60 miles northwest of Missoula on State 10, Mineral Co.

The ghost town of Ubet is located three miles west of Garneil, which is 26 miles north of Harlowtown on State 191, Fergus Co. It was first an old stagecoach station, then a railroad town, and finally, in the 1890s, a gold-mining center. Only a few buildings are intact.

The ghost town of Yellowstone City is on the Yellowstone River about 25 miles south of Livingston and a bit east of State 89, in the Gallatin National Forest, Park Co. It was begun in 1864 as a gold-mining city and lasted for only two years before the gold was exhausted and the Crow Indians raided the settlement and destroyed most of the buildings. Today only a store and saloon are still standing.

The ghost town of Zortman is located about five miles northwest of State 191 on the southern edge of the Fort Belknap Indian Reservation, Phillips Co. In 1929 a fire destroyed most of the town but a few other towns in the area have survived from the 1890s. There are a number of abandoned gold mines in the area.

The Crazy Woman Lost Gold Mine is on Going to the Sun Mountain, about fifteen miles west of St. Mary (State 89), Glacier Co. There is an abandoned gold-mining camp in nearby Logan Pass.

Somewhere along the bank of the Clark Fork River on the **Fort Missoula Military Post,** a miner of the 1880s buried about 200 pounds of gold nuggets after his mule broke a leg. When he returned several weeks later he was unable to locate the hiding place. The site is about three miles south of Missoula off State 93, Missoula Co.

Just before a member of the Plummer gang was hanged in 1864 in **Missoula,** he admitted to burying about $50,000 in gold from a Denver bank robbery about a mile east of the town

223

along the banks of a stream in a thick grove of high trees. An empty iron chest was found in the area the outlaw described, but not the buried loot.

The ghost town of Bearmouth is six miles north of the ghost town of **Beartown** and can be reached via a dirt road in Granite Co. There are many legends about miners burying caches of gold in this area. In 1964 two treasure hunters found four different caches of gold dust, nuggets, and ore—worth a total of some $18,500 at the time. Today the value would be five times as much since the price of gold has escalated.

On the banks of the Flint River about two miles south of **Philipsburg,** State 10A, Granite Co., a prospector in 1873, who was being attacked by Indians, hastily stuffed about 50 pounds of gold dust and nuggets in a tin can and buried it in the soft mud. He beat off the attackers but was unable to find his cache.

The Lost Springer's Gold Mine is located in the vicinity of the Bagg's Creek Drainage area, about a mile north of the junction of Baggs and Cottonwood Creeks, near Anaconda, State 10A, Deer Lodge Co. The finder and two other miners took over 300 pounds of pure gold in less than a month after its discovery, but they were unable to relocate the site afterwards.

The Plummer gang hid their largest cache consisting of about $800,000 in gold bullion and coins in a cave on **Hollow Top Mountain,** in the northern section of Deer Lodge National Forest, about seven miles northeast of Waterloo, County 287, Madison Co. They were all caught and hanged before ever coming back for the treasure.

Just before being hanged outlaw Henry Plummer swore that he had buried the $650,000 in gold bullion from his last job somewhere along Missouri River in the vicinity of **Haystack Butte,** which is close to Choteau, State 89, Teton Co. Many have searched unsuccessfully for this hoard.

The Lost Neepee Indian Gold Mine is located near Rogers Pass in the Little Rockies, about twenty miles northeast of Lincoln County 200, Lewis and Clark Co.

The Plummer gang hid about $150,000 in gold bullion and a small chest of gold coins near the banks of the Missouri River, within a mile of **Cascade,** U.S. 15, Cascade Co.

In 1897 a prospector buried about $50,000 in raw gold on the northern tip of **Holler Lake,** about three miles east of Wolf Creek, U.S. 15, Cascade Co. He died before being able to go back for his cache.

A gambler named Fleming is known to have hidden about $40,000 in gold coins, which he won playing cards, under his cabin on Bell River, about a mile northwest of **Monarch,** State 89, Cascade Co. He was killed soon after. When his will was found many years later his cabin had already disappeared.

Butch Cassidy is alleged to have buried between $50,000 and $100,000 in gold in the hills west of **Malta,** State 2, Phillips Co.

In 1901 the Curry gang held up the Great Northern passenger train near **Malta** and buried the $80,000 in gold and silver coins in the immediate vicinity.

During the depression of 1929, a wealthy merchant and rancher named William Kittering buried about $35,000 in gold coins on one of his many pieces of property in the town of **Fort Peck,** County 34, Valley Co. He died without telling his family the location of the cache.

NEBRASKA

Chimney Rock is off State 92, four miles south of Bayard, Morrill Co. Towering 500 feet above the nearby North Platte River, this rock was a famous guidepost for trappers and traders and a campsite for westward-bound settlers who followed the Oregon Trail during the nineteenth century. A number of ambushes were made by Indians here and remnants of the wagons and objects they carried should be easy to find.

Bellevue on the Missouri River, ten miles south of Omaha, Sarpy Co., is the state's oldest existing town. First established in 1823, it became an important riverboat port. The remains of two steamers are located on the west bank of the river near the town and there are vestiges of many old buildings around the town as well.

The site of Fort Atkinson is located one mile east of Fort Calhoun via a secondary road,

Washington Co. Built in 1819 and abandoned in 1827, it served as the westernmost link in a chain of forts designed to protect the flourishing fur trade from Indian attack and to prevent encroachment by British interests. The fort was also used by westward-bound settlers as a staging point. There are no visible remains today, but its exact site is marked. In 1956 some minor archaeological excavation took place here, yielding a great wealth of artifacts.

The site of Fort Robinson is on U.S. 20 near the present town of Fort Robinson, Sioux Co. The fort was built in 1874 to serve as a base for a number of Indian campaigns fought in the area, and a settlement soon sprang up around it. No traces of the original fort or settlement remain today.

Scotts Bluff is near the North Platte River, off State 92, three miles west of Gering, Scotts Co. The area was settled in prehistoric times, as is evident from the large number of artifacts of the Archic Indians which are found in the most used camping grounds. Settlers traveling along the Oregon Trail stayed at these campsites, also a favorite spot for Indian attacks on the wagon trains. Remnants of the old trail worn by wagon wheels can still be seen. Near the top of the Bluff, which rises 800 feet above the surrounding valley, there are a number of caves which contain artifacts of settlers who used them for refuge, probably after being attacked by Indians.

The site of Fort Kearney is on State 10 about eight miles from Kearney, Buffalo Co. Built in 1848 the fort served to protect settlers traveling along the Oregon Trail until it was abandoned in 1871. Today no visible traces of the fort remain but the exact site was determined by recent archaeological excavations.

The ghost town of Amboy is on the Republican River about five miles east of Red Cloud, County 136, Webster Co. It was once a flourishing mill town and farm center but today only a few buildings are standing, as well as a dam and millrace.

The ghost town of Bloomington is on the Republican River about five miles west of Franklin, County 10, Franklin Co. It was once an important trading center and the county seat. Today about 100 buildings remain, many of which date back to the early 1800s. Three miles to the west, also on the river, is the **ghost town of Brooklyn;** all of its buildings, with the exception of a large mill, are in ruins.

The ruins of Centoria are on the south side of the Platte River, opposite the city of Kearney, Buffalo Co. Very few foundations of buildings or other ruins now exist. They were probably covered by mud during flooding periods of the river. Treasure hunters have made some good finds in the area.

Devils Nest is in a tract of woodlands and rough meadow along the Missouri River, about five miles north of Linky, County 12, Knox Co. During the early 1800s and until after the Civil War, this was a favorite hideout for outlaws and desperados, who are alleged to have concealed a great deal of booty here. Many caves in the area show signs of having been occupied.

The ghost town of Dobytown is located one mile west of Fort Kearney on the Platte River, Buffalo Co. During the 1840s it was one of the wildest and wickedest towns in the West. Travelers along the Oregon and Mormon Trails and soldiers from Fort Kearney kept the town lively at all times; the cemetery is full of many men who died in gun battles. Several saloons and other buildings still stand.

The ruins of Factorville are near the Missouri River, about a mile southeast of Union, State 73, Otoe Co. Very few traces of the town remain as it was leveled in a fire in about 1925.

The ghost town of Lowell is on the south side of the Platte River, about ten miles east of Kearney, near U.S. 80, Kearney Co. It was once a booming cattle-shipping center on the Burlington and Missouri Railroad and in the 1880s had a population of 5,000. The terminus for many cattle drives, it was a tough city, like Dodge City or Wichita. Only a few buildings are still standing; the ruins of many others can be seen.

The ruins of Martinsville are on the Martin farm about nine miles west of Doniphan, County 11, Garfield Co. It was founded in 1850 and served as a supply center for the settlers traveling along the Oregon and Mormon Trails.

The ghost town of Neapolis is on the south side of the Platte River near Cedar Bluffs, about ten miles west of Fremont (State 30), Dodge Co. There was a small settlement here in 1858 when the place was selected as the state capital. The area suddenly boomed and opportunists hid large amounts of liquor and other merchandise to sell when they could build stores and saloons. Then suddenly the state legislature reversed its decision and the town was abandoned. Much of the hidden merchandise and liquor was left where it had been hidden.

The ghost town of Newark is about fifteen miles south of Kearney on State 6 and 34, and about one mile west of Minden, Kearney Co. It was once a thriving farm and frontier town and then bypassed by the railroad and abandoned. Many old buildings are standing in a large grove of cottonwood trees.

The ghost town of Oreapolis is located on the Platte River about two and a half miles north of Plattsmouth, County 34, Sarpy Co. It was a very important riverboat town from the early 1800s until it was destroyed by a flood in 1879. Only a few buildings stand today. Apparently a riverboat is wrecked close to the town as treasure hunters have been finding large numbers of American silver coins of the 1870s on the river bank after flood waters. On the opposite side of the river are the ruins of the **Moses Merrill's Mission Site.**

The ghost town of Springranch is on the little Blue River about five miles west of Fairfield, County 14, Caly Co. During the 1800s it was an important Pony Express and stagecoach station and also a cattle stockyard center. Many buildings are intact, including the railroad depot, stockyard, and many of the business buildings.

There are many tales of buried gold in the area of Crawford, State 20, Dawes Co. During the numerous Indian uprisings miners had to seek refuge in nearby **Fort Robinson** and other caches are believed to exist on the premises of this fort.

A famous miner and gambler named "Flyspeck Bill" is known to have buried several caches of gold and silver coins valued at about $100,000 in the vicinity of Rushville, State 20, Sheridan Co.

In 1857 a returning California gold miner buried a small chest of gold coins at a camping site known as **Point of Rocks,** located east of Bronco Lake near Alliance, State 385, Box Butte Co.

The Scott's Bluff National Monument, located on the south bank of the South Platte River near Scott's Bluff, County 92, Scott's Bluff Co., was a well-used camping site throughout the nineteenth century for settlers and travelers going both east and west. Numerous treasure caches are alleged to be hidden in the many caves in these hills.

A successful gambler buried about $20,000 in gold coins near **Mud Springs,** a mile north of Broadwater on the north side of the North Platte River, County 92, Morrill Co.

Cattle thieves buried about $25,000 in gold coins in the vicinity of the town of **Mullen,** County 2, Hooker Co.

A returning California miner was attacked and wounded by bushwhackers near **Senaca,** County 2, Thomas Co. He managed to escape and buried about $70,000 in gold coins and bullion along the banks of the Middle Loup River, about two miles east of the town. He died soon after from his wounds.

A band of outlaws called the Pony Boys robbed two stagecoaches and buried the loot, which consisted of an undetermined value of gold bullion and coins, near a stream in the vicinity of **Bassaett,** U.S. 20, Rock Co.

Bandits robbed about 400 pounds of gold nuggets from the Treasure Express Stagecoach in 1867 and buried it on south banks of the Lodgepole River about two miles east of **Sidney,** State 30, Cheyenne Co. They were apprehended and hanged soon afterwards and would only give this vague location for the gold. Empty bags and two chests were found near the river, so the nuggets are expected to be buried in the general area.

While fording the Lodgepole River near **Chappell,** State 30, Deuel Co., a wagon carrying an Army payroll of about $50,000 in gold and silver coins was swept away by the current. All of the money was lost.

There are many reports that throughout the nineteenth century treasures were buried in the areas of **Ash Hollow, Chimney Rock** and **Courthouse Rock** which are located on the north side of the North Platte River, within a few miles west of Lewellon, State 26, Garden Co. All three places were camping grounds much frequented by settlers, miners, and trappers. Because of the common danger of attack by Indians and bushwhackers in these places, campers would bury their valuables at night or when attacks were imminent. Since many lost their lives during the attacks it is natural that many hoards were also lost.

After robbing a bank at Kearney in 1921, bandits buried $40,000 in gold coins and a considerable amount of jewelry somewhere near the Middle Loup River about two miles south of **Sargent,** State 183, Custer Co.

Buffalo Bill Cody hid about $17,000 in gold coins somewhere near the **Scott's Rest Ranch** near North Platte, County 70, Lincoln Co. On the collector's market these coins would be worth a small fortune today. Several miles northwest of this site is **Buffalo Bill Ranch State Historical Park,** once owned by the famous Wild West hero. Relics found on this ranch, especially items such as weapons, branding irons, barbed wire, and so on, bring high prices on the collector's market.

During the late 1890s, a rancher named Wiggins buried numerous caches of gold coins and bullion on his ranch, located between the north side of the North Platte River and the town of **Gothenburg,** State 30, Dawson Co.

The ghost town of Rylander is located about three miles northwest of Franam, County 23, Dawson Co. It was founded in the 1860s and was an important cattle and agricultural center until being burnt down by an accidental fire in 1894. Only a few of the old buildings remain standing. Nearby in Gilmore Canyon, a prospector named Chase Gish hid a large hoard of gold nuggets before being killed by Indians. Close to Rylander is the McDermott Ranch, where several caches of gold coins and bullion were reported buried. While digging a post hole in 1951 a ranch hand discovered gold coins worth over $40,000. In the resulting stampede, a treasure hunter discovered a cache of about 20 five-pound gold bars.

Several chests full of gold coins and silverware were hidden on the **site of Plum Creek Massacre,** now a state park, located on the outskirts of Lexington, U.S. 80, Dawson Co. Several caches of gold robbed from miners are known to have been buried in and around the town.

There are many old tales about soldiers and gamblers burying caches of gold and silver coins in the vicinity of **Dobytown, Fort Kearney** and **Kearney.** It is one of the favorite treasure-hunting spots in the state and rarely a year passes that a major find isn't made. In 1975 a treasure hunter found a cache of 179 California gold coins which turned out to be worth over $150,000 because of their numismatic rarity. Large numbers of old weapons are also found in great abundance, and along the river bank large quantities of valuable old bottles are recovered, especially after flood waters.

Just prior to a raid by Quantrill's Raiders during the Civil War, many of the residents of **Bloomington** buried their valuables; during the raid many were killed. Five different caches of gold coins and jewelry have been found in this area in the past ten years. In nearby **Brooklyn** a hoard of about 200 gold and 350 silver coins were found by a treasure hunter in 1969, who discovered them while digging a hole to bury his trash before leaving after an unsuccessful weekend of searching the area.

In 1946 while plowing his fields a man found about $100,000 in Mormon gold and silver coins on his farm near **Wood River,** County 11, Hall Co. To avoid paying taxes and having problems with persons claiming to own the treasure, he reburied it on an island in the nearby Platte River. On his deathbed in 1950 he refused to tell any member of his family where the exact spot was, claiming it could only bring the family harm and he preferred "that the devil keep it."

A ferry operator on the Missouri River at **Decatur,** State 73, Burt Co., collected his tolls in empty nail kegs and when they were full he buried them near his home. In 1926 one of these kegs was accidentally discovered on his old property and many more are expected to be found in the area.

In 1924 about $500,000 in gold and negotiable bonds, taken during a three and a half million dollar mail-train robbery at Council Bluffs, Iowa, was tossed from the **Douglas Street Bridge** into the Missouri River between Omaha and Council Bluff. Months of dragging failed to find a trace of the money, which a great many persons witnessed being thrown into the river.

During the 1930s a bootlegger buried about $10,000 in gold coins and $25,000 in paper currency near the **Plattsmouth Bridge,** which crosses the Missouri River off State 34, Sarpy Co.

The Jesse James gang is alleged to have hidden a large amount of loot on the **Catron-Miyoshi Fruit Farm,** located about three miles southeast of Nebraska City, State 35, Otoe Co.

After a flood in 1972, several thousand gold and silver coins were found along the west bank of the Missouri River, about half a mile south of **Nemaha,** County 67, Nemaha Co. They probably were washed ashore from a river wreck. At the confluence of the Nemaha and Missouri Rivers nearby, a small boat overset in 1857 carrying five returning California gold miners; they lost about $50,000 in gold coins and bullion.

The ghost town of Yankton is near the banks of the Missouri River about a mile south of Rulo, State 73, Richardson Co. Only five buildings are still standing.

NEVADA

Austin is located on U.S. 50 below the crest of the Toiyabe Mountains, Lander Co. During the 1860s the town flourished as a silver-mining boomtown and was the state's largest city after Virginia City, boasting a population of over 10,000. The Austin Mines yielded over $50 million in silver before being closed down in the 1890s, causing the town to decline. Today the town only has a population of about 300 and the ruins of many of the old buildings are all over the area; the most impressive is **Stokes Castle** built in 1879 by the financier Anson Phelps Stokes, which is just outside of the town.

The site of the former **Berlin Mining Camp** is off State 21 near Ione, Nye Co. Gold was discovered here in 1863 and during the next seventeen years more than one million dollars in gold and silver was found here. No traces of the campsite remains today.

Carson City was founded in 1858 on the site of a trading post begun seven years earlier and became the state capital in 1861. After the discovery of the Comstock Lode, the town flourished as a supply point for the miners and the nearby ranching communities. Many of the original buildings are still standing today.

Dayton is off U.S. 50 about ten miles east of Carson City, Storey Co. The town got its start as a trading post on the Carson River for the California-bound settlers. Then in 1850 with the discovery of gold in nearby Gold Canyon, the town quickly grew in size and importance. Today the small, sleepy community of about 250 people still has many of the original structures standing from the gold-mining period.

Genoa is located off U.S. 395 in the Carson Valley, Storey Co. It was founded in 1849 and is the state's first white permanent settlement. It started off as a trading post along the California Trail and soon after was settled by many Mormons, but they all went back to Salt Lake City in 1855 and miners and ranchers soon took their place. Most of the original settlement was destroyed by fire around 1880.

Goldfield is on U.S. 95, 25 miles south of Tonopah, Nye Co. The discovery of gold here in 1902 created this community which boomed until 1918, boasting a population of 40,000 people. Now there are fewer than 200 people living in it. Between 1903 and 1940 over $100 million in gold was produced here. Many of the old buildings and remains of others from the town's heyday still can be seen.

The remains of **Las Vegas Mormon Fort** can still be seen on North Las Vegas Boulevard at Washington in the present town. In June 1855 Mormon missionaries established a small settlement here to convert the Paiute Indians, but abandoned it two years later and returned to Salt Lake City. Today only one of their adobe buildings still stands on the site.

Tonopah is located at the junction of U.S. 6 and 95, Nye Co. The discovery of silver here in 1900 started Nevada's second big mining boom; soon after gold was also discovered in the area. Around 1910 over 30,000 people lived here, but today the town has a population of fewer than 2,000. By 1920 when the mines were depleted, they had already yielded over $200 million in gold and silver. There are only a few of the original buildings left.

Virginia City is located about ten miles north of Carson City, Storey Co. Founded in 1859 as a direct result of the famous Comstock Lode discovery nearby, it flourished for about twenty years as the most prosperous mining metropolis in Nevada. By 1876 it had a population of over 30,000, but a fire that unfortunately destroyed the city in 1875 necessitated much rebuilding. However by 1880 most of the mines were depleted and the place made a sharp decline. Today parts of the ghost town have been restored and about 600 people now live there.

The Comstock Lode was one of the world's richest deposits of lode gold and silver and produced over $300 million during its twenty-year heyday. The capital not only helped build Virginia City, but San Francisco as well, and partially enabled the Confederacy to finance the Civil War. Today the sites of many of the mines are marked by large yellow dumps, which are now being reworked by amateurs on weekends.

The ruins of Fort Churchill are on U.S. 95A, about eight miles south of U.S. 50, near the village of Weeks, Storey Co. It was built in 1860 following an Indian uprising and served as a pony express station and trading center until being abandoned in 1871.

The Lost Pogue Gold Mine is in the Pancake Mountains, about 5 miles north of Pogue Station, in White Pine County.

The Lost Wilderness Gold Mine is near Sherman Peak in the Shoshine Mountains, about fifteen miles northeast of Gabbs, County 23, Nye Co.

The Lost Padre Martyr Gold Mine is in the vicinity of Mount Jefferson in the Toquima Range, about ten miles northeast of the town of Round Mountain, County 92, Nye Co. Several other abandoned gold mines are in this general area.

The ruins of Aurora are close to the California-Nevada state line about 25 miles southwest of Hawthorne on County 31 in the Excelsior Mountains, Mineral Co. During the Civil War the town had a population of over 10,000 but today only a few ruins are visible.

The ghost town of Belleville is at the base of the Monte Cristo Mountain range on State 95, about seven miles south of Mina, Mineral Co. It was once a prosperous mining town; and some of its mid-nineteenth-century buildings have survived.

The ghost town of Belmont is located about ten miles east of Bald Mountain and 45 miles northeast of Tonopah on County 82, Nye Co. It was a roaring mining town before the Civil War; many of its buildings are intact.

The ruins of Bonnie Clare are a few miles south of Gold Mountain and fifteen miles northwest of the California-Nevada state line just off County 72, which goes to Death Valley Scotty's Castle, Nye Co. Only one building still stands among the ruins of more than a hundred.

The ruins of Bristol Wells are about ten miles south of Fairfield Peak and 45 miles north of Caliente on State 93, Lincoln Co. It was founded in 1873 when the Bristol Silver Mine was opened and a large smelting operation made the town prosper. Today only 3 kilns and a few cabins are standing among the many ruins and abandoned mines.

The ruins of Bullfrog are in the Death Valley National Monument on County 58, about five miles southwest of Beatty, Nye Co. There are a number of abandoned silver and gold mines in the area.

The ghost town of Candelaria is located in the Monte Cristo Mountain Range, about fifteen miles northwest of Coaldale (State 95), Esmeralda Co. At one time this was the richest silver-producing area in the nation but today only hundreds of ruined buildings are left.

The ghost town of Charleston is on the east fork of the St. Mary River, a few miles east of Mt. Velma, and about 50 miles north of the town of Deeth (State 40), Elko Co. It can be reached only by horseback; very few buildings are still standing in this old gold-mining town.

The ghost town of Cortez is in the Cortez Mountains on County 21, about 45 miles northwest of Diamond, Eureka Co. It was a thriving mining town of 1,000 in 1868; today about ten people still live among the many standing and ruined buildings.

The ghost town of Gilbart is near Dry Lake about eighteen miles northeast of Coaldale, Esmeralda Co. It was an active silver-mining center at the turn of the century and then was reactivated for a few years after World War I. There are many standing buildings in a

229

Detection capabilities of modern one-touch instruments are not bothered by highly mineralized ground that is usually found in rugged mountain terrain.

Colorful frontier history of the United States is often associated with buried treasures that are waiting to be found in Nevada and the other Desert States remarkable state of preservation and a little silver mining is done during the summer months. The site can be reached only with four-wheel-drive vehicles or on horseback.

The ghost town of Gold Point is about five miles north of Gold Mountain, about ten miles east of the California-Nevada state line, and about eleven miles southeast of Lida, Esmeralda Co. Only about twenty buildings are still standing. Several buried caches of gold are hidden here.

The ghost town of Goodsprings is in the Springs Mountains, about seven miles northwest of Jean on County 53, Clark Co. More than 200 old buildings are still standing; the town has been used in several Hollywood Old West Movies.

The ghost town of Hamilton is located ten miles south of State 50 between the Nevada National Forest and Treasure Peak, Churchill Co. During the 1870s more than $75 million in silver was produced in the immediate area. Hamilton is one of the most picturesque ghost towns in the state because of its large number of nineteenth century buildings.

The ghost town of Jefferson is six miles north of Round Mountain (County 92) and 60 miles north of Tonopah, Rye Co. Mining began in the area in 1866; ten years later the community had over 1,000 residents. Today over 50 buildings still remain.

The ghost town of Johnnie is near Mt. Stirling, about fifteen miles north of Pahrump on County 16, Clark Co. There are many old buildings, including a silver refinery. A lucky winner at the Las Vegas crap tables is known to have hidden about $100,000 of his winnings somewhere in this ghost town before dying from a heart attack.

The ghost town of Ludwig is 17 miles north of Wellington (County 3), just east of the Washoe Indian Reservation, Lyon Co. It is one of the best-preserved ghost towns in the state with over 100 buildings still standing.

The ghost town of Manhattan is in the Toquima Mountain Range just south of Bald Mountain on County 69, about 40 miles north of Tonopah, Nye Co. It was a prosperous gold center in the late nineteenth century and still has a few inhabitants.

The ghost town of Midas is located between the Spring Branch and Willow Rock Rivers on County 18, about 60 miles east of Winnemucca, Elko Co. It was a mining boomtown in the early 1900s; a few old gold prospectors live in the community today. A large number of buildings are in a state of preservation.

The town of Mina is five miles west of Pilot Peak and 28 miles northwest of Coaldale on State 95, Mineral Co. Fewer than 400 people still live in this town that had over 4,000 residents in the late nineteenth century. There are many other ghost towns and abandoned mines in this general area.

The ruins of Oriental are in the Grapevine Mountains, about nine miles south of the ghost town of Gold Point, Esmeralda Co. The site can be reached only by horseback; there are foundations of a few buildings.

The ruins of Osceola are located in the Humboldt National Forest, four miles south of State 50 and 40 miles southeast of Ely, White Pine Co. The site, which can be reached only by horseback, was a gold-mining center in the 1870s, of which very few ruins remain.

The ghost town of Palisade is located near Emigrant Pass, about ten miles southwest of Carlin (State 40), via a dirt road about four miles south of the main highway, Eureka Co. Three railroads formed a junction here and at one time it was expected to be the largest and most important city in the state. There are more than 100 old buildings in Palisade.

The ghost town of Palmetto is in the Slate Ridge Range, about 35 miles southwest of Goldfield (State 95) and four miles west of the ghost town of Lida, Esmeralda Co. It can be reached only by horseback. Its mile-long main street is lined with hundreds of buildings, most of which are in ruins. Nearby are several abandoned silver and gold mines.

The ghost town of Pine Grove is just south of Mount Etna in the Toiyabe National Forest, below the East Walker River, Nye Co. The town is accessible only by horseback. Just a few of the old buildings in this gold-mining center remain.

The ruins of Rawhide are located near Buffalo Mountain in the Toiyabe National Forest, about 40 miles northeast of Luning (State 95), Nye Co. This mining town once had a population of 5,000 and now it is filled with hundreds of ruins.

234

The **ghost town of Rhyolite** is near the northern edge of the Amargosa Desert, on County 58, three miles west of Beatty, Nye Co. This rip-roaring mining town once had over 6,000 residents; today only the old railroad station and a few business buildings are still standing among the many ruins. The world-famous "Bottle House" built from discarded whiskey bottles is located here.

The **ruins of Rockland** are three miles south of the East Walker River, near Sugarloaf Mountain in the Toiyabe National Forest and can be reached only by four-wheel-drive vehicles or horseback. There are ruins of several hundred buildings on this site and several small treasure finds have been made in recent years.

The **ghost town of Searchlight** is located ten miles east of Crescent Peak on State 95, about 55 miles south of Las Vegas, Clark Co. A few residents still live here and there are many standing buildings.

The **ruins of Silver Peak** are located in the Silver Peak Range, about 22 miles north of the ghost town of Lida on County 47, Esmeralda Co. There are several other smaller ghost towns in the area as well as many abandoned silver and gold mines.

The **ruins of Sodaville** are in the Excelsior Mountains about three miles south of Mina and a short distance east of State 95, Mineral Co. Very few traces of this once prosperous gold-mining town mark the site.

The **ghost town of Tuscarora** is located at the 6400-foot level on Mount Blitzen in the Tuscarora Mountains, near County 11, about 50 miles northwest of Elko, Elko Co. It was a thriving mining town until about 1900 when the mines were exhausted and the miners left. Only a dozen buildings survive.

The **ghost town of Vernon** is in the Seven Troughs Mountain Chain, 25 miles northwest of Lovelock (U.S. 80), Pershing Co. Vernon is about three miles to the east of the ghost town of Seven Troughs. Both mining towns have large numbers of standing buildings.

The **Lost Black Rock Silver Lode** is located in the vicinity of Mud Meadows and Black Rock, a bit northeast of the immigrant trails in the northwest corner of Humboldt Co. The **Lost Peter Lassen Gold Mine** is in the same general area. The **Lost Tenderfoot Gold Mine**, the **Lost Mine of the Little Brown Men**, the **Lost Padre Gold Mine**, the **Lost Indian Gold Mine**, and the **Lost Frenchman Gold Mine** are all within a ten-mile radius of Pahute Peak.

The **ghost town of Rosebud** is a bit east of Rosebud Peak, about 32 miles west of Imlay (State 40), Pershing Co. The site can only be reached by four-wheel-drive vehicles or horseback. About 50 old buildings are still intact in this gold-mining town.

The **town of Gerlach** is on County 81, near Granite Peak in Washoe Co. In this same general area the ghost towns of **Ashdown, Leadville, Roop** and **Sheepshead** are located; the **Lost Pick and Shovel Gold Mine** and the **Lost Foreman Lead Mine** are somewhere in the same general vicinity.

During the 1880s a prospector buried about $250,000 in gold ore near Tohakum Peak, about two miles northeast of the northern tip of Pyramid Lake, Washoe Co. He was unable to find the cache after the winter snows melted.

In 1814 a band of Indians attacked a wagon train carrying a large number of Chinese laborers and robbed about $50,000 in gold coins. They playfully scattered the coins along the shores of Pyramid Lake right off Anano Island.

In the general area of **Lovelock,** State 40 and 90, Pershing Co., the following ghost towns are located: **Ollinhouse,** nine miles west of Wadsworth; **Jessup,** 30 miles southwest of Lovelock; **Hot Springs,** 40 miles southwest of Lovelock; **Ragtown,** eight miles east of Fallon; **Rabbit Hole,** seven miles south of Sulphur; **Farrell,** 30 miles northeast of Lovelock; **Arabia,** 21 miles northwest of Lovelock; **Scossa,** fourteen miles north of Lovelock; **Dun Glen,** three miles northeast of Mill City; **Oreana,** fifteen miles northeast of Lovelock; **Unionville,** 28 miles northeast of Lovelock; **Rochester,** twenty miles northeast of Lovelock; **American Canyon** (a Chinese gold camp until 1900), 30 miles south of Mill City at the foot of Buffalo Mountain; **Lassen's Meadows,** seven miles south of Lovelock; **Bolivia,** 34 miles southeast of Lovelock; **National,** four miles south of McDermit; **Queen City,** five miles north of Paradise Valley.

The **Lost Silver Mine of Humboldt** and the **Lost Nevada Lead and Silver Mine** are both located in the vicinity of Lovelock in the direction of Trinity Mountain to the west.

235

The following ghost towns are located in the general vicinity of **Winnemucca,** U.S. 80 and State 95, Humboldt Co.; **Daveytown,** 28 miles northwest of Winnemucca; **Adelaine,** eighteen miles southeast of Winnemucca; **Aura,** eighteen miles west of Mountain City; **Edgemont,** fifteen miles southwest of Mountain City; **Rio Tinto,** two miles east of Mountain City; **Cornucopia,** 28 miles southwest of Mountain City.

The Lost Easterly Gold Ledge is located near the ghost town of Midas, near the head of Willow Creek Rock and Monument Peak, Elko Co.

In 1962 a tourist accidentally found a huge cache of gold ore in the vicinity of the ghost town of Tuscarora and didn't realize what he had until weeks later. He was unable to relocate the cache on subsequent trips. In a nearby canyon is the **Lost Golden Eagle Mine;** within a mile of this lost mine five miners were massacred by Indians in 1864 after burying about $100,000 in gold bullion.

The following ghost towns are located in the vicinity of Gold Acres and Battle Mountain, U.S. 80, Lander Co.: **Galena,** eleven miles south of Battle Mountain; **Bannock,** thirteen miles southwest of Battle Mountain near the Reese River; **Betty O'Neal,** fourteen miles south of Battle Mountain; **Lewis,** ten miles south of Battle Mountain; **Gravelly Ford,** on the Humboldt River, 23 miles southwest of Carlin; **Hill Top,** eighteen miles southeast of Battle Mountain; **Tenabo,** seven miles northeast of Gold Acres; **Buckhorn,** seven miles southeast of Gold Acres; **Union,** 38 miles south of Carlin; **Mineral Hill,** 42 miles south of Carlin; **Alpha,** 36 miles north of Eureka; **Amador,** seven miles north of Austin; **Yankee Blade,** four miles north of Austin; **Perciville,** nine miles northeast of Austin.

The Lost Bonanza Gold Mine is on a small mountain in a chain of six snow-capped peaks, in the general vicinity of Austin, State 50, Lander Co.

The following ghost towns are located in the general vicinity of Mountain City, County 51, Elko Co.: **Patsville,** two miles south of Mountain City near the Owyhee River; **Rio Tonto,** three miles south of Mountain City; **Jarbridge,** about fifteen miles southwest of Murphy Hot Springs, Idaho; **Delano,** eighteen miles southeast of Contact; **Metropolis,** eleven miles north of Wells; **Montello,** thirteen miles northeast of Elko; **Loray,** 31 miles northwest of Wendover.

The ruins of Camp Ruby are located 25 miles south of Wells on State 93 and then 38 miles southwest on Ruby Lake Road, on the Te-Moak Indian Reservation, Elko Co. The camp has served as a military post, trading center, and outlaw hangout over the years and numerous caches of treasure are reported in the vicinity. In the same general neighborhood the **Lost Joshua Ward's Silver Mine** is located; as well as the **ghost town of Hobson** at the south end of Ruby Lake.

The town of Currie is located on the Nelson River and State 93, about 60 miles south of Wells, Elko Co. The **ghost town of Sprucemont** is 24 miles north of Currie; another named **Victoria** is sixteen miles northeast of Currie; and a third ghost town, **Dolly Verden,** is 22 miles northeast of Currie.

The following ghost towns are located in the general vicinity of Ely, State 50 and 93, White Pine Co.: **Ruby Hill,** two miles west of Eureka; **Newark,** fourteen miles northeast of Eureka; **Schellbourne,** 41 miles north of Ely; **Aurum,** 25 miles northeast of McGill; **Steptoe City,** nine miles north of Ely; **Hamilton,** 23 miles west of Ruth; **Ward,** five miles southeast of Ely; **Taylor,** seventeen miles southeast of Ely; **Atlanta,** 45 miles north of Pioche.

A Jim Pogue is believed to have hidden about $200,000 in treasure near his trading post on the west slope of the gap in the **Pancake Mountains,** a few miles to the west of County 20, near the corner of Nye, White Pine and Eureka Counties.

The Knight's Lost Gold Mine is near Sand Spring in the Painted Hill Mountains, Churchill Co.

The following ghost towns are located in the general area of the Toiyabe National Forest: **Clan Alpine,** 21 miles east of Eastgate; **Wonder,** thirteen miles northwest of Eastgate; **La Plata,** seventeen miles southeast of Stillwater; **Quartz Mountain,** twelve miles north of Gabbs; **Broken Hills,** 54 miles east of Fallon; **Ione,** twenty miles northeast of Gabbs; **Grantsville,** twelve miles southeast of Gabbs; **Berlin,** eighteen miles east of Gabbs; **Goldyke,** twelve miles southeast of Gabbs; **Pine Grove,** fifteen miles southeast of Wellington; **Rockland,** sixteen miles northeast of Sweetwater; **La Panta,** ten miles southeast of Hawthorne; **Tonopah Junction,** four

236

miles west of Mina; **Pahranagat,** three miles south of Sodaville; **Marietta,** two miles northwest of Coaldale; **Aurora,** twenty miles southwest of Hawthorne; **Belleville,** sixteen miles south of Mina; **Gilbert,** 22 miles east of Mina; **San Antonio,** sixteen miles southwest of Manhattan; **Candelaria,** fourteen miles northeast of Basalt; **Columbus,** six miles northwest of Coaldale; **Bony Springs,** four miles southeast of Silver Peak; **Silver Peak,** twenty miles north of Lida; **Weepah,** 25 miles west of Tonopah; **Barcelona,** 43 miles north of Tonopah; **Belmont,** twenty miles southeast of Round Mountain; **Baxter Springs,** six miles east of Tonopah; **Hannapah,** twenty miles northeast of Tonopah; **Treasure City,** three miles south of Hamilton; **Tybo,** fourteen miles north of Warm Springs; **Morey,** 36 miles northeast of Warm Springs; **Clifford,** six miles west of Warm Springs; **Reveille,** seventeen miles southeast of Warm Springs; **Silverbow,** twenty miles south of Warm Springs; **Tempiute,** 27 miles northwest of Hiko; **Hiko,** four miles north of Crystal Springs.

On September 13, 1913 a flash flood carried away about half of the town of **Goldfield,** State 95, Esmeralda Co. Many safes and countless other valuables were washed away by the flood waters and the whole area to the west of the town is a treasure hunter's paradise.

At **Spanish Spring** on County 82, about eight miles southeast of the ghost town of Manhattan, Nye Co., Spanish miners in the late 1700s are known to have buried about a ton in gold bullion after many in their party were killed during an Indian attack.

Around 1900 a mine official or assayer buried about $70,000 in gold bullion somewhere on Oak Springs Summit, about eight miles southwest of Caliente, State 93, Lincoln Co.

The ghost town of Coyote Springs is on State 93, about 25 miles north of Crystal Springs, in the Worthington Mountains, Lincoln Co. After being abandoned in the 1870s it served as an outlaw hangout for many years. Numerous caches of loot are believed to be hidden in the area.

According to stories, in 1857 Mormon leader Brigham Young buried about one and a half million dollars in gold bullion and coins between Ash Meadows and Cave Valley in northern **Lincoln County.**

The following ghost towns are located in the general vicinity of Las Vegas in the southern part of the state: **Hornsilver,** three miles south of Gold Point; **Pioneer,** seven miles north of Beatty; **Gold Center,** five miles south of Beatty; **Bullfrog,** six miles southwest of Beatty; **Carrara,** seven miles south of Beatty; **Wahmonie,** eight miles northwest of Mercury; **Potosi,** 29 miles southwest of Las Vegas; **Roach,** two miles north of Stateline; **Crescent,** twelve miles northwest of Searchlight.

The Lost Duckett Silver Mine is in the Black Mountains in the very center of the Nellis Air Force Range and Nuclear Testing Site.

The Lost Gunsight Gold Mine, found and lost in 1850, is located in the area of Bullfrog Hills, about eight miles northwest of Beatty, Nye Co.

In 1897 a miner buried two large chests of silver coins and bars near **Mountain Spring Summit,** northwest of Potosi Mountain, just off U.S. 15, about 20 miles southwest of Las Vegas, Clark Co.

The Lost Mormon Gold Mine is somewhere in the vicinity of the McCullough Mountains, about fifteen miles northwest of Searchlight, State 95, Clark Co.

The Comstock Lode, an area about ten miles north of Reno, was rivaled only by the California Mother Lode in its number of gold and silver mines and millions of dollars of their worth. It is a veritable labyrinth of abandoned mines, mining camps, and ghost towns—most so close they almost touch one another. It is one of the favorite treasure hunting spots in this state and many important discoveries are constantly being made.

There are many old buildings and ruins in and around Carson City, about twenty miles south of Reno. Various outlaws and law-abiding citizens hid much treasure in and around the city. The following three ghost towns are located north of Carson City: **Washoe City,** nine miles to the north; **Como,** five miles to the northeast; and **Dutch Nick's,** three miles to the north.

A prospector named Snowshoe Thompson buried a 420-pound cache of gold nuggets on the far side of Echo Summit, near the town of **Stateline,** County 19, Douglas Co. He died from a heart attack soon afterwards.

Bandits robbed the Virginia City Bank in October 1927 and hid the loot somewhere in **Six Mile Canyon,** a few miles east of Virginia City. They were hanged without revealing the exact location.

Somewhere in the ghost town of **Ramsey,** eight miles northwest of Silver Springs (State 50 and 95A), Lyon Co., a prospector returning from the California gold fields buried over $75,000 in gold coins and bars after his horse broke a leg. He obtained a new horse in Virginia City, but foolishly mentioned burying his cache, and was bushwhacked and killed before he could get back to pick up his gold.

The following is a list of all the abandoned mines of precious metals, other minerals and gem stones in the state, by county: **CHURCHILL CO. Fairview Silver Mine,** near Fallon; **La Plata Mine,** near Stillwater; and **Wonder Mine,** near Fallon. **CLARK CO. Barefoot Mine,** eight miles west of Goodsprings; **Bullion Mine,** five miles south of Goodsprings; **Cottonwood Mine,** seven miles east of Blue Diamond; **Crescent Turquoise Mine,** near Searchlight; **Double-Up Mine,** seven miles north of Goodsprings; **Golden Empire Mine,** five miles southwest of Nelson; **Green Monster Mine,** eight miles north of Sandy Hill; **Key West Mine,** sixteen miles northeast of the "Narrows" on Lake Mead; **Lincoln Mine,** six miles south of Goodsprings; **Lead King Mine,** 3 miles northeast of Dike Siding; **Lucky Jew Mine,** eight miles south of Goodsprings; **Milford Mine,** two miles east of Well, California; **Monte Cristo Mine,** five miles south of Goodsprings; **Patsy Silver Mine,** three miles west of Nelson; **Potosi Mine,** six miles southwest of Mountain Springs; **Red Cloud Mine,** five miles northwest of Goodsprings; **Robbins Mine,** nine miles north of 'Goodsprings; **Sultan Mine,** eight miles southwest of Goodsprings; **Xmas Mine,** eleven miles southwest of Jean; **Yellow Horse Mine,** five miles west of Goodsprings; and the **Yellow Pine Mine,** three miles west of Goodsprings. **ELKO CO. Blue Jacket Mine,** near Duckwater; **Bullion City Mine,** near Elko; **Edgemont Gold Mine,** near Elko; **Gold Creek Mine,** near Elko; **Grouse Creek Gold Mine,** on Boulder Creek in the northwest corner of the Shoshone Indian Reservation; and the **Sprucemont Mine,** near Wells. **ESMERALDA CO. Black Horse Mine,** twelve miles west of Coaldale; **Drinkwater Mine,** ten miles northwest of Silver Peak; **Fowler Mine,** seven miles west of the Fish Lake Maintenance Station on Indian Creek; **Garnet King Mine,** five miles southwest of the ruins of Pigeon Camp; **Gilbert Gold Mine,** near Tonopah; **Goldsmith Gold Mine,** seven miles south of Tonopah; **Klondyke Mine,** nine miles south of Tonopah; **Micro Metal Mine,** Columbus Salt Marsh, six miles off State 6 highway; **Mohave Gold Mine,** twelve miles south of the Dyer Post Office; **Mohawk Gold Mine,** eight miles south of the Dyer Post Office; **Montezuma Mine,** eight miles west of Goldfield; **Oro Monte Mine,** eleven miles northwest of Silver Peak; **Oriental Mine,** on Palmetto Mountain, seven miles south of the Tule Canyon River; **Palmetto Mine,** near Lida; **Phillipsburg Gold Mine,** near Goldfield; **Pinon Mine,** fourteen miles west of Coaldale; **Red Rock Mine,** seven miles northwest of the Fish Lake Maintenance Station; **Roosevelt Mine,** in Palmetto Mountains, five miles south of Tule Canyon Road; **Silver Moon Gold Mine,** six miles south of Gold Point; **Sylvania Silver Mine,** five miles southwest of Palmetto, in the Palmetto Mountains; **Weepah Mine,** near Tonopah; and the **Wiley Green Mine,** twelve miles south of Gold Point. **EUREKA CO. Buckhorn Mine,** near Beowawe; **Mineral Hill Silver Mine,** near Mineral Hill; **Richmond Mine,** on Ruby Hill; and the **Tenabo Silver Mine,** on Battle Mountain. **HUMBOLDT CO. Bolivia Mine,** near Winnemucca; **Getchell Mine,** near Golconda; **Golden Jacket Mines,** near Mill City; and the **Pueblo Mine,** near Mill City. **LANDER CO. Bannock Gold Mine,** on Battle Mountain; **Betty O'Neal Mine,** on Battle Mountain; **Canon City Mine,** ten miles northwest of Kingston; **Clifton Silver Mine,** near Austin; **Copper Basin Mine,** on Battle Mountain; **Cortez Gold Mine,** on Battle Mountain; **Dean Gold Mine,** on Battle Mountain; **Geneva Mine,** near Austin; **Guadalajara Gold Mine,** near Austin; **Kingston Gold Mine,** near Austin; **Lewis Gold Mine,** on Battle Mountain; **Pittsburg Mine,** on Battle Mountain; and the **Yankee Blade Silver Mine,** near Austin. **LINCOLN CO. Bristol Silver Mine,** near Pioche; **Bullionville Mine,** near Pioche; **Caselton Mine,** near Pioche; **Comet Mine,** eight miles west of Pioche; **Frieburg Mines,** near Hiko; **Groom Mine,** thirty-five miles southwest of Crystal Springs; **Ida May Mine,** six miles east of Bristol Wells; **Juka Gold Mine,** near Tybo; **Jackrabbit Mine,** four miles southeast of Bristol

Wells; **Lincoln Mine,** two miles south of Tempiute; **Lucky Star Mine,** five miles east of Bristol Wells; **Old Potosi Mine,** near Mountain Springs; **Pan American Mine,** nine miles southwest of Pioche; **Roset Mine,** eleven miles northwest of Crystal Springs; **Silver Stallion Gold Mine,** twelve miles northeast of Wilson Creek Mountain; **Southpoint Mine,** seventeen miles northwest of Crystal Springs; **Tempiute Mine,** near Tybo; and the **Woodbutcher Mine,** 6 miles south of Bristol Wells. **LYON CO. Buckson Mine,** near Wabuska; **Como Gold Mine,** near Dayton; and the **Ramsey Gold Mine,** near Virginia City. **MINERAL CO. Granite Gold Mine,** in the Lodi Hills; **Pinegrove Gold Mine,** near Yerington; and the **Rockland Gold Mine,** near Yerington. **NYE CO. Atwood Mine,** near Luning; **Bullmoose Silver Mine,** twelve miles southeast of Beatty; **Cascade Gold Mine,** eight miles east of Eden Creek Ranch; **Clay Mine,** ten miles northeast of Beatty; **Clifford Mine,** near Tonopah; **Downeyville Mine,** near Gabbs; **Ellsworth Gold Mine,** near Ione; **Flurspor Silver Mine,** six miles east of Beatty; **Goldyke Mine,** near Luning; **Hotcreek Gold Mine,** near Tybo; **Jefferson Mine,** near Tybo; **Johnnie Gold Mine,** four miles northeast of Johnnie; **Kawick Gold Mine,** near Tonopah; **King Tonopah Gold Mine,** three miles north of Tonopah; **Lodi Mine,** near Downeyville; **Mayflower Mine,** four miles southwest of Springdale; **Morey Silver Mine,** near Tonopah; **Northumberland Silver Mine,** near Belmont; **Ophir City Silver Mine,** near Austin; **Oswald Mine,** seven miles east of Reed; **Pioneer Mine,** near Springdale; **Pueblo Gold Mine,** near Austin; **Quartz Mountain Mine,** near Gabbs; **Reveille Mines,** near Tybo; **Royston Silver Mine,** near Tonopah; **San Antonio Silver Mine,** near Tonopah; **Silver Bow Mine,** near Tybo; **Tonopah King Mine,** three miles northeast of Tonopah; **Troy Gold Mine,** near Tybo; **Wahmomie Mine,** near Beatty; and the **Washington Silver Mine,** near Austin. **PERSHING CO. American Canyon Mine,** near Unionville; **Arabia Mine,** near Oceana; **Dun Glen Chinese Mine,** near Mill City; **Goldbanks Gold Mine,** near Winnemucca; **Rabbithold Gold Mine,** near Gerlach; **Rochester Silver Mine,** near Lovelock; **Rye Patch Silver Mine,** near Lovelock; and the **Seven Troughs Gold Mine,** near Lovelock. **STOREY CO. Gold Hill Mine,** near Virginia City. **WASHOE CO. Leadville Mine,** near Gerlach; **Olinghouse Mine,** near Wadsworth; and the **Poe City Mine,** near Reno. **WHITE PINE CO. Almeda Mine,** near Eureka; **Aurum Silver Mine,** twenty miles southeast of Schellbourne; **Eberhart Mine,** near Ely; **Joy Gold Mine,** near Eureka; **Mineral City Gold Mine,** near Ely; **Newark Hill Silver Mine,** near Eureka; **Pancake Mine,** near Hamilton; **Paymaster Mine,** south of Mineral City; **Taylor Mine,** near Ely; and the **Ward Gold Mine,** near Ely.

NEW HAMPSHIRE

Exeter in Rockingham County was founded in 1638 and has more Revolutionary War landmarks than any other place in the state. The state capital was moved here in 1775 from Portsmouth. Unlike most old Colonial towns which have been obliterated by progress, this town has fewer than 10,000 population and many interesting colonial buildings have been preserved.

Shaker Village is located west of State 106, twelve miles north of Concord, Merrimack Co. The town was founded in 1792 by the Shaker religious sect, part of it was burned down in 1804, and many of the original buildings have been restored in recent years. Vestiges of many old buildings can be found in surrounding farm land.

The ruins of Fort William and Mary are located in New Castle, near Portsmouth. A small village was built on the site of an earlier earthwork constructed some time in the 1600s as protection against pirates. It was renamed **Fort Constitution,** was manned briefly in 1806 and again during the War of 1812, then abandoned and fell into ruin. Many early colonial ruins also dot the surrounding countryside.

Portsmouth at the mouth of the Piscatagua River was first settled in 1623 and named Strawberry Banke, but renamed Portsmouth in 1653. The town was an important colonial seaport and shipbuilding center. Many of the old buildings have been preserved and the ruins of many others still exist.

Manchester in Hillsborough County is the state's largest town (90,000) and dates back to the colonial period. Many ruined houses are in the neighborhood. **Stark Fort,** built during the colonial war, lies hidden somewhere near Nutts Pond.

Durham in Strafford County dates back to the early Colonial period. A retired pirate named John Clifton is known to have died after burying a substantial amount of booty in 1716, which he acquired in the Caribbean. The site of the cache is believed to be near State 108 and the Oyster River.

Ruins of Fort Constitution are located near the intersection of State 1B and Wentworth St. in New Castle, Rockingham Co. It was first known as **Castle William and Mary** when built by the British around 1770. It was captured and renamed by Patriots in 1774 and used by them during the Revolution. Nearby are also the ruins of a lighthouse built in 1771.

The site of Pannaway Plantation is located on Odiorne's Point on State 1A just south of Seavey's Creek, close to Rye, Rockingham Co. This, the state's first settlement, was founded in 1623 and abandoned later in the same year. No traces remain today.

The site of Fort Number Four is located on the Connecticut River on County 11, about half a mile from County 12, Sullivan Co. This wooden fort was built in 1744 and attacked twice in 1746 by Indians who burnt all of the surrounding houses and farms. Then in 1747 it withstood a fierce three-day siege by 700 Frenchmen and Indians. During the Revolution it was used by the Patriots. There is nothing left of it now, but numerous ruins of Colonial buildings are in the area.

Near **Woodsville,** at the confluence of the Connecticut and Ammonoosuc Rivers, Orange Co., an old miser named John L. Woods, for whom the town was named, is reported to have buried a large treasure around 1829 near a sawmill he owned.

The Isles of Shoals are seven islands located about ten miles southeast of Portsmouth. In 1813 the Spanish brig **Sagunto** was lost among these islands and its crew buried a large treasure to keep it from being seized by American authorities. According to legends many pirates buried their booty among these islands and several large treasure finds have been made over the years by fishermen and treasure hunters. Blackbeard is supposed to have buried one large cache on Londoner Island and another on Smuttynose. Four large silver bars were found on Smuttynose in 1880. During the eighteenth century an unidentified British warship was wrecked on the east side of Appledore Island, carrying a considerable amount of silver bullion; specie and silver coins dating from that period have been found here after storms in recent years. The pirate John Quelch is reported to have buried nine pounds of gold and 190 pounds of silver on the west side of Appledore Island. In 1718 a privateer is known to have buried a large cache of plunder from the Spanish Main somewhere on the same island. Just before he and his crew were captured and hanged in 1704, John Quelch was seen burying a great deal of treasure on Star Island. In 1685 a British merchantman, **King Edward,** was wrecked at a point called Miss Underhill's Chair on Star Island and lost a considerable amount of silver and gold specie; occasionally coins are found here today. During the colonial period a fort stood on Starr Island which is now in ruins. Various pirates are reported to have hidden plunder on White Island. In 1867 a fisherman dug up about 100 pounds in gold bullion and an undisclosed number of silver and gold coins. Sometime between 1715 and 1718 a pirate named Captain Sandy Gordon buried a cache of plunder on White Island.

Around 1650 an Indian trader named John Cromwell buried a large cache of treasure on his trading post on the west side of the Merrimack River, near **Merrimack,** about two miles above the mouth of Pennichuck Brook, now known as Cromwell Falls, State 3, Hillsborough Co.

While fleeing in 1775 after the start of the Revolution, Governor John Wentworth buried a large strongbox with gold and silver coins, as well as six chests containing silver and gold plate in a wooded area somewhere between **Portsmouth** and **Smithtown,** Rockingham Co.

During winter northeasters, large numbers of English and Spanish silver coins dating from the mid-1700s are found on the beach at Seabrook, County 286, about fifteen miles south of Portsmouth, Rockingham Co.

Batsto is an abandoned town on the Mullica River in Burlington County, about ten miles east of Hammonton on N.J. 524. During the Revolution this community produced iron products, especially cannon, and was also an important glassworks until it was abandoned in 1848. The ruins of several hundred old buildings can still be seen.

Baylor Massacre Site is located on the Hackensack River in Bergen County on County Road 53 between Routes 116 and 90. In 1778 the British massacred a large number of American dragoons and a mass grave containing their remains was recently discovered. At this same time the British burnt and destroyed many homes and farms in the area and these are still waiting to be found.

Bound Brook on the Raritan River in Somerset County is the site of an important skirmish between Patriot and British troops in 1777. A large amount of military supplies is known to have been abandoned by both sides and await discovery.

In Burlington on the Delaware River, Burlington County, are still many colonial buildings. The surrounding area has British and American campsites, about twenty of which are marked.

Chestnut Neck on the Mullica River, Atlantic Co., was a thriving village with a shipyard and a number of storehouses, which served as an American privateering base during the Revolution. In 1778 the British totally burnt the town to the ground and the site is now covered by a boat yard. Ten large vessels were also burnt during the British attack. It is on U.S. 9 near the junction of County Road 575, two miles northeast of Port Republic.

Cooper's Ferry on the Delaware River was settled by Quakers in 1697. The place was an important ferry on the main colonial road between New York and Philadelphia. The modern city of Camden now occupies the site.

Cranbury in Middlesex County is one of the state's oldest settlements and vestiges of early colonial homes can be found there today. A number of important skirmishes took place in Cranbury during the Revolutionary War.

Crosswicks in Burlington County was settled in the late 1600s. Vestiges of many of its early colonial buildings are visible. A skirmish occurred there in 1778 a few days before the Battle of Monmouth.

Elizabeth is in Union County. Several important structures from the colonial and Revolutionary War period still survive and there are ruins of many others in the surrounding area.

Englishtown in Monmouth County is located a few miles northwest of the Monmouth Battlefield on the Patriot army's line of march to that place. Two buildings from this period have survived and many more are in ruins.

Fort Lee on the Hudson River is located at the western terminus of the George Washington Bridge. Urban development has destroyed most of this Revolutionary War site. On the 300-foot bluff near the river some traces of the outer works of the fort can still be seen. A major battle took place here in 1776.

Fort Mercer, located in the Red Bank Battlefield Park on the Delaware River, was a large earthwork with fourteen cannon during the Revolution. During an attack on this fort in 1777 British troops suffered 1,200 casualties and the Patriots lost fewer than 40 men. Traces of a moat that surrounded the fort and also of several brick buildings can be seen.

Gloucester Point on the Delaware River in Gloucester County was the first white settlement on the east bank of the Delaware, founded by the Dutch in 1623, who built **Fort Nassau.** The village started to grow only when Irish Quakers arrived in 1682. The site was occupied by 5,000 British troops in November 1777 with part of a British fleet anchored offshore. The British **H.M.S. Augusta** (64 guns) and **H.M.S. Merlin** (18 guns), were badly damaged by Patriot gunfire and were run aground on Gloucester Beach and blown up. Fragments of both wrecks can be seen on the beach at low tide.

Haddonfield, located about ten miles east of Camden along State 70, was the site where British troops under General Clinton camped for a number of weeks during the summer of 1778 before marching to the Monmouth Battlefield. The ruins of many colonial and Revolutionary War buildings are there.

241

Hopewell on County Road 518 in Mercer County was a village founded in the last decade of the seventeenth century and of little importance. However, in 1778 a squad of British troops guarding a wagon carrying over 100,000 pounds sterling in gold and silver coins, was attacked by Patriots and all were killed. The Patriots managed to bury the money before British reinforcements arrived but then they were all killed in the fighting. The site of the treasure was lost.

Little Egg Harbor Massacre Site is located three miles from Tuckerton, Ocean County. British forces led by Captain Patrick Ferguson surprised and completely annihilated six companies of Patriot troops commanded by Casimir Pulaski at this spot in 1778. Most of the Americans were asleep in three houses, which were burnt to the ground.

Middlebrook Encampment is located on the north edge of Bond Brook on County 527, Somerset County. It was used by General Washington and his army to bivouac during May and June 1777 and again in November 1778 through June 1779. Many men were buried here and much gear no doubt abandoned and lost.

Monmouth Battlefield is west of Freehold in Monmouth County. One of the major battles of the Revolutionary War was fought here on June 18, 1778 as General Sir Henry Clinton marched through from Philadelphia to New York and met the Patriots under George Washington. After sacking Philadelphia they filled over 1,500 wagons with supplies and plunder. Washington showed his genius and routed the British, who were forced to bury a great deal of what they had taken before fleeing towards New York City. Some was found by the Patriots, but a great deal, including treasure, is waiting to be discovered.

Morristown National Historical Park is located fifteen miles west of Newark in Morris County and is surrounded by a series of parallel ranges of hills. The Jockey Hollow area, which remains unspoiled, was the site of Washington's Army encampment during the terrible winter of 1779–1780. **Fort Nonsense** was built here in 1777 but no traces remain of it today.

Princeton Battlefield is located in a wooded area off U.S. 206 in the outskirts of Princeton in Mercer County. On January 3, 1777 the Patriots led by Washington defeated a much superior force of British troops, an event which many historians claim saved the American Revolution from ending prematurely.

Quinton Bridge. The piles of this old bridge are located a few hundred feet upstream from where N.J. 49 crosses Alloway Creek in the village of Quinton. During the Revolution the Americans suffered a minor defeat at this bridge and remnants of this encounter can be found.

Ringwood Manor and Iron Works is located on County Road 17 close to the New York State border in Passaic County. Iron deposits were discovered here about 1740; Ringwood mines, furnaces, forges, and manor house were soon built and the place began flourishing. During the Revolutionary War Ringwood supplied the American army with everything from simple hardware to the immense links of the great chains used to obstruct the Hudson River. The old manor house burnt down during the Revolution and a new one was constructed nearby. Many structures have survived.

Salem in Salem County was the first permanent settlement of English colonists on the Delaware, established by Quakers under John Fenwick in 1675. In 1682 New Salem, as it was originally called, became a port of entry and prospered until around the beginning of the Revolution, when many of the settlers began moving west. The town had a temporary revival during the Civil War. Many old ruins of buildings in the area span three centuries.

Shabbakonk Creek just south of Lawrenceville on U.S. 206, Mercer County, was the site of a delaying action fought by Patriots against British forces under Cornwallis on January 2, 1777. The Patriots had to abandon some of their gear before running off to safety.

Springfield Battlefield is located off U.S. 78, two miles south of the village of Springfield in Union County. In June 1780, it was the scene of two major Revolutionary battles of 1780, during which both sides suffered major losses of men and equipment.

Toms River. The original village site is located a bit north of the present fishing community in Ocean County. It was destroyed and burnt by the British in 1782.

Trenton, at the head of the Delaware River, was settled by Europeans in 1680, originally called **The Falls,** and renamed Trenton in 1719. During the Revolutionary War the city was occupied at different times by troops of both sides and a number of minor battles took place in and around the city. A few colonial and Revolutionary War structures still remain but most are covered by the present city.

One of the favorite treasure-hunting spots in the state are the miles of beaches at **Sandy Hook,** the treacherous point of land jutting out into New York Lower Bay that all ships must pass when entering New York or the mouth of the Hudson River. Over the centuries hundreds of ships were wrecked and many millions of dollars in treasure and artifacts were cast up on these beaches and are awaiting discovery.

Another area which has claimed a large number of ships is **Cape May,** the southern tip of the state that must be weathered by all ships entering Delaware Bay. Among the many lost here was the Spanish warship **Juno,** of 34 guns, which was wrecked in a bad storm in October 1802 carrying over 300,000 pesos in silver bullion and coins. Of the 425 persons on board, none survived the disaster.

Large numbers of gold and silver coins have been found along the beaches of **Little and Big Egg Harbor, Brigantine Beach,** and **Ship Bottom** on **Long Beach Island**—all located to the north of Atlantic City. On these beaches, many ships have been wrecked over the centuries, vestiges of which are visible after winter storms have carried away large amounts of sand.

A bandit named the Bunker Kid is alleged to have buried a large cache of loot near **Newton,** State 206, Sussex Co.

During the Depression a farmer named Arthur Barry buried about $100,000 in gold coins and paper currency somewhere on his farm near **Andover,** County 517, Sussex Co. He died without leaving directions to the hoard.

Somewhere on a farm presently owned by a Henry Walker near **Hanover Neck,** six miles east of Morristown, County 10, Sussex Co., the owner of the property in the early 1800s hid about $50,000 in gold coins under a big tree.

Somewhere on the estate of William Besthorn near **Caldwell,** County 506, Sussex Co., a cache of $12,000 in gold coins was buried and lost.

A wealthy farmer named Hendrick Dempster buried about $50,000 in gold coins on his farm near **North Bergen,** U.S. 95, Hudson Co.

In 1903 the barge **Harold** sank close to the shore off **Sewaren** in the Delaware River, west of Bridgetown (County 49), Cumberland Co. About 6,000 of the 100-pound silver ingots the ship was carrying were salvaged but about 1,800, weighing a total of 90 tons, were lost under the mud. Around 1950 several of these silver bars were found on the beach at Ben Davis Point.

Several pirate treasures are reported to be buried in the vicinity of **Cliffwood Beach** on Raritan Bay, County 35, Middlesex Co., including one hidden by Captain Kidd.

During the days of Prohibition several bootleggers are reported to have buried about one and a half million dollars in paper currency near **Lake Manetta,** just south of Lakewood, State 9, Ocean Co.

Captain Kidd is also reported to have buried treasures at **Sandy Hook** and **Red Bank** in Monmouth County.

Large numbers of early twentieth-century silver coins are found on the beach at **Ocean Grove,** just south of Asbury Park, County 66, Monmouth Co. They are probably washing in from an offshore shipwreck.

During the late 1700s a pirate named John Bacon had a base where the **Barnegat Lighthouse** is now situated, on the northern end of Island Beach, about ten miles north of Ship Bottom, Ocean Co. He is reported to have buried numerous caches of plunder in this area.

Large numbers of silver coins from the mid-eighteenth century are found on **Squam Beach,** just north of Ship Bottom, on Long Beach Island. Old timbers from several wrecks are also exposed in this area after storms.

Pirates are alleged to have buried treasure on the northern side of **Abescon Island** facing Reeds Bay, County 157, Atlantic Co. Some treasures were found there in the 1930s.

Captain Kidd was known to have obtained fresh water on several occasions at **Lilly Pond** near Cape May Point and is said to have buried a treasure in the area. Another pirate named Joe Bradish used Turtle Gut Inlet in this same area as a base of operations and is also supposed to have buried many caches. Survivors from several shipwrecks at Cape May also hid treasures on the beach.

A pirate treasure is believed to be buried on the Cedar River about a mile southwest of **Cedarville,** County 553, Cumberland Co.

A farmer named James Gilam hid a large treasure on his property at **Finns Point** on the Alloway River near Quinton, County 581, Salem Co.

Several caches of gold coins were buried in the late eighteenth century in or near the old **Seven Star Tavern** on the north banks of the Salem River near Sharptown, reached via a dirt road about two miles west of Woodstown (County 45), Salem Co.

During the Revolution some British officers are known to have hidden a large amount of plunder which had been taken during the sacking of Philadelphia, in the vicinity of **Palmyra,** County 453, Camden Co.

In 1921 a rich farmer named Vincent Conklin died after burying a large treasure near his barn on his farm about one mile east of the tiny village of **Tabernacle,** County 532, Burlington Co.

Retreating British troops during the Revolution buried two chests of gold coins on Apple Pie Hill, three miles southwest of **Chadsworth,** County 563, Burlington Co.

NEW MEXICO

Abo National Landmark is on U.S. 60 about three miles west of Abo, Torrence Co. An Indian pueblo started here around 1300 and continued being used by the Tompiro Indians until it was attacked and destroyed by Apaches in 1670. By 1620 many of the Indians had been converted to Christianity by Spanish missionaries who built a mission there. Today many ruins of adobe houses, a church, and convent still exist.

Acoma Pueblo is located on a 400-foot bluff near State 23, thirteen miles south of Casa Blanca, Valencia Co. Founded about 1300, it is believed to be the oldest continuously occupied settlement in the nation. In 1540 Spanish explorers led by Hernando de Alvarado visited the site and camped here. In 1629 the Franciscans founded the Mission of San Estévan de Rey which is still in use. The ruins of many adobe Indian homes and some Spanish dwellings are here.

Aztec Ruins Monument is on a secondary road about one mile north of Aztec, San Juan Co. On this site are numerous ruins of large Indian masonry dwellings dating back to 1100, which were abandoned around 1295 because of a great drought. Ruins of several abandoned mining camps are also in the area.

Chaco Canyon National Monument is on State 56, 64 miles north of Thoreau, Union Co. Today there are remains of twelve different Indian pueblos in this park, containing over 450 different ruins. Most date back to 1000, but were abandoned by 1225.

Rabbit Ears National Landmark is a bit north of Clayton, Union Co. This mountain, rising over 6,000 feet from the surrounding plains, was an important landmark for westward-bound travelers on the Cimmarron Cutoff of the Sante Fe Trail. Near the base of this mountain are vestiges of many campsites where travelers refreshed themselves and graves of many who were killed during Indian attacks in the area.

El Morro National Landmark, on State 53, two miles east of El Morro, Valencia Co., rises 200 feet above the valley floor close to the Continental Divide. It was called El Morro by the Spanish and later Inscription Rock by tens of thousands of settlers and miners who camped here and inscribed their names on the rock.

The ruins of Fort Union are on State 477, nine miles north of Watrous, Mora Co. The fort was built in 1851 near the point where the Santa Fe Trail's mountain route, leading across Raton Pass, joins its other route, the Cimarron Cutoff. It was the largest United States military post during the nineteenth century guarding the southwest frontier and it was garrisoned by Union troops during the Civil War. Abandoned in 1891, the adobe fort fell into ruins.

Gila Cliff Dwellings are on State 26, 47 miles north of Silver City, Catron Co. There are five cliff dwellings in these overhanging cliffs; Pueblo Indians divided the caves into 35 rooms and lived there between 1275 and 1400. Later the dwellings were used by bands of Apaches who preyed on the settlements of white men; tales of treasure being buried here by them are numerous.

Gran Quivira National Monument is on State 10, one mile east of Gran Quivira, Bernacillo Co. The ruins of this Mogollon Indian settlement were built in 900 and used until 1672 when severe droughts and Apache raids drove the Indians away. Near these ruins are others of **Pueblo de las Humanas,** founded by Spanish around 1590; it also contains the ruins of two large churches—**San Buenaventura** and **San Isidro**—also abandoned in 1672 for the same reason.

Bandelier National Monument is on State 4, twelve miles south of Los Alamos, Los Alamos Co. The ruins of more than twenty different Pueblo Indian villages, which thrived between the thirteenth and sixteenth centuries, are located in this site. Ruins of several early nineteenth-century mining camps are also seen here.

Pecos National Monument is on State 63, a bit south of Pecos, Taos Co. The site consists of a multistoried, 600-room quadrangular village built by the Pueblo Indians during the fourteenth and fifteenth centuries. It served as a campsite for the Coronado expedition of 1541 and as a base for other explorers who followed. In 1621 Franciscans established the **Mission of Nuestra Señora de Los Angeles de Porciuncula** on this site and a large Spanish settlement soon developed, all of which was destroyed during an Indian uprising in 1680. The village and mission were rebuilt in 1693 and continued in use until being abandoned in 1838. Today the ruins of a church, convent, two major pueblos, and a possible fort can be seen.

Quarai National Monument is on a secondary road about one mile south of Punta de Aqua, Torrance Co. Ruins of a Tiwas Indian pueblo and a large Spanish church named La Purissima Concepcion de Cuarac are found here. The pueblo dates back to the early 1300s and the church to the 1620s when Franciscans founded the mission, which was abandoned in 1672 after repeated Apache raids. No traces of the other Spanish buildings can be seen today.

Raton Pass in the Raton Mountains, near U.S. 85 and 87, on the New Mexico-Colorado border, Colfax Co., was the main danger area on the Cimarron Cutoff of the Santa Fe Trail. Countless westward-bound settlers were attacked and killed here by Indians; they left vestiges of numerous campsites.

The Barrio de Analco is located in the city of Santa Fe. Founded in 1610, it is one of the oldest European settlements in the nation. None of the original adobe buildings remain, but there are numerous vestiges of them around the more recent buildings in the area.

Glorieta Pass Battlefield is on U.S. 84-85, ten miles southeast of Santa Fe. On March 18, 1862 a decisive Civil War battle was fought and won by Union troops here against Confederate volunteers from Texas who were after control of the Colorado silver mines for the Confederacy. At the mouth of Apache Canyon nearby, the Confederates had a supply depot which was destroyed by the Union troops. Vestiges of this important battle can be found on both sites.

Santa Fe was the terminus of the Old Santa Fe Trail. Portions of the actual trail and its campsites can be found east of the present city.

Taos Pueblo National Landmark is three miles north of Taos, Taos Co. The site contains many five-story communal dwellings built by the Tigua Indians sometime before 1500. The site was visited by Spanish explorers as early as 1540. Missionaries in 1598 built the **Mission of San Geronimo** there, which was destroyed and rebuilt twice before being abandoned in 1680 because of an Indian uprising. In 1694 a new mission and settlement was founded and continued in operation until 1847, when it was destroyed by American cannon fire during the Taos Rebellion. The ruins of the mission can still be seen.

Hawikuh Ruin Landmark is twelve miles southwest of the Zuni Indian Reservation, McKinley Co. The Zuni Indian pueblo, now in ruins, was the largest of the fabled "Seven Cities of Cibola," whose alleged wealth inspired Francisco Vasquez de Coronado's expedition to the area in 1540. This was the first site he visited and finding no gold there, he used it as a base for several months while scouting the surrounding area. No traces of his campsite have been found yet.

The ghost town of Bingham is on State 380, about 28 miles east of San Antonio, Socorro Co. Nearby are the abandoned Carthage coal mines.

245

The **ruins of Bonanza** are just off U.S. 25 about fifteen miles southwest of Santa Fe, Santa Fe Co. It was a mining town used by various bands of outlaws, some of whom are believed to have buried caches here.

The **ruins of Canoncito** are located six miles southwest of Florieta on State 84-85, in the Sangre de Cristo Range, San Miguel Co. The town flourished around the time of the Civil War and was an important stage station.

The **ghost town of Cerrillos** is on County 14, about 20 miles southwest of Santa Fe, Santa Fe Co. It was once a prosperous mining and cattle town with 21 saloons and later was called the turquoise capital of the world because of the large numbers of these gem stones found in the area. About 50 old buildings survive.

The **ghost town of Chico** is on County 120, about 22 miles east of Maxwell, Colfax Co. It was a wild cattle town until being abandoned in 1892. Only a few wooden buildings are left.

The **ghost town of Chloride** is in the Black Mountain Range on County 52, about 30 miles west of Hot Springs, Sierra Co. It was a rich silver town founded in 1879 and abandoned by 1890 with a large number of buildings, including five saloons, remaining.

The **town of Colfax** is on the Vermejo River about 30 miles southwest of Raton (U.S. 25), Colfax Co. Only a small number of people still live in this near-ghost town of several hundred old buildings.

The **ghost town of Colmon** is on Ocaze Creek about eleven miles south of Springer (State 59), Colfax Co. A few miles to the south are two other ghost towns, **Nolan** and **Levy.** All three have large numbers of buildings still standing.

The **ghost town of Cuchillo** is on County 52 about eight miles northwest of Hot Springs, Sierra Co. There are only a few buildings left in this old mining town.

The **ghost town of Dayton** is located nine miles south of Artesia (County 505), Colfax Co. It was first a rugged cowtown and then an oil boomtown in the 1920s; today several hundred buildings remain.

The **ruins of Elizabethtown** are located near Baldy Peak, about five miles north of Eagle Nest via County 38, Colfax Co. It was a silver-mining town until being abandoned in the 1890s.

The **ruins of Endee** are located five miles from the Texas state line on U.S. 40, Quay Co. It was a wild and tough cowboy cattle town until the early 1900s.

The **ruins of French** are on the Canadian River about five miles south of Maxwell (U.S. 25), Colfax Co. It was an important railroad town and the terminus for many long cattle drives. During its heyday in the late nineteenth century it boasted 25 saloons and twelve brothels.

The **ghost town of Golden** is on County 14 near Placer Mountain, 31 miles southwest of Santa Fe, Santa Fe Co. It was a booming copper-mining town until 1918 and about 100 buildings have survived.

The **ghost town of Holman** is in the Sangre de Cristo Mountains on County 3, about 35 miles north of Las Vegas, Mora Co. It was an important supply center and stage station on the Santa Fe Trail and about 50 buildings are still standing.

The **ghost town of Kingston** is on State 180 about twenty miles west of Caballo, Grant Co. There are still about 40 houses hidden in a grove of trees.

The **ghost town of Las Palomas** is near the Rio Grande River on U.S. 25, about fourteen miles south of Hot Springs, Sierra Co. Nearby are the ruins of an Indian pueblo village.

The **ghost town of Madrid** is on County 14, about nineteen miles southwest of Santa Fe, Santa Fe Co. It is an abandoned coal-mining town with about 700 old buildings.

The **ghost town of No Aqua** is on the east side of Carson National Forest, about 25 miles south of the Colorado state line, just off State 285, Rio Arriba Co. It was once an important railroad center and cowtown.

The **ruins of Pearl** are in the Antelope Ridge, about 35 miles southwest of Hobbs (State 180), Lea Co. This site can be reached only by horseback; not much remains of this mining community.

The **ghost town of San Pedro** is in the Sandia Mountains, about eighteen miles northeast of Albuquerque, near County 344, Bernacillo Co. It was a copper-mining boomtown that died in 1918.

The **ghost town of Torrance** is on the east side of the Cibola National Forest, about ten miles northeast of Corona and a mile west of State 58, Torrance Co. It was once a thriving railroad center.

The ruins of Turley's Mill are on the Rio Grande River about two miles west of Arroyo Hondo (County 3), Taos Co. It was settled in 1830 and only the ruins of a distillery and several mills are left.

The ghost town of Yankee is on the East Fork of the Canadian River on County 72, eight miles northeast of Raton, Colfax Co. It was a coal mining town that was abandoned when the railroad failed.

A prospector hid about $60,000 in gold coins in a cave on **Shiprock Peak,** about five miles west of the town of Shiprock, State 550, San Juan Co.

During the 1930s a Mexican millionaire flew about $30 million in gold bullion into the United States and unsuccessfully tried to sell it to the U.S. government. He then buried the hoard somewhere in the deserted area where he had landed his private plane. A flat mesa was nearby, according to his pilot; Shiprock Peak was to the south, Mesa Verda National Park to the north, and the Ute Indian Reservation was to the east. This area is near the town of **Shiprock** in San Juan Co. The Mexican is believed to have been an ex-government official who amassed this fortune through graft and embezzlement.

In 1890 a miner named George H. Osteen found an old abandoned Spanish gold mine high in the Ute Mountains a few miles west of **Aztec,** State 550, San Juan Co. He removed about 50 pounds in gold, but could not find the mine when he came back to get more of the 500 or so pounds of gold lying at the mouth of the mine.

About $50,000 in gold coins and bullion from a stagecoach robbery in 1874 were hidden in the vicinity of a sandstone window rock, about one mile east of **Aztec.** In a rock shelter on the canyon tributary of nearby San Juan River, other outlaws are alleged to have buried about $60,000 in gold bullion.

The Lost Frenchman Gold Mine is located near Truchas Peak in the Nacimiento Mountains a few miles from Tierra, State 64, Rio Arriba Co. In the nearby town of Santa Clara, County 101, Jesse James is alleged to have buried some loot. The **Lost Waterfall Gold Mine** is also located somewhere in nearby Largo Canyon.

Texas outlaws buried a large cache of gold bullion in **Pump Canyon,** about five miles northeast of Newcomb, State 666, San Juan Co., just before being caught and hanged in 1876.

Prior to being attacked by Indians, Mexican miners concealed four wagonloads of gold bullion somewhere in an abandoned mine shaft on **Beautiful Mountain** in the Chuska Range in the southwest corner of San Juan Co.

A prospector named Alec Toppinton buried a large cache of gold bullion in a cave on the northern end of the **Carrizo Mountains** on the Navajo Indian Reservation near Tohatchi, State 666, McKinley Co.

Somewhere on **Powell Mountain** located along the Continental Divide, about 32 miles east of Gallup, McKinley Co., the Zuni Indians are known to have hidden a huge cache of gold, silver, and jewels when the Spaniards began exploring the area in the mid-sixteenth century. The Spanish tortured several hundred Indians to death trying to learn the location.

The Zuni Indians also buried several large caches of treasure, which the Spaniards called the **Laguna del Oro Treasures,** in the vicinity of Fort Wingate, about 23 miles east of Gallup on U.S. 40, McKinley Co.

Still another cache of Zuni treasure, hidden when the Spanish arrived in the mid-1500s, is on **Broom Mountain** along the Continental Divide near the El Moro National Monument in Valencia Co.

In the vicinity of **Bluewater Lake,** about four miles northwest of Anaconda, State 66, Valencia Co., there is a deep canyon on which a Jim Admans had a cabin in 1864. From a nearby stream he gathered over $100,000 in gold nuggets and hid them near his cabin. He left behind a diary telling of his cache. Nearby in the vicinity of the town of **Bluewater** another prospector is known to have concealed about $80,000 in gold bullion.

The Lost Sewing Basket Mine is located in the vicinity of Grant, State 66, Valencia Co. About $3 million in gold bullion is believed to have been buried on or near the **Lost Spanish**

In searching any area — especially ruins — treasure hunters are urged to make certain they are familiar with all local laws and customs.

Charles Garrett has worked closely with experienced prospectors to develop metal detectors especially suited for finding nuggets and gold deposits.

Mission of Malpais nearby. Also in this same general area the **Tadwell Treasure,** said to consist of $50,000 in gold coins, was buried near the Rio San Juan just south of Grant.

In 1936 an airplane crashed in the vicinity of **Mount Taylor,** about fifteen miles northeast of Grant. It was carrying about $100,000 in paper currency from California to New York to further the political ambitions of presidential candidate Al Landon. Although parts of the plane wreckage were found, the money was not. Just north of this mountain in the vicinity of a clear spring, four returning California miners buried a large amount of gold bullion when a band of Paiute Indians began trailing them. One survived the attack but was unable to locate the cache.

The Spanish had a mission, which is lost today, in the village of San Rafael, a few miles south of **Grant** on County 53, Valencia Co. Before being driven from the area by hostile Indians in 1674, the padres buried eighteen mule loads of gold bullion in the immediate vicinity. One gold bar was found in 1935 by a cow hand. The Zuni Indians also buried several caches of treasure in this area to prevent their seizure by the Spanish.

Prior to being attacked by Indians, a party of Franciscan missionaries buried nine mule loads of gold ore in a cave in the vicinity of the **Perpetual Ice Cave,** about eighteen miles southwest of Grant. The entrance to the cave was sealed off and later on they were unable to relocate the site. In this same area near the **Bandera Crater** on Agua Frio Creek, some train robbers buried about $100,000 in gold and silver coins before being caught and hanged in 1897.

In 1860 while fleeing from hostile Indians, a group of miners were forced to bury a mule train load of silver bars to the south of **Grant** at a place called the **"Narrows,"** about midway between the lava flow and Cebolleta Mesa. About 100 years earlier in this same area, a mule train carrying gold and silver bullion led by a group of Spanish miners and missionaries was also attacked by Indians. About six tons of precious metal was buried somewhere between the **"Narrows"** and **"Little Narrows,"** which is about fifteen miles south of Grant. This same area was a favorite hangout for outlaws in the 1800s, several of whom are known to have buried hoards in the area. A United States Army payroll was robbed in 1878 and buried in this same area. A posse searching for it discovered a cache of seventeen 25-pound gold ingots instead.

The **village of Quemado** is on the Wash River at the foot of Escondido Mountain. In the 1700s the Spaniards had a mission here and several gold mines, of which no traces now exist. During an Indian uprising in 1761, the Zuni killed all the priests and robbed all of their church treasures and a large hoard of gold bullion. This they buried somewhere near the peak of **Escondido Mountain.** During another uprising in 1799 fleeing Spaniards are reported to have buried twenty mule loads of gold bullion in this same general area.

Indians also forced Mexican miners to bury a wagon load of gold bullion somewhere along Alamocita Creek near the village of **Magdalena,** State 60, in the Cibola National Forest, Soccoro Co.

The **Lost Acoma Gold Mine** and a **Lost Silver Mine** are located in the general vicinity of McCarty's Station on the San Jose River and State 66 just west of Albuquerque, Valencia Co.

The **Lost Dupont Gold Mine** and a cache of hundreds of twenty-dollar gold coins hidden under a rock nearby are located in the Santa Fe National Forest on the west side of San Pedro Mountain, about ten miles northeast of Cuba (County 44), Taos Co.

A large cache of Mexican bandit loot is hidden in a box canyon two miles west of **Espanola,** State 84, Taos Co. The bandits were caught and hanged but refused to disclose the exact whereabouts of the treasure. Part of the hoard consisted of two huge silver bells weighing about 300 pounds each, taken from a Mexican church in Monterey.

The **Lost Spanish Queen Gold Mine** and the site of a Spanish mission are on the de las Vacas River, in the vicinity of the village of Jemez Pueblo, County 4, Sandoval Co. The Indian slaves revolted in the seventeenth century and killed all the Spanish overseers and priests. In this same general area several prospectors returning from California in the 1860s buried a large cache of gold bars. The place they claimed to have buried the bars was then named Canado de Conhiti but this place is no longer on current maps.

Near the confluence of the Rio Galisteo and Rio Grande Rivers, about 25 miles southwest of **Santa Fe** in Santa Fe Co., Trader Rico hid all his accumulated wealth before going to Mexico; while in that country Rico was killed.

In the general vicinity of the town of **Placitas** near Sandia Peak, about twelve miles northeast of Albuquerque, the Spaniards worked a gold mine during the late 1600s and buried a large amount of gold ore and bullion before being driven off by Indians. Within a mile or two of this peak some bandits dropped a Wells Fargo box full of gold bullion either in a mine shaft or vertical cave. The floor of the cavern was quicksand, preventing the bandits from recovering their gold.

Ladron Peak is so named because in 1894 outlaws buried about $50,000 in gold on it, taken in a train robbery. The mountain is located about 30 miles southwest of Belem (U.S. 25) and five miles north of the Salado River, Socorro Co.

The ruins of the **Mission of Nuestra Señora del Socorro** is located on the outskirts of the town of Socorro, U.S. 25, in the center of Socorro County. During an Indian uprising in 1741, the priests had to bury a large amount of church treasure and several years' accumulation of gold bullion from seven nearby gold mines. Those entrusted with burying the treasure were killed while fleeing to Mexico and others were not able to locate it. In 1880 the Catholic Church placed advertisements in several New Mexico newspapers offering a $1 million reward to anyone finding the treasure. Several small caches of gold bars have been unearthed but the main treasure was never discovered.

One of the biggest treasure finds publicized in the state occurred in 1964 when a treasure hunter found a whiskey barrel full of Mexican gold coins on the site of the **Turley Mill's Distillery**; since then several smaller treasures have been found. The distillery and settlement only flourished between 1830 and 1855, but after that period they served as an outlaw base. Several caches of loot such as the one found in 1964, have been buried here; the coins found were all dated in the 1870s—long after the place had been abandoned.

In the vicinity of **Taos Pueblo,** State 64, Taos Co., the Spaniards worked a very productive gold mine during the late seventeenth and early eighteenth centuries, which they were forced to abandon because of hostile Indians. Nearby they also had a small settlement. Before leaving, the Spaniards concealed about 500 pounds of gold ingots in a well shaft and filled it in with dirt. In this same area are two ghost towns—**Bland** and **Bonanza**—both gold-mining centers in the 1880s and 1890s.

There are a number of lost gold mines and abandoned mining camps in the area surrounding the **ghost town of Cerrillos.** Somewhere along the old wagon trail between Cerrillos and San Pedro, a group of Mexican soldiers were forced to bury about $250,000 in gold coins and bullion prior to being attacked by Zuni Indians. The few who survived were unable to locate the site when they returned with reinforcements. The **Mina del Tiro,** one of the first Spanish gold mines in this state, is within a half hour mule ride of Cerrillos.

The Lost Sanchez Gold Mine is on the eastern side of the Manzano Mountains about two miles west of Manzano, County 14, Torrance Co. The same Sanchez family that owned the gold mine in the 1700s had a large mansion in Manzano. They are alleged to have buried a great deal of gold bullion in an apple orchard behind the mansion.

There are ruins of a Spanish mission and a small settlement which flourished in the 1700s on the outskirts of the village of **Chilili,** about eighteen miles southeast of Albuquerque on County 14, Santa Fe Co. A huge fortune in gold and silver bullion is reputed to be hidden amongst the ruins of the settlement, which was destroyed by Indians after the massacre of all the Spaniards.

One of the most sought-after treasures in New Mexico is known as the **Gran Quivira Treasure.** According to local legend the Spanish missionaries who abandoned the San Buenaventura and San Isidro Missions in 1672 loaded about 200 burros full of gold and silver bullion, church treasures, treasures dug up from Indian graves, and some raw gold and silver ore. Just as they were ready to head for Mexico, they saw Indians approaching, so they dumped all the treasure into a vertical cave on a knoll overlooking both old mission sites. The cave was sealed off. This site is on the present Gran Quivira National Monument. The two Spanish missionaries who reached Mexico left documents telling that they were forced to abandon a great deal of treasure. But the amount and location of the treasure were undisclosed.

The Camaleon Hills, located about ten miles northeast of Corona, State 54, Torrance Co., were a hideout for many groups of outlaws during the nineteenth century. Several caches of loot are buried there. In one case some outlaws robbed a large group of returning California prospectors of about 200 pounds of gold bullion and some coins. The prospectors returned several days later with a posse; all of the outlaws were killed but the gold was not found.

The ghost town of White Oaks, is fifteen miles east of Ancho (just off State 54) in the Jicarilla Mountains, Lincoln Co. This site was first settled in the late seventeenth century by Spaniards who are believed to have buried several gold caches in the area. On nearby Lone Mountain two Spanish miners hid several burro loads of gold ore. About two miles north of White Oaks, a Mexican miner named Bonifacio Chavez buried two large ceramic jars full of gold dust near the junction of two streams and the ruins of several old cabins. In the late nineteenth century, the wealthiest man in the county, Jose Analla, hid about $200,000 in gold bullion and several jugs of gold coins somewhere on his ranch, about one and a half miles north of White Oaks. In 1882 several silver bars were found on the banks of Rio Bonito Creek, which cuts through the middle of the ghost town. In 1934 a cache of several hundred Mexican gold coins was found by a land surveyor.

The Lost White Gold Mine is located in the vicinity of Questa, County 3, Taos Co.

In the northern part of the Sangre de Cristo Mountain Range in the vicinity of the town of Red River, County 38, Taos Co., there is a place that has been called **Treasure Cave** for several hundred years. It is near the junction of three streams and a waterfall. Many believe a large treasure was buried somewhere inside of the cave. In the same general area, at Palo Flechado Pass, the outlaw Charles Kennedy concealed a great deal of gold bullion from his last robbery before he was hanged. Not far away is the **Mina Perdida,** worked during the eighteenth century by Spaniards who had a small settlement in the valley below the mine.

The old Santa Fe Trail cut through Raton Pass, located about ten miles north of Raton, U.S. 25, Colfax Co. In the mid-nineteenth century, a Billy Wooten operated a trading post in the pass. It was common knowledge that he had buried barrels full of gold and silver coins. In 1953 a treasure hunter found one barrel of American and foreign coins with a face value of about $600 but a numismatic value of over $75,000. Within a mile of the ruins of Wooten's trading post, a returning California miner hid a large cache of gold bars.

About two miles south of Raton on the Canadian River is a butte known as **Starvation Peak.** When Indians attacked a white settlement in the area, the inhabitants sought refuge on this peak. Before all of them died of starvation and thirst they buried their personal possessions in the area. About a mile to the southwest are the ruins of **the ghost town of Baldy,** consisting of a few house foundations and chimneys.

Outlaw Black Jack Ketchum is alleged to have buried a large cache of gold and silver coins near **Folsom,** County 72, Union Co. Another band of outlaws are also supposed to have buried plunder on Devoy's Peak, near Mount Dora, State 64, Union Co.

Somewhere along the Cimarron River, in the vicinity of Springer, State 56, Colfax Co., about $250,000 in gold coins were hidden in 1830 under a large rock "half as big as a house," which was near several abandoned mining shacks.

Near the fork of the Canadian and Vermejo Rivers stand the ruins of **the ghost town of Hilltop,** about three miles south of Maxwell, U.S. 25, Colfax Co. In the late 1800s outlaws who used this town as a base are reputed to have buried several treasures here.

During the Mexican Revolution a pack train carrying over $1 million in gold bullion and coins was sent by the Hildago family for safekeeping in the United States. **Near the confluence of the Mora and Canadian Rivers,** a few miles north of Sabinoso, County 65, San Miguel Co., the pack train was harassed by Comanche Indians and the hoard was hidden in a cave nearby. Only two Mexicans survived repeated attacks and were unable to locate the cave afterwards.

On the Peco River, about one mile southeast of Colonias, a tiny settlement about ten miles north of Santa Rosa (U.S. 40), Guadalupe Co., there are numerous ruins of an early Spanish settlement which was destroyed by Indians in the late 1700s. Before being massacred the residents are believed to have buried numerous valuables.

In the late 1850s Indians attacked a wagon train of returning California gold miners about four miles northwest of Tucumcari, State 54, Quay Co. The miners buried about $650,000 in gold bullion on a mesa near **the ruins of Fort Buscum,** now known as Rich Mesa. All were killed and the gold was never found.

Confederate troops being pursued by Union soldiers buried a large number of gold bars **near the Santa Fe Railroad** about two miles east of Tolar, State 60, De Baca Co. A heavy rain had erased all signs of the hiding place when they returned for it several days later.

The ghost town of Mogallon is on County 76, about eight miles east of Alma, Caron Co. It was a gold-silver mining camp in the late nineteenth century; nearby are the ruins of several other abandoned towns.

At **Gold Hill** in the Burro Mountains, about twelve miles northeast of Lordsburg, State 70, Hidalgo Co., the Spaniards had several gold mines which they worked until around 1810. In one of the shafts an American miner buried about $20,000 in gold bullion before being killed in a saloon brawl in 1856. In the same area a Swede hid a large cache of gold nuggets and bullion.

Bank robbers are believed to have hidden about $400,000 in gold coins and bars on **Cuchillo Mountain,** about ten miles northwest of Hot Springs, U.S. 25, Sierra Co.

The Lost Iron Door Gold Mine is located in either Blue or Turquoise Canyon near the Rio Grande River, a few miles southeast of Socorro, U.S. 25, Socorro Co. Around 1675 an earthquake trapped several hundred Spanish miners inside; they were lost along with a large amount of gold bullion that was also stored in a mine shaft. On nearby Socorro Peak several caches of gold bullion are supposed to be hidden. During the early 1800s a vast amount of church treasure and gold bullion was buried by fleeing Mexican priests and miners along the Rio Grande River between Socorro and the village of Caballo. During a flood in 1929 several boys found a large part of this cache.

In 1926 several cowboys discovered six saddlebags of gold nuggets and small gold bars among the ruins of **Fort Ojo Caliente,** in the extreme southwest corner of Socorro Co., and more treasure is believed to lie in these ruins.

In the Palomas Mountains, which run between Hot Springs and Hatch on U.S. 25 in Sierra Co. and Dona Ana Co., numerous treasures are reported to be hidden. Spaniards are believed to have concealed a great hoard of gold bullion near Pierce's Cave along the Rio Grande River, several miles east of Las Palamos Village. In 1610 the Spanish explorer Pedro Navarez left a map in Mexico City showing that 250 bars of gold and eighteen mule loads of silver ore had been hidden in these mountains, in the vicinity of the present Calallo Reservoir. On the eastern side of these mountains, near the town of Aleman, a Spaniard named Jose Colon concealed a large treasure of gold and silver bullion. Just before he was hanged in 1850, the leader of a band of renegade Comanches confessed to having buried about $4 million in gold bullion in a cave about eight miles southwest of Aleman. About five miles southeast of Hot Springs and one mile east of the Rio Grande River, Spaniards concealed a great cache of gold bullion in the early 1800s.

In recent years the famous **Victoria Peak Treasure** has received a great deal of publicity in the press. Its site is on the White Sand Missile Range in the Jornado del Muerto, near Humbrill Canyon, in the San Andres Mountains. In 1937 a man named Doc Noss claimed to have found a huge cache of gold bars "stacked like cordwood" in a cavern of this peak. The gold is reputed to be worth one and a half billion dollars—a figure probably greatly exaggerated by the press. Some claim that Spaniards buried this hoard; others that it is part of the famous Montezuma Treasure of Mexico. Several professional treasure-hunting firms are presently trying to obtain permission from the United States Government to search for the bars on the restricted military base.

In 1878 a Mexican miner named Demetrio Varela is believed to have found a large cache of gold and silver bars down an old mine shaft in a canyon just off **St. Augustine Pass** in the Organ Mountains, located at the southwest corner of the White Sand Missile Range. He was blinded in an explosion soon afterwards so the site was lost. In the neighborhood some Spanish missionaries concealed gold and silver bars in 1817 and this is what Varela may have stumbled upon. A number of other treasures are located in these same mountains. The **Lost Governor Otero Gold Mine** and the **Lost Soledad Gold Mine** are both located in this area. A

255

bandit named El Chato buried a huge cache of church treasure in the Soledad Canyon and in nearby Soledad Pass are remains of two abandoned gold-mining camps dating back to the late eighteenth century. During the 1760s when the Spanish missionaries were driven off by Indians, they are alleged to have buried about $4 million in gold bullion and church treasures in Soledad Pass in a cave which they sealed off. Mexican bandits are also thought to have concealed about fifteen mule loads of silver bars in this neighborhood, while being pursued by United States Cavalry troops in 1809.

Somewhere on the Netherlin Ranch, about midway between Tularosa and Weed, County 521, Otero Co., outlaws buried a large cache of gold bullion and silver coins in 1873 before being apprehended and hanged.

During the Mexican Revolution several wagon loads of gold bullion and coins were hidden in a limestone cave by a Mexican army captain entrusted with taking it from Mexico City to Santa Fe. The site is on the Penasco River about eight miles south of Artesia, State 82, Eddy Co.

A cache of gold bullion and coins was buried near the main house on the Gilbert Ranch located on the south bank of the Lower Penasco River about 7 miles south of Artesia, just off State 285.

In the late 1890s a bank robber buried about $75,000 in gold coins and an unknown quantity of silver bullion in a cave on the Guadalupe Mountains about two miles north of Carlsbad, State 285, Eddy Co. Near Grapevine Springs in the vicinity, some Spaniards in 1803 were forced to hide about twenty mule loads of silver bullion that was enroute to Mexico when they were attacked by Indians.

The ruins of the eighteenth-century Spanish gold mine, Santo Nino, is in the Real San Francisco del Tuerte, a few miles east of Santa Fe, Santa Fe Co. There are remains of several houses and an old church.

In Grant County there are ruins of three Spanish gold mines. The Santa Rita Mine is on the south side of the Rio del Norte River near Whitewater, about twenty miles south of Silver City. Nearby in the Sierra del Oro the Santa Rosalia Mine and the Mina del Compromiso are located.

The three most sought after lost mines in the state because of the great wealth they are known to contain are: the Lost Skelton Canyon Gold Mine, somewhere in Skelton Canyon, near Rodeo, in Hidalgo Co.; the Lost Jouranada de la Muerte Gold Mine, on the eastern slope of Mount Soledad, in the Andres Mountain, Sierra Co.; and the Lost Acoma Silver Mine is located somewhere between Acoma and Laguna in Valencia Co.

The following are the names of abandoned mines in the state listed by county: BERALILLO CO. Ferro Mine is on the Canoncito Indian Reservation. DONA ANA CO. Mountain Chief Mine, twelve miles east of Organ; the Stephenson-Bennett Mine in the Organ Mountains, 15 miles east of Las Cruces. GRANT CO. Alhambra Silver Mine, in the Burro Mountains, fifteen miles southeast of Silver City; Black Hawk Silver Mine, in the Burro Mountains, thirteen miles southeast of Silver City; Georgetown Silver Mine, in Mimbres Valley, nine miles northeast of Santa Rita; J. W. Carter Turquoise Mine, in the Burro Mountains, five miles southeast of Silver City; Naiad Queen Silver Mine, in the Mimbres Valley, nine miles east of Silver City; Piños Silver Mine, two miles north of Bayard; Rose Silver Mine, at the foot of Little Hatchet Mountain, two miles southeast of Hachita; Lady in the Mimbres Valley, nine miles northeast of Santa Rita; and the Silver Cell Mine, a mile southeast of Piños Altos. HIDALGO CO. American Silver Mine, eight miles southwest of Hachita; Apache Silver Mine, twelve miles southeast of Hachita; Ben Hive Silver Mine, in the Hatchet Mountains, three miles southeast of Hatchita; Gold Hill Silver Mine, thirteen miles northeast of Lordsburg; Hachita Turquoise Mine, 6 miles southwest of Hachita; Jack Doyle Silver Mine, at the foot of Little Hachet Mountain, two miles southeast of Hachita; Lady Franklin Silver Mine, eight miles southwest of Hachita; Leidendorf Silver Mine, in the Pyramid Mountains, fourteen miles south of Lordsburg; Paradise Gold Mine, near Chiricahua Peak, twelve miles west of Rodeo; Prize Silver Mine, eight miles southwest of Hachita; and the Steins Pass Mine, in the Chiricahua Mountains, seventeen miles southwest of Lordsburg.

McKINLEY CO. The **St. Michael Mine,** near St. Michael. **SANDOVAL CO.** The **Luciani Mine,** 4 miles west of La Ventana. **SAN MIGUEL CO.** The **Sarah Ellen Mine,** 12 miles northwest of Egnar. **SANTA FE CO. Cunningham Gold Mine,** at the base of the Ortiz Mountains in Cunningham Gulch, ten miles east of Golden; **Shoshone Gold Mine,** at the base of the San Pedro Mountains, ten miles southeast of Golden; and the **Golden Wizard Mine,** four miles north of Golden. **SIERRA CO. Las Aminas Gold Mines,** near Slapjack Hill, 2 miles north of Hillsboro. **TAOS CO.** The **Jay-Hawk Silver Mine,** three miles southeast of Pinos Altos. **VALENCIA CO.** The **Mirable Mine,** near Bluewater.

NEW YORK

Albany was discovered by Henry Hudson in 1609 and the Dutch trading post of **Fort Nassau** was built on an island in the Hudson off this city in 1614. Ten years later settlers arrived and built **Fort Orange** and colonists from Norway, Scotland, Germany, Denmark, and Holland began arriving in large numbers. In 1652 the village of Beverwyck was laid out around **Fort Orange,** which became Albany when the British took control of the place in 1664. The site of **Fort George** is located at the foot of State Street and a few blocks up the hill at the other end of this street **Fort Frederick**—the object of a British attack in 1777—once stood. At the corner of Pine and Lodge Streets is the site of a colonial hospital which treated large numbers of wounded patriots during the Revolution. Many old ruins of the seventeenth and eighteenth century surround the countryside.

Bear Mountain on the Hudson at the junction of the Palisades Interstate Parkway and U.S. 9W, Washington County, contains remnants of **Forts Montgomery** and **Clinton** which were captured by the British during the Revolutionary War.

Bennington Battlefield, located on N.Y. 67 near Walloomsac, Washington County, is the site of a famous battle between the British and Patriots on August 14, 1777.

Butlersbury Mansion, built in 1742 on Switzer Hill, near Fonda in the Mohawk Valley still stands. It was the ancient homestead of the much-dreaded Tory raiders John and Walter Butler. During the Revolution they amassed a great deal of plunder in raids against Patriot settlements all over the Mohawk Valley. Both escaped to Canada before the war ended and it is reported that they buried a vast amount of plunder somewhere near this mansion.

Mohawk settlements. Between 1580 and 1666 the Mohawks had sixteen villages, called Indian castles, in the Mohawk Valley, Montgomery County. All of these except one near Auriesville were burned in 1666. The four built to replace these castles were burnt in 1693, at which time these Indians were greatly reduced in number. The sites of the early castles are not known exactly, however, three which existed during the Revolution were near the villages of Fort Hunter, Fort Plain, and Indian Castle.

Continental Village. The site of this place was just north of Peekskill, two miles north of Gallows Hill Road, Putnam County. During the Revolutionary War the Patriots had a camp and supply center from 1777 to 1781.

Crown Point Campsite is located off the west end of the Lake Champlain Bridge, Essex County. The French built Fort Frederic here in 1731 and then blew it up in 1759 when British troops were approaching. From its ruins the British then built **Fort Crown** a short way inland, but it was accidentally burnt in 1773. Near the ruins of both forts is the campsite used by the British and Patriots at various times during the Revolutionary War.

Dobbs Ferry Site on the Hudson River, Dobbs Ferry, Westchester County, was the main crossing point of the lower Hudson. The shore line has been altered almost beyond recognition but there is still a great deal of unobstructed ground which contains colonial and Revolutionary War period artifacts.

Schuylerville on the west bank of the Hudson in Schuylerville off New York 29, a few hundred feet west of U.S. 4, Saratoga Co., is the site of a 50-acre open field. Here the 6,300 surviving British troops under Burgoyne surrendered on October 17, 1777 after the famous battle of Saratoga. Many relics are to be found on this former battlefield.

Fishkill Landing is a site on the east bank of the Hudson, opposite Newburgh and near U.S.

257

9, Dutchess Co. Here are the last vestiges of an earthworks called Fort Hill that was garrisoned by Patriots during the Revolutionary War.

Fishkill Village is located about five miles east of Fishkill Landing near the intersection of U.S. 9 & I-84, Dutchess County. The Dutch founded a village here around 1700 and during the war it served as the principal military depot for the Patriot army and there are vestiges of many of the old homes, earthworks, and encampments.

Fort Ann is located about midway between **Fort Edward** and **Whitehall** on U.S. 4, Washington County. Colonial and Revolutionary War wooden forts built here were the scene of a number of minor Revolutionary War skirmishes. Vestiges of the fort can be found around the northern edge of the modern village.

The site of Fort Dayton is located at the edge of the town of Herkimer near the junction of N.Y. 28 and U.S. 90, Oswego County. The stone fort was built in 1722 by Palatines who settled the area; remnants of this fort and colonial homes can be seen.

The site of Fort Delaware is located north of Narrowsburg on N.Y. 97, Sullivan County. It was built around 1750, but the site has been eroded away by the Delaware River.

The site of Fort Edward is located on Rogers Island in the Hudson River connected to today's village of Fort Edward by N.Y. 197, in Saratoga Co. The British built fortifications here in 1709, 1731, 1755, and 1757 and the site was used by both sides during the Revolutionary War as encampments.

Fort Hunter, strategically located where the Schoharie and Mohawk Valleys join, was settled at an early date by the Dutch and served as an important military post during the French and Indian Wars. In 1820 the old fort and other buildings were stripped of stones for the construction of the Erie Canal, but some vestiges can still be found.

Fort Klock is located in the Mohawk Valley on N.Y. 5, just east of St. Johnsville, Montgomery County. It was first built as a trading post in 1750 and much of it still survives. Just east of the fort a battle took place between Redcoats and Patriots on October 19, 1780.

Fort Niagara is located at the mouth of the Niagara River on Lake Ontario near Youngstown, Niagara County. The French had a fort here in 1726 which the British rebuilt in 1770. It was used by them during the Revolutionary War, taken over by Americans in 1783, and recaptured during a bloody battle by the British in 1813. The fort has been restored and the surrounding area could yield plenty of artifacts.

Fort Ontario, at the mouth of the Oswego River opposite the city of Oswego, was built in 1726 by the British, destroyed by the French in 1756, and rebuilt by the British in 1759. They abandoned it in 1796, but used it again in the War of 1812, and then demolished it at the end of the war. Only the ramparts survive today.

The Fort Plain fortifications are located near the village of this same name, near the junction of U.S. 90 and N.Y. 5S, Montgomery Co. Fortifications covering half an acre were built around a farmhouse in 1776 by Patriots and soon after attacked and demolished by Tories.

Fort St. George is located just off the William Floyd Parkway near Smith's Point Bridge and Mastic Beach on Long Island. The British built this fort in 1776 and it was demolished after being captured by Patriots in 1780. Some parts of it can still be seen.

Fort Stanwix, in the center of the city of Rome, Oneida County, was first built in 1725 by the British and was an important Indian trading post. It was enlarged in 1758 by the British and abandoned in 1769. The fort was used again during the Revolutionary War by both sides and a major battle took place on the site in 1777. Nothing remains of the site.

Gardiner's Island located between the eastern forks of Long Island has been used as an anchorage since the early colonial period. During the Revolutionary War the British used Gardiner's Bay as a minor naval base.

German Flatts refers to a ten-mile stretch of Palatine settlements which stood in the Mohawk valley around the present town of Herkimer, Herkimer County. The Palatines, who began settling the area around 1730, had many of their homes destroyed first by rampaging Iroquois and then during the Revolution by Tories. In this general area are the ruins of hundreds of their homes.

Ruins. The Hugenots settled New Paltz, near the N.Y. State Thruway, between Kingston

258

and Newburgh, Ulster County, around 1700. Remains of many of their stone and brick homes are still to be found in this area.

Ruins. Near Indian Castle Church on N.Y. 5S, about midway between Little Fall and Fort Plain, the vestiges of many early settlers' homes can still be seen, most of which had been destroyed during the French and Indian Wars. Traces of Mohawk villages are also visible in this area.

Johnstown, located at the junction of N.Y. 67 and State Road 30A, Fulton Co., was first settled in 1760. In 1781 a major battle took place here and much of the town was destroyed. The ruins of many old buildings dot the area.

Kingston in Ulster County was founded by the Dutch in 1615. Here they build **Fort Esopus,** which became a prosperous place. The town was totally destroyed by the British in 1777, but a new town was later built over the ruins.

Lake George Village is on U.S. 9 and I-87, at the lower end of Lake George, Warren County. The Americans won a major battle from the French in 1755 here, then constructed **Fort William Henry** a short distance away. Here they beat off a major French attack in 1757 but five months later surrendered. The Indians under the French massacred all of the Americans and threw their remains in Bloody Pond near the present town. The ruins of two other forts built during the Revolutionary War—**Gage** and **George**—are located nearby.

Minisink Ford is located on the Delaware River, opposite Lackawaxen, Penna., Sullivan Co. It was the site of a furious battle in which the Patriot forces were totally wiped out on July 22, 1779 by Indians and Tories. The exact site is at the junction on N.Y. 97 and Country Road 168.

Newton Battlefield State Park is located six miles southeast of Elmira on N.Y. 17. A major battle between 4,000 Patriot troops under General John Sullivan and 1,000 British, Indians, and Tories took place here on August 29, 1779, which the Americans won.

New Windsor Encampment located on Temple Hill, southwest of Newburgh, Orange County, was used by 8,000 Patriot troops during the winter of 1782-1783 and covers some 70 acres. The troops lived in some 700 wooden huts, of which there are some remains.

New York City. Not much of the city that was constructed during the colonial or Revolutionary War periods can still be seen today. During their occupation, the Dutch had a line of cannon from the foot of present Greenwich Street to the intersection of Whitehall and Water Streets. In 1693 the British constructed **Fort George;** part of it can still be found in Battery Park. The original settlement of Fort Amsterdam also stood in this same park. In Fort Tryon Park, which covers some 62 acres, are the remains of an important earthworks built by the Patriots during the Revolutionary War and a British-built **Fort Tryon,** of which no traces remain. On the New York City side of the George Washington Bridge once stood **Fort Washington,** built by the Patriots at the outbreak of the war. Here the Patriots suffered one of their worst defeats in November 1776; some traces of this fort and battle can be found in vacant lots around West 147th Street. The center of the Wall Street area near the corner of William and John Streets was called **Golden Hill** during the colonial period, for legend has it that a great golden treasure was hidden there. On Governor's Island the Patriots erected numerous fortifications in 1776, which played no major role in the war; all have since disappeared. A few traces of early colonial buildings can be found in empty lots in the Greenwich Village section of the city. On the high ground along the Hudson, north of 125th Street, Patriot forces on September 16, 1776 won an early Revolutionary victory known as the Battle of Harlem Heights. Sections of this area are still underdeveloped and some relics can be found. Another major battle occurred two months later at **Laurel Hill Fort,** on the west bank of the Harlem River near 192nd Street and Audubon Avenue. Staten Island fell into the hands of the British in July 1776 and served as an important base throughout the war, though the Patriots attacked it several times. Most of the early colonial buildings were destroyed during the Great Fire of 1776 in which most of the city was burnt to the ground. In 1853 the city again suffered another devastating fire which destroyed about half the buildings as well as many ships along the waterfront.

Oriskany Battlefield is a state park located on N.Y. 69 about five miles east of Rome, Oneida County. It was the site of a major battle in August 1777 in which many lives were lost on both sides.

Peekskill on the Hudson River in upper Westchester County was first settled by the Dutch in 1665 and served as a farmers' trade town for two centuries. During the Revolutionary War it saw much military activity and a number of minor skirmishes. In the countryside around Peekskill are the ruins of many old buildings.

Raynham Hill is seven miles north of Northern State Parkway, Exit 35, on Oyster Bay, Long Island. During the Revolution this site served as one of the main British encampments. Since the place is still underdeveloped, many traces of the camp may still be found.

Sag Harbor, Long Island is still a small village as it was during the Revolution when it was used as a base by British troops. A number of skirmishes took place here. Explore this area for remains of early colonial buildings.

Saratoga National Historical Park is on the Hudson River near the village of Bemis Heights, Saratoga Co. Here two of the bloodiest and most important battles of the Revolution were fought in 1777 and much equipment was lost by both sides.

The Schoharie Valley near Middleburgh in Schoharie Co. was settled around 1700 by large numbers of Palatines. One can see the ruins of hundreds of their homes, most of which were destroyed by Indians and Tories during the Revolutionary War. The remains of an old stone fort stand in the present village of Gallupville on N.Y. 443. Legend has it that most of the settlers hid their valuables before an Indian attack in 1734, during which they were all killed.

Setauket, Long Island, first settled by Puritans from Boston around 1650, was the only important village in the central portion of the island during the Revolution. Throughout the war, the town was held by the Tories; Patriots made two raids against the place in 1777 but were repelled both times. Ruins of a number of colonial homes are scattered around the area.

Sharon Springs Battlefield, off U.S. 20 between Sharon and Sharon Springs, Schoharie Co., was the site of a battle in which a small band of Patriots defeated a much superior force of Tories and Indians in July 1781. The terain is still open farmland and many artifacts have recently been found there by treasure hunters.

Springsteel's Farm is about one and a half miles west of Stoney Point, Rockland County. It was the campsite of Patriot troops under Anthony Wayne in July 1779.

The area of Stone Arbadia consists of some 20,000 acres in the Mohawk Valley in Montgomery County, bisected by N.Y. 10, which was granted to Palatine settlers in 1723. There are ruins of many of these early homes in the valley. In 1780 a battle was fought here just north of the village of Palatine Bridge. Nearby is the site of **Fort Keyser,** which had been built long before the Revolution, and was already in ruins when it began. Within a two-mile radius of this site, **Forts Frey, Wagner** and **Paris** are also hidden.

Stony Point Battlefield is near the community of Stony Point on the Hudson River on U.S. 9W, about twelve miles south of West Point. The Patriots won a major battle here on July 15, 1779.

Tappan is located two and a half miles west of the Hudson opposite Dobbs Ferry, Rockland Co. It was settled around 1675 by the Dutch and ruins of some of their early houses dot this unspoiled area. It served as Washington's headquarters on several occasions and was an important encampment for Patriot forces during the Revolution.

Ticonderoga is located on Lake Champlain near the north end of Lake George, Essex County. During the French and Indian Wars the French first fortified Crown Point about twelve miles north of Ticonderoga, but when the British began building **Fort William** on the south end of Lake George in 1755 the French started construction on Fort Ticonderoga. During a battle fought in 1758, the British suffered over 2,000 casualties and failed to take the fort. The French, however, abandoned the fort a year later and it was taken over by the British. They lost it to the Patriots at the beginning of the Revolution, but soon recaptured it. **Fort Mount Hope,** half a mile east of Ticonderoga, was built during the French and Indian War to protect the La Chute River, a stream connecting Lakes George and Champlain. It was occupied by both the British and Americans during the Revolution and has since been restored. After General Burgoyne's surrender at Saratoga in 1777 the British burnt all of their buildings and barracks on both sides of the lake. In these areas are a great many interesting artifacts for the avid treasure hunter.

Valcour Bay, located seven miles south of Plattsburgh on the west side of Lake Champlain, was a scene of a famous naval battle won by the British on October 11, 1776. Remains of two Patriot vessels lost in this battle are buried under the sandy shoreline of the bay and treasure hunters have found many other artifacts from this period here.

In the **village of Verplanck's Point** on the Hudson River opposite Stony Point the remains of **Fort Lafayette** are hidden. On June 3, 1779 the village was captured by the British and a year later recaptured by the Patriots.

West Point. Within the grounds of the military academy on the Hudson River and N.Y. 218 are the remains of a number of Revolutionary War fortifications. **Fort Putnam,** which dominates the rocky hill today, was built in 1780 and restored in recent years.

White Plains in Westchester County was the scene of a major engagement on October 28, 1776. The site of the main battle and other skirmishes are well marked today, as well as surrounding hills where artillery batteries stood at the time.

The site of Fort Brewerton is on U.S. 11 near Brewerton, on the western edge of Lake Oneida, Oswego County. One can see only the earthworks of this fort, which was built to protect the route between Fort Ontario and Albany, and used during the French and Indian War and Pontiac's Rebellion of 1763-1766.

Plattsburgh Bay National Landmark is east of Plattsburgh on Cumberland Bay in Lake Champlain. After a naval battle on September 11, 1814, in which the Americans prevented a British takeover of New York State, the British army of 11,000, which had been encamped here, were forced to flee to Canada leaving behind a sizable store of military supplies, a great deal of which was buried.

The site of a plantation called **Fort Crailo** lies near the outskirts of Rensselaer, Rensselaer Co. The site was settled by a wealthy Dutch family in 1630 but no traces of the original buildings remain. Ruins of a manor house built in 1704 and occupied until 1871 can still be seen.

Sackets Harbor Battlefield. This small harbor on Lake Ontario is off State 3, about ten miles west of Watertown, Jefferson Co. Because this was the main base for the United States Naval operations on Lake Ontario during the War of 1812, the British landed troops and attempted to capture it. All of the original defenses were dismantled in 1816 but vestiges of them can still be seen.

The 363-mile long **Erie Canal** between Buffalo and Albany was completed in 1825 for the purpose of connecting New York City and the Hudson Valley with the Great Lakes. Many of the locks, toll stations, maintenance buildings, and fragments of the canal still exist; they produce a great wealth of nineteenth-century artifacts and occasionally some old coins.

On **Isle Royal,** an island on the St. Lawrence River off the port of Waddington, Lawrence Co., a treasure was buried by the French commander of the fort before he surrendered it to the British in 1760. Estimates of its value range from $10,000 to $100,000.

During the eighteenth century, there were a number of silver mines in the vicinity of Mount Utsayantha in Schoharie County. The **Lost Blenheim Silver Mine** is located somewhere on the northern side of this mountain. It was sealed off during the Revolution to prevent the British from benefitting from it and soon after a landslide covered it and concealed it permanently.

Silver Creek located about eight miles northeast of Dunkirk (County 59) on Lake Erie, is so named because large numbers of silver coins are found along the beach after bad storms. They probably come from the steamer **Atlantic,** which was wrecked here in 1852 carrying over $60,000 in coinage.

Pieces of wreckage can also be seen on the beach of Lake Erie, about four miles northeast of Barcelona, County 60, Chataqua Co. There are unconfirmed reports that gold and silver coins have been found in the same area. In 1873 the steamer **City of Detroit** sank here carrying over $200,000 in gold and silver coins and a large cargo of copper ingots; currents and storms have washed some of the remains ashore here.

In 1893 the steamer **Dean Richard** sank close to shore off Jerusalem Cors on Lake Erie, about ten miles south of Buffalo. She was beat to pieces in a storm and all of her remains, including over $191,000 in gold and silver coins, were cast ashore and buried under the beach sands.

261

A wealthy French merchant named Clairieux is known to have buried several kegs of eighteenth-century coins near the ruins of his house and store on **Grand Island,** in the middle of the Niagara River between Buffalo and Niagara Falls. There are also ruins of several other colonial buildings on this island. In 1888 a cache of sixteenth-century silver and gold coins was found near the ruins of a round stone building. During the French and Indian Wars some French raiders are alleged to have buried about fifteen chests of treasure somewhere on this island.

On the Lake Erie shore, about half a mile east of Port Colborne, County 58 in Ontario, Canada, many pieces of a wrecked steamship can be seen along the beach, where numerous American gold coins have also been found. They probably originate from the American steamer **Anthony Wayne,** which sank here in 1850 carrying over $100,000 in gold and silver coins. This site is about ten miles due west of Buffalo.

About two miles west of the village of Warsaw, State 20A, Wyoming Co., somewhere on the farm of Wilbur Rogers, a cache of about $45,000 in gold coins was buried during the Depression by the father of the present owner.

The Loomis outlaw gang is reported to have buried about $40,000 in **Montezuma Swamp,** located near Seneca, County 96, Seneca Co.

Around 1900 a traveling medicine man buried two chests of treasure, now known as the **Sulphur Spring Treasure,** near the ruins of the Sulphur Springs Health Resort, between the villages of North Pitcher and Pitcher, County 26, Chenago Co. A few gold coins, but ones dated more recently, were found in this area several years ago.

Just off the campus of S.U.N.Y. College, about four miles south of **Oswego** on Lake Ontario, Oswego Co., silver coins and fragments of chinaware are found on the beach after storms. The sailing vessel, **Lady Washington,** was wrecked here in 1803 carrying a very valuable cargo, and may be the origin of these valuables.

Some of the favorite treasure-hunting spots in the state are the various islands of the **Thousand Islands Group,** located where the St. Lawrence Waterway enters Lake Ontario, between the New York and Canadian borders. All of these islands were settled by Indians over the centuries and many of their artifacts are still undisturbed. The French also had small settlements on several of these islands and left ruins of many colonial buildings. Numerous important finds are reported every year in this area.

Tiny **Treasure Island** is situated on the St. Lawrence River between Louisville and Roosevelttown, County 37, Lawrence Co. The island was so named because during the Revolution Lord Amherst secretly buried about $100,000 here.

A wealthy eccentric named Moses Follensby is believed to have hidden about $400,000 in gold coins and paper currency somewhere on his property near Follensby's Road, about two miles southeast of **Tupper Lake,** County 3, and 30, Franklin Co.

During the Revolution a defecting British paymaster hid about $150,000 in gold coins near the northern tip of **Lake Colton** near the town of Colden, County 46, Lawrence Co. A lost gold mine, also reported to be in this general area, had been worked by Indians and early settlers.

A number of lost mines are in the Adirondack Mountains; among the most famous are the **Lost Indian Gold Mine,** near Mt. Colden; the **Adolphus Lavigne Lost Mine,** in the middle of Hamilton Co.,; and the **Lost Nippleton Silver Mine,** around the southwest corner of Warren Co.

Three different treasures are supposed to be buried in the vicinity of **Ticonderoga:** a number of gold and silver coins are believed to be buried near Old Fort Amherst at Crown Point; near the banks of Long Pond retreating British troops buried another cache during the Revolution; Indians are believed to have buried a great deal of plunder in the Mount Pharaoh Range a few miles north of Ticonderoga.

In 1776 the Tory Robert Gordon buried a fortune estimated at about $75,000 before fleeing from Patriot troops. The treasure site is in some marshes called **The Haven** on the Poultney River, about a mile northeast of Whitehall, State 4, Washington Co. He was killed by some Patriots while trying to reach the British lines and his treasure was never found.

During the Revolution numerous treasures were lost in the area of **Saratoga Springs,** U.S.

87, Saratoga Co., when the British and Patriots destroyed many buildings in the area. After the Battle of Saratoga the British hid several caches of plunder on the northern shores of Lake Saratoga.

Before being driven out of the area the Indians concealed a great deal of treasure in a cave not far from the village of **Conesville**, County 30, Schoharie Co. On nearby **Blenheim Mountain** the Indians had a silver mine. They are said to have hidden near its peak a great deal of treasure, which they had obtained in raids on the white settlements.

Around 1900 a band of outlaws are reported to have hidden a large cache of gold coins in or near **Wynd Cave**, near the town of Knox, County 157A, Albany Co.

During the 1930s the notorious gangster Dutch Schultz concealed a large iron box containing over $7 million in paper currency, gold coins, negotiable bonds, jewelry, and uncut diamonds among a stand of stately pine trees on the banks of the **Ecopus Creek**, about five miles south of Phoenicia, in the Catskill Mountains, County 214, Ulster Co. This was to be his retirement fund but he died before getting a chance to use it. In this same general area a bootlegger in 1935 concealed a great amount of gold coins and paper currency, also on the same creek, but a bit closer to Phoenicia.

The Schlechtenhorst Lost Silver Mine is located within a five-mile radius of Woodstock, County 212, Ulster Co. During the Revolution some Tory raiders buried a great treasure in the woods on the northern side of the town.

The Lost Shawangunk Silver Mine is located in the Catskill Mountains between Lakes Mongaup and Hodge Pond, in the northern top of Sullivan Co.

During the days of Prohibition a New York City bootlegger is known to have hidden about two and a half million dollars in paper currency in several iron boxes on an old abandoned farm site on the northern side of **Ashokan Reservoir**, about a mile east of the village of Shokan, County 28, Ulster Co. FBI and other law enforcement agencies were unable to find this cache after apprehending the gangster. The **Lost Truman Hurd Gold Min** is located in this general vicinity. Also, a cache called the **Tongorara Treasure**, reputed to be over one million-dollars worth of gold and silver coins, lies somewhere between the southern edge of this reservoir and the city of Kingston, U.S. 87.

A miner named Rufe Evans buried a cache of silver ore and bullion in or just outside of the tiny village of **Accord**, State 209, Ulster Co.

During the Revolution a band of Tory raiders hid a large amount of plunder in a cave in the **Shawangunk Mountains** just outside of Summitville, State 209, Sullivan Co.

The will of the farmer Tracy Maxwell, who died in 1948 stated that he buried about $135,000 in paper currency as well as a great deal of old family jewelry in or near his barn. His family unsuccessfully spent over $20,000 in trying to find this treasure. The farm is **two miles west of Surprise** on County 81, Greene Co.

During the eighteenth century, river pirates based in the vicinity of the **West Point Military Academy** are reputed to have buried many caches.

During the Revolution numerous treasures were buried in and around **Peekskill** by Tories who were forced to flee for their lives. These might be located by studying old property records to determine where the Tories lived and might have concealed their valuables.

The narrowest place on the Hudson River is a spot called Kidd's Point. The famous rascal is alleged to have buried a great treasure in this area, which has been the subject for numerous treasure hunts over the years.

Another pirate hoard is believed to be buried in a cave on a bluff overlooking the Hudson River at **Stony Point**, just south of Peekskill. Several miles further to the south at Croton-on-the-Hudson, there is a place called **Money Hill** where a great treasure of unknown origin is reputed to be buried.

A wealthy recluse hid several caches, totaling about $750,000 in gold and silver coins, on his estate in **Hicksville**, County 135 on Long Island. In 1960 a bulldozer operator found one containing $89,000 in old coins.

In the late eighteenth century pirate Joe Brandish is said to have concealed several chests of treasure at **Orient Point**, on the northeastern tip of Long Island.

Of all the places that Captain William Kidd is reputed to have buried treasure, **Gardiner's Island** in Block Island Sound is the most publicized and has the most likelihood of containing one of Kidd's treasures. He and other pirates did use the island as a base of operations. Just prior to being apprehended and hanged, Kidd did stop there right after taking a valuable prize at sea. There is a spot known as Kidd Valley on this privately owned island where numerous symbols on the rocks are believed to be clues to where his treasure is hidden.

Pirates are also known to have frequented **Fisher's Island** lying a bit north of Gardiner's Island. Some of them are believed to have cached treasures here. Coins and other valuable items have been found on the island but they are believed to have been washed ashore from wrecks.

In the early 1800s a pirate named Charles Gibbs is reported to have buried a large treasure in the vicinity of **Southampton Beach,** County 27, Long Island. During the 1930s millionaire Walter Chrysler buried a sizeable cache of money just above this beach on his estate.

Gold and silver coins from the early 1800s are found washed ashore after storms on **Shinnecock Beach,** about one mile south of Shinnecock Inlet, on Long Island.

After winter storms have removed great amounts of sand on Long Island in the vicinity of **Fire Island,** timbers of several shipwrecks are visible on the beach and many valuable artifacts have been found with metal detectors. One of these hulks is probably the Dutch immigrant ship, **Prins Maurits,** which was wrecked here in 1657 while carrying a great deal of treasure.

Vestiges of numerous ships are also exposed on the beaches in the vicinity of **Montauk Point,** the eastern tip of Long Island, where many ships have been lost over the years. One of the richest wrecks cast up on this beach was an American privateer, **Marey,** lost in 1763 while carrying about $100,000 in gold coins and bullion. Right on the beach by the village of Montauk, have been found German gold and silver coins believed to be coming ashore from the German immigrant ship **Herbert,** wrecked there in 1710.

Treasure hunters have had good success working the shores of **Governor's Island,** off the tip of Manhattan, where numerous ships were lost over the years. Coins and many types of colonial artifacts have been found in this area. Nearby Staten Island has also claimed a large number of ships; relics are often found along its banks.

NORTH CAROLINA

The Alamance Battleground, on N.C. 62, six miles southwest of Burlington, Alamance County, was the scene of a major battle between Tories and Patriots in March 1771.

Bath on the Pamlico River, Beaufort County, settled about 1696, was the first incorporated town in the state. The town is much the same today as it was two centuries ago. Ruins of many old buildings are to be found in the area.

Beattie's Ford is a lost site on the Catawba River, four miles north of Cowan's Ford Dam, Richmond County. At this spot on January 31, 1781 the Patriots suffered a serious defeat at the hands of Cornwallis's troops.

Beaufort in Carteret Co., was one of the state's earliest seaports, settled some time before 1713. The place abounds with many tales of pirate treasures buried in the vicinity. Beaufort was captured in 1749 by a band of pirates who burnt it to the ground after failing to extract a ransom. During the Revolution and the War of 1812, it was a major privateering base for the Americans. One of the heroes of this latter war, Otway Burns, is interred in the Old Burial Ground beneath a cannon from his privateering vessel.

Bell's Mill on Muddy Creek near its junction with the Deep River, about two miles northwest of Randleman, Randolph County, was recently covered by a reservoir. In 1781 a band of Tory troops, which had been successfully plundering the countryside for months, are supposed to have buried a substantial treasure in the vicinity of this mill and were all killed before returning to recover it.

Bethabara, about ten miles northwest of Winston-Salem, Forsyth County, was called Dutch Fort or Old Town during the colonial period. The community was founded in 1753 as one of the first "Moravian Settlements." Nothing remains of this early settlement, which was abandoned shortly after 1790, but the church and several wells. However, the foundations of a large number of buildings are visible.

Bethania is another abandoned Moravian settlement located on N.C. 65 between N.C. 67 and U.S. 52, a few miles northwest of Winston-Salem and close to Bethabara, which was founded about the same time. Only a few ruins remain.

The ruins of Brunswick Town are located on the west side of Cape Fear River off State Road 133, fifteen miles below Wilmington. The town, founded in 1726, was the most important in the state until being overshadowed by nearby Wilmington. At the start of the Revolution it was shipping more naval stores than any other port in the British Empire. Brunswick Town had been the center of the Stamp Act resistance in 1766 and was one of the first targets to be attacked by the British when the Revolution began. They completely destroyed the city, which was abandoned and never settled again. During the Civil War the Confederates built the huge earthwork **Fort Anderson** over the northern portion of the old townsite and in February 1865 it was captured by the Yankees after a heavy bombardment. In the general area are a number of other ruined buildings, also demolished during the Revolution, the most famous being Russelborough, also known as "Old Palace"—the former residence of the state's early governors.

Charolle, the county seat of Mecklenberg County, was founded in 1768. A number of minor skirmishes took place in this area during the Revolution. The ruins of many homes destroyed during this and the Civil War are scattered over the area.

Clapp's Mill is near the junction of Beaver and Big Alamance Creeks in Alamance County. A skirmish occurred here on March 2, 1781 between the advance troops of Cornwallis and Greene. Before the Patriots were forced to retreat they buried a number of bronze cannon and munitions.

Cox's Mill is on Mill Creek near its junction with Deep River, between Ramseur and Coleridge, Randolph County. It was the campsite for several weeks for Patriots led by General Kalb, who in 1780 headed for the relief of Charleston. The ruins of the mill are still visible and many artifacts can be found here.

Deep River is located near Guilford in Randolph County near S.C. 22 and 42. After the British and Patriots left this area around 1782, a cutthroat named David Fanning with a large band of cronies began terrorizing the countryside—murdering hundreds of people and robbing everything he could lay his hands on. He fled to Nova Scotia when a large force was finally sent against him in 1787, but before doing so, he buried a huge amount of yet undiscovered plunder in a cave along this river.

Edenton at the head of Albermarle South, Chowan County, first settled in 1658, has a number of surviving colonial buildings and ruins in the surrounding area.

The site of **Etchoe,** also known as Nikwasi or Sacred Town by the Indians, is now occupied by the present town of Franklin, Mason County. It was the most important town of the Cherokee Nation. Twice it was destroyed and rebuilt until the Indians finally departed in 1819 and the whites took it over. Local lore has it that the Indians buried many golden objects in the area.

Fort Johnson was a wooden fort which has long since disappeared. Originally it stood near the present village of Southport at the mouth of the Cape Fear River, Brunswick County. It was built as a defense against pirates in 1748 and was burnt by Patriots in 1775 to keep it out of British hands. Another stone **Fort Johnson** was built in the same area in 1809, seized by the Confederates in 1862, and used by them for the duration of the war. Only the remains of the officers' quarters of this later structure remains.

Gilbert Town once stood just off U.S. 221, about four miles north of Rutherford, in Rutherford County. It was captured by the British and Tories in August 1780, burnt to the ground, and abandoned.

Guilford Courthouse located off U.S. 220, just north of Greensboro, was the scene of Cornwallis's major victory over the Continental forces led by Greene in March 1781 where both sides suffered heavy losses.

Over

Most hobbyists associate ghost towns with the Western U.S., but they can also be found in Eastern states such as North Carolina

Facing

Ethical treasure hunters do not destroy property and they always try to dig so that they will leave any area in better condition than they found it.

Over

Modern metal detectors and searhcoils are built of sturdy materials because they are meant to be used in rugged outdoor conditions.

Facing

Searching for deeply buried caches often requires use of the Depth Multliplier two-box searchcoil, which Charles Garrett calls his "Bloodhound."

271

Halifax on the Roanoke River, Halifax County, east of I-95 near the Virginia Line, was founded in the early 1720s and was an important economic center during the rest of the century. Today only a small number of people still live in the village; the ruins of many brick and stone structures can be found in the area.

Hillsborough off I-85 just west of Durham, Orange County, was founded in 1754 on the site of an ancient Indian village. Until after the Revolution it was the most important town in the western portion of the state. During the war it was taken and occupied by both sides and a number of minor battles took place in the area. Today only 116 structures of the late eighteenth and early nineteenth centuries still stand, but the ruins of hundreds of others lie in the rolling hillside around the town.

Moore's Creek Bridge National Park stands near Currie on N.C. 210 northwest of Wilmington, Pender Co. The first battle of the Revolutionary War in North Carolina was fought here on February 27, 1776. The Patriots won a decisive victory, shattering British hopes of a fast victory in the South. The victors followed up by destroying the homes and property of hundreds of British supporters in the area.

New Bern at the confluence of the Neuse and Trent Rivers, Craven County, is the state's second oldest town and was founded by Swiss and Germans in 1710. The ruins of many old colonial buildings and others destroyed during the Civil War are found here.

Orton Plantation on the Cape Fear River near the ruins of Brunswick Town, has one of the oldest and largest surviving mansions of the early eighteenth century. Upon the death of "King Roger" Moore, as the original builder and owner was called, it was revealed that within "100 paces of the great house" he had buried a fortune in treasure valued in excess of £75,000 sterling at that time. No trace was ever found of it.

A site known as "Pyle's Defeat" is located on the west bank of the Haw River, below Graham, Alamance County. It was the spot where Patriots troops ambushed and massacred about 90 Tories led by Colonel John Pyle.

Quaker Meadows on N.C. 181 just west of Morganton, Burke Co., was actually first settled by Moravians around 1765; the ruins of many of their early dwellings still survive. A minor skirmish took place here in 1780 between Tories and Patriots.

Rockfish Creek, about fifteen miles south of Fayetteville in the northwest corner of Bladen County, served as an encampment for a large number of Patriot troops in February 1776.

Shallow Ford on the Yadkin River, about eight miles east of Courtney in Yadkin County, was the site of a settlement dating from around 1700, of which no trace survives today. In 1780 the Patriots won a skirmish here against Tories.

Trading Ford was three miles north of Shallow Ford on the same river. There was an early settlement here also, of which no traces remain. In February 1781 it served as a campsite for British troops under Lord Cornwallis.

Troublesome Iron Works on Troublesome Creek, one and a half miles north of Monroetown, Rockingham County, first served as a camp for Cornwallis's huge army. Later, in March 1781, Patriot forces dug field fortifications and camped there for several weeks.

Wilmington at the mouth of the Cape Fear River, New Hanover County, was first settled in 1732, and served as a base for the British Army under Cornwallis after being captured on February 1, 1781. The ruins of many old dwellings are found in this area.

Fort Macon is on Bogue Point on the eastern tip of Atlantic Beach near Morehead City, Carteret Co. The area has traces of several earlier wooden forts built in the 1700's to protect the residents from incursions of pirates and Spaniards, who occupied and plundered nearby Beaufort in 1747. The present restored fort was built between 1826 and 1834 and was occupied by Confederate troops until being captured by the Federals on April 24, 1862.

The site of Fort Fisher is on U.S. 421, about four miles south of Carolina Beach, New Hanover Co. It was the largest earthwork fortification of the Confederacy. Its great strategic importance was to keep the port of Wilmington open for the blockade runners bringing in the badly needed supplies to fight the war. After a six-week siege, Fort Fisher was finally captured by Federal troops on January 15, 1865. Only small sections of the earthworks are still visible as the area has been battered a great deal by hurricanes over the years.

Bennett Place State Historic Site is located at the intersection of State 1313-1314, near Durham, Durham Co. At this farm house on April 26, 1865 General Joseph E. Johnson surrendered some 90,000 Confederate troops to General W. T. Sherman, seventeen days after Lee surrendered to Grant at Appomattox. The farm site and surrounding area are a treasure hunter's paradise, as the defeated soldiers discarded tons of equipment and thousands of weapons—most of which were buried to prevent them from being found by the Union troops.

The site of Fort Defiance is on State 268, a bit north of Lenoir, Caldwell Co. The wooden fort was built around 1700 to protect scattered settlers from Indian raids. All traces of it had disappeared by 1789 when a large plantation was established on the site, the ruins of which are still visible.

Town Creek Indian Mound Park is on State 73, five miles southeast of Mt. Gilead, Anson Co. The Mississippi Indians of the late prehistoric period, flourishing probably about 1500, established a ceremonial village here and many Indian remains can be seen.

Bentonville Battlefield is on County 1008, two miles north of Newton Grove, Johnston Co. The largest land action in the state during the Civil War occurred here on March 19-21, 1865. More than 90,000 troops participated in the action where Confederates under General Joseph E. Johnson suffered defeat by Sherman's Army. Today the remains of many earthworks, a field hospital, and the Confederate cemetery remain.

Fort Raleigh National Historic Site is on U.S. 158, four miles north of Manteo, Roanoke Island, Dare Co. The site was the scene of the earliest English attempt to establish a colony in the United States. Sir Walter Raleigh sponsored the first two settlements here in 1585, but most of the settlers returned to England in 1586. The following year when more new settlers arrived they could find no traces of those who had remained the previous year. The fate of these 116 settlers has never been determined but they were probably massacred by Indians. By 1591 the colony was completely abandoned and fell into ruin. Today the sites of both settlements have been located and excavations are being done there.

The site of Fort Dobbs is near the outskirts of Statesville, Iredell Co. This was a frontier area of the state during the French and Indian War. The fort was built in 1756, fought off two major attacks by the Cherokee Indians in 1759 and 1760, and was then abandoned in 1764 and soon fell into ruin. Only the earthworks of the fort are still visible.

The Old Salem Historic District is located near the center of downtown Winston-Salem. It was founded by a Moravian colony in 1766, burnt to the ground in 1803, rebuilt and then consolidated with Winston in 1903. A number of late eighteenth-century buildings have been restored and there are vestiges of others.

During the Tuscarora War in September and October of 1711, the Indians massacred thousands of settlers **along the Chowan and Roanoke Rivers** and burned all of their homes and farms to the ground. In the ruins of many of these, treasure seekers have been finding fine colonial artifacts and some treasure.

In 1750 four survivors from a sunken Spanish galleon made it ashore with about 200,000 pesos in gold and silver specie and bullion at **Cape Lookout,** about fifteen miles southeast of Morehead City, Carteret Co. They lugged the treasure to the highest bluff on the point, buried it, then were rescued by local fishermen. After a great deal of negotiations the Spaniards received permission from the British Crown to return for the buried treasure several years later. A hurricane had altered the landscape and they were unable to find it. Over the centuries more than 300 sailing ships are known to have been wrecked on this dangerous point of land jutting out into the Atlantic Ocean and numerous hulks lie buried along the beaches here. A large number of European gold and silver coins from the late 1700s have been found in recent years right under the lighthouse. They are believed to be washing ashore from the German immigrant ship, **Christian,** wrecked here in 1799 with an unknown amount of treasure aboard.

Along the whole **Outer Banks,** which extend from the Virginia-North Carolina border down to Cape Lookout for more than 160 miles, remnants of hundreds of old hulks are seen along the beaches, especially after hurricanes or bad winter storms have removed vast amounts of sand. Just in the vicinity of **Cape Hatteras** more than 3,000 ships were lost over the centuries along this treacherous coastline. Local residents and fishermen are very helpful in pinpointing the area where wreckage is seen on the beach or where coins and artifacts are generally washed ashore. For help in selecting the most lucrative areas one should consult my book **Shipwrecks of the Western Hemisphere,** also **Graveyard of the Atlantic** by David Stick. In recent years the most publicized areas where treasure hunters have found large numbers of old coins and other valuables are in the vicinities of **Duck, Kitty Hawk, Nags Head, Avon, Buxton, and three different spots on Portsmouth Island.**

Large numbers of British and American gold coins have been found on the beach in the vicinity of the large fishing pier jutting out into the ocean on **Wrightsville Beach,** eight miles east of Wilmington, County 132, New Hanover Co. They probably come from the Civil War blockade runner **Fanny and Jenny,** which was wrecked at this spot in 1864. On the ship at the time was a solid gold, jewel-studded sword, being sent to General Robert E. Lee from British admirers. The sword may some day be washed ashore like the coins and other artifacts.

There is a **Lost Indian Silver Mine** located in the Snowbird Mountains between the towns of Marble and Andrews, State 19, Cherokee Co. It was producing until around 1800 when the Indians were driven out of this area by the white man.

According to local legend a cache of gold coins was hidden near the mouth of **Nantahala Gorge** in the early 1800s. The Nantahala River passes through this gorge into the Little Tennessee River, near Lauada, State 19, Graham Co. In this same gorge Cherokee Indians are alleged to have buried about 20 mule loads of silver bullion which they robbed from a silver mine in the vicinity of Dahlonega, Georgia.

Cherokee Indians are also reported to have buried about $100,000 in gold and silver bullion in a sealed cave in the **Great Smoky Mountains** about three miles west of Smokemont, State 73, Swain Co.

A lucky gem prospector hid a bag containing about 50 pounds of emeralds between two rocks near the bridge at **Caler Fork,** ten miles north of Franklin, Franklin Co. He was struck by a car soon after and only gave a vague location of the emeralds before dying.

The Lost Sontechee Indian Silver Mine is in the Snowbird Mountains near Andrews, State 129, Cherokee Co. Before sealing the entrance to the mine the Indians hid a large amount of plunder they had accumulated by raiding white settlements in the early 1800s.

On Summit, a mountain peak about two miles north of the town of Black Mountain, State 70, Buncombee Co., early Dutch farmers hid several caches of treasure before being massacred by Indians. One large cache was recently found on the Amcel farmstead just outside the town's limits. It consisted of several hundred gold coins, about 25 ten-pound silver ingots, and over 100 pieces of beautiful colonial silverware.

The Lost Copper Hill Silver Mine is in the vicinity of Silver Creek Knob, a mountain peak in the northern corner of Rutherford Co.

During the Civil War numerous caches of personal loot were hidden in and around **Charlotte.** One hoard consisting of over $100,000 in gold coins was hidden around where Sugar Creek passes under Morehead Street. Another cache of gold coins of unknown value was concealed under the ruins of an old house at the corner of Elizabeth Street and Hawthorne Lane.

A number of small caches of treasure are believed to be concealed among the ruins of mining cabins on **Richardson Creek,** a branch of the Rocky River, in the vicinity of Anson Mine, about five miles south of Wadesboro, off County 109, Anson Co.

During the Civil War a large cache of gold coins and jewelry was concealed on **Julius Benjamin's farm,** about a mile north of Mt. Pleasant (County 49), Cabarras Co. Benjamin was killed in the war and his family were unable to locate his hiding spot.

In 1781 a British regiment under General Cornwallis buried about twenty chests and kegs of gold and silver specie and bullion, as well as jewelry and silver plate—plunder they had accumulated in raids all over the state. The site is just east of Lexington, State 70, Davidson Co., on the banks of **Abbott Creek,** a few hundred yards north of the U.S. 64 Highway bridge which crosses this creek. To prevent the Americans from finding the treasure, the British used gunpowder to cause a landslide which completely obliterated all traces of the hiding place.

In 1893 a Gaston B. Means died after burying a vast fortune estimated at around $500,000,

somewhere on his large estate in Concord, State 70, about fourteen miles northeast of Charlotte, Cabarras Co. The estate is still in his family's hands and repeated searches have failed to locate this hoard, which is absolutely known to exist on the property.

A William D. Wentworth, in 1854, buried a large satchel of gold coins in the **nearby woods behind Brummel's Inn** before turning in for the night. He died in his sleep and no one was ever able to find his gold. The inn was located on the old stage road between High Point and Greensboro in Guilford County.

During the Revolution a British officer hid a large cache of gold and silver coins at a place now called **the Campgrounds,** located just outside of Red Crossing, State 64, Randolph Co.

There are numerous legends about hundreds of iron cooking pits filled with gold coins being buried by Confederate soldiers at the close of the Civil War. They were supposed to have been taken from the Confederate Treasury and buried **along the tracks of the Old Southern Railroad** between McLeansville and Burlington, Alamance Co. Several of these pots of gold have been found over the years.

During the Civil War a Confederate paymaster was forced to bury two chests of silver coins and paper currency along the **Deep River,** about two miles south of Ranseur, State 64, Randolph Co. Pursuing Union troops caught up with him soon after and he was killed in a skirmish.

The owner of the Williamson Plantation buried a large cache of gold coins and silver plate during the Civil War before joining the army and being killed in action. His plantation is on **the west side of the Haw River,** one mile northwest of Bynum, State 15, Chatham Co.

In 1963 a Milwaukee banker embezzled over $500,000 from his bank and then buried the hoard in or near his fishing lodge on the **Cape Fear River** just south of Tarheel, County 131, Bladen Co. He died of a heart attack after being apprehended and law enforcement officers were unable to find the cache.

Over $200,000 in gold coins and bullion was concealed somewhere on the **McKinnon Plantation** during the Civil War and lost when the owner was killed in the war. The site is on State 401 about two miles west of Fayetteville, Cumberland Co.

A large cache of silver and gold coins was buried on **the Keener Estate** just outside of Pinehurst, County 2, Moore Co., during the Depression.

There are several **Lost Indian Gold Mines** in the vicinity of Raleigh in Wake Co. At the close of the Civil War most of the large plantations were burnt to the ground by Union troops and their ruins can still be seen in the surrounding area. Numerous treasures are reported to have been buried and lost during the war and occasional finds are made by treasure hunters. While dredging the nearby Neuse River to build a marina in 1956, workers found several hundred Spanish early eighteenth-century silver coins.

During the Civil War a company of Union troops captured a Confederate supply train near **Autryville,** County 24, Sampson Co. After pushing all of the wagons with their contents into the South Black River, they discovered that there had been four large chests containing about $350,000 in gold and silver coins concealed among the foodstores and munitions.

Pirate Blackbeard is known to have used the area around Elizabeth City, State 17, Pasquotank Co., as his main base when operating off the United States. He is alleged to have buried several different caches in the area. One possible site is in or near the ruins of an early colonial building on the south bank of the **Pasquotank River,** about three miles north of the city. Several small hoards of gold and silver coins have been found in the area and they are believed to have been concealed by members of his crew. History tells us that Blackbeard paid off the mayor and other local officials for protection when he was in the Elizabeth City. The mayor is known to have buried a chest of loot somewhere on his farm, about three miles east of the city.

While plowing his fields in 1857 a farmer found old Spanish silver and gold coins then valued at $6,000 and more is believed concealed on his farm which is near **Currituck,** County 34, Currituck Co. In the nearby village of Barco another farmer in 1934 discovered a large copper still containing several hundred English silver coins from the late 1600's.

Many pirates had a base on **Plum Point,** near Bath, County 92, Beauford Co., on Pamlico

Sound. On the point are ruins of colonial homes and some alleged caches. Recently a treasure hunter found about $10,000 in coins and artifacts near the foundation of one old brick ruin.

Numerous pirates, including Blackbeard, used **Ocracoke Inlet** on the south end of Ocracoke Island, between Pamlico South and the Atlantic Ocean, as a base and many are believed to have buried caches in the area.

During the Civil War a Confederate blockade runner was attacked by a Union gunboat and run aground on **Shaklesford Beach** located on the southwest side of Harkers Island, about ten miles south of Beauford (State 70), Carteret Co. The crew lugged a large chest of silver coins ashore and buried it among the high sand dunes. Union troops landed and the Confederates were all killed in a skirmish.

Between Wrightsville Beach and Kirkland, State 17, New Hanover Co., there is a place called **Money Hill** where eighteenth-century pirates are reported to have buried a large treasure.

During the Civil War about $30,000 in silver and gold coins were buried on the **Gander Hall Plantation** a few miles west of Wilmington, State 74, Brunswick Co.

The pirate Stede Bonnet is reputed to have buried a large cache of booty somewhere along the banks of the **Cape Fear River,** about four miles above Wilmington at a place now known as Buccaneer Point. A small cache of gold coins was found in this area in the 1930s by a boy digging for fishing worms.

Female pirate Anne Blythe is known to have buried a cache of gold bullion and silver coins in the vicinity of **Fort Caswell** at the mouth of the Cape Fear River, a few miles south of Southport, Brunswick Co. Other pirates also used this area over the centuries and may also have buried treasure.

Large numbers of Civil War mintage gold and silver coins are found on both sides of **Lockwood's Folly Inlet** in Brunswick Co. During the war six blockade runners were wrecked in this area and the coins are most likely being washed ashore from these wrecks.

NORTH DAKOTA

The ruins of Fort Abercrombie are off U.S. 81 a bit east of Abercrombie, Richland Co. The fort was built in 1858 and was the first Federal fort in the state. It suffered two major attacks by Sioux Indians in 1862, one of which was a five-week siege, and was abandoned in 1877.

The ruins of Fort Buford are situated near the confluence of the Missouri and Yellowstone Rivers, near Buford, McKenzie Co. The fort was built in 1866, used until 1881 when it was abandoned, and served mainly to quell disturbances made by the Sioux Indians. Only the stone powder magazine and officers' quarters are still standing.

The ruins of the Fort Union Trading Post are on the Upper Missouri River, several miles west of Buford, McKenzie Co. For almost 40 years after its construction in 1828 it served as the most important fur-trading post in this section of the country. After 1832, when the first riverboats reached the area, it became an important river port.

Whitestone Battlefield is off U.S. 281, 28 miles northwest of Ellendale, Dickey Co. The last major encounter east of the Missouri River between the Sioux Indians and Federal troops took place here on September 3-5, 1863; the soldiers won after suffering many losses.

Fort Totten is a bit south of the town of Fort Totten, Benson Co. It was built in 1869 and used as a military outpost until 1890 when it became an Indian agency. Today most of the original buildings are still in use.

The site of Fort Abraham is off County 6, five miles south of Mandan, Morton Co. This Federal fort was built in 1872, primarily to protect the men building the Northern Pacific Railroad, then abandoned in 1891. Several buildings of the fort have survived and there are many remnants of a surrounding Indian village.

The site of Fort Rice is on the west side of Lake Oake, 22 miles south of Mandan, Morton Co. It was built in 1864 and occupied for thirteen years by Federal troops until being abandoned. Only two blockhouses are still visible.

The site of Fort Dilts is located off U.S. 12, between Rhame and Marmarth, Bowman Co. The fort was built in 1864 and destroyed the same year after a wagon train bound for the Montana gold country sought refuge there. Indians attacked and burned it down after massacring everyone.

The site of Menoken Indian Village is one mile north of Menoken off U.S. 94, Burleigh Co. Many remnants of this Mandan Indian settlement can still be seen, but there are no traces of a fort built by French explorers who settled the area briefly.

Pembina State Park is off U.S. 29, 22 miles northeast of Cavalier, Pembina Co. Some remnants of the earliest white settlement in this state are seen in this park. The French had a trading post here in 1797–1798, then Scottish settlers founded a village in 1812 which lasted for about twenty years. There are remains of the Fort Pembina military reservation, which was in use from 1870 to 1895.

The site of Fort Mandan is on the Missouri River, fourteen miles west of Washburn, Mercer Co. It was built of wood by the men of the Lewis and Clark Expedition who spent the winter of 1804–1805 here; soon after it was destroyed by the Sioux Indians. Today a replica stands on the site.

The ghost town of Antelope is near Young Man's Butte on U.S. 94, about 30 miles east of Dickinson, Stark Co. More than 100 buildings from the late 1800s are still standing.

The ghost town of Arvilla is 22 miles west of Grand Forks, just south of State 2, Grand Co. It was a thriving college town in the 1880s, but when fire destroyed the college in 1893 the town was also abandoned.

The ruins of Ashtabula are located on the Cheyenne River about twenty miles north of Valley City (U.S. 94), Barne Co. It was a farming community which was destroyed by a flood in the late 1800s and very few traces of it exist.

The ghost town of Auburn is on State 81 about seven miles north of Grafton, Walsh Co. It was abandoned when the railroad bypassed it. Many wooden buildings are still standing.

The ghost town of Bartlett is about a mile north of State 2 and four miles west of Lakota, Nelson Co. It was a prosperous railroad town with 21 saloons—several of which are still standing—and the ruins of over 200 buildings remain.

The ruins of Belmont are on the west bank of the Red River, about fourteen miles south of Grand Forks, Forks Co. It was an active river port during the second half of the nineteenth century, until it was destroyed by a flood in 1897. At this time several safes containing large amounts of money were swept into the river and never recovered.

The ruins of Bowesmont are located between the present town of this name and the Red River, about 24 miles south of Pembina, State 81, Pembina Co. The town was also destroyed by the great flood of 1897.

The ghost town of Buford is near the present town of Buford and the ruins of Fort Buford near the Montana State line, McKenzie Co. The town was founded by the American Fur Company in 1828 and abandoned in 1881 when the fort was deactivated. Only about a dozen buildings are still standing.

The ruins of Deapolis are on the Missouri River two miles south of Stanton, County 200, Mercer Co. It was an important riverboat town until being destroyed by fire in 1888. Only a single grain elevator now marks the spot.

The ruins of the town of Fort Clark are on the south side of the Missouri River, about 30 miles north of Bismark. It was founded in 1829 as a trading post for the American Fur Company and destroyed by fire during an Indian raid in 1853. Only a few building foundations are left. Nearby are the **ruins of Fort Clark,** a fortified post used by the United States Army around the mid-nineteenth century.

The ghost town of Fort Ransom is on the Cheyenne River about 27 miles north of Oakes (County 1), Ransom Co. It was founded in 1818 near the military post of the same name. The post ruins are on a hill about a mile south of the town.

The ghost town of Grandin is about a mile east of U.S. 29 and 24 miles north of Fargo, Cass Co. Nearby is another ghost town named **Mayville**. Both flourished briefly in the late nineteenth century as part of the Grandin Brothers' land development scheme, which backfired.

277

The **ghost town of Grand Rapids** is on the James River about 40 miles southeast of Jamestown (State 10), La Moure Co. It was the county seat until 1886, but abandoned soon after when it was bypassed by the railroads.

The **ghost town of Bowman** (originally called Atkinson) is near Butte View, about eight miles northwest of Bowman, State 12, Bowman Co. It was a mining town that flourished only for a few years.

The **ruins of Hungry Gulch** are on Tabacco Garden Creek about six miles southeast of Wheelock (County 2), Mountainrail Co. The town was founded in 1902 as a result of a false gold rush and abandoned two years later. Many buildings are still intact.

The **ruins of Le Roy** are on the south side of the Pembina River about four miles northeast of Walhalla (County 32), Pembina Co. It was founded in the early nineteenth century by the Hudson Bay Company and can be reached only by horseback or on foot.

The **ruins of Little Missouri** are on the Fort Berthold Indian Reservation, about fifteen miles north of Killdeer (County 200), Dunn Co. Only a few cellar pits and foundations are still visible.

The **ruins of Manhaven** are on the east bank of the Missouri River, about fifteen miles north of Stanton, Mercer Co. It was founded in 1809 as Fort Manuel Lisa and abandoned in 1812. The buildings were occupied again in 1822 and a **Fort Vanderburgh** (in ruins) was erected nearby. By 1880 the town and fort had both been abandoned.

The **ruins of Medora** are on the west bank of the Little Missouri River, opposite the ghost town of **Little Missouri Cantonment,** and about 24 miles east of Beach, just south of U.S. 94, Billings Co. Both were booming cowtowns and railroad centers until being abandoned by 1900.

The **ghost town of Oakdale** is on the eastern slope of South Killdeer Mountain, about ten miles northwest of Killdeer (County 200), Dunn Co. It was a prosperous frontier town; however only a few of its buildings are still standing. Several abandoned gold mines are in the vicinity.

The **ruins of Ojata,** first called Stickney, are located near the Turtle River, about ten miles west of Grand Fork in Fork Co. It was a thriving railroad town until destroyed by a fire in the late nineteenth century.

The **ruins of Old Bottineau** are on Oak Creek, close to the Canadian border, about one mile north of present Bottineau (State 218), Bottineau Co. In recent years treasure hunters have had good success in finding several caches of treasures and a great wealth of artifacts here.

The **ruins of Old Ludden** are on the James River about a mile west of present Ludden, County 11, Dickey Co. It was founded in 1833 and abandoned in 1886 after a flood destroyed most of the town.

The **ghost town of Pleasant Lake** is located about 45 miles northwest of Devil's Lake on State 2, Benson Co. Only the old railroad station survives. Bank robbers are known to have hidden several chests of gold bullion here in the 1880s.

The **ghost town of Rock Haven** is on the Missouri River about two miles north of Bismark, Morton Co. It was once a thriving boat-building and dry dock center for the river traffic; now only a few buildings are left.

The **ruins of St. Joe** are near Lookout Point in the Pembina Mountains, about three miles west of Walhalla (County 32), Cavalier Co. It was established in 1851 as a trading post and soon after became a mining center. About twelve miles further west on the banks of the Pembina River are the **ruins of St. Joseph,** its sister city, also abandoned by the turn of the century.

The **town of Verendrye** is on the Souris River about eleven miles northeast of Velva (County 41), McHenry Co. Only a few people still live in this ghost town of several hundred buildings.

The **ghost town of Wamduska** is near Lake Wamduska about ten miles south of Lakota, State 2, Nelson Co. It was founded in the 1880s as a Great Northern railroad town but only flourished for a few years. Today a 75-room hotel and many other buildings are still standing.

The **ruins of Winona** are on the Missouri River opposite Fort Yates (County 24), Emmons Co. It was a rip-roaring cowtown until destroyed by a flood in the 1890s.

During an Indian attack a paymaster for the Hudson Bay Company was forced to bury about $40,000 in gold and silver coins on Big Butte, near the town of Lignite, State 52, Burke Co. He was killed and those with him were unable to find the cache later.

About $100,000 in gold coins and bullion from a bank holdup in 1893 was concealed in the foothills of the Turtle Mountains near Belcourt, State 218, Rolette Co.

The Lost Mountain of Gold was discovered in 1864 by a group of settlers led by Doctor Dibbs. The mine was somewhere in the vicinity of Belfield, U.S. 94, Stark Co. The settlers found many abandoned mine shafts on the mountain and in one of them they extracted several hundred pounds of gold from a very rich vein. They were later unable to relocate the site. The mines were probably worked by Indians before the white men arrived.

A large cache of gold coins robbed from an army paymaster was buried on **Sunset Butte,** about ten miles northwest of Amidon, State 85, Slope Co. In this same area at Chalky Butte, some Indian renegades buried a treasure before being killed by United States Cavalry troops in 1878.

In 1864 a returning California miner buried about $100,000 in gold dust and nuggets in the vicinity of **the junction of the Knife and Missouri Rivers,** about a mile north of Stanton, Mercer Co.

Another California gold miner buried about $200,000 in gold bullion along the banks of the Missouri River within the limits of the town of **Stanton.** After spending a week recuperating from an illness, the unfortunate miner discovered that the river had flooded and obliterated all traces of his hiding place.

During an Indian attack a group of miners returning from the Montana gold fields buried about $90,000 in gold nuggets along **the Missouri River,** about a mile east of Fort Clark, County 200A, Oliver Co. They were unable to find the spot several days later when they returned with Army troops.

In the late nineteenth century, a trader buried about $55,000 in gold and silver coins on the east bank of **the Missouri River** at the mouth of Burnt Creek, about a quarter mile north of the present day railroad bridge between Mandan and Bismark, Morton Co.

OHIO

The Chillicothe Towns were settlements of Shawnee Indians who caused such great destruction on the Kentucky frontier. The first Indian village by this name, which was destroyed by Kentuckians in 1787 was located near the present Chillicothe, founded by white men in 1796.The second village, where Daniel Boone was held captive, was on the Little Miami River near Xenia, east of Dayton. In 1780 it too was destroyed by white men. The third Chillicothe was on the Great Miami River where Piqua stands today; it was burned to the ground by frontiersmen in 1782.

Defiance on the north bank of the Maumee River, Defiance Co. was the site of a French mission in 1650; in the city park you can see vestiges of an earthworks built in 1794 by the British.

The site of Fort Laurens is on the Tuscarawas River, near Bolivar, Tuscarawas Co. This fort, built in 1779, was the only Revolutionary War defense post to be erected by United States forces in what is now Ohio. Here during the summer of 1779, British attacks were repelled on several occasions. Fort Laurens was demolished at the end of the war. Two miles southeast of this site is another ghost town once called **Zoar Village,** which was settled by German refuges in 1817 and abandoned in 1898.

Gnadenhutten Monument is a short distance south of modern Gnadenhutten on U.S. 36, Tuscarawas County. A Moravian mission was established here about 1773. The mission and settlement were destroyed by Patriot forces in 1782 and about 140 Indians who had settled with the Tory whites in Gnadenhutten were all massacred.

Fort Campus Martius on the Ohio River near the outskirts of present Marietta, Washington Co. was the name of a lost settlement founded in 1788 by American pioneers and destroyed during an Indian raid about ten years later.

279

Mingo Bottom is another lost settlement on the Ohio River near the present Mingo Junction, Jefferson County. It was settled by Iroquois in 1750. In 1766 the town was the only settlement—red or white—on the Ohio between western Pennsylvania and Louisville, Kentucky. The place was totally destroyed during an attack by white men around 1780.

Piqua Towns. The Piqua branch of the Shawnee Indians settled three towns in Ohio, all called Piqua. One was on the north side of Mad River, about five miles west of present Springfield in Clark County; this was destroyed by frontiersmen in 1780. The second stood near the modern town of Piqua on the Great Miami River. The third was about three miles to the north near the town of Pickawillany, where the Old Johnson Trading Post was built in 1749. No traces of any of these towns have survived.

Schoenbrunn Village is three miles east of New Philadelphia on U.S. 250A, Tuscarawas County. Moravian missionaries and Christianized Indians from Pennsylvania founded the first permanent white settlement at this place in 1772; it prospered until the Revolutionary War began and was then abandoned.

Battle Island Monument is located just north of Upper Sandusky near the intersection of U.S. 23 and Ohio 53. Here a battle was fought and won by Tories and Indians. The Patriots suffered a humiliating defeat and their leader, Colonel William Crawford, was tortured to death.

Mound City Group National Monument is on State 104, four miles north of Chillicothe, Ross County. This site was the cultural center of one of the most remarkable prehistoric civilizations in the Americas—that of the Hopewell Indians. There are 24 huge burial mounds within a thirteen-acre earthen enclosure.

The site of Fort Winchester is on the west bank of the Auglaize River opposite the town of Defiance. The fort was built in 1812 and destroyed when the Fort Winchester Bridge was constructed on the site.

Fort Recovery is located near the intersection of State 49 and 119, near the town of Fort Recovery, Mercer Co. On this site the Americans suffered a major setback in the westward expansion. On November 3-4, 1791 troops led by General Arthur St. Clair lost 900 men in a battle with Indians before they retreated. Two years later American troops returned to the area and built the fort. It withstood a major Indian attack in 1794 but soon after was abandoned and fell into ruin. Some portions of the fort have been restored recently.

The site of Fort Stephenson is located in a park of the same name in Fremont, Sandusky Co. It was constructed in 1813 by American troops; a few months later they successfully defended it against a major attack by British soldiers and then abandoned it at the end of the War of 1812. No traces remain today.

The site of Fort Greenville is near the corner of West Main Street and the Public Square in Greenville, Darke County. This wooden fort was built in 1793 and occupied only during that winter by the troops of General Anthony Wayne before being abandoned. Nothing is left of it now.

Fort Ancient National Historic Landmark is on State 350, seven miles southeast of Lebanon, Warren Co. On a hilltop here are prehistoric Indian earthworks and mounds built by the Hopewell.

Serpent Mound Park is on State 73, four miles northwest of Locust Grove, Adams Co. The mound is over a quarter mile in length, occupying a hill crest off Brush Creek. Remnants of a prehistoric settlement dating back to 1000 B.C. can barely be seen in the area.

Fallen Timber Battlefield is on U.S. 24, two miles west of Maumee, Lucas Co. On August 20, 1794 American troops under General Anthony Wayne defeated a large force of Canadian militia and Indians here. Remnants of earthworks still survive.

Mound Builder State Memorial is on State 79 near Newark, Licking Co. The park is rich in numerous prehistoric Hopewellian earthworks and mounds dating back to 650 B.C.

Fort Meigs is located on the outskirts of Perrysburg, Wood Co. A section of this fort built during the War of 1812 has been restored and many artifacts have been reported to been found around it.

On December 29, 1876 the Pacific Express Train plunged into a gorge near **Ashtabula**, State 20, Ashtabula County, when the bridge spanning the gorge collapsed. One car carrying $2 million in gold bullion broke into pieces and the gold tumbled out and fell below the muddy river bottom. It has never been recovered.

Large numbers of gold and silver coins from the late nineteenth century are found on the shores of **Lake Erie** about two miles east of Vermilion. State 6, Erie Co. They probably come from a nearby wreck.

During the Revolution a British warship carrying over £100,000 sterling in gold and silver coins was wrecked at Locust Point, about fifteen miles east of **Toledo,** Ottawa County. The survivors buried the treasure on shore; when they returned several weeks later they were unable to locate the spot because snow had hidden their markers.

During the French and Indian Wars a French army officer buried a great deal of plunder on tiny **Isle St. George** in Lake Erie, about fifteen miles north of Sandusky, Erie Co.

In 1862 a bank robber buried about $100,000 in gold bars on the west bank of the **Grand River,** about two miles from Lake Erie and near Fairport Harbor, County 535, Lake Co. On his deathbed he stated that the gold was about "three feet deep and 30 paces northwest of a large oak tree on the river bank."

Somewhere in a cow pasture on **the Pierpont farm** near the village of Leipsic, County 65, Putnam Co. John Dillinger is reported to have buried about one and a half million dollars in paper currency during the 1930s.

In or near the ruins of old **Fort Finley,** near the town of Finley, U.S. 75, Hancock Co., an army payroll was hidden during the War of 1812, just prior to an Indian attack. The officer who concealed the money was killed.

During the Revolution a cache of about $25,000 in gold coins was buried on **the farm of a John Ashland,** along the south bank of the Sandusky River, just outside of the town of Wyandot (County 231), Crawford Co.

During a 1913 flood which destroyed a great part of **Dayton,** many hidden hoards were lost. Treasure hunters are still successfully working the areas where the greatest damage was done.

In about 1790 a army payroll was buried on the river bank near **Fort Recovery** to keep it out of the hands of attacking Indians; it was never found. The site is just north of the town of Fort Recovery, County 119, Mercer Co.

In 1780 a band of Shawnee Indians being pursued by army troops hid a large amount of plunder along one of the bends of the **Little Miami River** near Old Town, about three miles north of Xenia, State 68, Greene Co.

During the Revolution about $25,000 in gold coins were buried on the north side of the **Sandy River,** about a mile south of Minerva, State 30, Carroll Co.

The Morgantown gang, who terrorized the area of Woodford and East Liverpool during the 1880s buried numerous caches of booty near their headquarters on the west banks of the **Ohio River,** about two miles east of East Liverpool, State 30, Columbiana Co.

During the War of 1812 fleeing British troops buried several treasures in or near the ruins of **Fort Wapatomica** on the Muskengum River, about two miles north of Zanesville, U.S. 70, Muskingum County.

About $125,000 in paper currency from a bank holdup in 1924 was buried on the **Lisman Farm,** located about two miles east of the village of Joy, County 555, Morgan Co.

Large numbers of gold and silver coins are being washed ashore from a river wreck on the west bank of the **Ohio River** near Cheshire, County 7, Galion Co.

Riverboat pirates had a base for many years on a bluff overlooking the **Ohio River,** about a mile northeast of Crown City, County 553, Galion Co. After the pirates had robbed more than $24,000 in gold and silver coins, as well as a large number of watches and jewelry from the passengers of a river steamer in 1876, a posse cornered the gang at their base camp and all were killed. The proceeds of the robbery were never found.

OKLAHOMA

Washita Battlefield is on U.S. 283 a few miles northwest of Cheyenne, Roger Mills Co. Here Custer attacked the sleeping Cheyenne village and massacred all the Indians living there, setting the stage for his fate eight years later at the Battle of the Little Big Horn in Montana. No traces of the village are left.

The site of Fort Gibson is off State 10 a bit north of the town of Fort Gibson, Cherokee Co. Built in 1824 by the United States Army, it served to protect the Seminole, Creek, and other Indian tribes, which had been forcibly transplanted here from their homelands in the southeast. Abandoned about 1840, it was again occupied during the Civil War by Union troops and remained in use until 1889. No traces of the original fort have survived but the log stockade and several buildings have been reconstructed.

Fort Sill National Historic Landmark is five miles north of Lawton on U.S. 66 and 277, Comanche Co. The original fort was built of wood in 1869 and played an important role in controlling the Indian tribes for two decades. Then it was abandoned; a much larger one built of stone is still being used today on this United States Army training base. There are no traces of the original fort.

The site of Fort Washita is near the junction of the Red and Washita Rivers, on State 199, southwest of Nida, Cotton Co. This fort was built in 1842 by troops of Zachary Taylor to protect the Chickasaw Indians in the newly created Indian Territory and as a stopping station for travelers moving along the Southern Overland Trail. During the Civil War it was occupied by Confederate troops; several buildings of the fort are still standing.

Before dying in around 1900 an old eccentric, who had mined gold all his life, buried about $80,000 in gold coins in a copper box near his cabin in the **Kiamichi Mountains** near the town of Cloudy, Pushmataha Co. This site is less than a mile from the junction of the Texas-Arkansas-Oklahoma state lines. Many treasure hunters have combed this area unsuccessfully.

In 1872 the Jesse James gang made a number of raids along the Texas-Mexico border and got more than $1 million in gold, most of it by robbing a caravan carrying gold bullion belonging to a Mexican insurgent general. With several posses hot on their trail, the gang buried the gold in the **Wichita Mountains** near the town of Geronimo and the Cache River, about ten miles south of Lawton, County 7, Comanche Co.

The ghost town of Bigheart is located a few miles west of Hulah Reservoir just off County 99, about midway between Herd and Boulangerville, Osage Co. It was a thriving Indian school center. Today the town consists of only five buildings.

The ruins of Boggy Depot are near Clear Boggy Creek, which is located about thirteen miles southwest of Atoka (State 69), Johnston Co. It was founded in 1837 and during the Civil War served as a Confederate outpost for four years. Later when the railroad bypassed the town it died quickly. In Boggy Depot are ruins of hundreds of buildings and traces of old streets.

The ruins of Camp Mason are on the east bank of the Canadian River about a mile south of Lexington (County 74), McClain Co. The place first served as an Indian trading station and later on as an army base before being destroyed by a flood in the late nineteenth century.

The ruins of Choctaw Town are located two and a half miles north of Bokchito (State 70), Bryan Co. The site was founded in 1844 as a school for the Choctaw Indians and was destroyed by fire in 1921.

The ruins of Cornish are about one mile south of Ringling, State 70, Jefferson Co. It was a rugged cowtown until being abandoned in the late 1800s. Very few ruins remain.

The ruins of Doaksville are near the Red River about a mile north of the town of Fort Towson, State 70, Choctaw Co. It was founded in 1821 and was a thriving trade center until being destroyed by Confederate raiders during the Civil War.

The ruins of Fred are located at the junction of the Boggy Depot-Fort Sill Road and the Chisholm Trail, about four miles south of Chickasha, State 81, Grady Co. This small trading center and stage station was wiped out by Indians around 1860. About two miles to the east on the west bank of the Washita River are a few ruins of a trading post and small settlement.

The ghost town of Gibson is located on the southern tip of the Gibson Reservoir, about three miles east of Okay (State 69), Wagoner Co. The town only existed between 1871 and 1886 when the railroads were being built in this area and then quickly died. A few people still live here among the many abandoned buildings.

The ghost town of Grand is on the Canadian River across from the Antelope Hills, about twelve miles south of Arnett (State 60), Roger Mills Co. It was a highly prosperous community during World War I and then during the duststorms of the 1930s the people all moved elsewhere, leaving a very picturesque ghost town. Treasure hunters have found numerous small caches of money here.

The ghost town of Ingalls is on the Cimarron River about three and a half miles east of Ripley, State 108, Payne Co. The infamous Trilby Saloon, which is still standing and heavily bullet-scarred, was the main hangout of the Dalton and Doolin gangs, who buried several caches in the area. A wealthy patent medicine king from New York built several mills here and a railroad which is long-gone. This man buried a large treasure before dying.

The ruins of Krebs are located on the southwestern tip of the Eufaula Reservoir, about three miles east of McAlester, County 31, Pittsburg Co. Near this former coal-mining town, which died in the 1930s, are also numerous ruins of the coal mines in the area.

The ruins of Mayhew Courthouse is on the Clear Boggy River, about four miles north of Boswell (State 70), Choctaw Co. Only a few foundations are left.

The ghost town of North Fork Town is on the North Fork of the Canadian River about two miles east of Eufaula, State 69, McIntosh Co. During its history the town has had three names: when it was founded in 1836 it was named Creek Indian Town; then the name was changed to Micco in 1853; and finally it was renamed North Fork Town in 1872 when the railroad reached it. An important trading center, it was at the junction of the California Trail and the Texas Road. A few buildings remain.

The ruins of Nunih Wayah are located one and a half miles west of Tuskahoma, State 271, Pushmataha Co. In this former capital of the Choctaw Nation, few traces of any habitations are left. There are also other ruins of Indian settlements in the surrounding area.

The town of Okay is on State 69 about thirteen miles north of Muskogee, in Muskogee Co. It is one of the oldest white settlements in the state and just too tough to die—a few hardy residents remain today. It was devastated by floods, fire, dust storms, and tornados but each time it was rebuilt. Amongst the many ruins here, there are the remains of stove, plow, truck, and airplane factories—all of which went bankrupt. About half a mile south of the town is the famous Three Forks, the confluence of the Verdigris, Grand, and Arkansas Rivers. In 1822 a large trading post was established here. Over the years there have been several different settlements, all of which were destroyed by floods. For a while before the Civil War, the United States Army also had a large wooden fortification on the site, which has disappeared. Several caches of bandit loot are reported to be buried in the immediate area.

The ruins of Perryville are located about eight and a half miles south of McAlester, and half a mile west of State 69, Pittsburg Co. After its founding in 1838 it served as a trading post; during the Civil War it was used as a Confederate supply depot and outpost. After the Battle of Honey Springs the Union troops pursued the Confederates to this site and badly beat them. The Federals then fired the town and it was never rebuilt.

The ruins of Salt Works, founded in 1820, are on the southern end of Tenkiller Reservoir, about seven miles north of Gore near County 100, Sequoyah Co. All that is left are ruins of the warehouses and a few homes.

The ghost town of Scullyville is on the south bank of the Arkansas River near State 271, about twelve miles south of Fort Smith, Arkansas. It was founded in 1822 and demolished by Federal troops at the end of the Civil War, after serving as an important Confederate outpost during the war. Numerous caches of treasure were hidden here by the fleeing Confederates. Some of its buildings remain.

The ghost town of Silver City is on the south bank of the Canadian River about two miles north of Tuttle (County 37), Grady Co. A wild and wicked cowtown, Silver City was destroyed by a flood in the late nineteenth century. On the eastern side of Tuttle, a twelve-ton boulder marking the Chisholm Trail was a widely used campsite for the westward-bound pioneers and miners. At one time there was also a large trading post on this site.

The ruins of South Coffeyville are on the Verdigris River across the state line from Coffeyville, Kansas, on State 75, Washington Co. It was a wide-open western town that boasted more than 50 saloons and a greater number of brothels. The town was burned down in the 1890s by some drunken cowboys.

The ruins of the Tullahasse School are located about eight miles northwest of Muskogee on County 518, Muskogee Co. A Presbyterian mission was started here in 1850 for the Creek Indians. It fared badly during the Civil War, then in 1880 the small settlement was burned down. Soon after, the mission was rebuilt and used for years to educate Indians and Negro freedmen.

The ruins of Union Mission are located ten miles southeast of Chouteau, State 69, Mayes Co. Founded in 1819, this Presbyterian mission served the Osage Indians and a settlement grew up around it. The French are believed to have begun a community much earlier at this same place. Numerous legends tell of the Indians having buried various treasures robbed from white men in and around these ruins.

Somewhere on Sugarloaf Peak about ten miles northwest of Boise City, State 56, Cimarron Co., there is believed to be about $2 million in gold bullion buried by a group of French miners who struck it rich in the California gold fields during the mid-nineteenth century. The miners concealed their cache on that mountain and went into Boise City to purchase supplies, where all four were killed in a saloon gun fight.

The Lost Bat Cave Platinum Mine is in the Slick Hills, north of the Deep Fork River, in the general vicinity of Edna County 6, Creek Co.

Ther are several Lost Spanish Gold Mines in the region of Devil Canyon, about ten miles north of Altus, State 62, Jackson Co.

The ghost town of Wildman is on the North Fork of the Red River, about five miles northwest of Synder (State 183), Kiowa Co. Only about ten buildings have survived. Within a three-mile radius of this town is the Lost Gold Bell Mine.

Several miles north of Wilburton (State 270), Latimer Co., is Robbers' Cave, used for many years by bandits who are believed to have hidden several small treasures here. In another sealed cave within a half mile of Robbers' Cave, bandits concealed over 100 mule loads of unrefined gold ore.

The Lost Devil's Half Acre Gold Mine is about eight miles south of Okemah (U.S. 40), Okfuskee Co.

A Lost Spanish Gold Mine is east of Spiro (State 271), somewhere in the vicinity of Buzzard Hill in the Poteau Mountains, Sequoyah Co. Mexican bandits are supposed to have buried loot in a cave on nearby Brushy Mountain, south of Sallisaw, U.S. 40.

During the Indian War of 1868 a cavalry officer buried $42,000 in silver coins near the banks of the Golf River, about two miles south of Sturgis, State 56, Cimarron Co.

During the 1870s outlaws buried $80,000 stolen from a West Texas bank in a cave in Gyp Sink near Casteneda, State 385, Cimarron Co.

Outlaws used the large caverns on the Black Mesa Plateau, located in Kenton, County 325, Cimarron Co., as a base for many years during the late nineteenth century. They are believed to have buried several caches here.

The Dalton gang used a cave in the Grass Mountains overlooking the Cimarron River, about three miles northwest of Orienta, State 60, Major Co. They are said to have stashed a great deal of their booty in the general area.

In 1874 a returning Montana gold miner buried a large cache of gold and silver coins somewhere in the Roman Nose State Park, about eight miles north of Watonga, State 270, Blaine Co.

During a Comanche raid in 1879 about a half million dollars in gold coins is reported to have been buried in a canyon off the Washita River, about four miles south of Clinton, U.S. 40, Custer Co.

Before being killed by Indians in 1853, a group of returning California miners buried several iron pots of gold on the bank of the Arkansas River near the Black Dog Trail Crossing, about eight miles east of Newkirk (State 177), Kay Co.

Outlaws buried a large cache of gold bullion along the banks of the Bird River near the village of Pearsonia, about twelve miles northwest of Pawhuska (State 60), Sage Co.

The outlaw Al Spencer buried about $30,000 from a one-man train robbery in 1923 on a farm in the Osage Hills, just outside of the tiny village of Okesa, about two miles south of

State 60, Sage Co. Several other bandit caches are buried in this same area near Nelagoney.

In 1932 bank robbers buried about $80,000 on a **farm then owned by an H. Kohlmeyer,** near the village of Bansdall, County 11, Sage Co.

Approximately three miles southwest of the **ghost town of Keystone** on the Cimarron River, about twelve miles west of Tulsa and overlooking Salt Creek, is **Dalton Cave.** In or near this hideout, the Dalton and Doolin gangs are alleged to have hidden several caches of booty. The Daltons also used the old Berryhill Farm just south of nearby Mannford Village and are believed to have hidden treasure there.

Outlaw Cole Younger is known to have concealed about $80,000 in gold bullion on the south side of the **Arkansas River,** a mile downstream from the Sand Springs Bridge, County 51, about five miles west of Tulsa. The Dalton gang are also alleged to have buried money on the farm then owned by a Jack Wimberley. In an area now called **Lost City,** about two and a half miles southeast of Sand Springs, outlaw Frank James concealed $88,000 in paper currency in a leather pouch, which he hid in a narrow crevice of a rock pile. In this same spot on the Arkansas River, a group of early nineteenth-century Mexican miners are alleged to have hidden a large amount of gold bullion before being killed in an Indian attack.

Outlaws are reported to have buried about $25,000 in gold and silver coins somewhere on Scaley Rock Mountain located between Claremore and Lake Claremore, State 66, Rogers Co.

During the early 1800s a large store of silver bullion was buried by Mexican miners some place along **Lost Creek** near the Phillips Ranch in the Osage Hills, just outside of Bartlesville, State 60, Sage County. This occurred just before the miners were attacked by Indians who killed most of them.

Just prior to being shot by a posse in the 1920s, Al Spencer hid an undetermined amount of loot in a wooded area about two miles south of **Caney,** Kansas. The location is just on the Oklahoma side of the state line, in the vicinity of a bridge that crosses a deep ravine and dry creek bed, about fifteen miles north of Bartlesville, Sage Co.

While the driver was crossing the **Verdigris River,** about a mile south of South Coffeyville, State 169, Nowata Co., a wagon carrying over $50,00 in gold coins and nuggest tipped over. Its treasure contents were spilled out and carried downstream by the swift current. The returning Montana miners were able to recover only a small part of their gold.

The Jesse James gang reportedly buried a large cache of loot on the banks of the **Neosho River** near Miami, U.S. 44, Ottawa Co. On the banks of the nearby Spring River a gambler buried a large cache of gold coins before being gunned down in a saloon brawl.

About five miles west of Pryor, State 69, Mayes Co., is a spot known as **Robber's Canyon,** one of the Cole Younger gang's favorite places for ambushing stagecoaches and wagon trains. Several caches of loot are believed to be buried in the area.

The Meadows gang are said to have buried about $135,000 in gold bullion on the outskirts of **Pryor,** just before being caught and hanged.

There are a number of **Lost Gold Mines** that were worked by the Indians, Spaniards, and Mormons on the east side of Lake Spavinaw, about ten miles northeast of Salina (County 20), Mayes Co.

A group of Spanish miners returning to Mexico with several years' accumulation of gold bullion were attacked by Indians in Flowers Canyon, a few miles northeast of **Fort Gibson** (County 10), Cherokee Co. They concealed the gold in a cave before fleeing for their lives.

Before their exodus from Oklahoma in the early nineteenth century the Cherokee Indians concealed a great deal of treasure in various caves in the area of **Horseshoe Bend** on the Illinois River close to Tahlequah, State 62, Cherokee Co. A band of renegade Indians led by Chief Blackface also buried their loot in this same area. Somewhere on **Park Hill** in Tahlequah, the Indians worked a silver mine which they sealed off before leaving their home. During the nineteenth century a rich merchant named Billy Stinnett ran a trading post on this hill for almost 50 years; now the place is in ruins. He is known to have buried a considerable fortune in the area. Just before the Civil War broke out the United States Government paid $50,000 in gold coins to four Cherokee Indian chiefs for a large tract of land; the Indians buried their gold for safekeeping about half a mile south of the town on **Tahlequah Creek;** soon after they were ambushed by outlaws and killed.

Charles Garrett evaluates this beautiful Western treasure hunting site and points out the many possible locations of hidden wealth.

The Depth Multiplier two-box searchcoil this treasure hunter is using permits a metal detector to detect large targets at depths of 18 to 20 feet.

Just prior to the Civil War Chief Opothleyoholo of the Creek Nation was paid $160,000 in twenty-dollar gold pieces. Because of problems he was having with other leaders of his tribe, he buried the money in the woods near the **Deep Fork River,** where the road branched towards Rigitsville, about two miles west of Checotah, State 266, McIntosh Co. On his deathbed he told of this event but no one was ever able to find the treasure.

During an attack by Arapaho Indians, Spaniards are alleged to have buried seven mule loads of gold bullion on **Lee Creek Slough,** about four miles north of Nicut, County 101, Sequoyah Co. An Indian legend tells about a group of French traders who were ambushed in this same area, about three miles north of **Lee Creek Crossing.** The treasure they were carrying was hidden in a nearby cave.

In 1860 a Phillip Ursay was killed by bandits, who were trying to force him to reveal the location of a large number of gold coins and some jewelry, which he had buried on his farm. The valuables were concealed in a tin box and buried close to an old spring by his house near **Sallisaw,** U.S. 40, Sequoyah Co.

The Winchester Outlaw gang buried a large cache of gold coins in a blind canyon midway **between the Red River and the town of Hollis,** State 62, Harmon Co., in the southwestern corner of the state.

Miners are reported to have buried gold bars somewhere along **Turkey Creek** near the village of Canute, State 66, Washita Co.

In Hobbs Canyon, **between Mt. Scott and the town of Meers,** County 49, Comanche Co., outlaws are believed to have buried $784,000 in gold bullion from a train robbery.

In 1924 a prospector named Keown discovered a fabulous ledge of platinum near **Bat Cave** in the Wichita Mountains, about fifteen miles northwest of Meers. He was killed in a mining accident before he could stake his claim, so its location was consequently lost.

Outlaw Frank James buried about $5,000 in gold and silver coins near the barn on **the old Billy Royce farm** in the rugged Keeche Hills near Anadarko, State 62, Caddo Co.

A Mexican pack train carrying 40 mule loads of gold bullion worth about $4 million was attacked by Indians. The mule drovers quickly buried the whole cache in an old spring or gully along the east branch of **Lost Creek,** about five miles south of Oklahoma City. The few survivors were unable to locate the site when they returned months later.

A large number of treasures are supposed to be buried in **Devil's Canyon,** in the Rainy Mountains in the northeast corner of Kiowa Co. The Spaniards are believed to have had a settlement and worked several gold mines in this area. During one Kiowa Indian raid they were forced to throw 40 burro loads of gold bars into a deep cavern, from which they were unable to remove the gold later on. A lost stagecoach lies under creek sands near **the old Perry Crossing** on the east bank of the North Fork of the Washita River, about two miles southeast of Devil's Canyon. Actually there are more than a dozen places in this canyon where Indians, Spaniards, and outlaws are reported to have buried treasures.

Outlaws buried an undetermined amount of money from a Wichita Falls, Texas bank robbery somewhere on **the Climers Ranch,** about three miles southwest of Grandfield, State 70, Tillman Co.

The Jesse James gang is said to have buried a wagon load of gold ore and nuggets and about $2 million in loot on the west slope of **Twin Mountain** in the Wichita Mountain range, between Keeche Hills and Fort Sill, State 277, Comanche Co. A Mexican bandit buried over $200,000 in gold coins and bullion on the north side of this same mountain. The Spaniards had numerous gold mines in this area from the late 1600s until around 1820 and there are many abandoned settlements and mines to be found. Spaniards are believed to have buried a treasure somewhere in **Spanish Cave,** about one mile southwest of **Treasure Lake.** The lake got its name because in the late eighteenth century a Mexican pack train carrying a large amount of gold bullion was attacked by Indians and the Mexicans threw all of the gold into this lake to prevent its being taken. Many outlaws used this area as their headquarters and many of them are believed to have hidden caches of loot. **In Wild Horse Canyon** about ten miles east of Twin Mountain, bandits are reputed to have concealed two wagon loads of gold ore. At nearby **Cut Throat Gap** an army payroll of $96,000 in silver coins was hidden by renegade Indians before they were killed by an army patrol.

Spaniards are alleged to have hidden a large cache of gold bullion on **the Williams farm** near Elm Springs Creek, about two miles west of Walters, County 53, Cotton Co.

Somewhere near **the ruins of the old Pecan School,** about fifteen miles south of Lawton on the Cache River, Mexicans buried seven mule loads of gold bullion while fleeing from a band of hostile Indians.

At **the old Fort Sill trading post,** a bandit threw four bags of gold and silver coins into a well, which has since been covered. About $100,000 from an 1892 stagecoach robbery was also buried in this same area in Comanche Co.

Outlaws attacked an army supply train in 1869 and made off with a large army payroll in gold and silver coins. They buried the loot **in a cave near Mill Creek** in the Arbuckle Mountains, about three miles northeast of Arbuckle in the northwest corner of Cotton Co.

A large hoard of coins, jewelry, watches, and weapons were concealed by bandits in a cave in the rugged Quachita Mountains, near Pine Knott Crossing on the Little River near the **ruins of Ringold,** Pottawatomie Co.

Prior to 1964, Standing Rock and a number of ghost towns in its neighborhood, stood on the north bank of Piney Creek, McIntosh Co. Then a dam was built, and Lake Eyfaula, the resulting reservoir, covered both the well-known rock and the ghost towns. Just before the flooding, a man found a large silver bar near the base of the rock, which had been a camping area for westward-bound settlers for many years. Many more bars are believed to be in the area. Spaniards are said to have buried a large number of gold bars in a cave near this rock.

In the area near Wilburton, State 270, Latimer Co. the Indian outlaw Black Face hid at least three caches of loot along a dry creek bed in the hills just north of the town.

OREGON

The site of Fort Astoria is at 15th and Exchange Streets in Astoria. The fort and a settlement were built here in 1811 by the Pacific Fur Trading Company, but fear of an impending attack by the British caused them to be abandoned two years later. The fort was restored to the United States in 1815 and present Astoria built up around it. A portion of the original fort has been reconstructed.

The site of Fort Clatsop is located at the mouth of the Columbia River near U.S. 101, five miles south of Astoria. This wooden fortification was built by Lewis and Clark and served as their winter quarters in 1805-1806 after their epoch-making exploration across the North American continent. No traces of the original fort remain but a replica has been built on the site.

The site of Fort Klamath is near the junction of State 62 and 232 near the town of Fort Klamath, Klamath Co. Built in 1863, it was garrisoned by the United States Army and militia for 27 years to protect settlers in the Klamath Lake area from hostile Indians. The fort served as the center of military operations during the Modoc War of 1872-1873. None of the more than 40 buildings that stood in this fort, or the fort itself, has survived; only a replica of the guardhouse now stands on the site.

The Oregon Trail Marker on Laurel Hill west of U.S. 26 near Government Camp, Hood River Co., designates the point where the Oregon Trail began to follow an old Indian trail in order to bypass the Columbia River rapids and Mt. Hood. Extending some 2,000 miles from Independence, Missouri to the mouth of the Columbia River, this famous emigrant route was first used in the early 1800s. By 1850 it had become a deeply rutted highway. The marker indicates a favorite camping spot of the westward-bound settlers; at this site, there were also many Indian attacks.

Jacksonville is on State 238, west of Medford in Jackson Co. Founded in 1852 after a big gold strike nearby, this mining boomtown flourished for 32 years, then went into decline after the railroads bypassed it in 1884. During its heyday more than 30,000 people lived in the town, which today has fewer than 1,600 residents. A few of the original buildings have survived but there are ruins of countless others.

291

The site of the town of Champoeg is above the falls of the Willamette River, off I-5, 28 miles southwest of Oregon City, Clackamus Co. The area was settled in 1818 and the town was founded in 1843 by American and French-Canadian settlers. By 1850 it was very prosperous as an important transportation and trading center. During a flood in 1861, all traces of the town, with the exception of one house that has been reconstructed recently, disappeared under a thick layer of mud deposited by the river. In a way its destruction was similar to that of Pompeii.

The site of the Salem Methodist Mission Station is on the Willamette River, about ten miles north of the present town of Salem, Marion Co. It was founded in 1834 and a community grew up around it; then the whole site was abandoned in 1841 and the settlers and missionaries moved south to found the present town of Salem. The original mission has disappeared.

The ghost town of Althouse is on County 46, midway between Cave Junction and the Oregon Caves National Monument, Josephine Co. Nearby are three other ghost towns: **Browntown, Grayback Camp,** and **Holland.** All have a large number of standing buildings and there are many abandoned mines in the area.

The ghost town of Auburn is on the Powder River about nine miles southwest of Baker (U.S. 80), Baker Co. It was founded in 1861 as a gold-mining center and became the county seat the following year. By 1864 Auburn had become the second largest town in the state with a population of over 5,000 When the gold rush began in Idaho in 1868, most of the miners headed for those parts. Within a few years Auburn was a ghost town. A wealthy Chinese merchant is known to have hidden about 400 pounds in gold dust and nuggets in the city somewhere near the Chinese cemetery.

The ghost town of Auroria is situated across the creek from the present town of this same name, 33 miles south of Portland on County 99E, Clackamas Co. Over 50 old buildings are still standing in this mining town.

The ghost town of Boston, twelve miles south of Albany on County 99E, Linn Co. was once a booming mill and trade center. When the railroad missed the town by two miles in 1871, it was abandoned. Among the many buildings still intact is the Thompson Flour Mill built in 1856.

The ghost town of Cecil is about fifteen miles south of Heppner Junction (County 74), Morrow Co. It was an early settlement at the Oregon Trail crossing of Willow Creek and a busy stage station. The Famous Oregon Trail well still can be seen in the center of the main street.

The ghost town of Copperfield is on the Snake River across from the Idaho state line, about twenty miles north of Robinette on County 86, Baker Co. It was founded in 1908 as a construction town for a power plant. In 1914 because of the lawlessness there, the National Guard was called in and martial law was declared. A few months later the whole town except a few buildings burned to the ground. Nearby is the ghost town of **Homestead,** in which only two saloons and a few homes are still standing.

The ghost town of Cornucopia, accessible over a dirt road, is twelve miles north of Pine, County 86, Baker Co. This town and the nearby ghost town of **Carson,** about four miles to the south, were thriving gold- and silver-mining towns in the nineteenth century; there are many abandoned mines in the area.

The town of Denio is located in one of the most deserted sections of the state, about 130 miles southeast of Burns, State 20, in the Blue Mountains near the Nevada state line, Malheur Co. It can be reached only on horseback. Once this was a wool and borax center with over 1,000 residents; today only a few dozen sheep herders still live here. The old hotel and many other buildings are still standing and there is a large dump with many bottles from the past century.

The ruins of Dixie are four miles north of Gold Hill (U.S. 5), Jackson Co. It was founded as a gold boomtown in 1862 and ten years later was abandoned when the gold was exhausted. Nearby is the ghost town of **Prairie City,** also in total ruins.

The ghost town of Elk, on the Elk River, about six miles east of Toledo (State 20), Lincoln Co. can be reached only by foot or horseback. It was founded in 1866 as a terminus on the

Wagon Road. Among the many buildings still standing are the blacksmith shop, several stores, and two saloons.

The ghost town of Elkton is on the Umpqua River about thirteen miles west of Drain (County 38), Douglas Co. It was founded in 1832 as a Hudson Bay Trading post and later was an important stage station. Only a few buildings are left.

The ghost town of Ellendale, on County 223 about two and a half miles south of Dallas, Polk Co., was founded in 1844; it was called O'Neal Mills and Nesmith Mills. Nearby are the ruins of several other unnamed ghost towns.

The ghost town of Fort Hays is on Clear Creek, about two and a half miles north of Selma, Jackson Co. It was founded in 1852 as a stage station and grew into a mining town. A battle of the Rogue River Indian War was fought here in 1856. One can see many of the original buildings.

The ghost town of Fort Rock, about five miles southwest of the lava beds and eighteen miles north of Silver Lake (County 31), Lake Co., can best be reached by four-wheel-drive vehicles. Fort Rock was founded in 1908. Among its many standing buildings are three stores, two saloons, a creamery, a cheese factory, a newspaper office, and a school.

The ghost town of Frankfort, on the Pacific coast, a bit west of State 101 and several miles north of Gold Beach, Curry Co., was once an important seaport. The docks were on the Sister Rocks, connected to the town by a bridge and wooden railway. Divers report that they have recovered large numbers of early nineteenth-century bottles and many interesting artifacts from several sailing ships wrecked here.

The ghost town of Frenchglen is at the dead end of County 205, some 64 miles south of Burns and two miles west of the Blitzen River, Harney Co. It was founded in 1875 and was a cowtown until about 1910. About a mile and a half to the southwest on the old "P" Ranch are numerous ruins.

The ruins of Galice are on the Rogue River, close to Hobson Horn Peak, about 21 miles northwest of Grants Pass, Josephine Co. Among the many ruins of this gold-mining town are the arsenal and powder house used during the Rogue River Indian War. Several abandoned gold mines are in the area.

The ghost town of Granite is on Granite Creek, about 41 miles west of Baker, Grant Co. The town was called Independence when it was founded in 1862 as a gold-mining center. Among the many intact buildings is the three-story Grand Hotel.

The ghost town of Hardman is on County 207, about twenty miles southwest of Heppner, Morrow Co. This community, formerly called Rawdog, then Dairyville, was a stage station and prosperous farming community.

The ghost town of Harney is on Rattlesnake Creek, about twelve miles east of Burns and about two miles north of State 20, Harney Co. Two miles to the north are the **ruins of Fort Harney.** Harney was a cowtown and many of its standing buildings are still equipped with their fixtures.

The town of Jacksonville is a near-ghost town with only a few residents and several hundred deserted old buildings. It is about midway between Medford and Ruch on County 238, Jackson Co.

The ghost town of Kerby, originally called Kerbyville, is on State 199, about 28 miles southwest of Grants Pass, Josephine Co. Founded in 1856 as a gold-mining center, it became the county seat with about 500 residents. When the placer deposits were worked out the town folded. Among the structures that have survived are the stage station and stage barn.

The ghost town of Malheur is on the South Willow River, near State 26, about twenty miles northwest of Brogan, Malheur Co. It was founded in 1872. Nearby are two other ghost towns—**Marysville** and **El Dorado.** All three have many standing buildings. A number of abandoned gold and silver mines are in the area.

The ruins of Merlin are seven miles northwest of Grants Pass (U.S. 5), Jackson Co. and can be reached only by four-wheel-drive vehicles. This area was mined in prehistoric times and one can see the ruins of pit houses. Merlin was a booming mining center for a few years in the 1870s; the most prominent ruin is the old assay office.

The ghost town of Mitchell is on Service Creek and State 26, Wheeler Co. It was founded in 1867 as a stage station on the Dallas-Canyon City route and over the years has suffered badly from fires, floods, and outlaw attacks. A few people still live among the many old buildings. On nearby Mitchell Service Creek Peak, outlaws concealed about 250 pounds of gold dust and nuggets before being caught and hanged in 1873.

The ruins of Oak Point are on the Columbia River about four miles north of Clatskanie (State 30), Columbia Co. Founded in 1810, the town quickly became an important river port and trading center. Near the end of the century it was destroyed by a flood and very few traces can now be seen. At the time of the disaster a great deal of treasure was lost and is now buried under the rubble and dried river mud.

The ruins of Parkersburg are on the south fork of the Coquille River, about four miles east of Bandon (State 101), Coos Co. Before 1900 it was a thriving boat-building, salmon-canning, and lumber-mill center, but the town folded in 1910 when a fire destroyed much of it.

The ruins of Scottsburg are on the Umpqua River, about eleven miles east of Reedsport (State 101), Douglas Co. It was founded in 1850 about the same time as another ghost town, Tower Town, two miles to the east. Both were destroyed by a flood in 1861 and never rebuilt.

The ruins of Sparta are three miles west of Eagle Creek and 21 miles east of Baker on County 86, Baker Co. It was founded in 1863 as a gold-mining center and had a life of only a few years before being abandoned.

The ruins of Sumpter are on the Powder River and County 220, about 25 miles west of Baker in Baker Co. When it was founded in 1862, a farming community grew around it; then with the discovery of gold the town really boomed. In 1900 it had over 3,000 residents but by 1915 all had left. Most of the buildings were toppled by an earthquake in the 1920s.

The ghost town of Syracuse is on the south side of the Santiam River opposite the ghost town of Santiam City. Both are located about one mile west of Jefferson, just off State 5, Marion Co., and were founded around 1850 as farming communities.

The ruins of Takilma are in the Siskiyou Mountains, about five miles east of O'Brien (State 199), Josephine Co. First Takilma was a gold-mining town and later became a center for extensive copper mining. The ruins of another ghost town, Waldo, lie one mile to the north.

The ruins of Wells Springs, abandoned in 1920, are fifteen miles south of Boardman (State 30), Columbia Co. There are ruins of about 300 buildings.

The Lost Four Dutchman Gold Mine is in a canyon in the Ochoco Mountain, just outside of Prineville, State 26, Crook Co. Several unidentified ghost towns are in this same area.

The Lost Soldier Gold Mine is somewhere along the West Fork of Cow Creek, about eleven miles west of Glendale and a few miles west of U.S. 5, Douglas Co.

The Lost San Pedro Gold Mine was one of the richest in the state. For many years before the first white American settlers reached the area, miners came from as far away as Mexico to work it. The mine was somewhere along Big Inlet Creek on the southeast slope of Diamond Peak, just north of Emigrant Butte Pass in Lane Co.

The Lost Sheepherder Gold Mine had originally been worked by Indians. It was rediscovered by a shepherd who dug out almost 500 pounds of pure ore in one day, before falling off a ledge and being killed. The mine is located somewhere in the vicinity of Coyote Wells, about midway between Freezeout Mountain and Monumental Rock, about 25 miles south of U.S. 20, Malheur Co.

The Lost Malheur Gold Mine is on the Owyhee Indian Reservation, midway between the Owyhee and Sucker Rivers, about 30 miles southwest of Homedale, Idaho, in Malheur Co.

The Lost Tillamook Gold Mine is west of Gale Creek somewhere between Edwards Butte and Tillamook, State 101, Tillamook Co.

The Lost Bear Creek Gold Mine is in the Wallowa Mountains, west of the Imnaha River, in the vicinity of Lookout Mountain, near the Idaho state line, Wallowa Co.

About twenty miles east of Glendale, U.S. 5, on Skelton Mountain in Jackson Co., a bandit confessed to having buried a payroll of $60,000 in gold coins, which he robbed from a stagecoach in 1880. He died in prison before being able to go back after his loot.

The area between Fort Stephens at the northwest tip of the state and Tillamook Bay about

294

50 miles to the south is called a "graveyard of ships." More than 200 vessels were dashed to pieces on this coast, making the beaches one of the most productive treasure-hunting places in the state. Countless finds of treasure and relics from nineteenth-century sailing ships are found each year. **On Clatsop Beach,** about ten miles southwest of Astoria, large numbers of Spanish sixteenth-century silver and gold coins are washed ashore during storms. It is believed that one of the famous Manila galleons was lost here. Nearby at **Cannon Beach,** pottery and other artifacts are washed ashore from a wreck dating from the 1700s, probably of Spanish origin. About 200 feet from shore, many of its cannons are visible in less than ten feet of water. About 25 miles further to the south **near the mouth of the Nehalem River** (just off State 101, Tillamook Co.) the remains of an unidentified Spanish ship was discovered buried under the beach sands around the turn of the century. Wooden timbers, ceramic shards, and large amounts of beeswax, one piece dated 1679, have been uncovered. It is possible that this hulk is one of the many missing Manila galleons lost on their long voyages from the Philippines to Mexico. If this is so there must be a great wealth of priceless treasure to be found on this site. Local Indian legends state that the wrecked ship was a rich treasure galleon and that the survivors buried vast amounts of riches in the nearby **Neahkahnie Mountains** just north of the river mouth.

A cache of about $17,000 was buried by an early nineteenth-century trader on **Deer Island** in the Columbia River, about ten miles north of Portland, Columbia Co.

About $100,000 in gems and jewelry from a 1923 holdup is reported to be buried in several large Mason fruit jars on **the west bank of the Columbia river,** about two miles north of the city limits of Portland. In this same area a bandit named Simms buried $6,000 in gold coins before being caught and hanged in the early 1800s.

Near the base of the south slope of Mount Hood, County 35, Hood River Co., outlaws buried $85,000 in gold bullion in a cave and then were unable to locate it. Somewhere on nearby Laurel Hill other bandits buried about $46,000 in gold coins. And in nearby **Horse Thief Meadows** at Barlow Pass, outlaws reportedly buried $35,000 in gold coins. Outlaw Ed Croy and his gang plundered the local gold mines in the late nineteenth century and amassed a fortune estimated at $200,000 in gold dust and nuggets. Their lair was at **Bennett Pass,** about ten miles north of Barlow Pass. Gang members buried all the gold in this area before being gunned down in an ambush set up by vigilantes.

Along the beach at Cascade Head, just west of State 101 on the Lincoln and Tillamook county lines, a Mexican pirate is known to have hidden a treasure when his ship was wrecked nearby. He and his crew were soon after captured and shot.

About twenty miles down the coast from Cascade Head is the **port of Newport** and several treasures are supposed to be buried here. A miner is believed to have buried several saddlebags of gold nuggets along the shore on the **north side of Yaquina Bay;** robbers in the 1930s buried a large cache of diamonds and jewelry near where the Elk River enters this bay; and a large number of gold bars was hidden somewhere along the beach by survivors from a shipwreck in the 1860s.

In the 1920s a wealthy politician and landowner buried a large quantity of money in a barn of some farm about **two miles south of Salem,** U.S. 5, Marion Co.

A miner concealed about $50,000 in gold bars and coins on **the north side of the Ochoco River** near Skelton Rock, a much-frequented campsite for miners and settlers, about two miles east of Prineville, State 26, Crook Co.

One of the most dangerous navigation points on the whole coast was **the mouth of the Umpqua River** in Winchester Bay, just west of Reedsport, State 101, Douglas Co. A dangerous sand bar and swift currents make it a difficult place to enter or leave. Between 1851 and 1858 eight ships carrying returning gold miners were wrecked in this area with a loss in gold of over $5 million. The surrounding beaches no doubt conceal a great deal of this shiny wealth.

A miner stored about $50,000 in gold dust and nuggets within a few hundred yards of **Golden and Silber Falls,** located in the Coast Range Mountains, about 23 miles northeast of North Bend, State 101, Douglas Co.

At the mouth of Coos Bay between North Point and Charleston village, State 101, Coos Co., two ships carrying large amounts of gold were wrecked in the mid-nineteenth century—the **Jackson** and the **Cyclops.** Fishermen have reported occasionally finding gold nuggets on the beaches in this area after some storms. About two miles to the north the gold coins sometimes found on the beach are believed to be from the vessel **Sunshine,** wrecked here in 1875 while carrying a keg containing about $28,000 in gold coins.

During an Indian attack several miners buried about $40,000 in gold bars on **the Randolph Trail** midway between Sugar Loaf Mountain and Coquille (County 42), Coos Co.

The ruins of Pacific City are on the coast about four miles west of Langlois (State 101), Curry Co. It was a thriving fishing port until being destroyed by a tidal wave in 1894; more than 400 people were lost and about 45 fishing boats were sunk.

Gold Beach is on the coast on State 101 and at the mouth of the Rogue River, Curry Co. It allegedly got its name when a Spanish treasure galleon was wrecked there and the survivors buried large quantities of treasure in many separate caches along the coast. Indians who supposedly witnessed the event dug up some of the treasure. In the late 1950s a farmer found a large cache of silver coins and plate which he foolishly melted down and sold for silver value. There are many unconfirmed reports of gold and silver coins from the late seventeenth century being found on the beach; Gold Beach residents often enjoy wearing these as pendants.

The Lost French Cabin Gold Mine is located along the Willamette River in the vicinity of Lowell, County 38, Lane Co. **The Lost Johnson Gold Mine** is somewhere on nearby Steamboat Creek.

The Trestle Creek Lost Gold Lode, The Lost Gold Mine of Fiddler's Green, and **The Lost Dutchman Gold Mine** are all located near North Steamboat Creek in the vicinity of Bohemia Mountain, about 35 miles southeast of Cottage Grove, U.S. 5, Lane Co.

There are over a dozen lost gold mines in **the Steamboat Mountains** as well as many abandoned mining camps and ghost towns. They are located in the general area of Deadman and White Rock Butte, between the North Steamboat Creek and South Umpqua River, about twenty miles southeast of Roseburg (U.S. 5), Douglas Co.

The ruins of Day's Creek are on the south Umpqua River, about seven miles northeast of Canyonville (U.S. 5), Douglas Co. Near this tiny gold-mining settlement several caches of gold nuggets were buried by miners in the late nineteenth century.

Somewhere in the vicinity of Sexton Mountain Pass on the Rogue River, about ten miles northwest of Grants Pass, U.S. 5, Josephine Co., Indians dumped twenty mule loads of gold bullion into a gully. They had captured it from a band of outlaw Indians who had accumulated a great wealth of gold by raiding the mining camps during the 1850s.

Another band of Indians captured a wagon train carrying about $40,000 in gold ore and several chests of gold bullion and coins. According to reports they cast it all into the **Rogue River,** about two miles northwest of Merlin, which is just a few miles west of Grants Pass.

Several caches of treasure are said to be buried on **Gold Hill** on U.S. 5, about twelve miles northwest of Medford, Jackson Co.: a prospector may have buried about $40,000 in gold nuggets and dust here, outlaws are reported to have buried about $48,000 in gold bullion from a stagecoach robbery, and the rich madam of a brothel in nearby Grants Pass is known to have concealed her life's accumulation of wealth somewhere on the hill before dying in 1895.

The ghost town of Sailor's Diggings is four miles east of O'Brien (State 199), Josephine Co. After being abandoned in the nineteenth century it became an outlaw lair. Several caches of loot are believed to be buried among the many ruins.

The ghost town of Williams is on the Illinois River near Holcomb Peak and about fifteen miles south of Murphy (County 238), Josephine Co. Gold miners are alleged to have concealed various caches of gold nuggets and dust among these old buildings in the late 1800s.

In the Jacksonville surroundings, County 238, Jackson Co., are a large number of abandoned gold mines and the ruins of several unnamed ghost towns. Gold nuggets are still being found in large quantities along the streams by modern prospectors. Bandits buried about $78,000 in gold bullion on the east slope of nearby Timber Mountain before being apprehended and hanged by angry vigilantes.

Near the tiny village of Pelican located at the southern tip of Upper Klamath Lake, near

State 97, Klamath Co., bandits concealed several chests of gold coins from a stagecoach robbery in 1874.

The Lost Forest Gold and Silver Mine is located near the town of Silver Lake, County 31, Lake Co. This mine was worked by Spaniards in the eighteenth century, so the ruins of their settlement must also be in this area.

Outlaws hid about $12,000 in gold and silver coins at Stage Gulch, on **the Umatilla River,** midway between Pendleton and Stanfield (County 80N), Umatilla Co.

The Lost Nez Perce Indian Gold Mine and **The Lost John Cash Gold Mine** are somewhere along the Lostino River near Mount Joseph on the east side of the Wallowa Mountains, about seven miles southeast of Enterprise (County 82), Wallowa Co.

The Lost Bear Creek Gold Mine is in the shadows of Sacajewea Peak in the Wallowa Mountains, midway between Enterprise and Lookout Mountain, in the southeastern section of Wallowa Co.

Indian renegades buried over $90,000 in gold bullion and coins on the outskirts of **Ontario** on the north banks of Willow Creek in Marion Co.

PENNSYLVANIA

Barren Hill in the northwest suburbs of Philadelphia was the campsite of Lafayette's troops, sent by Washington from Valley Forge, which were attacked by a stronger British force and wiped out in May 1778. Portions of the battlefield are still unspoiled.

The Battle of the Clouds, a major conflict between Washington's army and the British under Cornwallis, took place off U.S. 30 near Malvern, Chester Co. on September 16, 1777. Before the battle a record-breaking deluge caused the loss of much of the Patriots' equipment and baggage.

Brandywine Battlefield Park. The site of this famous battle on September 11, 1777 actually covers 30,000 acres, which remain unspoiled today. Markers denote the sites where the various actions took place. The Patriots lost the battle.

Bushy Run Battlefield is located on State 993, north of Jeannette and east of Harrison City. In August 1763 a relief force of British troops heading for Fort Pitt (in Pittsburgh) were attacked by a much larger force of Indians; both sides suffered heavy losses.

Carlisle in Cumberland Co. was first settled in 1720. The town served as the main military base in the state during the French and Indian Wars and as the jumping-off place for settlers moving to the west. Many historical structures still stand in this town and the ruins of numbers of others are nearby.

Chester on the Delaware River below Philadelphia is the second oldest settlement in the state, founded in 1643 by Quakers. There are ruins of many old buildings outside the present city. After his defeat at Brandywine, Washington retreated here in 1781; and his campsite is marked at a spot east of the present city line on U.S. 13.

Cornwall Furnace is located near the town of Cornwall on U.S. 322, Lebanon Co. It was established in 1742 after rich sources of iron were discovered in the area. During the Revolution this plant produced a great number of cannon and other items the Patriots needed. The iron works was closed down in 1883.

Coryell's Ferry is on the Delaware River where U.S. 202 crosses the river between Lambertville, New Jersey and New Hope, Pennsylvania. During the Revolution Washington's army camped there four times and Cornwallis used the site on one occasion.

The Crooked Billet Site is off Pa. 332 in Bucks Co. On May 1, 1778 a skirmish took place here between a much superior British force and Patriots, who suffered severe losses including all of their baggage.

The Durham Village site is located near Riegelsville, Bucks Co. Here the ruins of the village and the Durham Furnace, an iron works which functioned between 1727 and 1789, can still be seen. During the Revolution, cannon and other things were produced here for the Patriot cause, including large numbers of heavy-cargo boats, many of which were used by Washington in his famous crossing of the Delaware in 1776.

297

Easton, located at the junction of the Lehigh and Delaware Rivers, Northampton Co., was founded in 1752 and was an important communications hub throughout the colonial period. In the present town and surrounding area are the ruins of many buildings.

Ephrata is a ghost town near the junction of U.S. 222 and 322 near present Ephrata, Lancaster Co. German Baptists founded the town in 1728; it was abandoned around 1880.

Forks of the Ohio Point State Park, in Pittsburgh's Golden Triangle, was recently created by clearing away all of the modern buildings on the site. No traces of Fort Pitt have been found, but some vestiges of Fort Duquesne can be seen in the center of the park. The French first settled here in 1731 but were driven away by Indians soon after. The land changed hands many times among the French, British, and Indians in the years to follow.

Fort Augusta was located on Pa. 14 near Sunbury, Northcumberland Co. This wooden fort, built in 1756, was never attacked because of its large size and strong garrison. During the Revolution Patriot forces fought the Iroquois from this fort. Soon after the war it fell into ruin and has almost totally deteriorated.

Fort Bedford is located in Bedford Village in the south-central part of the state. The town was founded in 1750 and the fort, which has been restored, in 1757. The village was along the wilderness route connecting eastern and western Pennsylvania. During the nineteenth century it was a famous health resort and attracted the rich from all over the states.

The site of Fort Le Boeuf is in Waterford, near Lake Erie, Erie Co. It was built by the French in 1760 and destroyed in the Pontiac War three years later. Only the foundations remain today.

The site of Fort Ligonier is off U.S. 30 in Ligonier, Westmoreland Co. The wooden fort was built in 1758 by the British and withstood a bad attack by the French and Indians this same year. The town was founded in 1816 on the site of the fort.

Fort Necessity Battlefield is located on U.S. 40, about eleven miles east of Uniontown. The fort was built by George Washington in 1754. In a battle the same year, his men repelled French and Indian attackers. The exact site of the circular stockade has not been located but the fort and its earthworks have been reconstructed.

Old Orchard Camp, about a mile north of Fort Necessity, was the site of General Braddock's bivouac in 1755 during the French and Indian Wars. Braddock was buried here.

Fort Zeller, half a mile north of Newmanstown, Lebanon Co., is the state's oldest surviving fort. It was built in 1723 by pioneers, rebuilt in 1745, and used as a refuge during the French and Indian Wars.

Hannastown site is located off Pa. 819 just north of Greensburg, Westmoreland Co. It had the distinction of having been burned in the last action of the Revolutionary War on July 13, 1782. The ruins of many buildings can be seen today.

Hopewell Village is located on Pa. 23, five miles southeast of Birdsboro, Berks Co. Founded in 1770 as an iron-making center, it was abandoned in 1883. The ruins of over 25 brick structures remain.

Lancaster in Lancaster Co. was founded by English Quakers and Germans in 1717 and has the distinction of being the oldest inland town in the United States. The Continental Congress met here in 1777 after its flight from Philadelphia. Lancaster was the state capital from 1799 to 1812. During the Revolution British troops garrisoned here on several occasions. Many ruins are in the area.

Matson's Ford, first settled in 1747, is located just off Pa. 23 near Gulph Mills, Chester Co. Washington's army camped here for a few days in 1777. There are a number of ruined buildings here.

Moland House is near Pa. 263 just south of Jamison, Bucks Co. Washington used this building as his headquarters and in 1777, his troops had camped here for two weeks.

The Paoli Massacre site is on the outskirts of Malvern, Chester Co. The British troops of General Charles Grey pulled off a surprise attack on the encamped troops commanded by General Anthony Wayne and routed them after inflicting heavy casualties. The dead Patriots were buried here in a mass grave.

The Pennsbury Manor site is on the Delaware River near Tullytown, Bucks Co. William Penn, the founder of Pennsylvania built a manor house here in 1699; when he abandoned it two years later it fell into ruin. The manor has been recreated but the site of the actual building remains lost.

Philadelphia was founded in 1682 by English Quakers led by William Penn and it grew rapidly. Its first European settlers were Swedes. By the time of the Revolution it had 40,000 residents and was the second largest city in the British Empire. The British, who captured and occupied the city in 1777, held it for ten months. A large number of colonial buildings have survived; vestiges of others can be found in empty lots in the oldest section of the city.

Swede's Ford, on the Schuylkill River in Norristown, Montgomery Co., was an important communications hub from about 1690 and served as a campsite for both sides during the Revolution.

Thompson Island is located on the Allegheny River, off U.S. 62, nine miles southwest of Warren, Warren Co. The only Revolutionary War battle in this section of the state was won by the Patriots here on August 15, 1779.

Valley Forge State Park, on the Schuylkill River in Chester Co. was the famous winter quarters for Washington's Army in 1777-1778. Of the 10,000 soldiers who camped here, 3,000 died and were buried on the site. The park comprises some 2,000 acres; markers indicate where the various campsites, quarters and hospitals once stood.

Washington Crossing State Park, on the Delaware River near New Hope, Bucks Co., is where Washington began his famous Delaware crossing during the night of December 25, 1776 to surprise the British garrison in Trenton—one of the most dramatic events of the war. Four miles north of this site on Pa. 32 is the spot where his troops camped for two weeks before the crossing.

Whitemarsh, on the Wissahickon River near the intersection of U.S. 309 and Pa. 72, Montgomery Co., was the campsite of Washington's army before they wintered at Valley Forge in 1777. A few minor skirmishes took place here.

Wyoming Village, first settled around 1753, is located on the Susquehanna River about six miles northeast of Wilkes-Barre, Luzerne Co. The place was attacked by 900 Tories and Indians in July 1778. Almost every one of the Patriots, including women and children, were massacred. The raiders then destroyed over 1,000 houses in the village and surrounding valley and carried off a great deal of plunder.

Fort Wyoming. There are some vestiges of this fort in the main public square of today's Wilkes-Barre. It was built in 1771; during the same raid that obliterated Wyoming Village, it was destroyed along with 23 homes that surrounded it.

York in York Co. was founded in 1741. When the Continental Congress took refuge here in 1777 there were about 300 houses. York has the distinction of being the place where the Patriots printed the first paper money during the Revolution. It also served as an important Patriot military base and prisoner-of-war center. On the outskirts of the present town several sites are marked; there are also many ruined buildings around today.

The site of New Sweden is located on the Delaware River in the Printzhof National Historic Park, about five miles northeast of Chester, Delaware Co. This first permanent white settlement in what became the colony of Pennsylvania was founded by Swedes in 1638. In 1643 the Swedes also settled on Tinicum Island in the river close to this settlement, building a fort there. Both settlements were destroyed by the Dutch in 1655 and have completely disappeared.

Gettysburg National Military Park is on State 134 outside of Gettysburg, Adams Co. Here the Confederate army under General Robert E. Lee suffered a major defeat at the hands of the Union forces led by General George G. Meade on July 1-3, 1863. More than 1,400 markers describe where different phases of this action took place.

The Village of Hopewell is on State 915, five miles south of Saxton, Bedford Co. The village flourished between 1770 and 1883 when it was abandoned and represents the beginnings of America's iron and steel industry. These early mills even employed charcoal furnaces. All of its mills, factories, and houses are in ruins today.

The site of the Pennsbury Manor Plantation is on the Delaware River south of Morrisville, Buck Co. This plantation was built in 1683 by William Penn; only the foundations of the great manor house and out-buildings are left.

Nazareth is on State 33 about thirteen miles northeast of Allentown, Northampton Co. The town was settled by Moravians in 1740 and has kept many of its original buildings. Ruins of others are to be found in and around the town.

Old Fort Mifflin is located on the Delaware River, on the eastern edge of the Philadelphia International Airport. The fort's construction was begun in 1771 and it was held by Patriot troops when the British took Philadelphia in 1777. But after a six-day siege it was captured and destroyed by the British. In 1798 it was completely rebuilt and stands today. Number of relics here make for good treasure hunting.

Old Economy is on State 65 several miles northeast of Ambridge, Beaver Co. This prosperous industrial community flourished between 1825 and 1905 and then fell into ruin after being abandoned. Today only seventeen of the original buildings are still standing in this ghost town.

The site of Fort Raystown is located in Fort Bedford Park in present Bedford, Bedford Co. The wooden fort was built in 1758 and was used by troops as late as 1794 to put down the Whiskey Rebellion. Today it is completely gone.

Bethlehem is off U.S. 22, Lehigh Co. It was first settled by Moravians from Bohemia and Saxony in 1741 and 21 of their original buildings still stand in this city. Ruins of many of their homes and farms can also be seen in the surrounding countryside.

During the War of Jenkin's Ear in 1742, two privateering vessels captured the Spanish merchantman **San Ignacio El Grande,** and then headed back for their home port of Philadelphia. To deprive the English king of his share of the plunder, which consisted of 22 tons of mercury in ceramic flasks and 38,000 pieces of eight, they decided to conceal it before reaching the port. They took it ashore on the west bank of **the Delaware River,** about two to three miles southwest of Chester, and buried it along the river bank. Several weeks later a flood deposited great amounts of mud along the river bank and they were unable to locate the valuable cache.

Gold coins have been found along the shore of Lake Erie in the vicinity of **Lawrence Park,** County 955, Erie Co. They are believed to be from the steamer **Erie,** which was wrecked in this area during a storm, while carrying over $200,000 in gold coins. About twelve miles northeast at **Orchard Beach,** fragments of an old wreck are occasionally exposed on the beach after winter storms. Large numbers of American silver dollars from the late nineteenth century are found by the local residents.

In around 1890, about $60,000 in gold coins and paper currency was robbed from the Emporium Bank and buried on one side of **the Kinzua railroad bridge,** which crosses Kinzua Creek about five miles northeast of the town of Mount Jewitt, State 6, McKean Co.

About $5 million in gold and silver bullion was buried in 1812 by the old eccentric millionaire Colonel Noah Parker. It lies somewhere along the banks of **the Potato River** near the village of Crosby, County 46, McLean Co.

During the Revolution a band of Tory raiders are known to have buried several chests of treasure on **the McMillan Farm** two miles east of Bloosberg, State 15, Tioga Co., near the Tioga River.

Confederate raiders robbed several banks in central Pennsylvania, then buried the loot in barrels in the vicinity of **Mountain House,** near the summit of Snowshoe Mountains in the Allegheny Range, about a mile west of Wingate, State 220, Centre Co.

Outlaw David Lewis buried a sizable treasure within sight of the jail in **Bellfonte,** State 220, Centre Co., before his death in 1820.

Somewhere along the banks of the **Jacks River,** a few miles north of Lewistown, State 22, Mifflin Co., the outlaw Joe Fracker is supposed to have buried a large cache of gold and silver coins. Outlaw David Lewis is also said to have buried a saddlebag containing about $10,000 in gold coins on the banks of the **Juanita River** at Juanita Terrace just south of Lewistown. High water eroded the river bank and carried his gold away before he got back to retrieve it.

During the Civil War Confederate raiders robbed about fifteen tons of silver bullion destined for the mint in Philadelphia. Then with Union troops hot on their heels the raiders secreted it in **a cave about two miles north of Uniontown,** State 40, Fayette Co. After sealing off the cave they headed back to Virginia in haste.

During the Revolution in 1775, when his wagon train was attacked by Indians, the paymaster quickly buried about $150,000 in gold and silver coins, destined for the soldiers of General Braddock. The paymaster was killed in the attack and the location lost. The incident occurred on **Laurel Hill** near the town of Farmington (close to Fort Necessity), State 40, Fayette Co.

There are a number of **lost Indian gold and silver mines** in the vicinity of McConnellsburg, in the nearby Cove and Dickeys Mountains, Fulton Co. They were mined until the white settlers arrived and forced the Indians to head further west.

There is a spot named **Spanish Hill** on the Susquehanna River, about a mile south of Sayre (close to the New York state line), State 220, Brafford Co. Here, according to legend, a large cache of Spanish treasure was buried long before the first settlers reached the area.

In 1888 a bandit named Michale Rizzalo robbed a bank of $12,000. Before being caught and shot he buried the cache near **Laurel Run Creek** in the Laurel Run Mountains, about four miles east of Wilkes-Barre, Luzerne Co.

In 1948 a small plane carrying about $250,000 in paper currency developed engine trouble and crashed into **Mount Carmel** near the town of Ashland, County 54, Northcumberland Co. Just before the plane crashed someone threw the money out a window, according to one of the survivors. To date no one has admitted finding it.

Throughout the area surrounding **Reading** in Berks Co., there are countless caches of personal treasures, since even today most Pennsylvania Dutch, who distrust banks, hide their personal wealth on their property. There are numerous abandoned buildings and farms in this area, some of which surely contain such caches.

During the Revolution in 1775, a band of Tories led by a Captain Doane terrorized the area between Lancaster and Reading. Just before Patriot troops moved in to contain them, they buried about $100,000 in gold and silver coins, silver plate, and jewelry in **an abandoned well, about a mile south of Wernersville,** State 422, Berks Co.

The Lost Bear Jaspar Mine is located in the vicinity of Raubville, along the Delaware River, County 32, Northcumberland Co.

Another band of Tory raiders buried a great deal of plunder in **a cave overlooking the Delaware River,** about two miles north of Easton, State 22, Northcumberland Co.

After a bad flood in 1947, large numbers of British, French, and Spanish silver coins from the late eighteenth century were found along the west bank of **the Delaware River,** in the vicinity of Lumberry, County 32, Bucks Co. They were probably washed ashore from a river wreck, but may have been from a cache buried along the river banks.

An associate of Captain Kidd, Doctor John Bowman, is reputed to have buried a great deal of plunder on his property, **Bowman's Hill,** located in the Washington Crossing State Park along the Delaware in Bucks Co.

During the Revolution a British spy confessed to burying a large number of gold coins **near a tavern on Pond Street,** directly opposite Burnington Island on the Delaware River in the town of Bristol, which is about four miles northwest of Philadelphia. Fleeing British officers are also known to have hidden a great deal of plunder along the banks of the river near Bristol when they were expelled from Philadelphia.

Hessian soldiers are alleged to have tossed a cannon filled with gold coins into **the Delaware River** near Chester during the Revolution.

Many colonial relics are found on **Petty Island** in the Delaware River near the main center of Philadelphia. There are numerous ruins on the island and several old sailing ships were wrecked here.

The ghost town of Sizerville, founded in 1838, is located about three miles from present Sizerville, County 155, Cameron Co. Most of it burned down in 1897, then the place was abandoned.

The town of Austin, County 607, Potter Co., was once one of the most prosperous in northern Pennsylvania. On September 30, 1911 the giant Bayless Dam just two miles north of the town burst open and destroyed Austin, as well as the town of **Costello,** about three miles further south. About 100 persons were killed and property damages were over $5 million. The residents of these two towns reported losing near half a million dollars in money and jewelry. Numerous safes of stores and other businesses were also buried under the dirt of the surrounding flatlands. This is one of the favorite treasure-hunting spots in the state.

In the vicinity of the village of **Gardeau,** County 155, McKean Co., more than one and a half million dollars in silver bars was buried by a Captain Blackbeard (no kin to *the* Blackbeard) of the British Admiralty in 1812. The silver was being taken overland to Canada from Mexico to avoid its being captured at sea during this period of war. When the British officer reached this town and discovered that his nation was at war not only with France, but now with the United States as well, he quickly hid the treasure and rushed for Quebec to avoid being captured. A landslide is believed to have further concealed the cache.

RHODE ISLAND

Forts on the Island of Rhode Island. This fifteen-mile long island in Narragansett Bay was also called Aquidneck Island during the colonial period. During the Revolution there were twenty separate forts scattered over the island; the actual sites of most of them have been lost. The **Butts Hill Fort site,** fortified by the British in 1777, is located off R.I. 138 in Portsmouth; its earthworks can still be seen. The site of **Arnold's Point Fort** is located on Lehigh Hill and the ruins of many old homes are scattered in the area. The **Bristol Ferry Fort** was in the vicinity of the Mount Hope Marina east of the present Mount Hope Bridge. A number of major battles were fought all over the island and most of them are well marked. Vestiges of a number of earthworks and old ruins can be seen on the outskirts of present Newport. A report by the Portsmouth Historical Society published in 1897 stated that the ruins of more than 1,000 structures predating 1800 were scattered all over the island.

Block Island was first visited by explorer Verrazano in 1524 and again by the Dutchman Adriaen Block in 1614. It was considered a sacred island by the Indians and countless numbers of them were buried here. Settlers first came in 1661; remains of their homes are found at several locations on the island. During the Revolution a number of major naval actions occurred close to Block Island, which served as a refuge for criminals and deserters during this war. Both privateers and pirates used it as a base, the former during the French and Indian Wars and the latter at various times.

Bristol located about midway between Providence and Newport was settled in 1669 and was a major shipbuilding center during the colonial period. In October 1775, the town suffered heavy damage during a British naval bombardment. The British pillaged and burned it down in May 1778. As recently as 1940 the vestiges of an earthwork could be seen on the outskirts of the town, but it has since been lost. Many historical houses are still standing and the ruins of many others abounded in the vicinity.

The Fort Barton site, on a bluff near Tiverton in Newport Co., was built in 1777. Traces of the fort can be seen in a park surrounding it today.

Gaspee Point is located about seven miles below Providence on the west side of Narragansett Bay. One of the first overt acts of American defiance occurred here in 1772 when the British schooner **Gaspee** ran aground at this spot. After patriots had overcome the crew, they set the vessel afire and it blew up, covering the beach with debris.

Green End Fort is located in the town of Middletown, Newport Co. The town was founded in 1743 and destroyed by the British in 1776, who then built this fort. Earthen ramparts of it can still be seen.

Newport was founded in 1639 and quickly became one of the major seaports of New England, because of its fine natural harbor. During the French and Indian Wars it was a major smuggling port and soon after became an important slave-trading center as well. The British captured the city in December 1776 and held it until October 1779. Then the French occupied it in July 1780 held it for a year. Many battles were fought at Newport during this war and the city suffered very badly. It regained its former importance only recently. **At Brenton's Point,** the Patriots started a fort in 1776, which the British completed. When the British withdrew in

302

1779, they destroyed it and burned all of the surrounding barracks. In 1793 **Fort Adams,** which still stands, was built on this site. On Goat Island in the harbor the British built **Fort George** about 1778, but no traces of it remain today. The Patriots built **Fort Greene** early in 1776 somewhere between Washington Street and the harbor, in what is now called Battery Park.

Portsmouth, Newport Co., founded in 1638, was the most important settlement in the state until eclipsed by Providence and Newport. Many historical landmarks have survived and there are ruins of others all over the place.

The Prescott Farm is located on R.I. 114 near Union Street in Portsmouth. The main house of this farm built in 1710 is presently being restored along with a number of other buildings. During the Revolution it was owned by one of the richest families in New England, the Overings, and was occupied by the British. Legend tells that the British General Richard Prescott buried a substantial amount of gold coins somewhere on this farm, before being captured by Patriots during a surprise raid.

Providence, the first settlement in the state, was first inhabited in 1636 by religious dissenters from Massachusetts. Vestiges of the early colonial settlement can be found on the east bank of the Providence River. Nothing remains of the nine forts that once stood in and around this town during the colonial and Revolutionary periods; their sites are now occupied by modern buildings. The site of **Fort Washington,** built in 1775, was known until recent years when it was levelled by hydraulic guns during the enlarging of the port facilities. Remains of a small number of old buildings can be found on the outskirts of the present city.

The Smith's Castle site is located on U.S. 1, about one and a half miles north of Wickford on Narragansett Bay, Washington Co. A large trading post by this name, built here in 1678 over the site of an earlier building, was burned during the King Philip's War, but restored recently. The ruins of other colonial buildings are nearby.

A Revolutionary War campsite is located about a mile east of Potterville on Town Farm Road, Providence Co. Both sides used these camp grounds very frequently during the Revolutionary War. A large number of wells and fireplaces can still be seen there.

The Great Swamp Battlefield is off State 138 near Kingston, Washington Co. Here a decisive victory of the King Philip's War was won by 1,000 New Englanders over 3,000 Narragansett Indians on December 19, 1675. An obelisk now marks the site where more than 1,000 Indians were slain and the settlers lost 80 men.

The site of Founders' Brook, originally called Pocasset, is off Boyd's Lane in Portsmouth. Founded in 1638, it was the state's second settlement. In 1738 a ship, **The Palatine,** bringing wealthy German Palatines from Rotterdam, was wrecked during a blinding snow storm on Block Island; some say the ship was attracted by false lights. The crew mutinied, killed all the survivors, and plundered the loot, which they buried on the island before setting off for the mainland. Here all were drowned in another storm. The account was reported by a small child who survived the massacre.

The pirate captain William Kidd is said to have buried treasure at seven different places in this state: **Hog Island, Patience Island,** in **Pirate's Cave** on Conanicut Island, **Block Island,** at **Skakonet** in Newport Co., near **Watch Hill** in Washington Co., and at **Brenton Point** in Rhode Island Sound.

It was reported in 1949 that a treasure chest belonging to the pirate Charles Harris, who buried it in 1723, was found along the beach at the base of **Newport Cliffs,** just south of the city of Newport. Before the finder could return with lifting equipment, the tide came in and covered the massive chest again. The pirate, who was hanged in Newport, admitted burying the chest in the area where it was allegedly found.

The pirate Thomas Tew reportedly buried about $100,000 in booty somewhere in **Newport.** Other hoards were concealed here during the Revolution, when the island fell into the hands of the British and many of the residents had to flee to the mainland.

In recent years treasure hunters have found many artifacts and some coins at **Sandy Point,** the northern tip of Block Island. In 1738 the German ship **Princess Augusta** was dashed to pieces on this point with a horrendous loss of life and great personal wealth belonging to the immigrants. At Southwest Point there are reports of coins being found on the beach that

Beachcombers are famed for their keen eyesight, but a modern metal detectors lets them "see" beneath the sand where valuable lost objects lie hidden.

South Carolina and nearby states still abound in Civil War relics which can be found with proper research and the use of a modern computerized detector.

probably come from the Irish merchantman **Golden Grove,** wrecked there during a winter gale in 1765.

Over the years many artifacts and ship's fittings have been found along the beach at Point Judith near the mouth of Narrangansett Bay. They are believed to be washing in from two British warships—**H.M.S. Syren** of twenty guns and the **H.M.S. Triton** of sixteen guns—which were dashed to pieces here in 1777 during a lusty gale.

Vestiges of an old wreck are reported along the beach at **Misquamicut State Park,** about five miles south of Westerly in Washington Co. The hulk is most likely the American merchantman **Minerva,** lost while in ballast, so there isn't much likelihood of finding any treasure other than some artifacts on her

After a winter storm in 1923 a fisherman found several hundred gold and silver Spanish coins of the mid-eighteenth century on tiny **Hope Island,** lying off the west side of Prudence Island in Narragansett Bay. More treasure is probably still hidden there.

SOUTH CAROLINA

Beckham's Old Field is located near the junction of S.C. 97 and 99, near Beckhamville, Chester Co. Here the Patriots won their first victory in June 1780, causing the British to abandon all of their weapons and baggage and flee.

Beech Island, on the Savannah River just south of Augusta, Georgia, served as an encampment for the Patriots in 1781. A minor skirmish was fought there this same year.

Bee's Plantation is located on the Edisto River just below Jacksonboro, Colleton Co. No vestiges of this huge plantation have survived, except its name. A skirmish between Tories and Patriots was fought here in 1780.

Belleville Plantation is on the Santee River, just east of the U.S. 601 bridge in Calhoun Co. The plantation was occupied by the British in 1780 and became a fortified base and supply depot. During the war a number of battles were fought here and it exchanged hands several times. The remains of the earthworks, a cemetery, and the foundations of a number of brick houses can be seen.

Biggin Church is located on the Cooper River near S.C. 44, about a mile south of U.S. 17A, opposite the town of Moncks, Berkeley Co. The ruins of this brick church and cemetery can still be seen. The town that once stood here was settled in 1706. The church was built in 1712, rebuilt in 1756, accidentally burned in 1776, rebuilt the same year, and burned again by the British after they had used the town as a base in 1781. A number of minor battles were fought in this area but the exact locations of the actions are not known today.

Black Mingo Creek is located at the junction of S.C. 41 and 51, near Rhems in Williamsburg Co. The town of Willtown was settled on the banks of this creek in 1750. By 1800 it had become the largest settlement in the region, but it has since disappeared. About a mile downstream from the town the British had a campsite which was successfully attacked by Patriots in September 1780. Scattered about this swampy area are the remains of many colonial homes and plantation manors destroyed during the Civil War.

Blackstock Battlefield is located on S.C. 51, about three miles from Cross Keys, Union Co. The site, which touches on the Tyger River, is far removed from civilization and is surrounded by deserted, swampy land, where there are vestiges of many colonial homes. In November 1780 the Patriots won a major battle here, forcing the British to abandon many supplies and munitions before departing.

Blue Savannah Battlefield, on the Little Pee Wee River near U.S. 501, south of Ariel Crossroads, Marion Co., was the scene of a small battle won by the Tories in 1780.

Brierly's Ferry was located somewhere near the junction of the Broad and the Saluda Rivers in Richmond Co. A settlement was founded here about 1700, of which no traces exist today. The town was the scene of several minor skirmishes during the Revolution and a British military post in 1780.

The Battle of Waxhaws site is nine miles east of Lancaster, near S.C. 522, Lancaster Co.

Here on May 29, 1780, the Patriots suffered a humiliating defeat which has been called the Buford Massacre. The dead from both sides were interred in a common grave; many of the Patriots' weapons were buried with them.

Camden on U.S. 1, just off I-20, Kershaw Co., still retains much of its historical charm. Fortunately the site of the original town founded in 1730 remains undeveloped and vestiges of many house foundations can be seen. The British used the town as a major military post during the Revolution. In the famous Battle of Camden, fought on the outskirts of the city on August 16, 1780, the Patriots suffered a major defeat.

Cedar Spring is located at the Junction of S.C. 56 and 295 on the southeast outskirts of Spartanburg. At this spot the Wofford Iron Works were built around 1750; during the Revolution two minor battles were fought here in 1780. After winning the second action the Tories set fire to all of the homes in the area.

Charleston. In 1670 the English settled at Albemarle Point on the west bank of the Ashley River, about three and a half miles from where the river joins the Cooper to form Oyster Point. No trace of the settlement has been found to date but in this general area divers have recovered many artifacts dating from this period. Oyster Point soon proved to be a better location than Albemarle Point and the settlement was moved there around 1672. But around 1680 most of the colonists abandoned this site as well and founded Charleston. The city began thriving as an important colonial seaport and it was the fourth largest city in the American colonies at the time of the Revolution. In 1776 and 1779 the British made major efforts to capture Charleston but failed. However, after a long siege it was captured on May 12, 1780 and held until December 14, 1782. Although about 550 buildings from the eighteenth and nineteenth centuries survive none of the earlier buildings remains. The city suffered a great deal during the Civil War and was heavily damaged again during a devastating earthquake on August 31, 1886.

Cheraw village, on the Great Pee Wee River in Chesterfield Co., was settled by the Welsh in about 1752. It was used as a British military base during the Revolutionary War and a number of minor skirmishes took place nearby. During the Civil War Cheraw served as an important Confederate supply depot until captured and destroyed by Sherman in 1865. There are many remains of many old buildings.

Chehaw Point is near the U.S. 17 bridge, which crosses the Combahee River in Georgetown Co. Here can be seen the remains of an old fort where the Patriots suffered a defeat by British troops in 1782. There are ruins of a number of large plantation houses within several miles of this place.

The Cowpens Battlefield site is about twenty miles west of Kings Mountain, near the intersection of S.C. 11 and 110, and about two miles southeast of Chesnee in Spartanburg Co. The Patriots led by General Daniel Morgan won a major battle here on January 17, 1781; the British lost almost 1,000 men. As they fled, they abandoned a great deal of supplies and war materials.

Dean Swamp, a bit northwest of Salley in Aiken Co., was the scene of a skirmish won by Tory and British troops in May 1782.

Drayton Hall, on the Ashley River near the junction of S.C. 57 and 61 in Charleston Co., is one of the best surviving examples of a colonial plantation house. It was built in 1738 and occupied by the British during the Revolutionary War. The manor was one of the few not destroyed by Sherman's troops during the Civil War. There are tales of several different treasures being buried in the area. Ruins of a number of other colonial buildings can be seen nearby.

The Eutaw Springs Battlefield was located somewhere in the vicinity of the present village of Eutaw Springs, on S.C. 6 and 45, Orangeburg Co. The actual site is now under the waters of Lake Marion. One of the bloodiest and last battles fought in the South during the Revolutionary War took place here on September 8, 1781.

Fairforest Creek is located a few miles south of Union, near U.S. 176 in Spartanburg Co. It was the scene of a major battle between Whigs and Tories in 1775 and a large number of houses in the surrounding area were destroyed at the same time.

Fish Dam Battlefield is located where the bridge on S.C. 72 crosses the Broad River, Chester Co. A minor battle was fought here on November 9, 1780; the British were scattered after losing some of their artillery and supplies in trying to cross the river.

Fishing Creek Battlefield site is located near Catawba Ford, just north of Great Falls, Chester Co. The Patriots suffered a defeat here when attacked by British cavalry on August 18, 1780. Over 150 Patriots were buried in a mass grave on the site, along with their weapons.

Fort Charlotte, built during colonial times, was located near the Savannah River off S.C. 91 in McCormick Co., but is now under the Clark Hill Reservoir. One of the first overt acts of the rebellion occurred here when Patriots seized the fort on July 12, 1775. It was the scene of a number of battles and changed hands a number of times.

Fort Dorchester is on the Ashley River and on S.C. 642, about six miles south of Summerville, Dorchester Co. A settlement was established here in 1696 but had already been abandoned when this fort was built in 1775. The British captured the fort in April 1780 and held it until the approach of Patriot forces on December 1, 1781. At this time the British made the mistake of thinking that a much greater force was approaching than actually was. They threw all of the artillery and other war materials into the river and burned the fort before taking flight. The ruins of the fort and that of another settlement which sprang up after the war and lasted until 1788 are here.

Fort Galphin is on the Savannah River about twelve miles below Augusta on Silver Bluff, near S.C. 32, Allendale Co. It was a wooden stockade built by the Tories around the beginning of the Revolutionary War; some earthworks remain.

Fort Johnson on James Island in Charleston Harbor was built during colonial times as the principal fort guarding the harbor and town. It played a major role in the British capture of the city in 1780. Today only the brick powder magazine is left.

Fort Motte is on the Congaree River near its junction with the Watergee, Calhoun Co. Here the British had one of their principal supply depots during the Revolutionary War, which in 1781 was attacked, captured, and burned by the Patriots. A town also named Fort Motte grew up here but was abandoned some time before 1900. Although the site is shown on present road maps, no roads go near it and it can be reached only by boat.

Fort Watson is located on U.S. 15 and 301, about eight miles southwest of Summerton and less than a mile from the Lake Marion Bridge, Clarendon Co. The British constructed a large wooden fort on top of an ancient Indian burial mound, then known as Wright's Bluff, in 1781; this fort had the distinction of being the first captured by Patriots, who later burned it. The earthworks encircling the mound can still be seen.

Georgetown is on Winyah Bay in Georgetown Co. The Great Pee Wee and three other rivers empty into the sea here. The town was founded in 1735 and became a very busy port, serving the hundreds of surrounding indigo and rice plantations (all of which were destroyed during the Revolutionary War). While the British occupied the town in 1780 it was attacked several times by Patriots. Before leaving in 1781 the British burned most of it to the ground. Many vestiges of colonial buildings can be found here.

The Great Cane Brake on the Reedy River is about six miles southwest of Fountain Inn, Greenville Co. In December 1775 more than 4,000 troops camped here; after most of them had departed leaving a small garrison behind, Tories attacked and were repelled with heavy losses. The "great cane brake" still covers this swampy area, concealing all traces of the site.

The Lost Hammond's Store site is located near where S.C. 72 is intersected by S.C. 49, two miles northeast of Mountville, Laurens Co. Patriot troops surprised a band of some 250 Tory raiders camped in and around this store on December 28, 1780. They killed most of the raiders, then burned the store and surrounding homes.

Hampton Plantation, on U.S. 17 and 701, about a mile west of the Santee River Bridge, Charleston Co., is one of the finest surviving plantation houses in the South and dates back to 1735. It was used by the British as a base during their occupation of Charleston. Legend has it that before being forced to flee several high-ranking British officers buried a substantial amount of treasure under the main mansion.

Hanging Rock is just south of Health Springs on S.C. 467, Lancaster Co. Here the British established a major base after the fall of Charleston and in August 1780 a bloody battle took place in which the Patriots were beaten. When the British were forced to abandon the site they placed over 25 bronze artillery pieces and "thousands of arms and other accrutements" in a nearby cave, which they sealed off by an explosion of gun powder.

The High Hills of Santee are in Sumter County. A narrow ridge extends about 40 miles along the east side of the Wateree River and early explorers reported that along this ledge there were hundreds of caves which showed signs of having been lived in by early Indians. During the Revolutionary War many refugees lived in the same caves. In July 1781 General Nathanael Greene with his whole Patriot army spent six weeks recuperating from their recent battles in these hills. After the war thousands of the defeated Tories settled in the area; today the ruins of hundreds of their brick buildings can be seen in this totally undeveloped area.

Hunt's Bluff is on the Great Pee Wee River just off S.C. 57, about five miles west of Blenheim, Markboro Co. A large barge carrying over ten tons of military supplies for British forces was accidentally overturned at this spot on the river and nothing was recovered.

Jacksonboro is on U.S. 17 near the Edisto River, Colleton Co. Nothing remains except the name of this town, which was founded in 1735 and was the provincial capital of the state for several months in 1782.

Juniper Spring is about one mile northwest of Gilbert, Lexington Co. On June 18, 1781 the British ambushed a force of 150 Patriots at this spot and put them to flight after killing a few of them.

Kings Mountain is just south of the North Carolina-South Carolina line off Interstate 85, Cherokee Co. It was the scene of an important American victory over a large Tory force on October 7, 1780. A number of caves here are reported to contain prehistoric Indian artifacts.

Kingstree Village is near the present town of this name, off U.S. 52, on the Black River, Williamsburg Co. The village, founded in 1732 by Irish Calvinists, was destroyed by the British in 1781; another town of the same name was built nearby.

Somewhere on North Island in Winyah Bay, Georgetown Co., a band of Tory raiders landed in 1781 and buried a great deal of gold and silver plunder. All were killed before being able to return for it. Many unsuccessful searches for the treasure have been made already.

Leneud's Ferry is on the Santee River near U.S. 17A and Jamestown, Berkeley Co. The site was settled by French Canadians in 1755 and was abandoned before the Revolution began. Here on May 6, 1780 British dragoons decimated a much larger force of Patriot troops, which suffered over 100 casualties.

Matthew's Bluff is on the Savannah River at the dead end of S.C. 41, Allendale Co. A skirmish took place here in 1781 and after winning the battle the Patriots threw several bronze artillery pieces, which they had captured from the British, into the river.

Mepkin Plantation is on the Cooper River about 30 miles above Charleston, Berkeley Co. Today this 3,000-acre plantation is a Trappist monastery and tree farm. The original plantation house, built in 1724, and the ruins of more than 40 other brick colonial structures are on this property.

Middleton Place Gardens are on the Ashley River, fourteen miles northwest of Charleston, Berkeley Co. In 1741 the Middleton family built one of the largest mansions in the South; during the Revolutionary War the place was occupied by the British and partially destroyed by them when they left. It was again rebuilt and retained by the same family. Upon the approach of Sherman and his army, the plantation owner buried a large treasure near the mansion, which was totally destroyed by Yankee troops. The owner died from wounds received in trying to defend his property.

Moncks Corner on the Cooper River is located about a mile northeast of the town of this same name, just south of the U.S. 52 bridge over the canal connecting the Cooper and Lake Moultrie, Dorchester Co. A plantation was founded here in 1735 and a small settlement sprang up soon after. By the outbreak of the Revolution it had become an important commercial center. It was a critical Patriot supply base during the British siege of Charleston and protected by 500 troops. In April 1780 the British with 1500 troops attacked and easily captured the place and after stripping it, burned it to the ground.

311

Mulberry Plantation on the Cooper River about 30 miles above Charleston, Berkeley County, can be reached only by boat. Its rice fields, dikes, canals, and its mansion, dating from 1714 are in excellent condition. During the Yamasee War of 1715-1716 a band of renegades who were captured and hanged claimed to have buried an immense treasure of gold coins and jewelry in the area.

Musgraove's Mill is on the Enoree River near the bridge on S.C. 56, about 27 miles south of Spartanburg, Union Co. A skirmish took place here on August 18, 1780; it was important for being one of the few times that untrained militia were able to defeat seasoned British soldiers. The old mill stood in a good state of preservation until being burned by vandals in 1971.

Ninety-Six Battlefield is located off S.C. 248 about two miles south of the present village of Ninety-Six, Greenwood Co. In 1730 a trading post was established on this site and soon afterward, a sizable settlement grew up. Between August and November 1775 three different battles were fought here between Loyalists and Patriots. The British seized the town in 1780 after the fall of Charleston. In May 1781 the Patriot Army under General Nathanael Greene besieged the place for almost a month, but the British held it. The area has been spared urbanization and remains much the same as it was two centuries ago. Vestiges of the defenses, siege works, the village, and the burial ground remain.

Orangeburg on the Edisto River, Orangeburg Co., was founded in 1730 by German and Swiss settlers. During the Revolution it was occupied for several years by the British, who burned the town to the ground before leaving. Another town by this same name now covers the ruins.

Parker's Ferry Battlefield is on the Edisto River in Colleton Co. The settlement, founded some time before 1700, was an important colonial way station on the main highway. A major battle took place here in August 1781. Recently, substantial earthworks were discovered on the site and several iron cannons were unearthed. The best way to reach the battlefield is by boat, otherwise a long trek by foot is required.

Pon Pon Chapel ruins are near the intersection of S.C. 64 and County Road 40, near Jacksonboro, Colleton Co. This church, which was built in 1725 and destroyed by fire in 1801, had the distinction of having John Wesley preach in it in 1737.

Port Royal Island, Beaufort County. During the sixteenth and seventeenth centuries, both the French and Spanish established missions and settlements on this island but they have since disappeared. In 1710 the British founded Beaufort, the second oldest city in the state after Charleston. In 1715 the Yamasee Indians killed all the settlers, except a handful who managed to escape by ship, and burned the town, which was rebuilt soon after. After a bloody battle the British captured the town, causing grave harm to many of the buildings. Beaufort also suffered severe damages during the Civil War. There are traces of the early settlement in many areas of the present town.

The site of Prince's Fort is located between I-26 and S.C. 123, near Inman, Spartanburg Co. A minor battle between Tory and Patriot forces took place here in July 1780. The wooden stockade was burned down about two years later.

Quinby Bridge Battlefield is about a mile above where the Quinby River feeds into the East Branch of the Cooper River, near Hugar Crossroads, Berkeley Co. A major battle was fought here on July 17, 1781 when both sides suffered heavy losses. In the center of the site are the ruins of the Quinby Plantation mansion, which was built before 1750.

Ratcliff Bridge is over the Lynches River, just south of U.S. 15 and S.C. 34, near Bishopville, Lee Co. The Patriots suffered a major defeat here at the hands of a Loyalist battalion on March 6, 1781. A great deal of weaponry and other things were lost in the river at the time.

Rocky Mount is just south of the Great Falls on the Catawba River, Fairfield Co. On July 30, 1780 Patriots defeated the garrison holding this British outpost and burned it to the ground.

Round O is on U.S. 17A, eleven miles east of Walterboro, Colleton Co. This was the largest Patriot encampment of the Revolutionary War. The remains of several wells, fireplaces, and a blacksmith shop are at this site and many relics must be buried under the topsoil.

The Rugeley's Mill site is on County Road 58 near the bridge over the Grannies Quarter Creek, about ten miles from Camden, Kershaw Co. This campsite was used by the armies of both sides during the Revolution; today parts of Rugeley's house, barn, mill, and well can be seen.

The Seneca Old Town site, located on the Clemson University Campus, Pickens Co., was settled at some early date by Cherokees. When they initiated hostile actions against the Patriots in 1776, a Patriot force attacked and burned this town down, as well as many other Indian settlements in the area. Later this same year the Patriots built **Fort Rutledge** on this site, but it is now gone.

The ruins of Shelton Church are located at the junction of S.C. 21 and 235, north of Shelton, Beaufort Co. Isolated in the lonely woods, this was one of the most elegant churches in the South. It was first built in 1746, burned by the British in 1779, rebuilt, and then burned again by Sherman's undisciplined troops in late 1864. The church has remained in ruins since then.

Singleton's Mill was located somewhere in the southwestern corner of Sumpter Co., but the exact spot has not been found. A settlement was started here around 1725 and captured by the British shortly after the fall of Charleston. When forced to withdraw the British destroyed the 100 or so houses which comprised the town.

Snow's Island was a settlement in the southeast corner of Florence Co., somewhere in the vicinity of present Kingsburg. In 1780-1781 the Patriots used this as one of their most important supply depots; in March 1781 it was attacked and destroyed by British forces. To keep the vast amount of war materials out of enemy hands, the defenders threw most of the supplies into the Lynches River before retreating.

Stono Ferry Battlefield is a mile south of Rantowles on S.C. 318, Charleston Co. The battle, which resulted in a draw, took place on June 20, 1779 between 1,500 Patriots and 900 British. Both sides suffered heavy losses.

Strawberry Ferry is on the Cooper River at the end of S.C. 44, Berkeley Co. Located about 25 miles up the river from Charleston, this site was an important communications hub from early colonial times. During the Revolutionary and Civil Wars it was the center of much military activity by all combatants. The foundations of a number of colonial brick buildings are nearby.

Sullivan's Island in Charleston Harbor was settled soon after Charleston but all traces of the colonial settlements and Revolutionary War period fortifications have been obliterated by shifting sands and modern urbanization.

Skirmish on the Black River near S.C. 50 and U.S. 301 in Clarendon Co. is where an important battle took place between Tory and Loyalists on October 25, 1780; the conflict was won by the Loyalists.

Thicketty Fort, also known as **Fort Anderson,** was probably located near the present village of this same name, on U.S. 29, about five miles southwest of Gaffney, Cherokee Co. The large wooden fort was attacked and captured by Tories in July 1780 and burned to the ground; the cannon were thrown into a nearby creek.

Wadboo Plantation was located near the junction of Wadboo Swamp with the Cooper River in the vicinity of Moncks Corner, Dorchester Co. Three different Revolutionary War skirmishes took place on this property. During the last the British burned the great mansion and about twenty other buildings in the area, the ruins of which are hidden today in the woods.

Walnut Grove Plantation near I-26 and U.S. 221, south of Spartanburg, was built in 1765 near the North Tyger River and has been recently restored. As news of the approach of Sherman's army reached the owners in late 1864, they threw all of their considerable valuables into an unused well, then had it filled with dirt. Later they were unable to locate the spot.

The Fort Carey site is located on the Wateree River just south of Camden where the I-20 bridge crosses it, Kershaw Co. During the recent construction of a new bridge here, remains of this Revolutionary War fort were discovered on the river bank and a large collection of priceless artifacts and some coins were unearthed by workmen. This fort was in the hands of the British when the Patriots made an unsuccessful attack against it in August 1780.

Wiboo Swamp was on the Santee River but is now located on a branch of the man-made Lake Marion, due south of Manning and west of S.C. 260, Clarendon Co. A major Revolutionary action took place here during March 1780 and both sides lost many men and war materials.

The Williamson's Plantation site is on S.C. 322 about four miles east of McConnel, York Co. In a surprise raid on July 12, 1780, the Patriots attacked this plantation and killed the notorious Captain Huck and his band of Tory raiders. The Tories had accumulated a great amount of plunder in a period of five years and it was believed to have been buried somewhere on this site.

Winnsboro is on U.S. 321, about 28 miles from Columbia, Fairfield Co. It was the main camp for the British under Lord Cornwallis from late October 1780 to early January 1781 before they launched their second offensive to capture North Carolina. A little village now stands on this campsite, of which there are yet many vestiges.

Witherspoon's Ferry is where the S.C. 41 bridge crosses the Lynches River near Johnsonville, Florence Co. A battle took place here in 1780. Before they were routed, fleeing the Tories threw a large amount of war material into the river, including a number of bronze cannon.

The Ruins of the Wofford's Iron Works are somewhere on Lawson Fork Creek, probably near the dead-end dirt road running off S.C. 47 between Glendale and Spartanburg. The works were started around 1773, although the area had been settled several decades earlier. A major battle was fought and won here by the British on January 15-16, 1780. They destroyed the iron works and burned the houses before departing.

Fort Moultrie is on Sullivan's Island opposite the city of Charleston. Actually three forts were built on this site over the years. **Fort Sullivan,** the first, was built of palmetto logs and sand. An important battle was fought here on June 28, 1776 when Patriots in the fort were able to defeat a British squadron of nine ships. Fort Sullivan was later razed when the British took Charleston in 1780; another was built soon after which was destroyed by a hurricane. The present fort was built between 1807 and 1811 and partially demolished during the Civil War.

Fort Sumter National Monument in Charleston Harbor is where the Civil War first broke out on April 12, 1861. Construction on the fort began in 1829 and continued until 1860. For a twenty-month period beginning in 1863 the fort was the scene of a continuous Federal siege, but it wasn't surrendered until the approach of Sherman's army. Sections of the fort have been restored. On the surrounding beaches there have been found many interesting Civil War relics.

The site of Charlesfort is located somewhere on Parris Island, in Port Royal Sound, Beaufort Co. where the United States Marines have a large training base. In 1562 French Huguenots founded a settlement here to challenge Spain's claim to all of North America, but it lasted only a year. In January 1976 the site of this settlement was accidentally found and a large number of artifacts from the period were discovered.

Pendleton is off State 123, twenty miles southwest of Greenville in Oconee County. Founded in 1790, it is one of the oldest towns in the northwestern part of the state. In the present town are the ruins of many old buildings. Nearby are the ruins of numerous plantations as well.

Fort Frederick, in the town of Port Royal on Port Royal Island, was built in 1718 by the British. It is the oldest surviving fort in the United States built of tabby (lime with shells, gravel, and stone).

After General William T. Sherman captured Columbia in 1865, his troops spent two days throwing 43 cannon, several four-inch mortars, 10,000 rifles and muskets, and more than one million musket balls and other ammunition into the **Congaree River** to prevent them from falling back into the hands of the Confederates. Now these relics would be valued at over $1,000,000 if found in good condition. The town was then burned to the ground.

On August 24, 1893 over 1,000 lives were lost and great property damages inflicted by a terrible cyclone at **Charleston and Savannah.**

During the Civil War a wagon train bringing about six tons of silver bullion from Arizona was ambushed by Union troops near the village of **Saluca.** The bullion was thrown into the nearby Saluda River to prevent the Confederates from recapturing it. The site is about ten miles northeast of Greenwood in Greenwood Co.

More Civil War treasures lie at the bottom of the **Congaree River** about two miles north of Sandy Run, County 176, Calhoun Co. Union soldiers ambushed a fleet of Confederate supply boats at this spot on December 12, 1864. One of the boats carrying over $125,000 in gold coins and bullion overturned and its contents were lost.

Confederate raiders captured a Union payroll of about $100,000 in silver and gold coins and buried the cache along **the Santee River** in the vicinity of St. Stephen, County 45, Berkeley Co., before being caught and shot.

During the Revolution about $63,000 in gold and silver coins is known to have been buried in or near **the manor house of the Hampton Plantation,** on the banks of the Santee River near Jamestown, County 41, Berkeley Co.

The Little River Inlet, located close to the North Carolina state line and north Myrtle Beach was a pirate hangout for many years in the seventeenth and eighteenth centuries. Numerous treasures are believed to be buried in the area. In the ruins of nearby **Fort Randall,** treasure hunters have recently been doing a great deal of searching for several Civil War treasures reported to be buried here.

Several small caches of gold and silver Spanish coins have been accidentally discovered in the vicinity of **Murrell's Inlet,** midway between Georgetown and Myrtle Beach, Horry Co. Pirate treasure is alleged to be buried here. There are many colonial ruins in the general area.

In 1520 after a Spanish ship commanded by a Captain Lucas Vazquez de Ayllon wrecked at **Cape Romain,** about midway between Georgetown and Charleston, the Spaniards camped for several months while waiting to be rescued. Finally in desperation they abandoned the place, leaving behind a great deal of gold that had been obtained in Mexico by Cortez's soldiers, and started heading south. Only one of the 90 odd men survived. Later when he was brought back to locate the treasure he was unable to find the spot where it had been buried. Over the centuries many other ships have been wrecked in this area and their remains are scattered on the surrounding beaches.

Charleston has suffered from numerous hurricanes over the years and more than 100 ships were lost in Charleston Harbor as a result of these storms. Remains of these ships and their cargoes can be found all around the shoreline of this harbor. Many Civil War blockade runners were also deliberately run aground and set afire to prevent capture by Union forces. These too may produce interesting artifacts and possibly some treasure. On the beaches of **Morris Island** just south of the port, fishermen have found large numbers of coins after storms. Since they date from three different centuries, they are probably coming from three different shipwrecks.

On the northern tip of the Isle of Palm at Dewees Inlet, about ten miles northeast of Charleston, treasure hunters have reported finding large numbers of Civil War vintage silver coins, musket balls, and pottery.

SOUTH DAKOTA

The site of Gordon Stockade is in Custer State Park on U.S. 16, three miles east of Custer, Custer Co. The first settlers who came to the state seeking gold built this stockade as protection against the Indians in the winter of 1874-1875. Most of the original buildings no longer remain but the stockade itself has been restored.

Deadwood is on State 385, Lawrence Co. Soon after the discovery of gold in the Black Hills in 1874, this town was established and quickly became a boomtown. It attracted such famous personages such as Wild Bill Hickok, Calamity Jane, and others, some of whom ended up in nearby Boot Hill Cemetery. A few original structures and many ruins still remain. On the west end of the town are the remains of **The Broken Boot Gold mine,** which operated from 1878 to 1904.

Around **Homestake Gold Mine** (operating since 1878), located on U.S. 14A and 85 near Lead, Lawrence Co., there are vestiges of many homes dating back to the time of the first gold discovery in the area. There are also a number of abandoned mine shafts in the nearby hills.

The site of Old Fort Pierre is on the west bank of the Missouri River, about three miles above the mouth of Bad River, a few miles south of Pierre, Stanley Co. This fort was strategic to the fur trade business and so had three trading posts. The first lasted from 1817 until 1819, when it was destroyed by Indians. In 1822 the Columbia Fur Company had built **Fort**

Tecumseh, which was used until 1832, when it was replaced with **Fort Pierre.** In 1855 this fort was sold to the United States Army, but they never used it. The fort vanished without a trace like the previous two posts.

Fort Sisseton stands twenty miles west of Sisseton, Marshall Co. It was built in 1864 primarily to protect wagon trains against Sioux attacks and abandoned in 1888. It is now undergoing restoration but very little of it actually remains.

Wounded Knee Battlefield is about ten miles northeast of Pine Ridge, Shannon Co. This is the famous site where on December 29, 1890, American troops are alleged to have massacred more than 100 Sioux Indians after first disarming them.

The ghost town of Old Ashton is on the Mud River opposite the present town of Ashton, two miles east of State 281, Spink Co. Only a few buildings are still standing in this farming town.

The ghost town of Bloomington is on a small creek about five miles north of Vermillion (State 77), Clay Co. The town was destroyed by a band of outlaws in 1877. Several small caches of treasure are known to be buried here.

The ruins of Bugtown are about three miles north of Custer on State 385 and four miles west on a dirt road. It was once a prosperous gold-mining town. Several caches of treasure are believed to be buried in the area. Nearby are several abandoned gold mines.

The ruins of Crook City are near Lookout Peak on State 14A, about seven miles from Whitewood, Lawrence Co. The town once had 3,000 residents until the railroad bypassed it. It was abandoned in 1888; an accidental fire destroyed most of the town around 1900.

The ruins of Fosyer City are on the Mud River, about 24 miles south of Aberdeen, Spink Co. It only boomed for a few years in the 1870s until being bypassed by the railroad.

The ruins of Le Beau are on the River Indian Reservation, on the west side of Lake Oake, about 25 miles southwest of Selby (State 83), Dewy Co. It was a cowtown and trading center until the residents left in the 1890s.

The ruins of Leroy are on the west bank of the Big Sioux River, about five miles northwest of Watertown, Codington Co. Only the foundations of a few buildings are left.

The ghost town of Medary is located just outside of the city limits of Brookings (U.S. 29), Brookings Co. It was founded in 1857 as the first town in Dakota Territory. Today only a few buildings remain standing.

The ruins of Minnesela are on the Belle Fourche River on the old St. Onge Road, about five miles southeast of Belle Fourche (State 85), Butte Co. An old hotel is all that is intact, but there are ruins of several saloons, many stores, a blacksmith shop, a harness shop, and a hardware store.

The ghost town of Nelson Roadhouse is now called Custer Farmhouse, as Custer used it during his expedition to the Black Hills in 1875. It is on the Canyon River, about five miles west of the town of Custer in Custer Co. The town was first a military outpost, then prospered during the gold rush of the late 1870s. Only a few buildings are left.

The ghost town of Ordway is on the Ash River about ten miles northeast of Aberdeen (State 281), Brown County. This formerly thriving mining town was once a prospective state capital.

The town of Rochford is in the Black Hills National Forest about fifteen miles south of Lead (State 85), Lawrence Co. It was founded in 1877 due to the discovery of gold by a hunter. Two years later, when the Standby Mine began operating at full blast, it boasted a population of over 2,000. Today only a few people still live here, but there are many standing buildings.

The ghost town of Rockerville is located at the foot of Storm Mountain in the Black Hills just off State 16, about twenty miles southwest of Rapid City, Pennington Co. It was founded in 1876 and by 1882 was one of the largest gold-mining centers in the state. Today about twenty buildings are still standing. Nearby are several other ruined ghost towns and numerous abandoned gold mines. A gold miner named Carl Bufford is known to have concealed a large cache of gold bullion in the old cemetery.

The ghost town of Sheridan is on State 385, about six miles north of Hill City, Pennington Co. Its original name was Golden City when prospectors discovered rich deposits of placer gold in 1875. By the following year it had more than 5,000 residents, and its name was changed to Sheridan. It became the county seat and the first federal court west of the Missouri River was established here. After the gold petered out the town collapsed, but a large number of picturesque buildings are left.

The ghost town of Silver City is on State 85A, just north of Silver Peak and about twenty miles west of Rapid City, Pennington Co. It was founded in 1876 as the result of the discovery of gold and silver in the area. Today only a church and general store remain. It was a wild town, that boasted almost as many saloons and brothels as homes. Nearby are the ruins of five other ghost towns, one of which is **Camp Gordon.** There are many legends about miners, outlaws, and gamblers burying caches in the area. One of the favorite hiding places for wealth was the **Wildcat Caves,** about seven miles east on County 44.

The town of Terry is on State 385, about two miles south of Lead, Lawrence Co. It was a thriving gold-mining town of over 1,000 residents in the 1870s and 1880s and now only a few dozen people still live there. On nearby Sugarloaf Mountain there are numerous caves and large caverns where a number of prospectors are known to have hidden their wealth. In nearby **Icebox Cave** a band of outlaws are supposed to have concealed about 150 pounds of five-pound gold ingots before being caught and hanged.

The ruins of Tigerville, are on the Rapid River, about five miles northwest of Hill City (County 385), Pennington Co. It was named for the **Bengal Tiger Mine** which closed down in 1887. At that time the town had over 500 residents. Today only a few stone chimneys mark the site.

In 1879, **somewhere on Bear Mountain,** about ten miles southwest of Hill City in Pennington Co., two prospectors named Humphrey and Shafer made a gold strike estimated at over $1 million. They concealed the gold somewhere near their cabin on the west side of this mountain and were killed by outlaws when they refused to reveal the location.

Outlaws buried over $160,000 in gold bullion right where **the Owl River enters the Belle Fourche Reservoir,** nine miles northeast of Belle Fourche (State 212), Butte Co.

The Lost Theon Stone Gold Mine is in the vicinity of Spearfish, State 14, Lawrence Co. The Indians worked other gold mines in this same area. After ambushing a band of miners, some Indians buried over $25,000 in gold nuggets near the peak of Lookout Mountain. About a mile to the south in Blackstain Gulch, a miner buried over $40,000 in raw gold before being bushwhacked and killed. Indians attacked another group of miners in Bear and Potato Creek Gulch and hid seven horse loads of raw gold in a cave before being caught and shot.

Numerous treasures are said to be hidden in the area of **Deadwood,** U.S. 90, Meade Co. One cache known as the **Four Direction Treasure** is reported to consist of $46,500 in gold coins and to be hidden somewhere in the town. In another case, outlaws robbed a $30,000 payroll of gold and silver coins from the Holy Terror Mine and buried it in the town before being caught and hanged. A third group of bandits netted about $85,000 in gold bullion from the Deadwood Stage and buried it somewhere on nearby Deadwood Mountain. The Gordon Party returning from the Montana gold fields were ambushed by Indians in the 1870s and robbed of $45,000 in gold bullion, which the Indians buried in the vicinity of Sturgis, a few miles north of Deadwood. A gambler named Archie McLaughlin buried about $10,000 in gold coins and several leather pouches of gold dust under one of the many saloons in the town.

The Lost Cabin Gold Mine is in the vicinity of Whitewood in Lawrence Co. Nearby are several other abandoned gold mines and the ruins of several mining camps.

In 1879 outlaws robbed the Cheyenne-Deadwood stagecoach and made off with about 450 pounds of gold bars, which they buried in the vicinity of **Lame Johnny Creek,** just north of Sturgis, County 34, Meade Co., before a posse caught up with them and killed them all.

During the gold rush days **Rapid City** was a wild and booming town which boasted over 50 saloons and more than 300 professional gamblers. There are tales of many caches of treasure being buried in the area. Occasionally modern construction unearths one of these caches. Among the most famous treasures are these: a large number of gold coins hidden in the limestone caves just outside the city limits; about $50,000 worth of raw gold hidden by a prospector in a cave on the south side of the city; another cache of $26,000 in gold bullion dropped into the pool at the waterfall in Spring Creek, a few miles southwest of the city.

On the **Burnt Ranch** located just outside of Redfern, County 385, near the Pactola River in Pennington Co., a miner buried about $3,000 in gold bars and was unable to find them.

There are many tales about **lost gold mines** in **the Black Hills** in the general vicinity of Horse Thief Lake and Castle Creek, near Silver City in Pennington Co. Among the most famous are **The Signal Mountain Mine, The Four Crosses Mine, The Scruton Brothers Mine, The Gratz Duke Mine,** and **The Brilliant Fire Mine.** The outlaw Squeeky McDermit robbed about $35,000 in gold bullion from a Homestake Mine shipment and buried it somewhere between Silver City and Mystic along the banks of Rapid Creek.

Just north of Mount Rushmore in the vicinity of Keystone, State 16, Pennington Co., a band of renegade Indians robbed about $75,000 in gold bullion from the Homestake Mine and buried it in a cave.

In 1887 stagecoach robbers obtained an unknown amount of money and jewels from the passengers and concealed it all near their lair on **Hat Creek,** near Battle Creek, just south of Hermosa, County 79, Custer Co.

During an Indian massacre in 1876, the Joseph Metz family were all killed. Their personal wealth was buried near their home on the old stage road in **Red Canyon,** about two miles north of Edgemont, State 18, Fall River Co.

One of the largest stagecoach robberies took place in 1878 when the bandits made off with $400,000 in raw gold and bullion. Then they buried the cache somewhere in the vicinity of Canyon Spring and Horsehead Creek Crossing in **Wind Cave National Park,** Custer Co. They were apprehended and hanged without revealing the whereabouts of the money.

In 1891 other outlaws robbed a stagecoach of some $140,000 in gold coins and bullion and concealed it along the **Pierre Trail** just west of Spring Creek Crossing, several miles west of Fairburn, just off State 79 in Custer Co.

During the late 1870s a group of miners returning from the Black Hills who were being attacked by Indians buried about $100,000 in gold bullion. The treasure is about 100 to 200 yards from the Missouri River in what is now called **Riverside Park** in the city of Pierre, State 14, Stanley Co. The hiding place was near the base of a giant cottonwood tree, according to one of the survivors who was unable to locate it later when he returned with soldiers to protect him.

During a stagecoach holdup outlaws made off with 5,000 ounces of gold bullion. When they lost a wheel of their wagon with a posse hot on their trail, they dumped the cache in **San Creek** near Buffalo Gap just outside of Custer, State 16, Custer Co.

In 1875 a prospector buried a large cache of gold nuggets along the banks of French Creek, about 25 miles southeast of Custer in **Wind Cave National Park.** Flood waters erased his markers, and the cache was lost.

A chest containing $30,000 in gold and silver coins from a train robbery was hidden along the banks of **Hat Creek,** just outside of Rumford, County 52, Fall River Co.

Over $200,000 in gold bullion was robbed from the Sidney Stage and buried along the banks of the **Hat River,** near Ardmore, State 71, Fall River County.

Outlaws netted over $240,000 from the Deadwood Stage in 1879. A posse was in pursuit so they were forced to hide the loot somewhere on **Sheep Table Mountain** in the Badland National Monument, about five miles south of Scenic, County 44, Pennington Co.

In the 1870s a prospector named "Mexican Ed" buried a large cache of gold coins and bullion near his cabin on **Dirty Woman Creek** near Grindstone Butte, about fifteen miles northwest of Phillip, State 14, Haakon Co.

In the 1850s a steamboat carrying over $250,000 in gold bullion and coins caught fire and sank on the Missouri River near the **Farm Island Recreation Area** just south of Pierre in Hughes Co. Coins from this wreck have recently been found on the river banks by treasure hunters from the local area.

Large numbers of silver coins dating in the mid-nineteenth century turn up after flood waters on the west bank of the **Missouri River just north of Chamberlain,** U.S. 90, Brule Co. They are most likely being washed ashore from a river wreck.

Many artifacts and small numbers of gold and silver coins from the late 1800s are found along the banks of the **Missouri River about half a mile north of the Platte River** near the town of Platte, County 44, Charles Co.

The ghost town of Fisher Grove is on the James River about a mile west of Frankfort, State 212, Spink Co. Only a school house and a saloon are still standing.

In 1862 an Indian named Gray Foot are alleged to have buried a flour sack containing $56,000 in gold coins which he robbed from a bank in Lorton, Minnesota. The money is concealed between two willow trees near the east shore of **Long Lake,** just east of Lake City, County 23, Marshall Co.

A member of the Jesse James gang is alleged to have buried a cache of loot somewhere in the vicinity of **Garretson,** County 11, Minnehaha Co.

TENNESSEE

Chickamauga Battlefield Park is on U.S. 27, nine miles south of Chattanooga. This was the scene of two fierce Civil War battles fought in September and November of 1863 for control of Chattanooga, a strategic railroad center and the gateway to the heart of the Confederacy. The 66,000 Confederate troops won an important victory over the Union Army with 58,000 men in the first battle. The Union won the second battle, forcing the Confederates to abandon Chattanooga and flee to Georgia.

Fort Donelson is on the Cumberland River near U.S. 79, one mile west of Dover, Stewart Co. One of the first Union victories took place here on February 16, 1862, when 27,000 Union troops under General Ulysses S. Grant, aided by gunboats, defeated a force of 18,000 Confederates under General Simon B. Buckner. The Union captured 14,000 of the Confederates. Some of the original earthworks and trenches have survived here.

Franklin Battlefield is on U.S. 31, south of Franklin, Williamson Co. One of the bloodiest battles of the Civil War was fought here on November 30, 1864 between the Union Army under General Jacob D. Cox and the Confederate Army of Tennessee under General John B. Hood. The Confederates lost over 6,000 men, including six generals, and the Union suffered 2,326 casualties.

Jonesboro is on U.S. 411 in the northeast corner of the state, Washington Co. The town, founded in 1779, is one of the oldest settlements in the state; there are a large number of ruined buildings dating back to this period in and around the town.

The Chucalissa Indian site is in Fuller State Park on the Mississippi River, about five miles south of Memphis near U.S. 61, Shelby Co. Indians first settled the region around 900 and abandoned it around 1600–1650. The Spanish explorer Hernando de Soto camped here for several weeks in 1541. These ruins contain a number of large mounds.

Shiloh National Military Park is on State 22, ten miles south of Savannah, Hardin Co. On April 6–7, 1862 the Federals won a stunning victory here, in which more than 100,000 men participated. A large number of casualties were suffered by both sides.

Stones River Battlefield is on U.S. 24, about five miles northwest of Murfeesboro, Rutherford Co. The Federals under General William S. Rosecrans won a major victory here over the Confederates under General Braxton Bragg on December 31, 1862. Only a few breastworks remain on the battlefield.

Bean Station, now covered by Boone Lake, is located eight miles east of Ruthledge off U.S. 11W, Grainger Co. This was the first permanent settlement in eastern Tennessee, founded in 1776. Many old, ruined homes were submerged by this man-made lake.

Eaton's Fort was located about nine miles southwest of Bluntville on U.S. 11W, Sullivan Co. This was one of the first fortified frontier stations in the state and the site of the first and only mint in the Southwest Territories. No traces are left today.

Fort Loudoun is on the Little Tennessee River a bit south of U.S. 411 and several miles northeast of Hopewell Springs, Monroe Co. Colonists from South Carolina built this isolated fort in 1756, deep in Indian country and the Cherokee laid siege three years later, finally forced the whites to surrender, and then burned the fort. The Indians promised the whites safe passage back to South Carolina but three days later they attacked them at the junction of Cane Creek and Tellico River, about eight miles south of Madisonville, and massacred most of them.

Fort Robinson stood on Long Island at the South Fork of the Holston River, near Kingsport, Sullivan Co. The fort was built in 1761 by Virginians who tried to build a settlement, but withdrew in a few years. Other whites came into the area around 1770 and settled around the fort on this island. In 1776 the Cherokee attacked and were soundly defeated by the settlers, starting the Cherokee War of 1776. The site became a jumping-off spot for settlers moving into new areas to the west and south. A shipyard which produced various types of river vessels also flourished there for many years. The western third of this island is now covered by housing and industrial developments, but the remainder is undeveloped and has vestiges of many historical landmarks.

Nashville on the Cumberland River was first settled by a French trader in 1710 but the town wasn't founded until 1779. **Fort Nashborough** was built soon after, but the pioneers still suffered from many Indian attacks. The present city has obliterated all traces of the fort and homes of the early settlers.

The site of Fort Watauga is located on Tenn. 91 three miles west of Elizabeth, Carter Co. When it was first settled in 1769 the town was named Sycamore Shoals. The fort was built the next year and both the village and fort were destroyed by Indians about ten years later. The homeless settlers moving on.

The Lost Delosie Silver Mine is somewhere in Sevier Co. close to the North Carolina state line near Gatlinburg, State 441, near the Great Smoky Mountains.

During the Civil War a Confederate paymaster buried about $60,000 in gold and silver coins the day after the Federal victory at nearby Fort Donelson in February 1862. The money is concealed in the vicinity of **Bear Springs**, County 49 on the west side of Lake Barkle, Dover Co. Fleeing Confederate officers and soldiers are supposed to have buried more loot about four miles to the south in and near the village of Carlisle. In 1962 a treasure hunter found a cache of gold and silver coins from the Civil War period in nearby **Dover**, also probably hidden by the retreating Confederates.

Other Civil War treasure is said to be buried among **the ruins of Fort Henry** on the east side of Kentucky Lake, Stewart Co. A short distance to the south at Paris Landing, where the bridge on State 79 crosses this lake, a large cache of weapons and bronze cannon were hidden by the retreating Confederates in 1862.

During the Civil War a John Winters buried a large cache of gold coins and silver plate on his **farm near the Cumberland River**, about two miles north of Erin, County 13, Houston Co.

During an ambush on a Union supply train, a chest containing over $50,000 in gold and silver coins was cast into **the Buffalo River**, about two miles northwest of Flat Wood, County 48, Perry Co.

The outlaw John Murrell is said to have buried over $1 million in gold near his stone house about **three miles south of Dancyville**, County 76, Fayette Co.

Union troops are alleged to have amassed between $1 and $2 million in plunder of various types during the Civil War. When they were in jeopardy from advancing Confederate troops they buried the entire cache on **Owl Creek**, about two miles north of Lexington, County 20, Henderson Co. After the war several came back together and were unable to locate the cache.

The bandit Joseph Thompson Hare terrorized and robbed travelers on the Natchez Trace for many years and is believed to have concealed most of his accumulated booty along the banks of **Wolfe Creek**, just outside the village of Rossville, County 57, Fayette Co.

The ghost town of Fuller is located between Memphis and the Mississippi River in the southwestern corner of the state. Only a few buildings still stand here today.

In the 1860s a miserly old farmer named Cefe Wenton is alleged to have buried a large fortune in gold coins on his **farm near Hillsboro**, State 41, Coffee Co. He and his wife were tortured to death by robbers without revealing the location. One small keg of coins was found on his farm in 1923, but this is believed to be only a small part of his treasure.

After sacking Atlanta Union troops reportedly buried a great deal of Civil War loot **in a cave on Monteagle Mountain,** just outside Monteagle, U.S. 24, Marion Co.

A returning California gold miner is supposed to have buried a large cache of gold bullion and coins on **the bluff overlooking Big Clear Creek,** a few miles west of Wartburg, County 62, Morgan Co.

The Lost Indian Silver Cave Mine is somewhere on **Cumberland Mountain** near Crossville, State 127, Cumberland Co.

Cherokee Indian raiders are reported to have buried about $500,000 in gold bullion in **an old Indian mound near Log Mountain,** about six miles northeast of Luttrell, County 61, Grainger Co.

There are several **lost gold mines** which were worked by the Cherokee Indians in the **Bald Mountains** around Big Butte, which is ten miles southeast of Greenville, State 411, Greene Co.

A substantial amount of treasure was concealed in the vicinity of **Cove Creek Cascades** by fleeing Confederates during the Civil War. The site is a few miles northwest of Gatlinburg just off State 441, Sevier Co.

TEXAS

The ruins of Fort Griffin are on the clear fork of the Brazos River off U.S. 283, fifteen miles north of Albany, Shackleford Co. The fort was built in 1867 to defend the area from hostile Indians. A number of minor skirmishes were fought around the fort, which was abandoned in 1881 and fell into ruin.

The site of Fort Brown is on the north bank of the Rio Grande River at the foot of Elizabeth Street in Brownsville. General Zachary Taylor built the fort in 1846 to defend the Mexican border and to protect the settlers from hostile Indians. Several minor skirmishes were fought here during the Mexican War. During the Civil War three battles were fought at the fort, which changed hands with each encounter. A number of the fort buildings have survived.

Resaca de la Palma Battlefield is just north of Brownsville on Parades Line Road, Cameron Co. The last battle fought in Texas during the Mexican War took place here on May 9, 1846. The Americans under General Zachary Taylor won a stunning victory over the Mexicans led by General Mariano Arista.

Mission Nuestra Senora del Carmen is still standing in the Ysleta section of El Paso. It is the oldest settlement in the state, founded in 1681 by Spanish refugees and Indian converts, who were forced to flee from New Mexico during an Indian uprising. Many of the old adobe structures of the original settlement have survived.

Fort Davis is in Limpia Canyon off State 17 near the town of Fort Davis, Jeff Davis Co. It was built in 1854 to protect travelers using the El Paso-San Antonio Road, which was a segment of the Overland Trail to California. Troops stationed there were kept quite busy fighting Indians and protecting wagon trains and stagecoaches. The Confederates held the fort at the beginning of the war, but when they abandoned it in 1862 the Apaches completely destroyed it. The Army built another fort on the same site in 1867, and it was garrisoned until being abandoned in 1891. Of the original 50 buildings of the second fort only twenty have survived.

Fredericksburg is on U.S. 290 in the center of the state, Gilles Co. The town was founded in 1846 by German immigrants who signed a peace treaty with the Comanches. It was one of the few early settlements in the state that wasn't attacked by Indians. Many of the original buildings are still standing.

Presidio Nuestra Senora de Loreto de la Bahia is off U.S. 183, two miles south of Goliad, Goliad Co. This Spanish frontier town was established in 1749 to protect several nearby missions. During the Hidalgo Revolt of 1812, in which the Mexicans fought for independence from Spain, a battle was fought here and the place captured by the rebels. During the Texas Revolution in 1835, another encounter was fought and won by Americans. The following year

Over

Proper research can reveal where old river fords, popular treasure hunting sites, are now located on beaches and shores of man-made lakes.

Facing

Enjoyment of beautiful scenery and everything else offered by the great outdoors is a "side benefit" to the hobby of treasure hunting with a metal detector.

Over

On the trail of a large cache, this Texas treasure hunter is using a Depth Multiplier two-box searchcoil which will give his detector maximum depth.

Facing

This treasure hunter is wearing headgear that will protect him during long days of searching under the hot Texas sun.

the Mexicans retook the town and massacred the 343 inhabitants; some adobe buildings still survive.

Old Fort Parker is on State 14, four miles north of Groesbeck, Limestone Co. It was built in 1834 to protect settlers against Indian attack. Two years later it was the scene of brutal massacre in which Comanches killed everyone except for five children whom they enslaved.

San Jacinto Battlefield is off State 225, 21 miles east of Houston, Harris Co. The Americans under Sam Houston gained their independence from Mexico by winning a decisive battle here on April 21, 1836. Because of this victory Texas eventually became a state.

The site of Fort Richardson is off U.S. 281, a mile southwest of Jacksboro, Jack Co. The fort was built in 1867 to protect the settlers from the depredations of the Kiowa and Comanche Indians and was abandoned in 1874. Only a few of the fort's buildings have survived.

Fort Belknap is on State 251, three miles south of Newcastle, Throckmorton Co. Built in 1851 as one of the largest forts in northern Texas, it weathered a number of fierce Comanche attacks and also served as a stop on the Butterfield Overland Mail Route. In 1867 the fort was abandoned and fell into ruin.

Fort Concho is on the forks of the Concho River just south of San Angelo, Tom Green Co. It was built in 1867 where several east-west trails converged and served as the point of departure for most southern expeditions to the far West. The fort was abandoned in 1889 and a number of its structures are well-preserved.

The Alamo National Historic Landmark in San Antonio was originally built in 1718 as the Mission of San Antonio de Valero; then it was converted into a fortress around 1793. The famous Texas Revolution battle of March 6, 1836 took place here, in which 188 Americans were slaughtered by Santa Anna's Mexican Army of 5,000. Nearby on Mission Road stands the Mission of Nuestra Senora de la Purisima Conception, which was built in 1731 and is still in remarkable condition. During an Indian attack in 1781 when most of the inhabitants of the mission were massacred, a great deal of church treasure was hidden on the site and never found again.

Mission San José y San Miguel de Aguayo is on U.S. 281, about six miles south of San Antonio. It was founded in 1720 and soon became one of the most important missions on the northern frontier of New Spain. By 1750 a settlement of over 2,000 people surrounded the mission, of which no traces remain. There are vestiges of old adobe houses about two miles to the east of the site.

La Villita in downtown San Antonio is an authentic restoration of this village which was founded in 1722 and originally settled by poor soldiers and their Indian wives. It became a fashionable residential district after 1819, when a flood destroyed most of the rest of the city. Some vestiges of the original buildings remain.

The site of the community of **San Felipe de Austin** is located in Stephen F. Austin Historic Park in San Felipe, Austin County. The community was founded in 1823 and became the first Anglo-American colony in the state, but by 1870 it had been abandoned. Today very few traces of the settlement can be seen in this park.

The site of Mission Tejas is on the Neches River, off State 21, southwest of Weches, Houston Co. The Spaniards founded a mission and settlement here in 1690 to prevent French encroachment into the area, but very little is known about its history after its founding. Today no traces survive, but a replica has been built on the site.

The Lost Nigger Bill Gold Mine is located in the vicinity of Reagan Canyon in the Big Bend National Park, Brewster Co.

The Lost Silver Ledge Mine is in Croton Brakes Canyon in Dickens Co.

The Lost Jim Bowie Silver Mine is on the San Saba River near Menard in Menard Co.

The Lost San Saba Gold Mine is on the San Saba River just above the remains of an old military fort, a bit south of Menard in Menard Co.

The Lost Spanish Fort Gold Mine is about 30 miles north of Bowie, County 59, Montague Co. There are ruins of an early French settlement and several abandoned mining camps near the mine.

One of the most lucrative treasure-hunting places in the state is in **the old section of Galveston.** On September 8, 1900, a tidal wave struck and over 6,000 people were killed. Property damages were over $17 million and almost every building was destroyed. Around the foundations of these old buildings many caches of hidden personal wealth are to be found. The area is a mecca for bottle collectors.

The ghost town of Adobe Walls is on the Canadian River about 25 miles northeast of Borger, County 136, Hutchinson Co. The famous Battle of Adobe Walls was fought here. Many of the town's structures are intact.

The town of Buffalo Gap is about fifteen miles south of Abilene on County 89, Taylor Co. Only the ruins of the courthouse and jail have survived from its heyday in the late nineteenth century. All the other buildings were burned down during an outlaw raid. Today a few people still reside here.

The ghost town of San Saba is on the San Saba River on State 87, about eleven miles south of Brady, McCulloch Co. It started out as a Texas Ranger fort and then flourished briefly as a gold-mining center.

The ruins of Center City are on State 84, about nine miles east of Goldthwaite, Mills Co. This cowtown was razed by a tornado in 1897.

The ruins of Doan's Crossing are on the south bank of the Red River, about a mile north of Carnes on County 283, Hardeman Co. It was a supply center during the trail herd days but now only one adobe house is left.

The ruins of El Copono are located on Copono Bay about twenty miles north of Corpus Christi on County 136, Refugio Co. It was founded in 1749. Numerous treasures are reported to have been buried here during the Mexican War when the inhabitants fled back to Mexico.

The ruins of English are on County 114 about six miles northwest of Avery, Red River Co. Founded in 1840 it thrived as a wild cowtown until being destroyed by Union troops near the close of the Civil War. At this time a wealthy rancher who was shot is known to have buried a large cache of silver coins somewhere in the town.

The town of Gail is one of the few authentic cowtowns that has survived until the present time. In the numerous ruins of old buildings and abandoned homes on nearby ranches one could find artifacts and possibly some treasure. The town is on County 669, about 35 miles west of Snyder in Borden Co.

The ruins of Idianola are on Lavaca Bay at the dead end of County 316, Calhoun Co. It was once one of the most important towns in the state and boasted a population of over 7,000. Several hurricanes reduced the town to rubble. Numerous caches of treasure are known to be here.

The ghost town of Helena is on the San Antonio River and on County 792 about five miles northeast of Karnes City, Karnes Co. It was a supply town on the old Chihuahua Trail, founded in 1852. Today only a few buildings are still standing.

The ruins of Kenney's Fort are on State 79, about two miles east of Round Rock, Williamson Co. The ruins of a wooden stockade and a few buildings have survived.

The ruins of Mount Sterling are on the Angelina River, about eight miles northeast of Wells (State 69), Nocagdoches Co. It was founded in the 1840s as a booming shipping and trade center and was destroyed by Union raiders in the Civil War.

The ruins of Nashville are on the west bank of the Brazos River, six miles southeast of Hearne, State 79, Robertson Co. A flood ravaged the town, leaving just the cemetery.

The ruins of Oakville are on County 9 about seven miles east of Three Rivers, Live Oak Co. It was an outlaw hangout until Texas Rangers drove them out in 1876 and burned the town to the ground. Several valuable caches are believed to be here.

The ruins of Ochiltree are on Wolf Creek near State 83, about fifteen miles south of Perryton, Ochiltree Co. It was a wild cowtown and outlaw hangout until razed by a tornado in the 1910s.

The ghost town of Old Preston is on the south shore of Lake Texoma, about fifteen miles west of Denison, State 75, Grayson Co. The town was founded in the 1830s; in 1840 the Texas

Republic established Fort Preston nearby, which is now in ruins. A large number of old buildings have survived well.

The ruins of Spanish Fort are on the Red River, County 102, about seventeen miles north of Nocona, Montague Co. It was founded in 1759 and by 1860 had a population of over 1,000. Today mounds cover the old Spanish fort and many buildings.

The site of Old Stone Fort is on the Rio Grande River about half a mile north of San Ygnacio, State 83, Zapata Co. Near the fort are the ruins of a settlement which also stood here during the late eighteenth and early nineteenth century. The fort was destroyed by a flood, but some treasure is believed to lie among the ruins.

The ghost town of Tascosa is on the banks of the Canadian River in one of the most unspoiled parts of the state, about 22 miles north of Vega (U.S. 40), Oldham Co. Giant cottonwood trees surround the site and over 50 of the old adobe buildings are still standing. There are many tombstones on nearby Boothill; and several caches of outlaw loot are supposed to be buried on the site.

The ruins of Zavalla are in the Angelina National Forest, about 25 miles north of Woodville (State 69), Angelina Co. It was a wild cowboy town on the old Beef Trail to Louisiana.

The ruins of Orient are located just outside of Aspermont, State 380, Stonewall Co. The town of several thousand people prospered briefly when a "salted silver mine" started a stampede for riches. The most prominent remaining feature is the abandoned, nonproducing mine.

The ruins of Pinery are on State 180, about 35 miles northeast of Signal Peak near the New Mexico state line in Culberson Co. It was an old stage station and cowboy supply center. Only a saloon remains.

The ruins of Rath City are in the Double Fort Mountains, about ten miles southwest of Aspermont (State 380), Stonewall Co. This supply center for buffalo hunters and prospectors was ravaged by fire in 1875.

The ghost town of St. Mary's, founded in 1840, is on Copona Bay near Bayside (County 136), Refugio Co. The town was an important seaport for pirates and privateers until late in the century. There are numerous tales of booty buried here.

The ruins of San Felipe are in Stephen Austin State Park, about eight miles northeast of Sealy (U.S. 10), Austin Co. It was founded in 1823 and served as an outlaw lair during the later nineteenth century.

The ghost town of Santa Rita is four miles northeast of Brownsville on County 281, Cameron Co. It was the home of Juan Cortina, the "Mexican Robin Hood," who is alleged to have buried plenty of plunder in the area.

The ghost town of Scottsville is eight miles east of Marshall (State 59), close to the Louisiana state line, Harrison Co. Religious camp meetings have been held here since 1840 and many of the old revival-town buildings are still standing. In the areas where the tent towns spring up for the religious meetings, many modern coins, rings, and jewelry are found by treasure hunters.

The ghost town of Sutherland Springs is just off State 87, about 32 miles east of San Antonio, Wilson Co. About 50 late nineteenth-century buildings remain intact.

The ruins of Tee Pee City are on the South Pease River, about ten miles west of Paducah (State 70), Motley Co. This old frontier town was destroyed by Indians and never rebuilt.

The ruins of Tower Hill are on the North Concho River near State 87, about eight miles southeast of Sterling City, Sterling Co. The ruins of an old fort are here and treasure hunters have found many artifacts, some treasure, and numerous skeletons.

One of the state's most famous lost treasures is the **Lost Bowie Silver Mine,** located somewhere in the vicinity of the town of San Saba, State 190, San Saba Co. In the 1750s it was the most productive silver mine outside of Mexico and the Spaniards had a sizable garrison stationed there to protect it. When a large band of Indians attacked in 1759 the Spaniards had over $33,000,000 in silver bullion, which was just being prepared to be sent in a large wagon train down to Mexico. The miners stored all of the silver in the mine, which was sealed off by a gun powder blast. During the battle most of the Spaniards were killed. The survivors made their way back to Mexico. The following year they returned with reinforcements but were unable to locate the mine or treasure because a landslide had further concealed its location.

The state's most famous outlaws were the Sam Bass gang. By the time Bass and his cohorts were gunned down in 1878, they had already robbed more than $3,000,000 in gold and silver—worth at least ten times that amount today. The gang is said to have hidden their ill-gotten booty in at least eighteen different places: at **Cove Hollow** near Rosston in Cooke Co., in an abandoned old Spanish mine near **Chalk Hill** in Dallas Co., along the **Trinity River** in the Oak Cliff section of Dallas, around **Schnault Springs** in North Dallas, somewhere in the city of **Denton,** in Denton Co., **near Bowie** in Montague Co., **near the base of Skeen's Peak** near Weatherford in Parker Co., along the banks of **Hubbard Creek Lake** near Breckenridge Pass in Stephens Co., in a cave near McNeil in Travis Co., near **Round Rock** in Williamson Co., along **Hickory Creek** about twelve miles northwest of Denton in Denton Co., on **Pilot Knob Mountain** in Denton Co., along **Duck Creek** just outside of Dallas, at **Pilot Point** in northeastern Denton Co., in **Longhord Cavern** a bit north of Dallas, along **Wise Creek** in Wise Co., along **Pond Creek** in Cooke Co., and at **Black Springs** near Jacksboro in Jack Co. To date none of these treasures has been found.

The ruins of Fort Hancock are on the Rio Grande River near the present town of this name, State 80, Hudspeth Co. It was called Fort Rice when it was founded in 1883.

The ruins of Fort Quitman are on the Rio Grande River about 80 miles below El Paso, about ten miles southwest of Finlay (State 80), Hudspeth Co. The fort was built in 1849 and abandoned in 1877.

Old Fort Cibolo is still standing in Presidio Co. near the village of Adobes on the Rio Grande River. During the Mexican War several caches of money were buried on the site and remain lost. Nearby on the Alamito Cienaga River are the ruins of **Fort Cienaga,** which was built in 1850.

The ruins of Fort Butterfield and the ruins of nearby **Fort Pine Springs** are both just outside of Singal Peak, State 180, Culberson Co. Both were built in the 1850s and abandoned by 1880.

The ruins of Fort Stockton are in the city of Fort Stockton, State 290, Pecos Co. It was built in 1859 and abandoned two years later.

The ruins of Fort Lancaster are on the Pecos River, about three miles south of Sheffield (U.S. 10), Crockett Co. It was built in 1855 and abandoned in 1861.

The ruins of Fort Hudson are twenty miles north of Comstock and a few miles west of County 163, Val Verde Co. It was built in 1857 and abandoned in 1868.

The ruins of Fort Clark are now on a dude ranch about 30 miles east of Del Rio (State 277), Kinney Co. It was built in 1852 and abandoned by 1870.

The ruins of Fort Duncan are in the town of Eagle Pass on the Rio Grande River, State 277, Maverick Co. It was built in 1849 and in continuous use until 1922.

The ruins of Fort Terrett are just outside Roosevelt, U.S. 10, Kimble Co. It was built in 1854 and abandoned two years later.

The site of Fort Ben Ficklin is four miles south of San Angelo (State 87), Tom Green Co. It was built in 1875 and destroyed by a flood in 1882.

The ruins of Fort Kelley, built in 1867, are three miles southeast of San Angelo in Tom Green Co. Several small treasures are supposed to be buried on the site.

The ruins of Fort Chadbourne are near the town of this same name on State 277, Coke Co. Founded in 1852 and abandoned in 1867, the fort was one of the most important supply centers on the Butterfield Overland Trail.

The ruins of Forts La Rena and McLaughlin are just outside of Carrizo Springs, State 277, Dimmitt Co. Both were founded in the 1870s and abandoned within ten years time.

The ruins of Fort McIntosh are on the Rio Grande River just north of Laredo in Webb Co. The place was first established as a Spanish presidio in 1757 and the fort was built there in 1849. It was abandoned in 1859. Another, built about a half a mile to the south, has since disappeared.

The ruins of Fort San Ygnacio are on the Rio Grande River about three miles north of the town of this same name, State 83, Zapata Co. It was built by the Spaniards in the 1700s and still in use in the 1840s.

The **ruins of Fort Lapas** are located about five miles northeast of Zapata, State 83, Zapata County. Spaniards built the fort in the mid-eighteenth century and only its foundation is left.

The **ruins of Fort Ewell** are on the old San Antonio Road, about 25 miles southeast of Cotulla (U.S. 35), La Salle Co. It was built in 1852 and abandoned in 1859.

The **ruins of Fort Ringgold** are on the eastern outskirts of Rio Grande City, State 83, Starr Co. It was built in 1848 and abandoned in 1865.

The **ruins of Fort Brown** are located in Brownsville on the north bank of the Rio Grande River, Cameron Co. It was founded in 1846 and used sporadically until the 1920s.

The **ruins of Fort Lipantitlan** are a few miles north of Robstown, State 77, Nuces County. There was an Indian village on this site as early as 1690. The Spaniards built the fort in 1734 and it was still being used as late as 1870.

The **ruins of Fort Marcy** are in Corpus Christi, Nuces Co. The structures were built in 1846, abandoned in 1857, reoccupied by the Confederates in 1863, and demolished by the Federals in 1865.

The **ruins of Fort Ramirez** are near State 281 on the southern boundary of Live Oak Co. Spaniards built the fort at an unknown date; Indians destroyed it during a massacre in 1813.

The **site of Fort Merrill** is on the Nueces River near George West (State 59), Live Oak Co. Founded in 1855, it was abandoned five years later.

The **ruins of Fort Esperanza** are located about ten miles southwest of the northern tip of Matagorda Island on the Gulf of Mexico in Calhoun Co. Early in 1863, the fort was built; a hurricane in November of the same year demolished it.

The **ruins of Fort Inge** are on the Old Chihuahua Trail just outside of Uvalde, State 83, Uvalde Co. It was constructed in 1849 and abandoned in 1869.

Fort Lincoln is still in a good state of preservation near the village of O'Hania, State 90, Medina Co. It was constructed in 1849 and abandoned three years later.

The **ruins of Fort Forilla** are next to the ruins of a Spanish mission and settlement which flourished during the eighteenth century. The community is located a few miles north of Bandera, County 16, Bandera Co.

The **ruins of Fort Moore** are on Monument Hill just south of La Grange (State 77), Fayette Co. The fort was founded in 1828 and abandoned after the Civil War.

The **ruins of Fort McKavett**, founded in 1852 and abandoned in 1883, are near the town of this same name on County 864, Menard Co.

The **ruins of Fort Mason** are in the town of Mason, State 87, Mason Co. It was built in 1851 and abandoned in 1869.

The **ruins of Fort Bend** are located on a bend in the Brazos River near Richmond (State 59), Fort Bend Co. This fort was built and only used during the Civil War.

The **ruins of the town of Velasco** are at the mouth of the Brazos River on the Gulf of Mexico, a few miles south of Freeport (County 288), Brazoria Co. There are ruins of an old fort and numerous buildings in this old Spanish port, which dates back to the mid-eighteenth century. Because pirates were based here in the nineteenth century treasure is believed to be buried here.

The **ruins of Fort San Jacinto,** constructed in 1836 and rebuilt in 1898, are located on the eastern end of Galveston Island in Galveston Co. About ten miles to the southwest is the **site of Fort Magruder,** of which no trace exists today. It was built by the Confederates in the Civil War and garrisoned by them throughout the war.

The **site of Fort Bankhead** was on the west side of West Bay inside of Galveston Island, about four miles south of La Marque on U.S. 45. During the Civil War the Confederates built and garrisoned this large stone fort; nothing is left of it now. About eight miles north near the town of Hitchcock, the Confederates manned **Fort Herbert,** which is also gone. Four miles to the east of this site are the **ruins of Fort Crockett,** built in 1897. The site is close to Alta Loma on County 6.

The **ruins of Fort Bolivar,** built in 1844, are on the southern tip of the Bolivar Peninsula opposite Galveston. Nearby is the site of **Fort Green** over which a new fort called **Fort Travis** was built in 1898.

The **ruins of Fort Sabine,** also known as **Fort Griffin,** are located at the mouth of the Sabine River on the Louisiana state line. It was built in 1862 by the Confederates, badly damaged during various attacks by Union gunboats, and then demolished in 1865 by Union soldiers.

The **ruins of Fort Colorado,** founded in 1836, and called **Fort Prairie,** are on the Colorado River just south of Austin, Travis Co. Several caches of treasure are rumored to be hidden on the site.

The **ruins of Fort Kinney** are east of Round Rock on State 79, Williamson Co. This fort, built in 1839, was ravaged two years later during an Indian attack. In 1857 it suffered a bad fire and was rebuilt.

The **ruins of Fort Crogan** are one mile south of Burnet, State 281, Burnet Co. Founded in 1849, the fort was abandoned two years later.

The **ruins of Fort Tenoxtitlan** are located just outside of Caldwell, County 21, Burleson Co. It was built in 1830 and abandoned in 1860 after being destroyed by Indians.

The **ruins of Fort Little River** are located on the Little River just outside the town of Little River, County 95, Bell Co. It lasted from 1836 until the end of the Civil War.

The **ruins of Fort Sullivan** are just above the mouth of the Little River near Cooks Point (County 21), Burleson Co.

The **ruins of Fort Boggy** are on the old Camino Real, about five miles south of Centerville, State 75, Leon Co. It was constructed in 1840 and continued in use until the late 1890s.

The **ruins of Fort Arkosisa** are on the Trinity River, about five miles west of Hardin (County 146), Liberty Co. This old Spanish fort and settlement date back to the mid-1700s.

The **ruins of Fort Teran** are near Nancy (County 69) in Angelina Co. It was built in 1834 and abandoned in 1865.

The **ruins of Fort Graham** are on the old Chisholm Trail near the Brazos River, about midway between Hillsboro and Meridan in Hill Co. Built in 1849, it was used for only four years.

The **ruins of Fort Smith** are eight miles east of Itasca (U.S. 35W), Hill Co. It was built in 1843 and still occupied during the Civil War.

The **ruins of Fort Worth,** located in the present city of Fort Worth, are what is left of a fort that was built in 1849 and abandoned four years later.

The **ruins of Fort Kings,** built in 1840, are about four miles southeast of Kaufman, State 175, Kaufman Co. Recently a treasure hunter from Dallas found a cache of about 300 Spanish silver coins of the mid-nineteenth century.

The **site of Fort Sherman** is on the Big Cypress River in the general vicinity of Mount Pleasant (State 271), Titus Co., but the exact location has been lost.

The **ruins of Fort English** are one mile east of Bonham, State 82, Fannin Co. The fort was built in 1836 and demolished in 1962 as a hazard to the public. On the opposite side of Bonham a **Fort Warren** was built in 1836, abandoned the following year, and is entirely gone.

The **ruins of Fort Johnson,** constructed in 1840, are on the south banks of Lake Texoma, four miles north of Pottsboro, County 1417, Grayson Co. The stockade was used until the turn of the century. The ruins of nearby **Fort Preston,** which was erected in 1840, are now under Lake Texoma, about a mile north of **Fort Johnson.**

The **ruins of Fort Fitzhugh** are three miles southeast of Gainesville (State 82), Cooke Co. It was built in 1847 and destroyed by Indians in 1874.

The **ruins of Fort Pickerville** are two miles north of Breckenridge (State 180), Stephens Co. This fort, built in 1854, was destroyed by fire in 1875.

Near the banks of the Rio Grande River opposite the Country Club in the section of El Paso that used to be called Piedras Parades, a wagon load of treasure was buried during the Mexican War.

Just north of El Paso are **the Franklin Mountains.** A great number of treasures are alleged to be buried in this area. Near the settlement of La Esmelda, at the foot of these mountains, beneath a large rock near a clump of scrub oaks, a bandit hid a cache of gold coins. A letter in the Mexico City National Archives states that in 1616 a large cache of church treasure and silver bullion was hidden on this mountain by missionaries fleeing for their lives from hostile Indians. The most valuable treasure is rumored to be about 300 burro loads of gold and silver bullion, which Jesuit missionaries sealed in an old mine shaft after they were expelled from the American colonies. Pancho Villa's vast accumulation is also alleged to be hidden in these mountains, within walking distance of downtown El Paso. A James B. Leach is reported to have buried about $250,000 in gold and silver coins. Several **lost silver mines,** which had been worked by Indians and Spaniards, are known to be in these mountains.

Mexican bandits are alleged to have buried a large cache of booty on the north side of the **Rio Grande River** near Acala, State 80, about 40 miles southeast of El Paso, Hudspeth Co.

The Quick Killer Lost Silver Mine is located in the Guadalupe Mountains near Finlay Peak in Hudspeth Co. The renegade Indian Geronimo is rumored to have had a secret gold mine in this same area. A Mexican miner named Policarpo Gonzalez made a big gold find and buried it somewhere on Sierra Blanca Mountain.

Mexican miners buried about $300,000 in gold bullion near Victoria Peak in the Sierra Diablo Mountains. They could not find the spot when they returned with supplies and enough mules to transport the gold back to civilization.

The Guadalupe Mountains are located in the northwestern corner of Culberson Co. The only settlement in this desolate part of the state is Signal Peak on State 180. There are a large number of **lost gold and silver mines** and the ruins of several ghost towns and mining camps in the area. The Ben Sublett's lost gold cache is near the southern end of these mountains, on the east end of a canyonlike chasm, sheer on both sides and about 75 feet deep. There he hid about 200 pounds of raw gold in a cave but lost the site. During the Mexican Revolution a group of banditos came to these mountains with eighteen burro loads of plunder estimated to be worth close to $30,000; they concealed it all in the vicinity of Grapevine Springs. In 1930 a prospector named Jesse Duran found a cave between the upper end of Rader Range and Juniper Springs, which is about 50 miles south of Carlsbad, New Mexico. In it were three skeletons and several large iron strongboxes full of gold and silver coins. He took as much gold as he could carry—a small part of the overall hoard—but lost the location of the cave.

About two miles north of Pecos State 80, Reeves Co., on the Pecos River are the remains of an **old fort.** Several hundred paces away is a small hill on which a group of returning California miners are said to have hidden a great deal of gold during a surprise Indian attack. In the early 1900s a Mexican is reported to have found one small chest of this treasure, but more is believed to be hidden.

The Lost Eagle Gold Mine is near the Overland Trail and Eagle Springs somewhere around Eagle Flats, about five miles north of Allamore (State 10), Hudspeth Co. Outlaws had a hangout in this area during the 1870s and 1880s. They concealed in a cave about 1,200 rifles and a great deal of shot, which they robbed from a United States Army supply train.

During the Mexican Revolution a band of Spaniards escaped with 105 mule loads of treasure and documents. These men turned themselves over to United States authorities, obtained diplomatic immunity, and were eventually shipped back to Spain. Then they admitted having buried the great cache of treasure somewhere in **Pinto Canyon** in the Chispa Mountains, about 23 miles southeast of Van Horn (U.S. 10) in Jeff Davis Co.

The ghost town of Shafer is on State 67, eighteen miles north of Presidio, Presidio Co. In the town are over 50 adobe buildings; the ruins of **Fort Cibola** are close by. About a half mile east stand the ruins of Mission Julimes. A group of Apache Indians are alleged to have hidden a strongbox full of gold dust in a cave along Cibolo Creek near the town.

The ruins of the **Spanish mission San Cristobal** are located just outside of Presidio on the Rio Grande River, State 67, Presidio Co. In one of the many other adobe ruins in this neighborhood, an undetermined amount of gold coins and paper currency from a 1924 Mexican payroll robbery is hidden.

A Confederate shipment of gold bullion from Genoa, Nevada was buried in the vicinity of **Toyahvale,** State 290, Reeves Co., to keep it out of the hands of pursuing Union Troops.

The ghost town of El Muerto is located on Casket Mountain a few miles north of Fort Davis, County 17, Jeff Davis Co. It was a mining town for a few years in the late nineteenth century; now only a few buildings are left. The **Lost San Antone Gold Mine** is located in this same area. The Red Curley gangs are supposed to have buried 25 mule loads of gold and silver bullion from their raid into Monterey, Mexico, and several train and bank robberies, in an old abandoned mine shaft a few miles west of Fort Davis, in the vicinity of Barrel Springs in the Davis Mountains.

There are said to be several **lost gold mines** in the vicinity of **Marfa,** State 67, Presidio Co. The most famous is the **Lost Chino Mine.** In one abandoned mine shaft a band of Mexican soldiers are believed to have hidden a large cache of plunder, including about half a ton of gold bars.

The Lost Ranger Gold Mine and the **Lost Spanish Blanco Mine** are located in the vicinity of **Yellow Horse Peak** between the Maravillas and San Francisco Rivers in Brewster Co. On **the Neville Ranch** between Black Peak and Elephant Mountains, on the east bank of the Calamity River, the notorious Mexican bandit Manuel Ortega hid about a dozen wagon loads of plunder from his many raids along the Mexico-Texas border, before he was killed in 1817.

In the **Big Bend National Park** there are several well-documented treasures. About two miles north of Boquillas, State 385, Brewster Co., on the Tornillo River bank, Mexican bandits buried several chests of gold bullion from a bank holdup in 1846. About eleven miles up this river from Boquillas is the **Lost Chisos Gold Mine,** located in the vicinity of Juniper Canyon. During the Mexican Revolution about twenty wagon loads of booty were hidden in this mine and then sealed off by insurgent soldiers. **The Lost Phantom Silver Mine** is located in this same general area. Near the entrance of another lost silver mine Mexican bandit Luis Terrazas buried over $3 million in gold bullion before being caught and shot.

About two miles west of the **ghost town of Tascora,** State 87, Oldham Co., on the banks of the Canadian River, a prospector hid over $75,000 in gold bullion and was unable to locate it later.

In 1859 a party of Kiowa Indians attacked a group of Mexicans. The attackers then buried a cache of ancient Aztec gold relics and about $40,000 in gold coins near a spring on **the old George Griffis Ranch,** about ten miles south of Higgins, County 213, Lipscomb Co.

The ghost town of Mobeetee is located on the Sweetwater River, about two miles south of present Mobeetie, County 152, Wheeler Co. Only a saloon and church are still standing. Within half a mile of the southern side of this ghost town, outlaws buried several chests of silver coins from a stagecoach robbery in 1867.

In 1874 bandits buried about $40,000 in newly minted twenty-dollar gold coins in a dry well in **Palo Duro Canyon** in the Palo Duro State Park, which is eight miles northeast of Wayside, County 285, Armstrong Co.

The Double Mountains are in Kent Co. near Clairemont, State 380. Several Indian legends tell about a group of Spanish conquistadors who robbed a great deal of Aztec booty in Mexico around 1540 and buried the hoard in these mountains. There are a number of **lost silver and copper mines** in these mountains. The **Spider Rock Treasure,** consisting of three large chests of church treasures, is buried near the ruins of a Spanish mission and settlement near Salt Forks on the eastern slope of these mountains.

An Aztec treasure estimated to be worth about $10 million is reported to be buried under the rubble of a Spanish mission chapel in the vicinity of Aspermont, State 380, Stonewall Co.

The ruins of Judkins are located between Wink and Kermit on County 15, Winkler Co. Somewhere in this same area is an abandoned **silver mine.** Prospectors who were being shadowed by hostile Indians hid a great deal of raw gold and then were unable to find it afterwards.

When the members of a wagon train were massacred in 1835, an undetermined amount of treasure was buried in the **Monahans Sandhills** a few miles north of Monahans, State 80, Ward Co. In this same area the Indian chief Yellow Wold buried a wagon full of silver ore before being caught and shot by Cavalry soldiers in 1878.

On the north side of the Pecos River at Horsehead Crossing, ten and a half miles southwest

335

of McCamey, State 67, Pecos Co., there are a large number of caves. In 1867 two brothers, Clell and Oliver Shepard, buried fifteen chests of gold bullion and coins from a wagon train robbery in one of these caves. Legend has it that for years the brothers came back to gather just enough of the loot to sustain themselves for a year at a time. Both died in a farm accident in 1887 and it is believed that much of their cache is still hidden in the limestone cave. In the same immediate area an army wagon spilled its contents while crossing the river. Two brass cannon and several boxes of rifles were lost on the muddy river bottom.

Somewhere on Seven Mile Mountain, five miles northeast of the town of Fort Stockton, State 290, Pecos Co., mid-sixteenth century Spanish explorers concealed a large cache of armor, weapons, and supplies while being pursued by hostile Indians. While searching for this cache several years ago a treasure hunter found a leather pouch containing about eight pounds of gold nuggets and a skeleton lying nearby.

On Castle Mountain, about ten miles southeast of Crane, State 385, Upton Co., several different treasures are said to be buried. A group of Mexican soldiers en route to Mexico are reported to have concealed a wagon load of gold ore after being attacked by Indians. A large cache of gold and silver coins from a stagecoach robbery in 1860 is supposed to be buried in a cave about 100 yards from a small spring in **Castle Gap Canyon.** In nearby **Rattlesnake Cave** a large store of gold ore was hidden. And a band of outlaws are reported to have hidden several safes of loot in another cave in the same area. There are ruins of several abandoned mining camps and silver mines on this mountain.

On Santiago Peak, fifteen miles west of the Maravillas River in the center of Brewster Co., a group of Mexican miners are reported to have concealed about 300 pounds of raw gold during an Indian attack. They could not locate it afterwards.

The Lost Seminole Bill Gold Mine discovered in 1887, with the ore assaying at $80,000 a ton, is somewhere near the Rio Grande River in the southwestern corner of Terrell Co., about fifteen miles southwest of Dryden, State 90.

About a mile west of the ruins of **Fort Belknap** on State 281 in Throckmorton Co., a dying bandit confessed to having buried $18,000 in gold in a bean pot in a grove of prickly pear trees, on the banks of a dry stream, within a hundred paces of the ruins of an adobe house. A bandit named Andy Duke buried a cache of gold bars and silver coins within several hundred paces of the fort ruins.

About midway between Albany and Baird, just off State 283 in Shackleford Co., on **Hubbard Creek,** near the old Greer homestead, two Mexican bandits buried about $50,000 in gold bullion and coins. They were caught near here and hanged without revealing the whereabouts.

A man-made lake now covers **the site of the old M. L. Dalton Ranch** near Palo Tinto, State 180, Pinto Co. A treasure of about $25,000 in gold and silver coins was buried on this ranch by its owner, who was killed by Indians in 1865.

In 1925 a man is reported to have buried about $35,000 in gold coins in a milk can in **Benbrook Lake,** near Fort Worth; but since that time the lake has been enlarged. Before his death in 1928, a farmer named William Riddle buried his life's fortune of around $100,000 somewhere on his ranch in this same area.

Dallas has a large number of treasures reported hidden in and around the expanding city. The **ghost town of La Reunion** is located near the southwest corner of the city limits. Recently vandals burned down the last of its standing buildings. Outlaws are said to have buried about $16,000 in gold coins about 100 yards from the first bridge on the Northwest Highway, going west from Flagpole Hill in the city. Jesse James and many other outlaws are known to have hidden various caches in the city.

Some Spaniards are known to have dropped a great deal of gold and silver bullion and church treasure into a deep spring near the east fork of the **Trinity River,** about ten miles northwest of Garland, a suburb of Dallas, during an Indian attack in the early 1800s.

Right after Texas won its independence in 1839, a group of Mexican merchants and traders dropped a large cache of gold and silver coins into a deep hole in the bottom of **Little Cypress Creek,** just north of Gilmer, State 271, Upshur Co.

336

According to legend, about $2 million in silver bars stolen by the pirate Jean Lafitte from the Spaniards was being shipped from southern Texas to Alabama. When United States troops began trailing the wagon train carrying the booty, the train leaders were forced to throw all the silver into **Lake Hendricks.** This lake is on the old Trammel Trail near the junction of Harrison, Panola, and Rusk county lines, about three miles southwest of Darco, County 43. Reportedly three of these bars were fished out of the lake in the 1920s.

During the 1850s a band of outlaws, who reportedly had netted about $107,000 from four bank holdups, buried it on the east slope of **West Mountain,** about midway between Abilene and Buffalo Gap, State 277, Taylor Co. Several caches of prospector's gold are alleged to be buried in the Buffalo Gap area.

In 1927 the Turgen gang buried a cache of $38,000 in gold and silver coins in a dry well at the end of a cattle trail, near some old oil derricks, about **eight miles west of Cisco (State 80), and three miles north of this same highway,** Eastland Co.

There are several treasure caches in the vicinity of **San Saba,** State 190, San Saba Co. Outlaws are known to have buried a cache of gold bullion along the banks of the San Saba River, about two miles northwest of the town. The **Lost Las Iguanas Silver Mine** is near the fork of the San Saba River and Silver Creek. Before Mexican miners sealed it off they stashed away over 2,000 fifty-pound bars of silver to keep it out of the hands of Indian attackers. In the late eighteenth century, a group of Spaniards are believed to have concealed several carloads of gold and silver bullion about three and a half miles up **Buck Creek,** which empties into the San Saba River. Near **where the Colorado River flows under State 190,** about ten miles east of San Saba City, the outlaw Jim Beasley hid several saddlebags of gold and silver coins before being caught and hanged.

There is a legend that Jim Bowie captured a Mexican wagon train carrying over twenty tons of silver bullion en route to Mexico. He buried it on the banks of the **San Saba River,** about two miles west of Menard, State 83, Menard Co. Close to Menard at a spot called **Pegleg Crossing,** which was a widely used campsite for many years, outlaws in 1883 buried about $30,000 in gold bullion from a stagecoach robbery. Near the old corral on **Jack Wilkerson's ranch** just outside of Menard, about $10,000 in gold coins were buried in 1872 by a horse thief who was caught and hanged.

During the late nineteenth century many outlaws used **Longhorn Cavern,** about ten miles southwest of Burnet (State 281), Llanos Co., as their headquarters. There is a good chance that loot has been buried near the cavern. Several miles to the east near **Sudduth,** outlaws being chased by a posse dropped a safe containing about $40,000 in gold coins into a deep well.

In 1832 fleeing Mexican priests hid a large cache of gold coins and church treasure in **Gholson's Gap** near the Lampasas River, a few miles north of Adamsville, State 281, Lampasas Co. The Comanche Indians are said to have hidden a cache worth about $3 million in gold and silver ore somewhere in the vicinity of Adamsville.

Hooker's Cave, located eleven miles south of Hillsboro on U.S. 25, Bosque Co., was used as an outlaw lair for many years. Several treasures are believed to be buried there. Nearby are the ruins of a stagecoach station where many coins and artifacts have been found by modern treasure hunters. There are many legends of a fabulous treasure being buried on the nearby **Hooker Farm** by early Spanish explorers, but to date nothing has been found.

There is a well-known legend that early Spanish conquistadors buried a fabulous fortune in the shaft of an abandoned Indian mine near the south side of the **Stillhouse Hollow Reservoir,** in the rugged hill country approximately eighteen miles southwest of Belton (State 190), Bell Co. Many persons have searched unsuccessfully for this treasure, which some believe to be worth over $20 million.

The famous **Steinheimer's Treasure** is alleged to consist of ten mule loads of gold ingots and other treasure valued at over $5 million. It is rumored to be buried at the confluence of the Leon and Lampasas Rivers where they form **the Little River,** close to U.S. 81, a few miles south of Temple in Bell Co.

A cache known as the **Santa Ana Treasure** is believed to be buried on the banks of **Shoal Creek,** a short distance from its confluence with the Colorado River, close to Austin. Another well-known legend states that Spaniards buried 75 mule loads of gold and silver ore to keep it out of the hands of attacking Indians. The ore lies near the **Colorado River** on the southeast side of Round Mountain, a few miles northwest of Austin.

There are at least twenty different places in the city of **San Antonio** where the Mexican bandit Pancho Villa is alleged to have concealed great caches of treasure. Most of these reported treasures are near old mission churches or cemeteries. The best-documented treasure in the area consists of $75,000 in gold coins which were buried on the top of a small hill, right below the Presidio Crossing of the **Nueces River,** just outside of the city.

During an Indian attack some Mexicans are supposed to have buried or hidden about 27 cartloads of gold and silver bullion in a cave in **Carrizo Pass,** near Carrizo Spring, State 83, Dimmit Co.

An outlaw cache of $12,000 in gold coins was buried on a **hill between the Coma and Tigre ranches** in the Nueces Flats, about five miles south of Olmos, U.S. 37, Live Oak Co.

The famed Rock Pens are in **the mountains on the Nueces River,** about 35 miles southwest of Tilden, County 16, McMullen Co. Attacking Indians forced a group of miners to bury 31 burro loads of gold ore here. All the miners were killed except one, who left a map that wasn't too accurate.

Gold and silver coins have been found along the northern bank of **the Rio Grande River** in the vicinity of Rio Grande City. They most likely come from the steamer **Carrie Thomas,** which sank here in 1880 while carrying over $125,000 in treasure.

There are two towns of Bagdad in Texas. One is just off the **Brownsville Channel** near the southernmost tip of the state. During the nineteenth century it was one of the main smuggler and outlaw lairs in the state. Many known caches of treasure are here. The site of this Bagdad is now covered by marshland, but the ruins of some buildings can still be seen. About $50,000 in Confederate treasure was recently discovered on nearby Long Island.

Just outside of Brownsville at **Palo Alto,** a Mexican army payroll of about $250,000 was buried after the Americans defeated the Mexicans in 1846. At nearby Resaca de la Palma numerous treasures are known to have been concealed by fleeing Mexicans.

Large numbers of old coins and artifacts are to be found along the beaches on **Brazos Island** at the mouth of Brownsville Harbor. Among the many ships lost here are the **Enterprise,** in 1846, with $20,000 in coins aboard; the **Lea,** in 1880, with $100,000 in gold and silver coins; the **Colonel Harvey,** in 1846, with $10,000 in coins; the **Globe,** in 1851, with $105,000 in gold and silver coins; the **Cincinnati,** in 1853, with $25,000 in coins; the **S. J. Lee,** in 1873, with over $100,000 in gold and silver specie; the **Ida Lewis,** in 1875, with $20,000 in coins; the **Texas Ranger,** in 1875, with over $200,000 in gold and silver specie and bullion; the French ship **Reine Des Mars,** in 1875, with over $110,000 in gold and silver coins and a large cargo of wines and liquors; and the **Clara Woodhouse,** in 1877, with over $80,000 in coins. None of these ships can be salvaged because of the swift currents and poor underwater visibility. All of their wealth will eventually wind up on this island's beaches.

Many other coins are to be found in the area of **Port Isabel** a few miles north of Brazos Island, near the southern tip of Padre Island. Among the many ships lost here, those carrying the most treasures yet unsalvaged were the **Columbia,** in 1931, with $800,000 in gold bullion; the Spanish galleon, **San Pedro,** in 1811, with $500,000 in gold and silver specie; the **Frontier,** in 1846, with $210,000 in gold and silver specie and bullion; and the **Mary Elizabeth,** in 1897, with $300,000 in gold bullion and silver coins.

Over the centuries such a large number of ships have been lost along the 100-mile length of **Padre Island** that a complete book could be written on this subject. For lack of space I am unable to cover them here. With the exception of Florida's east coast, Padre Island is the richest and most productive area in North America for finding old coins and artifacts on beaches. There isn't a mile-length of beach that doesn't have at least one old wreck lying offshore. Thanks to the winter storms from the Gulf of Mexico, most of the objects once on these ships end up on Padre's beaches.

Legend states that there is an **old Spanish city** now lost under the sands on **Padre Island,** about 25 miles north of the southern tip, almost due east of the Cameron and Willacy county lines. A large chest of gold coins is rumored to have been found in the area buried below two crossed swords sticking out of the sand. Several miles to the north two hermit brothers lived for years in a shack collecting old coins on the beaches. They accumulated a large fortune in treasure before being killed by someone trying to rob them of their loot.

During the Civil War a John A. Singer buried a fortune estimated at $80,000 in silver bars and gold and silver coins, jewelry, and silver plate. This treasure lies in a place now called **Money Hill,** six miles north of Santa Cruz on the Laguna Madre side of the island. He buried it between two oaks, but when he returned to get the cache a hurricane had blown away the trees and he couldn't find the spot.

The pirate Jean Lafitte is alleged to have buried about $1 million in treasure during the 1820s on **Sand Point** in Lavaca Bay, Calhoun Co. Other pirates also used this area as a base and may have buried caches as well. The Spaniards built **Fort Francisco** on Gracitas Creek at the head of Lavacas Bay in 1685, but it was destroyed two years later by pirates and the site is now lost. When General Santa Ana was defeated at the Battle of San Jacinto there were four Spanish settlements on this bay. The residents who quickly fled for Mexico took what they could carry, leaving behind many valuables. Soon afterward, all of their homes were destroyed by Texans.

Buried treasure belonging to pirate Jean Lafitte is alleged to be in more than 100 places on **Galveston Island** and in the surrounding countryside, but to date not a single cache has been discovered. He did make the island his headquarters for many years; both before and after the time of Lafitte other cutthroats also used Galveston.

An Enoch Brinson operated a ferry near **Morgan's Point** on San Jacinto Bay, about fifteen miles east of Houston. This man buried a large cache of treasure in a grove of trees just west of La Potre when Santa Ana marched his army through the area in 1836. Brinson was killed in a skirmish and his treasure site lost. Just north of Brinson's home General Sam Houston surprised Santa Ana's army camped on the surrounding plains. During the battle a Mexican paymaster buried over $12,000 in gold coins and couldn't find the spot after the battle.

At **Piney Point** just west of Houston a rich rancher buried $18,000 in gold during the Civil War. After the war had ended his memory failed him and he could not recall where his money was.

UTAH

The ruins of Old Cove Fort are near the junction of I-15 and State 14, near Beaver, Iron Co. It was built under the auspices of Brigham Young just after the start of the Black Hawk Indian War in 1867 to protect settlers and travelers using the Salt Lake-Pioche stage line. There are vestiges of other old buildings in the neighborhood.

The site of Camp Floyd is on State 73 about half a mile from Fairfield, Utah Co. It was built by United States Army troops in 1858 and by 1859 it had over 3,000 soldiers quartered there to suppress the Mormon insurgents and to capture the great number of outlaws in the territory. When the army pulled out in 1861, the fort was then taken over by the first Gentile community of the state. Only a few of the original buildings have survived.

The state has over 100 **abandoned railroad camps** that were used by the thousands who laid track for the Central Pacific and Union Pacific Railroads during the 1860s. Many artifacts can be found on these sites.

The ghost town of Cainesville is on the Fremont River and County 24, about twenty miles west of Hanksville, Wayne Co. It was founded as a Mormon farm colony in 1879 and abandoned because of the droughts during the 1930s. Many buildings still stand and there are several other small deserted settlements in the surrounding area.

The town of Eureka is on State 6/50 in the northeastern corner of Juab Co. At present the community has a population of about 1500 but around 1880 ten times that number lived in Eureka. There are many deserted buildings and ruins here. The whole area extending west to the Nevada line is desert. There are about a dozen other ghost towns in this area of which only five are identified by name: **Callao, Dunlap, Gandy, Gold Hill,** and **Ibopah.**

The **ghost town of Frisco** is just south of Frisco Peak and County 21, about sixteen miles west of Milford, Beaver Co. Founded in 1875 it was one of the wildest mining towns in history during the heyday of the **Horn Silver Mine.** It boasted over 10,000 residents and 26 saloons. Then in 1885, a serious mine disaster closed the town down overnight. A few buildings—including a store, a kiln, and a saloon—are still intact and there are hundreds of others in ruins.

The **ghost town of Grafton** is seven miles east of Springdale, just off County 15 on the south edge of Zion National Park, Washington Co. Mormons founded the town in 1859 about one mile down the Virgin River from its present site. But because of numerous floods and irrigation problems it was moved to its present site and by 1900 it was totally abandoned. No traces of the first site are now visible. A Hollywood movie company now owns the town and has restored a number of the standing buildings for use as a movie set.

The **ruins of Harrisburg** are near U.S. 15, about fifteen miles northeast of St. George, Washington Co. In 1861 this Mormon farm community was begun, but droughts forced it to be abandoned by 1895. The ruins of many stone buildings and fences can still be seen.

The **town of Hatton** is on U.S. 15, about three miles northwest of Kanosh. This Mormon farming town, founded in 1854, soon became an important stage station. Only a few people still live here and many old buildings are still intact.

The **ruins of Hebron** are just off County 120, about five miles west of Enterprise in the Dixie National Forest, Washington Co. It was founded in 1862 as a farming community by the Mormons and by 1910 it was completely deserted. Only cellars, foundations, and the cemetery now mark the site. About ten miles south of Enterprise is the **Mountain Meadow Massacre site,** which is a good spot for finding weapons and other relics.

The **ghost town of Knightsville** is two miles south of the **ghost town of Eureka** on State 6/50, Juab Co. It started out in 1897 as a farming community of 250 residents, but the discovery of silver caused a sudden boom. Over 1,000 residents moved in and a smelter was built. It is the only known mining town without a saloon in the West. Only a few old buildings are still standing. A small cache of coins was recently found near the foundation of the old schoolhouse.

The **ruins of La Plata** are about 60 miles northeast of Ogden near Laketown on County 30, Rich Co. This area was worked for gold and silver by Indians and Spaniards for several centuries before the white settlers arrived. When the **Sunset Silver Mine** was started in 1893 the town was begun, but when the silver was exhausted the mine and town folded up quickly. There are also other abandoned silver mines in the area.

The **ruins of Mercury,** also known as **Lewiston,** are ten miles west of Cedar City (U.S. 15), Iron Co. It was founded in 1869 after the discovery of silver, abandoned in 1880, started again in 1883 after the discovery of gold, and abandoned again by 1897. There are numerous abandoned mines in the area. The site can be reached only by four-wheel-drive vehicles or on horseback.

The **ghost town of Newhouse** is in the Wah Wah Valley, about two miles north of County 21 and 23 miles west of Milford, Beaver Co. It was a mining town for three different brief periods during the 1870s and 1890s. Today only a few buildings are standing.

The **ghost town of Paria** is on the Paria River, about 38 miles northeast of Kanab (State 89), Kane Co. The town was founded in 1868 as a Mormon farming center and also served as a gold-mining center. Floods and droughts forced it to be abandoned in the 1930s; among its many surviving buildings are an assay office and a mill.

The **ghost town of Pine Valley** is 22 miles north of St. George on County 18, Washington Co. It was once a thriving Mormon farming community. A number of buildings, including the 90-year-old church are still standing.

The **ruins of Silver City** are just off State 6/50, about four miles south of the ghost town of Eureka, Juab Co. It was founded in 1870 and flourished for only a few years as a silver-mining center. Then the mines were flooded and the 750 residents left.

The **ghost town of Silver Reef** is near County 91, about twenty miles northeast of St. George, Washington Co. It was founded in 1875 as a result of a silver boom and died in 1888 when the silver was exhausted. Several miles away the **ruins of Bonanza City** are visible. On nearby Tecumseh Hill there are over twenty abandoned silver mines and a well-preserved Wells

Fargo Office. Within a ten-mile radius of these two ghost towns are about ten others—all in ruins—which had brief lives during the silver-mining period.

The ghost town of Widtsoe is located near the junction of Sweetwater Creek and the east fork of the Sevier River, just off County 22, Piute Co. When founded as a mining town in the 1880s it was named Winder, changed in 1915 to Widstoe; during the droughts of the 1930s the town was abandoned. Today about 50 buildings are still standing.

A treasure estimated to be worth several million dollars is located somewhere in **Johnson Canyon,** in the vicinity of the Indian petroglyphs, about twenty miles northeast of Kanab between Black Rock Peak and the Paria River, Kane Co. The cache consists of a great amount of gold nuggets, dust, and bullion; silver bullion and coins; gold and silver plate; jewelry; ancient weapons; and a great variety of precious stones. All this was smuggled out of Mexico during the Revolution by a wealthy politician who was shot after he returned to the country. He left a map showing where the treasure was hidden, but it was too crude to be of much use other than giving a general location.

The Lost Spanish Gold Mine is near Margum Pass in the Confusion Mountain Range, about 50 miles west of Hinckley (State 6/50), Millard Co. From the mid-seventeenth century until around 1800 it was worked by the Spaniards, who also had a small settlement and fort in the area. About ten miles to the northeast near Swasey Peak the **Lost Margum Pass Gold Mine** is located. It was worked by Indians for many years; then the Mormons worked it briefly during the 1860s, until driven away by hostile Indians.

The following are the abandoned silver and gold mines in the state listed by county: **CACHELO CO. The La Plata Silver Mine** is about five miles northeast of Ogden. **BEAVER CO. The Horn Silver Mine** is forty-eight miles west of Milford; the **Newhouse Silver Mine** is a few miles west of Milford. **JUAB CO. The Diamond City Silver Mine** is close to Eureka; the **Emma Silver Mine** is in Little Cottonwood Canyon in the Wasatch Mountains, twenty-eight miles west of Salt Lake City; the **Eureka Silver Mine** is on the east slope of Wasatch Mountain, thirty-two miles west of Salt Lake City; the **Knightsville Silver Mine** is close to Eureka; the **Ontario Silver Mine** is on the east side of the Wasatch Mountains, thirty-two miles west of Salt Lake City; the **Silver City Silver Mine** is near Eureka; and the **Sunbeam Gold Lode Mine** is a few miles southwest of Eureka. **SALT LAKE CO. The Alta Silver Mine** is just outside of Salt Lake City. **TOOELE CO. The Sparrow Hawk Gold Mine** is in Manning Canyon of the Opuirrh Mountains, twenty-eight miles north of American Fork; the **Last Chance Gold Mine** is in the same area; the **Marion Gold Mine** is also in the same area; the **Mercury Silver Mine** is also in the same area but about three miles north on the American Fork River.

Chimney Rock Pass, on the west side of Lake Utah in Tooele Co. was an important camping ground for westward-bound settlers and miners during the 1800s. Many parties were attacked by Indians in this area and a number of small caches of personal treasures are believed to be hidden here.

In the general vicinity of a spot marked "well" on modern maps of the state in the **Dunway Mountain Range** about eight miles southeast of Granite Peak on the southeastern edge of the Salt Lake Desert, Tooele County, a group of starving California miners buried about $70,000 in gold coins and small ingots in 1854 and after obtaining supplies and returning to the area they were unable to relocate the spot.

Near Silver Island Mountain and Wendover just a bit north of the Bonneville Salt flats in the northwest corner of Tooele County a cache known as the **Donner Party Treasure** is rumored to be hidden.

About four miles northeast of Knolls, U.S. 80 in the **Great Salt Lake Desert,** Tooele Co., a Mormon treasure believed to be valued at $500,000 was buried in an abandoned well during an Indian attack.

The outlaw Eugene Wright is said to have buried a large amount of silver bullion from an 1882 train robbery near the town of **Mantua** on the western side of Cache National Forest, State 89, Cache Co. Four miles to the north of the Bear River bandits are supposed to have buried about $100,000 in cash and $35,000 in jewelry in 1921. In this same area other outlaws robbed $62,000 in gold coins from the Corrine Stage and buried it before being caught and hanged.

This abandoned house in the beautiful red rock high desert country of southern Utah presents many potential hiding places for treasure.

Well rewarded by their day spent treasure hunting with a metal detector, these two enthusiasts are ready to plan more adventures for tomorrow.

On the Bear River near Collinton, bandits are reported to have buried over $150,000 in silver and gold. Flood water erased their markers and they were unable to find the cache. About five miles to the east in Logan, State 89, other bandits in 1889 buried $78,000 in silver coins under one of the town's many stores.

Just north of Salt Lake City, where the Strevelle Train crosses State 89, outlaws are alleged to have buried about $90,000 in silver bullion.

The Lost Truelove Manhart Gold Ledge with gold assaying at $50,000 a ton is located in the vicinity of Park City, State 189, Summit Co.

A rich gold lode alleged to have been discovered by Brigham Young is in **Ferguson Canyon** in the Wasatch Mountains, just east of Heber City, State 189, Wasatch Co.

The ghost town of Iosepa is along an unmarked dirt road fifteen miles south of U.S. 80 and seventeen miles southeast of Grantsville (County 138), Tooele Co. About 40 buildings are still standing and several small caches of treasure have been located in recent years.

The Lost Crossland Gold Mine is located within a five-mile radius of Tooele, County 112, Tooele Co.

Outlaw loot totaling over $125,000 is said to be buried on Silver Island Mountain in the Cedar Range, about 40 miles southwest of Tooele City. About 24 miles southwest of Tooele City the ruins of the **ghost town of Ajax** are located. It was a silver-mining town for only a few years in the 1860s.

The ghost town of Mercury Springs is two miles south of Indian Peak in the Needle Range, in the southwest corner of Beaver Co., and can be reached only by horseback. About ten buildings, including a saloon, are still standing.

Another rich **lost gold mine** rumored to have been found by Brigham Young is on the west side of the Oquirrh Mountain Range, a few miles southwest of Salt Lake City.

A **lost silver mine** is located in the foothills of the House Mountains between the Sevier River and Trout Creek, about eight miles west of Kinckley (State 5/50), Millard Co. It was found and worked during the Depression by several miners who made a fortune and then moved back East.

There are ruins of six ghost towns in the area surrounding Eureka, State 6/50, Juab Co.: **Mosida,** on the west side of Eureka city limits; **Knightsville,** two miles south of Eureka; **Silver City,** four miles south of Eureka; **Diamond City,** about six miles southeast of Eureka; **Homansville,** one mile east of Eureka; **Dividend,** six miles east of Eureka.

The Lost Nephite Gold Mine is about five miles east of Spanish Forks (State 89), Unitah Co.

The ghost town of Connellsville is the Manti-La Sal National Forest, about twelve miles east of Fairview (State 89), Sanpete Co. It can be reached only by horseback. A small number of buildings are still intact.

The famous outlaw Butch Cassidy is believed to have buried a portion of the loot from his Castle Gate robbery in 1897 somewhere in **Horseshoe Canyon,** a few miles north of Price (State 6/50), Carbon Co.

The Lost Temple Gold Mine is in the vicinity of Gilbert Peak in the Unitah National Forest in Duchesne Co. Indian legends tell of a cave piled full of gold ore in this same general area. **The Lost Mine of the Lost Souls,** a very rich gold mine worked by the Spaniards in the 1700s, is in a remote canyon near the confluence of three streams in this same general area. A nearby cave containing a large number of skeletons and piles of silver bars was reportedly found around 1910 by a prospector, who could not locate the site when he returned with pack mules.

The Lost Ewing Gold Mine is located near Brown's Hole between Manila (County 43) and Horseshoe Canyon, Daggett Co. In this same canyon the Wild Bunch outlaw gang are known to have hidden $30,000 in gold coins and a wagonload of gold ore.

Four different treasures are alleged to be hidden in or around the town of **Vernal,** State 40, Unitah Co. A wealthy businessman who died in 1923 is known to have hidden his life's accumulated fortune somewhere on the Double "T" Ranch just west of town. The Black Jack Ketchum gang used the area as a base for several years and cached away at least three different hoards.

At the confluence of the Green and Willow Rivers, about 28 miles southeast of **Fort Duchesne** (State 40) Unitah Co., a band of Indians being pursued by the Cavalry are known to have hidden a great wealth of gold bullion before being killed by the soldiers. In this same general area are numerous abandoned mining camps and gold mines.

The ghost town of McCormack is in the Fishlake National Forest about 22 miles north of Fillmore (U.S. 15), Millard Co. Only a church and schoolhouse are still intact.

Outlaw loot totaling about $60,000 in gold and silver coins and jewelry is buried somewhere in the town of **Castle Dale,** County 10, Emery Co. About ten miles southeast of this town in Buckhorn Wash in the Coal Cliffs, Butch Cassidy and his gang buried $72,000 in gold and silver coins.

The famous Golden Plates of the Mormon Church are believed to be buried about three miles east of **Fillmore** (U.S. 15), Millard Co.

The Lost Silver Ledge of Santa Clara is near where the old Spanish road crossed the Santa Clara River, about ten miles southwest of St. George (U.S. 15), Washington Co. Mormon leaders are reported to have hidden substantial treasure in St. George during the Mormon War of 1857. Brigham Young himself is supposed to have buried over $3 million in treasure in this town. Three different Mormon caches were discovered in 1963 and 1964. The **Lost Dixie Silver Mine** is located between the towns of Santa Clara and St. George.

During the Mormon War of 1857 John D. Lee and other Mormon leaders are known to have hidden large amounts of money in **Cedar City,** including a cache of over 400 pounds of gold ingots. Cedar City is on U.S. 15, in Iron Co. Between this town and St. George in the vicinity of Navajo Lake several **lost gold mines** are located.

One of the most famous, but probably nonexistent hoards in the state is the **Montezuma Hoard,** reputed to be worth between $10 and $100 million in various types of treasure. Aztecs removed it from Mexico to keep it from Cortez and his conquistadors. It is reported to be somewhere in a maze of honeycombed passages on White Mountain near Kanab, State 89, Kane Co. Thousands have searched for this treasure unsuccessfully.

A large golden image that caused a war between the Navajo and Hopi Indians, is known to be hidden somewhere on **Canaan Mountain,** about fourteen miles northeast of Cannonville (County 12), Garfield Co.

The Treasure of the Golden Jesus, said to consist of a huge solid gold crucifix and 40 burro loads of other treasure, was supposedly hidden in 1810 in a cave **between Escalante and Boulder,** close to the Escalante River and near County 12, Garfield Co.

The Lost Josephine Gold Mine with ore assaying at $50,000 a ton is located in the vicinity of other abandoned gold mines in the Henry Mountains, near Waterpocket Canyon in Garfield Co. The **Lost Wolverton Gold Mine** is also in this same general area.

Near the confluence of the Colorado and Dolares River a band of returning California miners were attacked by Indians in 1856. Before being killed they are believed to have buried their gold. About ten miles up the Colorado River from this spot, just east of Cisco (County 128), Grand Co., a barge overturned in 1876 and several chests of silver coins for a nearby army garrison were lost in the river.

The Jack Wright Lost Gold Mine is on the Colorado River in Spanish Valley, just southwest of Moab (State 163), Grand Co.

The Lost John Howard Gold Mine is in the vicinity of Abajo Peak in the Manti-La Sal Forest, eight miles southwest of Monticello (State 163), San Juan Co. **The Lost Pot Hole Gold Mine** is in this same area.

During the Mexican Revolution a hoard of about $5 million in booty is supposed to have been buried by insurgent soldiers in the vicinity of **Moonlight Creek,** near Navajo Twin Rock, about two miles north of Bluff, State 163, San Juan Co.

The Lost Sam Brooks Gold Lode is near the Valley of the Gods in the Comb Range, about fifteen miles northwest of Bluff in San Juan Co.

Indians are alleged to have buried a great deal of gold ore on **Bears Ears Peak** in the Elk Ridge, about 22 miles west of Blanding (County 163), San Juan Co.

The Allen Farm site is on Lake Champlain, near Burlington, Chittenden Co. During the Revolutionary War a number of skirmishes took place on this site which also served as an encampment for both sides. There are ruins of many colonial buildings on and near this property.

Bennington, first settled in 1761, was an important Revolutionary War supply base for the Patriots, who also had several campsites around the outskirts of the present village. A major battle was fought nearby and won by the Patriots on August 16, 1777.

Button Mold Bay is on Lake Champlain, Addison Co. In this tiny, unspoiled cove Benedict Arnold ran his ship **Congress** and four smaller Patriot vessels aground and burnt them on October 13, 1776, after his defeat in the Battle of Valcour Bay. After storms remains of these ships are exposed on the beach.

Chimney Point is on Lake Champlain, near Vt. 17, Addison Co. It was settled by the French in 1690. A small fort was built, then rebuilt and enlarged in 1730. The French abandoned the settlement in 1759 and the following year the Mohawk Indians burned it to the ground. The place is so named because only the chimneys of these homes are still visible. During the French and Indian Wars the Patriots built a wooden fort here but no traces remain today.

The site of Fort Drummer was located on the Connecticut River just south of Brattleboro, Windham Co. The first English settlement was established here in 1724 when the fort was built, but the place was abandoned in 1763. Today the site is under the waters of the river as a result of the Vernon Dam being built.

Hubbardtown Battlefield is near Hubbardtown, eighteen miles northwest of Rutland, Rutland Co. About 1,000 patriots were ambushed and badly beaten here on July 7, 1777 and the dead from both sides were buried in two separate mass graves.

Isle La Motte is located in the northern part of Lake Champlain, Grand Isle Co. The French settled here in 1665 and constructed Fort St. Anne, but after several years abandoned it. No traces remain today.

Mount Independence is off State 22A, three miles northwest of Orwell, Addison Co. Located directly opposite **Fort Ticonderga** on the Vermont side of Lake Champlain, this wooden bluff was the site of a heavily fortified position during the Revolutionary War. Retreating Patriot forces buried a great deal of equipment, supplies, and weapons in this area.

In 1864 Confederate raiders robbed three banks in St. Albans for a total of $114,522 in gold coins and paper currency. The robbers are known to have buried the loot in the vicinity of **Highgate Springs,** just off U.S. 89, near Lake Champlain in the northwestern corner of the state, Franklin Co. They were caught soon after burying the money, but refused to reveal the exact location before being hanged.

In 1773 while under Indian attack, some British officers buried about $75,000 in gold coins near **Cedar Beach** off State 7, Chittenden Co. Only two soldiers survived the battle and they were unable to locate the cache.

In the early 1800s, a rich tradesman named Levi Bailey had a mill **on a stream between Mount Ascutney and Reading** (County 106), Windsor Co. On his deathbed he admitted burying a large cache of treasure in the vicinity of his mill, but it has never been found.

The Lost Birch Hill Silver Mine is located between Sherbourne Pass and Pico Peak, about fifteen miles northeast of Rutland (State 7), Rutland Co.

During the Revolution a treasure now known as the **Hell's Half Acre Treasure,** consisting of £75,000 sterling in British gold and silver coins, was buried on the southern shores of Lake Mephremagog near Newport (State 5), Orleans Co., by British officers fleeing from Patriots.

The Lost Slayton Gold Mine is somewhere on Mount Mansfield in the Green Mountains in the southwest corner of Lamoille Co. About ten miles to the east at Smugglers Notch several hoards of treasure are believed to be buried.

A cache called the **St. Francis Treasure** consisting of about $40,000 in church plate and gold and silver coins is reported to be hidden along the west bank of the Connecticut River near Bloomfield, County 105, Essex Co.

During the Revolution numerous caches of treasure were hidden and lost in **Burlington** on the eastern shore of Lake Champlain. Several small caches were found in the 1940s and 1950s, but these are believed to have belonged to a rich steamboat magnate, who hid many caches all over the city during the 1930s.

During the French and Indian Wars a band of Indians being pursued by white settlers from Rutland are known to have hidden several cartloads of booty on **Sable Mountain** in the Delectable Mountain Range, about ten miles north of Sherbourne Pass in Windsor Co.

A large cache of pirate treasure is rumored to be buried in or near **Money Cave** in the Green Mountains, just east of South Wallingsford, State 7, Rutland Co.

Near the Bennington Battle Monument just west of Bennington, State 7, Bennington Co., Patriot raiders, who robbed about $90,000 in gold and silver coins from a British supply train during the Revolution, buried it near this site before being caught and shot.

On Harmon Hill about five miles southeast of Bennington, the British buried several kegs of silver coins after being defeated at the Battle of Sarasota.

On the site of Fort Dummer on the Connecticut River, about three miles southeast of Brattleboro (State 5), Windham Co., treasure hunters in recent years have found five small caches of Revolutionary War period gold and silver coins.

VIRGINIA

The town of Albemarle was situated on a sharp bend of the James River near present Scottsville, Albemarle Co. It was founded some time before 1700 and no traces of it survive today.

Alexandria located on the Potomac River, seven miles south of Washington, D.C. was settled around 1670 and soon became an important seaport. Many of its colonial buildings have survived. Relics can be found on the muddy banks of the former port area, also on empty lots around the old section of the present town. During the Civil War it was one of the main Federal military bases. **Fort Ward,** built in 1861, is located in Fort Ward Park.

Belhaven was located near the mouth of Great Hunting Creek on the Potomac in the vicinity of Mount Vernon. The settlement began in 1657 and was abandoned around 1700. No traces exist today.

Belvoir Plantation. The ruins of the mansion and other colonial buildings are located on the Fort Belvoir Military Reservation, nine miles south of Alexandria, near U.S. 1 and Mount Vernon. The place was built in 1741, destroyed by fire in 1783, and then totally demolished by the British in 1814.

Berkeley Plantation is on the James River just off Va. 5, seven miles west of Charles City in Charles City Co. It was first settled in 1619, abandoned after an Indian massacre in 1622, resettled in 1636, and the plantation houses were built soon after. In 1862 the plantation served as General McClellan's headquarters. The main mansion has been restored and there are ruins of many colonial buildings on the property.

Boswell's Tavern is located on the South Anna River in Boswell Village, Louisa Co. This building which was constructed in the 1750s still stands today. Several Civil War skirmishes occurred here and a treasure was supposedly buried somewhere on the property during the Revolution.

Carter's Grove Plantation on U.S. 60, about six miles southeast of Williamsburg, was built early in the colonial period and has been restored today. During the Civil War several different treasures are supposed to have been buried on the property.

Castle Hill is located near the village of Cobham on Va. 231, Albemarle Co. This mansion built in 1764 has recently been restored. Near the house a skirmish took place on June 3, 1781.

Chiswell Lead Mines on the banks of the New River, are located near the intersection of U.S. 52 and County Road 619, near Austinville, Wythe Co. When the mine was discovered in 1756, a number of settlements sprang up nearby, none of which exist today. During the Revolution many forges and furnaces were built. The place was attacked at least six times by Tories and the British, as it was one of the main sources of lead shot for the Patriots' firearms. Vestiges of the mines and settlements can be found today.

The site of Fort Chiswell is located six miles north of the lead mines, near the intersection of U.S. 52 and County Road 619. This wooden fort was built about 1820 and abandoned long before the Civil War. The ruins can still be seen.

Corotoman Plantation stood on the Rappahannock River near the present village of Kilmarnock, Middlesex Co. It was settled in 1650 and was one of the largest and richest plantations in the state, but today its exact location is lost.

Colonial Heights on the Appomattox River, near U.S. 1 and 301, opposite Petersburg, was first established in 1665. Both sides had campments here during the Revolutionary War and several skirmishes took place in 1781. There are remains of a number of colonial buildings; nearby at Violet Bank are the ruins of a large mansion built in 1770 and burned in 1810.

Elk Hill on the James River is close to the small village of Georges Tavern, near Va. 6 and County Road 608, Albemarle Co. An estate owned by Thompson Jefferson stood here. It was occupied by Cornwallis in June 1781 and destroyed by his men. Rebuilt some time afterwards, it was sacked and destroyed in 1865, but the ruins still exist.

Another Fort Chiswell is located in the present town of Fort Chiswell on I-81, Wythe County. A pyramid of boulders is all that remains of this fort built in 1760 and destroyed during the Revolutionary War.

Fredericksburg, settled in 1671, was an important trading center and tidewater port in colonial days. Today a number of colonial buildings have survived and there are ruins of many others, especially many destroyed during the Civil War.

Great Bridge, on the Intracoastal Canal in Chesapeake, Norfolk Co., was the scene of the first major battle between British troops and Patriots after Bunker Hill. This encounter, which took place here on December 9, 1775, was won by the Patriots.

Green Springs Battlefield, located near the junction of State 5 and County Road 614, between Jamestown and Williamsburg, was the scene of a major battle in October 1781 with heavy losses on both sides.

Gwynn Island is in the Chesapeake Bay, Mathews Co. This place was settled some time around 1650. There are remains of more than 50 colonial buildings on this 2,000-acre island. During the Civil War the Confederates had a small fort on the east side of the island, but it was demolished after the war.

Hite's Fort is located on U.S. 11, about two miles north of Stephen's City, Frederick Co. The broken stone walls of this fort built in 1734, and of other Colonial buildings, can be seen here.

Jamestown, on the James River near Williamsburg, was founded in 1607, served as the capital of the state until 1698, and soon after fell into decline and was abandoned. Great restoration work has gone on in recent years. A portion of the settlement has been covered by the river.

Mechuck Creek near U.S. 250, six miles east of Shadwell, Albemarle Co., was the encampment for the American army under General Lafayette. His men dug trenches here in June 1781, but fought no battles.

Norfolk was laid out as a city in 1682. The residents burned it down in 1776 to keep it from falling into the hands of the British. It was rebuilt and heavily damaged during the Civil War. Few traces of the colonial period remain today.

Petersburg Fort was built in 1645 at the Falls of the Appomattox River but no traces of it have survived. Nearby a trading post was established in 1733 and the town of Petersburg founded on the site in 1784. During the Revolution a number of battles were fought in and near the town causing heavy damages. The same thing happened when several important Civil War battles were fought here between June 1864 and April 1865. Many earthworks and trenches can still be seen.

Point of Fork on James River is on Va. 6, about a mile west of Columbia, Fluvanna Co. This site was an important military base and supply depot for the Patriots, but was leveled by Tory raiders in 1781, and "thousands of weapons were lost in the fire."

The site of Fort Nelson is located on the grounds of the United States Naval Hospital in Portsmouth. This fort was built in 1745 and destroyed by the British in May 1779. In July 1781 the site was used as a major camp for British troops. Nothing is left of it today.

Richmond was first settled in 1609 but abandoned two years later because of hostile Indians.

350

A trading post was established in 1637 and a **Fort Charles** built in 1645, but the actual town was not founded until 1733; it grew rapidly. The city was plundered and destroyed by the British under Benedict Arnold in 1781, but rebuilt soon after. During the Civil War it served as the Confederate capital and in 1865 it was evacuated and burned down by its own people to keep it out of the hands of the Union army. Very few historical landmarks exist today.

Shadwell Plantation on U.S. 250 is about three miles east of Charlottesville, Albemarle Co. It was built around 1737 and was the birthplace of Thomas Jefferson in 1743. The first great mansion was destroyed by fire in 1770 and another larger one was built soon after. This fell into ruin and its exact location was unknown, until it was accidentally discovered in 1955.

Shirley Plantation, on the James River off Va. 5, about 25 miles southeast of Richmond, was first started in 1660. There are vestiges of numerous colonial buildings scattered all over this 800-acre property.

Suffolk is on the Nansemond River, Nansemond Co. First settled in 1618, Suffolk became a thriving town until it was totally destroyed by British raiders on May 13, 1779. Cornwallis's army camped here for a week in July 1781. Very few traces of the colonial period are left in this small village but a large number of ruins are scattered about nearby.

Westover is on the James River, seven miles west of Charles City, Charles City Co. It was established in 1619, but the place was destroyed and the settlers massacred by Indians in 1622. A large plantation was begun here in about 1690. During the Revolution and Civil Wars, the land was used as a campsite. No traces of the early settlement have been found.

Williamsburg. Colonial Williamsburg is an amazing restoration project that contains more than 80 original seventeenth- and eighteenth-century structures, along with several hundred others that have been reconstructed. There are ruins of other colonial buildings in the surrounding countryside.

Winchester in Frederick Co. was an important communications hub from prehistoric times, as indicated by the great number of prehistoric artifacts found in caves and under the soil. The town was founded in 1744 and **Fort Loudoun** was built in 1755; both have disappeared. A number of major battles were fought here during both Revolutionary and Civil Wars. There are many ruins in the surrounding hills.

Yorktown is on U.S. 17, about thirteen miles east of Williamsburg. Here in 1781, Washington and Rochambeau laid siege to the British under Cornwallis which resulted in the Patriots winning the war. The town had been settled in 1631, but most of the colonial houses were destroyed during this famous battle and later, during the Civil War in 1862, when McClellan's Union troops attacked.

Appomattox National Historic Park is on State 24, three miles northeast of Appomattox, Appomattox Co. The Civil War ended here on April 9, 1865 with General Lee's surrender of the Army of Northern Virginia to General Grant. Before laying down their arms, many of the Confederate soldiers buried their weapons and other personal possessions to keep them out of the hands of the Yankees.

The Fredericksburg and Spotsylvania National Park is located off U.S. 95 west of Fredericksburg. This sprawling park includes sections of four major Civil War battlefields. In the Battle of Fredericksburg, fought on December 11–13, 1862, Union forces were unable to dislodge the Confederates from their entrenchments to the west and south of the town. The Battle of Chancellorsville in May 1863 also ended in failure for the attacking Federals, who suffered heavy losses. The Union Army met with the same lack of success during the Battles of the Wilderness and Spotsylvania Courthouse, fought in May 1864. Many relics of these battles can be seen throughout the 3,672-acre park, but remember that sections of all four battlefields are outside of the park area and thus open for treasure hunters to search.

Fort Monroe in Hampton off U.S. 64, York Co. faces Norfolk across Hampton Roads. It was built between 1819 and 1834 on the site of a fort constructed in 1609 by the Jamestown settlers to repel any Spanish attack. During the Civil War Fort Monroe played a major role as the nearest Federal base to the Confederate capitol of Richmond. This well-preserved fort has been made into a museum.

Manassas Battlefield Park is on State 234, 26 miles southwest of Washington, D.C., Prince

William Co. The Confederates won two important victories here—the first on July 21, 1861 and the second on August 28-30, 1862, which was the key to Lee's invasion of the North. Many remnants of these battles can be seen today.

Cedar Creek Battlefield is on I-81 between Strasburg and Middletown, Frederick Co. The Confederates won a victory here on October 19, 1864 by surprising the sleeping Union troops. A great deal of war material was flung into the creek by the fleeing Union troops.

New Market Battlefield on State 305, about two miles north of New Market, Shenandoah Co. The Confederates led by General John C. Breckinridge won a victory here on May 15, 1864; many relics of the encounter are still visible.

Five Forks Battlefield is on County 627, twelve miles west of Petersburg. The Federal troops won a decisive battle here on April 1, 1865, cutting off Lee's last supply line in his defense of Richmond and Petersburg.

The Richmond National Battlefield Park contains sections of the land that saw eight different Union drives to capture the city between 1862 and 1865. Hundreds of earthworks, trenches, and gun batteries can still be seen.

At **Cape Henry,** reached via U.S. 60 through the Fort Story Military Base, north of Virginia Beach, the colonists who founded Jamestown in 1607 first landed and camped here for four days before starting up the James River. Their campsite has not yet been discovered.

During a hurricane in October 1785 more than 50 ships were lost in the Hampton Roads area between Norfolk and Newport News. At Portsmouth several large ships loaded with general cargoes and some treasure were lifted up by the high seas and thrown into the woods behind this port. Hundreds of houses were totally destroyed and many priceless treasures lost with them. The ruins of some can still be found in the **Benns Church and Carrollton areas** to the west of Portsmouth.

During the Civil War a wealthy plantation owner named Abraham Smith buried about $60,000 in gold coins and other valuables in **an abandoned old saltpeter mine in the Poor Valley,** between Allison's Gap and Saltville (County 91), Smyth Co.

Also during the Civil War fleeing Confederate troops in 1864 secreted sixteen wagonloads of weapons **in a cave in the Jefferson National Forest** about two to three miles east of Tannersville (County 16), Tazewell Co.

On Mount Rogers, the highest peak in the state, Indians worked several gold mines before the arrival of the white men. A Confederate major is known to have hidden about $350,000 in treasure taken by his raiders in Pennsylvania and Maryland during the early days of the Civil War.

In 1948 a local historian published a report stating that during the Civil War, the residents of **Roanoke,** U.S. 81, Roanoke Co., are known to have secreted over $1 million in many small caches, which they were unable to recover after the war for various reasons. In 1974 a treasure hunter discovered a cache of silver plate and coins worth about $20,000 in a park right in the center of the city.

During the last days of the Civil War a Confederate general and some slaves concealed more than $4 million in gold coins and bullion **on the McIntosh Farm** a mile south of Forest, County 811, and a few miles west of Lynchburg. One version states that the gold was thrown into a deep well; in another it was buried near a barn and the slaves were shot to keep the site a secret.

The famous **Beale Treasure,** said to consist of iron chests containing 2,921 pounds of gold, 5,088 pounds of silver, and $13,000 in gems and jewelry, is supposed to be hidden in the Blue Ridge Mountains near the village of Montvale, about four miles north of the ruins of the old Buford Tavern (built in 1820), Bedford Co., about twelve miles northeast of Roanoke.

Near the end of the Civil War with the Union troops closing in on the area, the residents of **Lynchburg** buried almost everything of value. Because many buildings were burned and people were killed in the conflict, at least $2 million in treasure is believed to be hidden yet, in and around the town. Several small caches have been found along the banks of the James River in recent years.

During the late eighteenth century, a large treasure of unknown contents and value was hidden somewhere on **Peaked Mountain** in the Massanutten Range near McGaheysville (State 11), Rockingham Co., by German and Swiss settlers under attack by Indians. The few who survived could not find the hidden cache.

Legends tell about Indians having buried large amounts of raw gold and plunder from raids made on white settlements in and around **Shenandoah Caverns,** about five miles north of New Market, State 11, Shenandoah Co. At the opposite end of the Shenandoah Valley is **Powell's Fort,** a natural rock fortress in the Fort Mountains near Waterlick. A trader named Edwin Powell buried a large cache of treasure near this spot under a large rock with a horseshoe carved on it.

There are a number of **lost Indian silver mines** in the vicinity of Passage Creek Gap, near Strasburg, U.S. 81, Shenandoah Co.

During the Revolution a British supply train was ambushed near Winchester, and the Patriot raiders, who were being chased by a larger body of troops, threw three chests of silver coins into a stream near Round Hill, about five miles north of **Winchester** in Frederick Co.

A cache known as the **Bureau of Engraving Treasure,** consisting of $31,700 in freshly made paper currency and a set of twenty-dollar-bill printing plates in a leather pouch, were hidden along a creek bed just north of Warrenton, State 211, Fauquier Co., in 1911.

In the late eighteenth century pirate William Kirk is alleged to have buried about $50,000 in silver coins somewhere on the 386-acre **Snow Hill Farm,** about a mile south of Bristow, County 619, William Co.

Confederate guerrilla Captain John Mosbey is known to have buried a cache between two large pine trees **between Culpeper and Norman,** close to County 522, Culpeper Co. The treasure, valued at several millions, consists of tons of gold and silver objects of many kinds from coins to church plate, and even a large number of weapons.

Because of the great amount of destruction that took place in **Richmond** during the Civil War and the countless personal fortunes hidden there, the city is the most productive treasure-hunting area in Virginia. Numerous caches of treasure and Civil War weapons and artifacts are found every year. Just before the Union soldiers entered the city, the Confederate treasury was emptied and various sums were hidden all over the city. One treasure consisting of $3 million in gold bullion was buried along the banks of the James River about two miles south of the city.

Petersburg and the surrounding area is also a choice treasure-hunting spot. Several large caches of Civil War valuables have been buried along the Appomattox River near the city.

Local legend has it that during the Civil War the British Government loaned the South $10 million in gold coins and bullion. The money was buried along the banks of the **James River** near the Berkeley Plantation, just east of Hopewell (County 10), Prince George Co.

Over the centuries large numbers of ships have been wrecked at and near **Cape Charles,** the northern tip of land at the mouth of the Chesapeake Bay. Many coins and artifacts have been found along the beaches in this area. Two other excellent treasure-hunting areas are Ship Shoal Island and Wreck Island, located a bit northeast of Cape Charles. Large numbers of gold and silver coins are found on the beaches of both islands after winter storms. Some people live on Wreck Island most of the year supporting themselves just by working these beaches for treasure and artifacts.

Pirates worked out of **Hog Island Bay,** about twenty miles north of Cape Charles. Several caches of treasure are believed buried in this area.

During the colonial period more than 75 ships were wrecked on the coast in the vicinity of **Cape Henry** located between Norfolk and Virginia Beach. Many relics and coins are found in this area. During a hurricane in 1708 a fleet of 24 British merchant ships were cast ashore here. One of them had over 300,000 pieces of eight aboard, which was never recovered. In 1770 the British merchantman **Gorel,** with over £100,000 sterling in gold coins, was also wrecked at this cape.

Hog Island, located about 25 miles northeast of Cape Charles, has also claimed a large share of ships over the years. In 1741 the English merchantman **Sea Nymph** went to pieces on this island with over £75,000 sterling in Spanish silver and gold coins aboard. The British ship

Swan with over $75,000 in gold and silver coins met the same fate in 1791. The merchantman **Inclination** carrying eighteen chests of gold and silver specie of unknown value also was cast ashore here in 1798.

WASHINGTON

Chinook Point Landmark is on U.S. 101, about four miles southeast of Chinook in the Fort Columbia Historical State Park, Pacific County. A small settlement of trappers once stood on this site soon after the Columbia River was discovered in 1792 but virtually nothing is known about it after its original founding. **Fort Columbia** still stands and it was one of three forts built here during the Spanish-American War. Nothing remains of the other two forts.

Horsethief Lake State Park is on Highway 14, six miles east of Lyle, Klickitat County. The park is one of the richest archaeological sites in the nation along the Long Narrows of the Columbia River. It was a spot where during the summer months Indians from many different tribes traveled long distances to come and trade. A great wealth of artifacts have been recently found in a number of excavated mounds and middens.

Fort Flagler is on the north end of Marrowstone Island, opposite Port Townsend, Kitsap County. This fort was founded along with Forts Worden and Casey in the 1890s to protect the approaches to Seattle and Tacoma and it continued in use until the end of World War I. Treasure hunters report that it is a choice bottle hunting area.

Steptoe Battlefield is on U.S. 195 a bit south of Rosalia, Whitman Co. On May 17, 1858 the American Army suffered a dreadful defeat here at the hands of the Indians and many of the soldiers who sought refuge in the nearby hills were hunted down and killed. There are also ruins of several mining camps in the area.

San Juan National Historical Park is 75 miles north of Seattle and can be reached by car ferry. British and American fur trappers both settled on the island early in the nineteenth century and between 1859 and 1872 the sovereignty of the island was disputed and a number of battles were fought. Remains of homes as well as British and American fortifications can be seen on the island.

The Pioneer Square District is near First Avenue at James Street in downtown Seattle. The first settlers founded a village across Elliott Bay at Alki Point in 1851, of which no traces remain, and the following year they relocated at this site. In 1889 a fire burned down this settlement, as well as all of the waterfront, and present Seattle was built over the site.

The site of Spokane House is in Riverside State Park, nine miles northwest of Spokane. When a trading post was established here in 1810 by the North West Company, Spokane House became the first permanent white settlement in the state. It was soon the most important trading center west of the Rockies, but Indian hostilities forced the residents to abandon it in 1826. Nothing now survives.

Fort Nitqually is located in Point Defence Park in Tacoma. A Hudson Bay Company trading post was erected on the site in 1833 and became the first permanent white settlement on Puget Sound. The fort was built in 1843 and occupied by the British until 1869, when it was abandoned and fell into ruin. A number of the buildings have been restored.

Cowlitz Mission is two and a half miles east of I-5 on old U.S. 99 near Toledo, Lewis Co. The mission was established by two Catholic priests in 1838 as a refuge for newly arrived settlers. Most of the original buildings have survived.

The ruins of Fort Vancouver are located on State 500 several miles east of Vancouver, Clark Co. Established in 1824, it served for two decades as the headquarters of the British Hudson Bay Company. At the height of its prosperity in 1845 the fort contained 22 major buildings and many smaller ones. After 1846, when the area became a part of the American territory, it quickly declined and soon fell into ruins. Vestiges of the original stockade and many of the buildings can still be seen.

The site of the Whitman Mission is on U.S. 410, seven miles west of Walla Walla, Walla Walla Co. Protestant missionaries built this mission in 1836 to convert the Cayuse Indians. It remained in operation until 1847, when an epidemic of measles killed most of the Indian tribe. In retaliation, the Indians killed the missionaries and white settlers who brought this disease and then completely destroyed the mission buildings.

The ruins of Fort Simcoe are at the western end of State 220, 38 miles southwest of Yakima, Yakima Co. The fort was built in 1855 by the United States Army after a flareup in Indian hostilities and garrisoned for four years until peace was restored in the area. Five of the original buildings have been restored.

The ruins of Asotin are on the Snake River and County 129, about six miles south of Clarkston, Asotin Co. It was a mining town that failed after a few years. The most prominent feature is the ruins of a flour mill.

The ghost town of Attalia is on the Columbia River and State 395 close to Fort Walla Walla and Wallula, Wall Co. In this former railroad town only a few buildings are intact.

The ghost town of Blewett is just north of Blewett Pass on State 97, about nine miles southwest of Cashmere, Chelan Co. It was once a booming gold mining town in the Wenatchee Mountains; now only a few cabins are left.

The ghost town of Brady is on the Satsop River opposite the town of Satsop, about fourteen miles east of Aberdeen (State 101), Harbor Co. In the late nineteenth century Brandy was a center for gold miners; today just a few of its buildings remain.

The ghost town of Burnett is three miles south of Buckley on State 5, King Co. It was abandoned when the coal mines closed after World War II. Many buildings are still intact.

The ruins of Cashup are four miles north of Steptoe near State 195, Whitman Co. This important trading post was burned to the ground in 1879.

The town of Colbert is on State 194, about thirteen miles north of Spokane, Spokane Co. Remains of five sawmills, three saloons, five stores, three livery barns, two blacksmith shops, two brothels, and many homes are still there, but the town has only a few inhabitants.

The ruins of Collins are on the Union Flat River just north of Uniontown (State 195), Whitman Co. This small community catered to the stage and freight lines in the early days of the state.

The ghost town of Conconully is on the Salmon River near Granite Mountain about seventeen miles northwest of Okanogan (State 97), Okanogan Co. It was the county seat until it burned down in 1892. The residents rebuilt it the next year, but abandoned in 1915. Many mining and logging buildings are still standing.

The ruins of Dalkena are located on County 6 about eleven miles northwest of Newport, Pend Oreille Co. Daltena was founded in 1902 as a lumber town; it burned down in 1935.

The ruins of Dodge are located at the junction of State 12 and County 127, about 45 miles west of Clarkston, Garfield Co. This stage station and mining town was destroyed in an earthquake.

The ruins of Eagle Cliff are on the Columbia River near County 409, about nine miles east of Cathlamet, Cowlitz Co. In 1865 this first salmon cannery in the United States was built. The remains of a large shed are all that is left.

The ruins of Fort Rains are on the Columbia River and County 14, about half a mile east of North Bonneville, Skamania Co. The fort was built in 1856 and has been restored. Nearby are ruins of other buildings.

The ghost town of Gold Basin is on the Stillaguamish River and near County 92, about 31 miles east of Marysville, Snohomish Co. It was a booming gold-mining town; nearby is the ghost town of **Silverton,** once a thriving copper-mining center.

The ruins of Golden are on the south end of Waunacut Lake, about ten miles southwest of Oroville (State 97), Okanogan Co. Very few traces of this once-prosperous mining town remain. It can be reached only by horseback.

The ghost town of Grange City is located at the junction of the Snake and Tucannon Rivers, about twelve and a half miles west of Delaney (County 410), Franklin Co. This river port was ravaged by a flood.

The ghost town of Jerry is located six miles southwest of Clarkston (County 12), Asotin Co. Only a few buildings remain in this booming horse town from the stagecoach days.

The **ghost town of McCormick** is on State 12, about 26 miles northwest of Chehalis, Grays Harbor Co. Along the 53-mile stretch between Chehalis and Raymond on State 12, there are over a dozen ghost towns, some in ruins, all former logging centers.

The **ghost town of Milan** is on the Little Spokane River and State 2, about 24 miles north of Spokane, Spokane Co. The lumber town was only recently abandoned when the sawmill closed down. There are many standing buildings.

The **ghost town of Newcastle** is on U.S. 5 just north of Renton, King Co. It is one of several abandoned coal towns in the area, all of which have numerous standing buildings.

The **ruins of North Dalles** are on the Columbia River near State 197, just opposite the town of The Dalles, Oregon, Klickitat Co. It was founded in 1880 and abandoned by 1900.

The **ruins of Patha,** also called Favorsburg and Waterstown, are 30 miles west of Clarkston near State 12, Garfield Co. The town was founded in 1861; its most prominent features are the ruins of several flour mills.

The **ruins of Pinkney City** are near the **site of Fort Colville,** about three miles east of Colville (County 20), Stevens Co. It was the first county seat and a logging center.

The **town of Republic** is on the Sanpoil River and County 20, Ferry Co. Only about 800 people still live here but in 1900 it was the fifth largest city in the state. Hundreds of abandoned buildings, including 28 saloons, two dance halls, and an opera house, are still standing.

The **town of Rogersburg** is located at the confluence of the Snake and Grande Ronde Rivers, about 25 miles south of Clarkston in the southeastern corner of the state, Asotin Co. It can be reached via a dirt road off County 129. Rogersburg was a prosperous riverport and gold-mining center; now about 25 people live here among the many old buildings.

The **ghost town of Salkum** is on County 99 about ten miles east of Mary's Corner (U.S. 5), King Co. It was a boomtown in the logging days; a bit further to the east are the ghost towns of **Mayfield** and **Rifee.**

The **ghost town of Silcott** is on the Snake River just off State 12, about nine miles west of Clarkston, Garfield Co. It was a thriving riverboat town until being burned down in 1885. Part of it was rebuilt, but the town was soon after abandoned.

The **ghost town of Spokane Bridge** is on State 10, about ten miles east of Spokane, near the Idaho state line, Spokane Co. It was a boomtown in the 1860s and now only a few buildings, including a store, are still standing.

The **ghost town of Wallula** is near the junction of the Columbia and Walla Walla Rivers on State 395, about fifteen miles southeast of Pasco, Walla Walla Co. Miners and cattlemen flocked to this boisterous river town. Nearby are the ruins of **Fort Walla Walla.**

The **ruins of Willapacific** are on State 101 and the east side of Willapa Bay, about 54 miles south of Aberdeen, Pacific Co. The town was built in 1900 on pilings driven into the bay waters and now only the pilings can be seen. Divers report that it is an excellent area for finding old bottles.

In 1852 a Captain James Scarborough, a wealthy merchant and trader, buried a barrel containing $127,000 in gold coins and bars on the **Fort Columbia Military Reservation** along the banks of the Columbia River near State 101, just opposite Astoria, Oregon in Willipa Hills Co.

The **Lost Shovel Creek Gold Mine** is on the Snake River near Craig, about twenty miles south of Clarkston, Asotin Co.

The **Lost Ostrander Creek Gold Mine** is in the vicinity of Ostrander, U.S. 5, Cowlitz Co.

The **Lost Swauk Creek Gold Mine** is on Swauk Creek, about four miles west of Liberty and south of Redtop Mountain in Kittitas Co.

The **Lost Spanish Gold Mine** is on the northern slope of Mount Adams, near the head of the Lewis River in the southwestern corner of Yakima Co.

Three different treasures are reported to be in the vicinity of **Port Townsend,** County 20, Jefferson Co. A cache of $80,000 robbed from a British paymaster is supposed to be somewhere on the banks of Discovery Bay. In 1870, saloon owner Harry Sutton buried $11,000 in gold coins in the Hammond Orchard in the town and never told the exact location. In this same orchard a wealthy jeweler named S. S. Buckley buried a large fortune of money and jewelry in the 1860s; it has never been found.

Just north of Port Townsend on **Protection Island,** about $75,000 in gold bullion is supposed to have been buried in 1874 by an unlucky prospector, who forgot the exact location of his treasure.

In 1864 bandits robbed the Canadian Pacific Railroad of about $60,000 in British gold sovereigns and buried it on the grounds of **the old Chevy Chase Inn** on Port Discovery Bay in the Straits of Juan de Fuca.

In 1861, Treasury Agent Victor Smith absconded with $9,000 in gold coins and buried it in a strongbox along the shore of the **Straits of Juan de Fuca,** in the vicinity of Port Angeles, State 101, Clallam Co. About two miles west of this city large numbers of American double eagle gold coins are found along the beach after storms. They probably come from a shipwreck.

In the 1870s a lumberman named Lans Hanson buried $75,000 in gold coins on **Vashon Island,** near the village of Portage in Tramp Harbor, which is located in Puget Sound between Seattle and Tacoma.

A large safe containing $2,400 in paper currency and $1,290 in gold coins owned by the Northern Pacific Railroad was accidentally dropped into **Connecticut Bay.** It is said to be near the present stevedoring docks at the mouth of the Tacoma waterway; now it lies covered by silt or mud.

Timbers of an old ship are exposed at certain times of the year at **Cape Alava** on the Pacific Ocean on the northern end of Olympic National Park in Clallam Co. When this occurs, treasure hunters report finding many silver coins dating in the late nineteenth century and many artifacts.

Near Cape Flattery—the northwestern tip of the state near the Straits of Juan de Fuca—on the Makah Indian Reservation, Clallam Co., many coins and relics are found by treasure hunters. The Spaniards had a settlement in this area in 1792 and a few buildings' foundations are still to be seen.

Large numbers of bottles and artifacts are washed ashore from a late nineteenth-century shipwreck at Cape Elizabeth, just north of Taholah, on the **Quinault Indian Reservation** in Grays Harbor Co.

Coins and relics from shipwrecks are also found along the beaches of **Cape Shoalwater,** at the mouth of Willipa Bay (near North Cove, County 105) and Ocean Park, County 103—both in Willipa Hills Co.

Before dying in 1918, a wealthy cattle rancher named Chief Smitken buried $18,000 in gold coins near the **St. Mary Indian Mission** in Omak, State 97, Okanogan Co.

The ruins of Fort Okanogan are on the Columbia River across from Rocky Butte (County 173), Okanogan Co. It was built in 1811 and destroyed during an Indian raid in 1874. Several caches of treasure are believed to be hidden on the site.

Between Adams Mountain and Fruitland (County 25), Stevens Co., is a place called **Robber's Roost.** Many caches are believed to have been buried there by the countless outlaws who used the place for many years as their headquarters. On nearby Stensger Mountain in 1853, a band of renegade Indians buried or hid in a cave four wagonloads of gold ore before being caught and shot.

Outlaw loot is supposed to be buried on **the site of the old Collins Roadhouse,** which was the headquarters for the freight and stage lines, just outside of Uniontown, State 195, Whitman Co.

The Lost Wheelbarrow Gold Mine is located near Bishop, about ten miles northwest of Uniontown. Several other abandoned gold mines and the ruins of mining camps are in this area.

Along the banks of the Snake River in the vicinity of Penawawa, about three miles east of County 127, Garfield Co., prospectors buried about 200 pounds of raw gold during an Indian attack and were unable to find it later on.

In the early 1900s a man named Parsley buried $43,000 in gold and silver coins along the banks of the **Grande Ronde River** near the tiny village of Mountain View, about five miles west of County 129, Asotin Co.

In 1879 outlaws are known to have buried about $30,000 in gold bullion in a cave on **Sentinel Mountain** in the Saddle Mountain Range, about three miles southeast of Beverly (County 243), Grant Co.

Bandits hurled three chests of gold bullion into the **Columbia River** on the north side at Plymouth, just west of the toll bridge, County 14, Benton Co. One chest was dredged up in 1911; the others remain buried under the swift-flowing river's muddy bottom.

WEST VIRGINIA

Rich Mountain Battlefield is off U.S. 250, six miles south of Elkins, Randolph Co. Federal troops under General George B. McClellan decisively defeated a Confederate force under General Robert Garnett on July 11, 1861 at this site. The ruins of earthworks and several houses damaged during the battle are here.

Carnifex Ferry Battlefield is off State 90, fifteen miles southwest of Summersville, Nicholas Co. On September 10, 1861 a Union force under General William S. Rosecrans defeated Confederate troops under General John B. Floyd. The trenches and the graves of the fallen can still be seen.

The site of Fort Lee is located at the confluence of the Elk and Kanawha Rivers in Charleston, Kanawha Co. The fort and a settlement were established here in 1786 and the city of Charleston grew up around them. Vestiges of the original settlement can be seen after floods have eroded the river banks.

Droop Mt. Battlefield is off U.S. 219 between Droop and Hillsboro, Greenbrier Co. On November 6, 1863 Union forces under General William W. Averell defeated a Confederate army under General John Echols here, ending all Southern resistance in the state. Breastworks, graves, and several ruined buildings can be found at this site.

Fort Ashby is in the town of Fort Ashby off State 220, Mineral Co. This fort was built by General George Washington in 1755 as one in a chain of frontier posts designed to protect the trans-Allegheny frontier. It has been restored, and nearby there are numerous ruins of buildings which date from the late eighteenth century.

Grave Creek Mound Park is on the Ohio River in Moundsville, Marshall Co. The site is one of the largest Indian burial mounds in the nation and is representative of the Adena culture, which dates back to 500 B.C.

Point Pleasant Battleground is at the confluence of the Kanawha and Ohio Rivers, two miles north of Point Pleasant, Mason Co. On October 10, 1774 a fierce battle was fought by 1,100 Virginia militiamen, who defeated a much larger Shawnee Indian force, thus breaking their power in the Ohio Valley. Three wooden frontier forts were built on this site between 1774 and 1786 but no traces of them remain. There are, however, ruins of many old stone and brick homes of the early nineteenth century.

The site of Fort Henry is on Main Street between 11th and Ohio Streets in downtown Wheeling. Five years after the town was first settled, this fort was built in 1774 to protect the early settlers from hostile Indians. One of the last battles of the Revolution was fought here in September 1782, when a British and Indian attack on the fort was repelled after a bloody, two-day siege.

During Pontiac's War in 1763 a wealthy farmer, who was killed by the Indians, buried a large cache of gold and silver coins in the old burying ground in **Charleston,** U.S. 64, Kanawha Co.

The Lost John Swift Silver Mine is somewhere east of Point Pleasant, County 62, Mason Co. The miners working this mine were attacked and killed by Indians. It is known that they had a great store of silver ore and bullion inside the mine.

Vestiges of a river steamer are seen along the south bank of **Ohio River** at Paden City,

County 2, Tyler Co. Local residents occasionally find American silver coins after the river floods.

Large numbers of bottles and other artifacts are found on the bank of the **Ohio River at Raven Rock,** County 2, Pleasants Co. They are also probably coming ashore from a river wreck.

During the 1930s, someone buried $2,000 in gold and silver coins on the Carpenter farm, about half a mile from **Bear Fork Creek** near Groves Hollow, in the central part of Gilmer Co.

During the Civil War $300,000 in Confederate gold bullion was buried on the banks of the left fork of the **Buckhannon River,** near the junction of Bear Camp Run, about a mile down river from Palace Valley in Upshur Co.

Just prior to his death in 1923, a miserly old farmer buried a large fortune in several iron chests along the **Guyandot River,** about half a mile north of Chapmanville, County 10, Logan Co.

In the early 1800s Indians were still working a silver mine near the present Javell farm, **between Workman's and Meadow Creeks,** just outside of Beckley (State 21), Raleigh Co. Before fleeing the area they are believed to have buried a large cache of silver bullion and other treasures inside the mine before sealing it off.

In the early 1900s a Dennis Atkins is alleged to have buried about $200,000 in gold coins along the east bank of the **Tug Fort River,** near the toll bridge, just north of Kermit, State 52, Mingo Co.

During the Depression a farmer named Kelly Cooper buried his life's savings near the barn on his farm on the east bank of the **Tug Fork River** near Sprigg (County 49), Mingo Co.

During the Civil War a Grover Bergdoll is supposed to have buried $150,000 in gold and silver coins along the west bank of the **Potomac River** in Harpers Ferry, State 340, Jefferson Co.

Also during the Civil War, Confederate raiders being pursued by Federal troops are known to have pushed several wagonloads of plunder into the **Potomac River** near Cherry Run, across from the Maryland state line in the northeastern part of Morgan Co. Several chests containing gold bullion were lost with the other treasures.

Somewhere on the campus of the Davis and Elkins College just south of Elkins, State 290, Randolph Co., robbers buried about $50,000 in bank loot in 1928 before being caught and shot.

WISCONSIN

The Nicolet Statue on State 57, near the city of Green Bay, commemorates the founding of the state's oldest settlement. French explorers visited the area in 1634; in 1669 Jesuits founded the mission of St. Francis here; the first French settlers arrived in 1745; then in 1763 Green Bay fell into British hands; finally the Americans took it in 1816. **Fort Howard** built in the same year still stands.

Madeline Island, the largest of the Apostle Islands in the Chequamegon Bay region of Lake Superior, was the ancestral home of the Chippewa Indians. After the 1680s, French, British, and American fur traders built large trading posts here: the French in 1693, the British during the 1790s, and the Americans in 1835. Nothing remains of these trading posts.

Aztalan National Historic Landmark is on State 89, three miles east of Lake Mills, Jefferson Co. One can see parts of a stockaded Indian village of the Middle Mississippi culture dating back to around 1200.

Pendarvis is off State 151 near Mineral Point, Iowa Co. In this ghost town are many stone and log buildings of a rough-and-tough mining community that flourished in the 1830s and 1840s. The place was founded by miners from Cornwall, England who came here to work in lead mines. The mines were quickly depleted, and the people left the area.

Oconto Site National Historic Landmark is in Copper Culture Park in Oconto, Oconto Co.

Excavations at this site indicate that copper-culture Indians settled in the area as early as 5500 B.C. The many copper implements found here may be evidence of the earliest use of metals in the world.

The sites of the two Fort Crawfords are located near Prairie du Chien, Crawford Co. French fur traders built the first fort in 1816 on St. Feriole Island in the Mississippi River, but it was destroyed by a flood. The second was built on the east bank of the river near Prairie du Chien in 1829; only the old hospital has survived from this site. There are a number of old ruins on St. Feriole Island, including a Georgian-style mansion that was constructed on top of a 2,000-year-old Indian mound in 1843.

Brule-St. Croix Portage site is off State 27 on the Brule River northeast of Solon Springs, Douglas Co. This was one of the most heavily traveled trails between the Mississippi River and Lake Superior from 1680 to 1880. In this part of the country there was abundant fur trapping; here also, travellers had to be wary of Indian attacks. Many old ruins, some dating back to the late 1600s, can be seen along the trail.

Lizard Mound State Park is one mile east of State 144 near West Bend, Washington Co. Indians of the Effigy Mound culture flourished here between 600 and 1000; their burial grounds or earthworks were made in the shape of animals and birds. Only 31 of the mounds are still preserved.

On October 28, 1892 the Great Milwaukee Fire razed 26 acres of homes and did over $5 million in property damages. The ruins of some of these buildings still stand in empty lots where treasure hunters have had good success in locating artifacts and some treasure. During a dredging operation in 1952 a large number of late nineteenth-century silver coins were deposited along the shore of **Sheridan Park,** probably from one of many ships that sank during the last century.

Several gold coins have been found on the shore of **Lake Superior** in the city of Superior. They seem to be from the ship **Benjamin Noble** which was carrying over $100,000 in gold coins when it sank.

During the Revolution a British officer buried a chest of silver coins on **Sand Island,** one of the Apostle Islands in Lake Superior. In 1760 an iron box containing $128,000 in gold coins was buried on nearby York Island by some British soldiers to keep it out of the hands of attacking Indians. A few miles further to the east on **Otter Island** lived a recluse named William Wilson. Before dying in the 1860s, he buried about $90,000 in gold and silver coins near his cabin. Since he had no known source of income and spent a great deal of money on the mainland, it was believed that he had found a great treasure on his island. On nearby **Hermit Island,** a Frederick Prentice in 1895 built a large home named Cedar Bark Lodge. He is supposed to have buried a large fortune near his home, which was torn down in the early 1930s. On nearby **Stockton Island** British soldiers are believed to have buried numerous caches of Revolutionary War plunder. In the old graveyard at La Pointe on **Madeline Island,** several treasures may have been buried during the French and Indian War.

In 1934 outlaw John Dillinger is reported to have buried about $700,000 in paper currency in several suitcases in the woods about a quarter mile behind **the Little Bohemia Lodge,** approximately eight miles southeast of Mercer, State 51, Iron Co.

When a wealthy businessman named R. C. Bennett died in 1950, he left his wife directions to a treasure. Following his instructions she found 60 tin boxes containing over $40,000 in nickels, dimes, and quarters under the floor of the basement in his home in **Eagle River,** State 45, Oneida Co. He is known to have buried another cache of about a million dollars in paper currency, which has not been found.

Prior to an Indian attack, a group of miners returning from Montana buried a wagonload of about $200,000 in gold bullion in a swampy area just south of Balsam Lake, about seven miles northeast of **St. Croix Falls** (State 8), Polk Co. Heavy rains caused the bullion to sink in quicksand-like soil and the miners were unable to recover it.

The Maxwell gang are reputed to have buried about $40,000 in loot in the vicinity of the tiny village of **Elk Mound,** State 12, Dunn Co.

Between the villages of Pepin and Stockholm on the east shore of Lake Pepin, a wealthy Illinois businessman concealed several caches of money in 1928 and he died without revealing the locations.

The remains of a paddlewheel steamer are visible at low water on **the Mississippi River,** about a mile south of De Soto, County 82, Crawford Co. Occasionally coins and artifacts are found along the shore.

Another unidentified riverboat was lost in the vicinity of **Glenhaven,** on the east side of the Mississippi River, about five miles west of County 133, Grant Co. Treasure hunters have found small silver bars and other artifacts along the muddy shore.

At the junction of the Black and East Fork of the Black River near Hatfield Village, four miles east of State 12, Jackson Co., there is a possible treasure. Indian legend tells about French explorers having buried a large cache of golden Indian artifacts which they discovered in an Indian mound.

The Jesse James gang is rumored to have buried a safe and two iron boxes full of loot from several bank and train robberies in the vicinity of **Wildcat Mountain,** just west of Ontario, County 33, Vernon Co.

Just prior to an Indian attack, in which they all were killed, soldiers buried four saddlebags of 1832 gold coins, destined for a payroll to frontier posts along the Mississippi. The cash is concealed on the highest bluff near **Fort Crawford,** just outside of Prairie du Chien, County 60, Crawford Co. on the Mississippi River.

In 1891 a Paul Seifert and his friend found a cave containing a fortune in priceless Indian relics made of gold and silver. After showing many of the local farmers some of the relics, they started out with about a dozen pack horses to gather the treasure and were never heard from again. They are believed to have been killed by outlaws who were after their find. The cave is reported to be in the vicinity of **Bogus Bluff** near Gotham and the Wisconsin River, County 133, Richland Co.

In the 1880s two Indian bandits robbed a riverboat of several chests of gold. After being caught they confessed to having buried the loot near **Coon Rocks Bluff** just outside of Dodgeville, State 151, Iowa Co.

There are many tales about a riverboat carrying over $100,000 in gold bullion having sunk on **the Wisconsin River** in around 1870. Apparently there is some truth to the tale—a boy swimming near where the ship allegedly sank found three ten-pound gold bars in 1953. The site is on the east river bank, about half a mile south of Portage, State 151, Columbia Co.

A wealthy furniture manufacturer died, leaving a note saying that he had buried about $500,000 in 1931. There were no directions to the fortune, but it is known to be somewhere along the shores of **Lake Winnebago,** within walking distance of the city of Oshkosh, State 45, Winnebago Co.

About $16,000 was buried in glass jars on the property of the Thomas Burke house. When the widow was evicted in 1962 and the house razed to build an expressway, workmen found $7,700 of the cache. But the old lady claims that the rest is still buried under or near the expressway in **West Allis,** a suburb of Milwaukee.

During the 1930s a gangster named Sam Amatuna is reported to have buried about $50,000 in paper currency wrapped in a canvas bundle, near County 120 **a few miles north of Pell Lake,** Walworth Co.

WYOMING

Independence Rock is on State 220, 50 miles southwest of Casper, Natrona Co. This 200-foot rock, towering over the surrounding plains, was situated along the Oregon Trail near the Sweetwater River. It was a favorite campsite of the westward-bound travelers, who left many vestiges of their presence here.

The Upper Green River Rendezvous site is on the Green River above and below the town of

Daniel, Sweetwater Co. Between 1820 and 1840 this was the most popular rendezvous site of the Rocky Mountain fur traders, who held a trading fair here every spring. Supply caravans from St. Louis exchanged goods for the furs brought by traders, trappers, and Indians from throughout the West. It was a two-month scene of wild times with gambling and shameless women.

The site of Fort Fetterman is off I-25, eleven miles northwest of Douglas, Converse Co. Strategically located on the North Platte River near the crossroads of the Oregon and Bozeman Trails, this military outpost was established in 1867 to defend the region from hostile Indians. It was abandoned in 1882 and in the entire fort only the officers' quarters are standing today.

Fort Bridger State Historic site is on the Blacks Fork of the Green River, off U.S. 30S, Uinta Co. In 1843 this fort was erected as a trading post by the famous mountain man Jim Bridger. It soon became the second most important outfitting point—next to Fort Laramie—for travelers on the Oregon Trail going from the Missouri River to the Pacific Coast. In 1857 the Mormons used the fort as a supply base for their converts heading for Salt Lake City. Between 1867 and 1869 it was an important supply center for the Union Pacific Railroad and the gold rush to the northwest. A village of 150 people now stands on the site but no traces of the original fort remain.

Fort Laramie is off U.S. 26, three miles south of Laramie, Albany Co. Built in 1834 at the confluence of the North Platte and Laramie Rivers and on the Oregon Trail, it played an important role in the westward migrations and bloody Indian wars. It also served as a pony express and overland mail station. The fort was abandoned in 1890, but eleven of its 21 extant structures have been restored.

The ghost town of South Pass City is off State 28, 33 miles south of Lander, Fremont Co. This gold-mining boomtown was founded in 1867 after the discovery of the Clarissa Lode on the Sweetwater River. By 1874 when all of the gold had been extracted, the town was abandoned. Several hundred of the original buildings survive.

The ruins of Fort Phil Kearney are just off U.S. 87 near Story, Sheridan Co. The fort was built in 1866 to protect the travelers along the Bozeman Trail. During the next two years it was under almost continual siege in the Chief Red Cloud War. As a result it was abandoned late in 1868. The stockade and officers' quarters have been reconstructed. Many battles were fought in this area between Indians and westward-moving whites, and the Sioux and Cheyenne waged a continual but losing battle to prevent the miners from trespassing on Indian hunting grounds on their way to the Montana gold fields. Souvenirs of many of these encounters can be found in the surrounding area—mainly pieces of broken wagons.

The ghost town of Almy is in the Bear River Valley, about six miles north of Evanston, County 89, Uinta Co. It was a prosperous coal town in the 1870s and 1880s. In 1895 a mining accident claimed 67 lives and the miners refused to work afterwards. The town then ceased to be.

The town of Atlantic City is on the south side of Shoshone National Forest, about four miles southeast of County 28 and about 40 miles northeast of Farson, Fremont Co. In 1870 it had over 2,000 residents. The two people who now live here run a restaurant and tavern for passing tourists. It is one of the most picturesque ghost towns in the state with many standing buildings.

The ruins of Reartown are fifteen miles south of Evanston (U.S. 80), Uinta Co., and can be reached only by horseback. Reartown was once a construction camp center on the Union Pacific Railroad.

The ruins of Blair's stockade are one mile north of Rock Springs (U.S. 80), Sweetwater Co. It was established as a trading post in 1866; and it was destroyed along with most of the surrounding houses by a gun powder explosion set off by two drunken miners in 1891.

The ghost town of Bonanza is at the junction of Norwood and Paintrock Creeks about thirteen miles east of Manderson (State 16), Big Horn Co. A false oil discovery in 1887 started a boomtown which quickly died and now only one house is standing.

The ruins of Bothwell are fifteen miles west of Alcova on County 220, near Horse Creek

Laramie County. Founded in 1865 and abandoned sometime before 1900, it was big enough to have its own newspaper and post office. Several caches of treasure have been found here in recent years.

The ruins of **Brown's Hotel** are across the Laramie River from old Fort Laramie, State 26, Goshen Co. During the 1860s the hotel and other buildings were situated here as a recreation center for the soldiers and passing settlers. When the army stopped the whisky traffic the town folded.

The ruins of **Bryan** are just north of U.S. 80 about thirteen miles west of Green River, Sweetwater Co. In 1868 it was established as a Union Pacific Railroad overhaul depot. When the railroad moved its tracks the town faded away.

The ghost town of **Carbon** is situated seven miles southeast of Hanna (State 30), Carbon Co. In this old coal mining town that was abandoned in 1902 many buildings are still standing.

The ghost town of **Cummins City** is just off County 230, about 40 miles southwest of Laramie in the Medicine National Forest, Albany Co. It was founded when a John Cummins salted the area with gold causing a mining stampede overnight. A nearby ghost town named **Jelm** also began with a false gold discovery.

The ruins of **Dillon** are on the Encampment-Baggs Road to the south of Rawlins (U.S. 80), along the Continental Divide, Carbon Co. This former mining town has the ruins of several hundred old buildings. Nearby are the remains of the ghost town of **Rudefeha** as well as numerous abandoned gold mines.

The ghost town of **Encampment** is on the Encampment River in the Bow Forest on County 70, about 20 miles south of Saratoga, Carbon Co. This famous trapper rendezvous dated from 1851.

The ruins of **Fairbanks** on the North Platte River two miles northwest of Guernsey (State 26), Platte Co., have been turned into a picnic grounds called Kelly's Park. It was a famous copper town in the 1880s; now only one cabin is still standing.

The ghost town of **Marbleton** is on State 189 about half a mile north of Big Piney, Sublette Co. It was abandoned a few years after its beginning in 1912, because all of the residents moved to Big Piney, founded in 1888.

The ghost town of **Orin** is near present Orin on the northwestern tip of Glendo Reservoir on U.S. 25, Converse Co. The old railroad station and many buildings are still standing.

The ruins of **Portuguese Houses** are about eleven miles east of Kaycee on the Poder River and County 192. Only a few ruins are left. About sixteen miles further to the east along the same road are the ruins of **Fort Conner** and another mile to the east are the ruins of old **Fort Reno.** Two other unidentified ghost towns in complete ruins are about four miles north of this last fort.

The ruins of **Rambler** are on the Encampment-Baggs Road near the shores of Battle Lake in the Medicine Bow National Forest, close to the Colorado state line, Carbon Co. There are ruins of many other mining centers and abandoned mines in the surrounding area.

The ghost town of **South Pass City** is four miles south of County 28, about 38 miles northwest of Farson, along the Continental Divide, Fremont Co. It is an historic old mining town with many well-preserved buildings. The city was founded in 1867 and by 1870 had over 4,000 residents. It died in 1873. About four miles to the east stand the ruins of **Fort Stambaugh.** Recently a cache of coins and some weapons were found in these fort ruins.

The ruins of **Tubbs Town** are two miles southeast of Newcastle (State 18), Weston Co. It was founded in 1888 and only boomed for two years before being abandoned.

There are several hundred other ruins of tiny settlements or camping grounds throughout the state, especially along the **Oregon, Mormon, and Bozemen Trails** which cut across the state and were traveled by tens of thousands of westward-bound settlers and miners. **Along the stage and Pony Express routes** there are also countless abandoned stations and homes. All are potential hunting spots for treasure and artifacts.

The **Lost Docony Gold Mine** and the **Lost Martinez Gold Mine** are located somewhere in the Laramie Hills, Medicine Bow National Forest, in the southeast corner of Albany Co.

Near the junction of the North Platte River and Glendo Reservoir in Platte Co. the

Spaniards had a rich and famous gold mine in the eighteenth century. Because of repeated Indian attacks it was shut down and the site was lost.

Somewhere among the many ruins surrounding **the Carissa Lode Mine on Willow Creek,** located about twelve miles northeast of South Pass City ghost town, a miner is known to have hidden over 100 pounds in raw gold before dying in a mine accident.

The Brigg's Lost Gold Ledge is located on Deer Mountain, Yellowstone National Park, in the northwest corner of the state. Its ore assayed out at $20,000 in gold and $3,000 in silver per ton.

Along Cache Creek, so named because a treasure is known to be concealed there, in the Jackson Hole Winter Sports Area of Teton Co., an outlaw buried about $150,000 in gold and silver coins and bullion before being shot by a posse. Another gang of bandits are rumored to have buried a like sum of money in the same area. Many gold nuggets are found along this creek and the ruins of numerous mining shacks are seen in the area.

Butch Cassidy is supposed to have buried about $70,000 in gold and silver coins in the vicinity of **Wind River Mountain** near Crowheart, State 26, Fremont Co.

The ghost town of Bald City is between Bald Mountain and State 14A, Big Horn Co. A few mining buildings are still standing in this mining center of the 1890s.

The Lost Walker Gold Mine is near the Conner Battlefield site in the Big Horn Mountains, just west of Sheridan (U.S. 90), Big Horn Co.

The Lost Cabin Gold Mine is located along Crazy Woman Creek in the Big Horn Mountains west of Buffalo (U.S. 90), Big Horn Co. Nearby are numerous abandoned gold mines and the ruins of miners' shacks.

In 1878 robbers got away with $240,000 in gold bullion from **the Homestake Mine** and buried it somewhere in the Black Hills close to Canyon Springs Station, about fifteen miles east of Sundance (State 14) in Crook Co.

The ghost town of Cambria is just off State 85, about nine miles northwest of Newcastle near the Flying V Ranch, Weston Co. This coal mining town was abandoned in 1928; many of its buildings are intact.

After robbing the Canyon Springs Stage of $140,000 the outlaws buried the loot along **Stockade Beaver Creek** about twelve miles southwest of Newcastle, Weston Co.

During the 1870s a stagecoach was robbed just outside of Newcastle and the $37,000 in loot was buried in the immediate vicinity. More stagecoach booty was buried in 1879 along the banks of **Whoop It Up Creek,** about five miles southeast of Newcastle.

A strongbox containing gold bullion was robbed from the Birdseye Stage Station in 1897 and buried along the banks of **the Wind River,** about three miles south of Thermopolis (State 16), Spring Co.

The Lost Soldier Gold Mine is in the vicinity of Arminto, ten miles north of Waltman (State 20), Natrona Co.

The Hole-in-the-Wall gang is said to have buried about $65,000 in a box canyon close to U.S. 25, **about two miles north of Casper,** Natrona Co.

In the vicinity of Muddy Gap along the Continental Divide, two miles south of the town of Muddy Gap (State 287), Carbon Co., miners are known to have hidden several large caches of raw gold before being killed by Indians in 1854.

The ghost town of Silver Cliff is one mile west of Lusk (State 85), Niobraba Co. Several small caches of treasure have been found there in the past decade.

Slade Canyon, near the town of Sunrise (County 270), Platte Co., is so named because the Jack Slade gang had their headquarters there for many years and are believed to have hidden numerous caches of loot in the area. Nearby **Sawmill Canyon,** a few miles northeast of Guernsey is alleged to be another of their hiding places.

Several treasures are believed to be buried around the town of **Fort Laramie** on the North Platte River, State 26, Goshen Co. The **Billingsley Treasure,** a cache of undetermined value, is hidden along the banks of the river near the town. In the 1880s several chests containing about $30,000 in gold bullion were buried near the stagecoach station. An army payroll of $20,000 in silver coins was buried near the ruins of the old fort.

364

Along the west bank of the Salt River, about a mile west of Smoot, State 89, Lincoln Co., a cache of $90,000 in gold and silver coins was buried by bandits from a stagecoach robbery in 1896.

The ghost town of Miner's Delight is on the Sweetwater River about 22 miles south of Lander (State 287), Fremont Co. Several small caches of treasure are supposed to be buried in the town, which has a large number of surviving buildings and several abandoned gold mines nearby.

PN 1562100

THE GARRETT LIBRARY

These standard-size 5.5" x 8.5" format books offer treasure hunting techniques, hints and history from Charles Garrett and other RAM Books authors. Each book is soft cover format unless otherwise noted.

Visit garrett.com often to watch for new titles!

PN 1501500

PN 1508600

PN 1508200

PN 1508300

PN 1501700

PN 1545500

PN 1505470

PN 1500000

PN 1500300

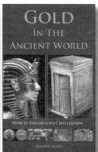

PN 1546100

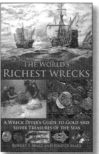

PN 1509810 hard cover
PN 1509800 soft cover

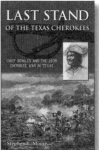

PN 1509900